WITHDRAWN

THE NEW ECONOMICS OF GROWTH

A Strategy for India and the Developing World

The Twentieth Century Fund is a research foundation engaged in policy oriented studies of economic, political, and social issues and institutions. It was founded in 1919 by Edward A. Filene, who made a series of gifts that now constitute the Fund's assets.

THE NEW ECONOMICS
OF GROWTH

A Strategy for India and
the Developing World

JOHN W. MELLOR

A Twentieth Century Fund Study

CORNELL UNIVERSITY PRESS
ITHACA AND LONDON

First published 1976 by Cornell University Press.
Published in the United Kingdom by Cornell University Press Ltd., 2–4 Brook Street, London W1Y 1AA.

International Standard Book Number 0-8014-0999-3
Library of Congress Catalog Card Number 75-38430
Printed in the United States of America by Vail-Ballou Press, Inc.
Librarians: Library of Congress cataloging information appears on the last page of the book.

Foreword

In the current atmosphere of increasing anxiety about the world's capacity to produce sufficient food to support future population growth, it may be difficult to recall the euphoria generated in the last decade by the "green revolution" in agricultural technology. But even at the peak of that euphoria, some observers of the developing countries were skeptical that technological achievements in agriculture could by themselves engender self-sustaining economic growth or that the governments of the developing countries would prove capable of taking advantage of these achievements. The Twentieth Century Fund, which had sponsored Gunnar Myrdal's *Asian Drama* and other works on related subjects, had a continuing awareness of the basic problems confronting the development efforts of India and other struggling nations. Six years ago, therefore, the Fund's trustees invited John W. Mellor of Cornell University, a leading authority on agricultural economics who was recently named to the post of chief economist for the Agency for International Development, to examine the green revolution and its prospects for contributing to economic development.

Mr. Mellor initially proposed to focus on development in India and the extent to which the benefits of the new agricultural technology might contribute to growth in other sectors of the economy. But his analysis of empirical data on Indian economic development eventually evolved into a new integrated growth strategy based on the increased employment made possible by an expanded food supply. In this book, Mr. Mellor demonstrates how an agriculturally-based economic strategy can lead to growth in industry and trade and, more important, give the poor an opportunity to become active participants in and beneficiaries of economic growth. Although his research dealt primarily with the Indian experience, Mr. Mellor also considers the applications of his employment-oriented strategy—with appropriate adjustments for local conditions—to other low-income countries.

Like Gunnar Myrdal before him, John Mellor is sensitive to the interaction of political, social, institutional, and economic forces. The strategy he develops is not automatic. It requires changes in government policy that will be opposed by those who supported—and received the main dividends from—the capital-intensive growth strategies favored in the past. The political significance of decisions about development strategy has been recently re-emphasized in India, where Indira Gandhi won her sweeping electoral victory in 1972 and made her latest turn toward authoritarianism with policies promising a new approach to economic growth that would give a bigger share to the millions of poor. Mr. Mellor, who himself argues for development based on measures to increase food supplies, points up the need to undertake broad changes in other sectors of the economy as well as in institutional arrangements if growth is to be more sustained and broader based than in the past.

There is good reason to stress accelerated development of the rural sector. As Mr. Mellor points out, its present relative neglect has not only impeded overall growth but also led to great internal strains and conflict in developing countries. He does not suggest a simplistic concentration on agriculture. Rather, he calls for an integrated strategy that involves fundamental changes in all of the forces that determine development. As such, his work represents a fresh and significant departure in development theory and practice.

The Fund is grateful to Mr. Mellor for the time and effort he put into his study, which is a worthy addition to previous Fund projects on development in both its careful scholarship and its independent thinking.

M. J. ROSSANT, Director
The Twentieth Century Fund

February, 1976

Contents

Tables

APPENDIX

FIGURES

Preface

Too many books on economic development have tended to regard agriculture as an impenetrable mystery, unyielding to the tools of economic analysis and incapable of being integrated with other sectors of the economy. Agriculture tends to be relegated all too often to a single, isolated section of the book, late in the presentation. It is because of this inability to recognize agriculture's positive role that the bulk of the literature on the "green revolution" has either eulogized agriculture—but solely for its contribution to increased food supplies—or maligned it on the basis of the "second generation" problems of distribution it creates.

This book gives agriculture a leading role. The book presents an employment-oriented strategy for economic growth—a strategy that uses technological change in an initially dominant agriculture as a major stimulus to a broadly participatory pattern of rural and urban development.

The strategic choices are real and involve major differences in the processes of planning and the allocation of resources. The shift in development strategy can be implemented only by decisions involving major political and institutional changes that affect the distribution of power and therefore require attention at the highest levels of government.

The strategy set forth here might have been inappropriate to many low-income nations in the 1950s and may still be inappropriate to some for economic reasons—including inadequate knowledge of the specific requisites for agricultural growth and insufficient breadth of industrial structure—and for political reasons—particularly including the need for centralization of authority in pursuit of national unity and international power. The strategy may also be unacceptable now because it would threaten the newly powerful vested interests that have developed from the old strategy and have, perhaps, been reinforced by past historical circumstances. But it suggests an approach to alleviating poverty that may be less naive than current nostrums and more effective than decades of economic stagnation.

The intent is not to analyze the politics of the choice of strategy but rather to elucidate the basic economic relationships. The approach to poverty is particularly relevant to a new theory of growth because, in contrast to many current attitudes, it treats the solution of the problem not as an issue of public welfare expenditure and redistribution of income but as a function of the structure of growth.

In many ways, India—with its 600 million people and 3.3 million square kilometers of area—is an ideal laboratory for the analysis of an employment-oriented growth strategy emphasizing agriculture. As the cradle and then stronghold of the capital intensive approach to economic growth since the mid-1950s, India provides an abundance of data for analysis and a wealth of debate over causes and results. The experience of India precludes easy generalizations. It supplies not so much the prescription for other countries as the perspective for posing the right questions—and then evolving toward effective solutions.

Despite its popularity in the development literature, much of the old, capital intensive strategy of growth practiced in India was never applicable to the many small countries of Asia and Africa. The rural employment-led strategy set forth in this book does not have large economies of scale in its individual production systems and hence has widespread applicability. In the extraordinary heterogeneity of India's nonurban sector—from the extraordinarily dynamic Punjab to the high-yield areas of coastal Andhra to the low-productivity, high-potential areas of Bengal, to some of the very poor and generally resource-deficient areas of Madhya Pradesh, to Bihar, with its disheartening tenure situation—there are extensive opportunities to understand the complex bases for success and failure of a parade of programs. In the past, many countries have equated modernity with capital intensive, large-scale industry and mechanized, commercial agriculture—an approach at best narrowly applicable. As it becomes recognized that genuine modernity requires a viable, dynamic, broad-based agriculture, the breadth of India's rural experience becomes increasingly relevant.

Similarly, if this book contributes to an understanding of the efforts of developing nations to improve slowly from what is now by no means a desperate state, through evolutionary processes, perhaps the problems and the approaches to their solution will be seen as not very different from those of energy, poverty, and world position, which are approached with a similar slowness and hesitation in the rich countries. And from that perception may come the mutual respect necessary for cooperative solution of the great problems of the world.

This book gives little specific attention to such much debated issues as "black" money, corruption, Plan "holidays," and subverting of the Fifth Plan, which are generally considered of great importance by specialists on the Indian economy. These problems, however, have been more the result of past strategy and its weaknesses than the cause of failure. Thus, the emphasis of this presentation is intentionally positive: to formulate an alternative approach to those past strategies and to define that approach in some detail.

Perhaps nothing indicates the scope, the method, and the bases for the arguments in this book better than a statement of my indebtedness to colleagues. The work on the manuscript has taken over four years. The effort simply could not have reached fruition without the participation of a large number of people. The basic conceptualization is the product of collaboration with Uma Lele which resulted in two major papers: one provided a mathematical test of the consistency of a number of key assumptions; the other placed those views in a policy framework.[1] The important input analysis of agricultural production is, of course, based directly on Uma Lele's earlier published work. The chapter on foreign trade is largely based on her analysis of low-income-country imports and exports, and the conceptualization of rural development processes draws upon her most recent book, *The Design of Rural Development*.[2] Finally, no one gave a more critical reading to the early drafts or was more demanding of improvement.

The strategy espoused here depends absolutely on the potential for accelerated growth in foodgrains production. Gunvant Desai made the judgments and time-consuming calculations that provide those estimates. The whole agricultural analysis also owes much to frequent and long discussions with Desai about those processes. A second crucial argument of the

---

[1] See Uma J. Lele and John W. Mellor, "Technological Change and Distributive Bias in a Dual Economy," Department of Agricultural Economics, revised Occasional Paper No. 43, Cornell University–USAID Employment and Income Distribution Research Project (October 1972); and Uma J. Lele and John W. Mellor, "Jobs, Poverty and the Green Revolution," *International Affairs*, 48:1 (January 1972).

[2] Uma Lele, *The Design of Rural Development: Lessons from Africa* (Baltimore: The Johns Hopkins University Press, 1975).

book is put forth with respect to the scope for changing capital intensity in the industrial sector through a change in industrial structure. Uttam Dabholkar provided a laborious and intelligent analysis of the data on capital intensity. Mohinder Mudahar played a key role in developing the simulation model that is so important as a test of the argument of Chapter VII specifically and the strategy generally.

Arthur Goldsmith and Debra Biamonte performed the bulk of the development and presentation of data and references which are so critical to the final backing of the arguments. Alice Wells performed the task of administering the details of a large research and graduate program, including meeting deadlines for budgets, reports, and publications which were essential to effective completion of this effort.

A search of the literature on growth and planning procedures was made by Gillian Hart in support of Chapters I and XI and of the discussion of labor-supply relationships that appears in Chapter IV. Chandrashekhar Ranade made a substantial contribution to expansion of the original model and to the precision of the discussion of growth models. Bupendra Desai, Michael Schluter, and Graeme Donovan completed micro-oriented research on various matters treated in the agriculture chapters and provided a detailed perspective on farmers' expenditure patterns, risk and uncertainty influences on small farms, and the effects on employment of changes in technology and prices. Shakuntala Desai undertook a detailed price analysis, which is reflected in Chapter IV. The analysis of small-scale industries was dependent on the microresearch of Jan van der Veen and his critical reading of the industrialization chapters. The chapter on health and education owes much to Richard Shortlidge's detailed analysis of village education, to Shubh Kumar's search of the literature and her own work on health and family-planning programs, and to James Levinson's microresearch and careful review of early drafts. I have drawn heavily on data developed by Ram Yadav, which supplement the information from the basic working paper by Uma Lele on which the foreign trade chapter is based. Raquibuz Zaman contributed to the trade and aid chapters, as did Gorantla Doraswamy. Although he was not at Cornell during the period of work on this book, I owe a special debt to T. H. Lee, whose study of intersectoral resource transfers was seminal to much of this analysis and who introduced me to the economy of Taiwan, where several elements of what I espouse have undergone the test of time.

Much of the substantiation in this book is drawn from detailed micro-studies of farmers and merchants conducted in my continuing program prior to the initiation of this study—including the work of U. S. Bawa, Ashok Dar, Osman Farruk, Uma Lele, T. V. Moorti, V. P. Shukla, Sheldon Simon, and Thomas Weaver. The care and detail of their earlier work gave the basis and the confidence for tackling this larger task. In the early months of the research, data were pulled together by Roger Selley and Allyn Strickland, while Roger Selley made a preliminary effort to formulate a simulation model for viewing the key relationships.

Dorothy S. Wigod and Ted Young performed extensive editing. Rebecca Lacey typed with dispatch and accuracy a long series of drafts and redrafts. Joe Baldwin produced the graphs. Again, I am grateful for their contributions.

A word of encouragement and a goad at a crucial time are always important to a task of this kind; Sir John Crawford, Wolf Ladejinsky, and John P. Lewis provided those.

Finally, a word about the patience of the Twentieth Century Fund and Carol Barker. A one-and-a-half-year project, ostensibly dealing largely with the green revolution, was expanded into over four years' effort concerned with the crucial problems of employment-oriented growth. I am grateful for the encouragement and forbearance that were the response to this delay.

JOHN W. MELLOR

Ithaca, New York

I Introduction

When Jawaharlal Nehru died on May 27, 1964, a few lines by Robert Frost were found at his bedside:

> The woods are lovely, dark, and deep,
> But I have promises to keep,
> And miles to go before I sleep,
> And miles to go before I sleep.

This poem carries a sense of direction from a simpler era. As the times have changed, other lines from Frost have become appropriate. Perhaps now:

> Two roads diverged in a wood, and I—
> I took the one less traveled by,
> And that has made all the difference.

and

> Yet knowing how way leads on to way,
> I doubted if I should ever come back.[1]

This book is largely about the economic factors that determine the choice of a development strategy. The focus is on increased employment and greater participation of the poor in economic growth rather than on the redistribution of existing output. In India specifically, but more generally in the less developed world, past growth has done little for the poor. The emphasis on employment reflects an optimism that growth can be restructured to provide more jobs for more people, although powerful in-

---

[1] From "Stopping by Woods on a Snowy Evening" and "The Road Not Taken," *The Poetry of Robert Frost,* edited by Edward Connery Lathem; copyright 1916, 1923, © 1969 by Holt, Rinehart and Winston; copyright 1944, 1951 by Robert Frost; reprinted by permission of Holt, Rinehart and Winston, Publishers, Jonathan Cape Ltd, and the Estate of Robert Frost.

terest groups will not relish the complex economic changes and political decisions necessary to implement the chosen strategy.

India, the Bellwether of Change

For the past two decades, India has been the object and source of alternating attitudes toward economic development. Most notably, the Second Five-Year Plan (1955–60), developed by P. C. Mahalanobis, helped to turn attention away from growth strategies that emphasized labor mobilization and small-scale production toward a plan that stressed the acquisition of capital goods and modern industrial power. A decade and a half later, Indira Gandhi's 1971 electoral appeal to the masses coincided with a worldwide shift in concern back to direct emphasis on employment. Then, a renewed search began for means of integrating increased employment and a broadened distribution of income into a basic blueprint of economic growth.

India's post-independence economic history epitomizes the interaction of a changing political context with the evolution of economic theory and shows how that interaction may, over time, lead to a substantial shift in the strategy of growth. The economic debate on the shape and substance of the Second Five-Year Plan, while open and vigorous, was probably decided substantially on political grounds.[2] That decision then molded much of the subsequent development literature. Highly sophisticated, multisectoral, intertemporal planning models grew out of the Indian experience; many of these were designed specifically to meet the increasingly complex needs of Indian planning. But fifteen years later, a changed political emphasis demanded alternatives to the unfortunate employment and income distribution consequences of these sophisticated techniques and their accompanying theory.

The theory behind the Mahalanobis plan was elegantly simple, internally consistent, and suitable to an economy presumed to have poor prospects for agricultural and export growth.[3] The power and the relevance of

[2] In a comprehensive survey of contributions to Indian economic analysis Jagdish N. Bhagwati and Sukhamoy Chakravarty have argued similarly; see "Contributions to Indian Economic Analysis: A Survey," *American Economic Review*, 59:4, Supplement (September 1969), 2–73, esp. p. 3.

[3] The most comprehensive statements of the intellectual foundations of the Second Plan are to be found in P. C. Mahalanobis, "Some Observations on the Process of Growth of National Income," *Sankhya*, 12:4 (September 1953), 307–12, and P. C. Mahalanobis, "The Approach of Operational Research to Planning in India," *Sankhya*, 16:1 and 2 (December 1955), 3–130.

the model should not be underrated. The source of growth was capital goods and the means of growth was the allocation of resources for their acquisition. It was recognized that poverty and welfare considerations would limit the initial proportion of the economy's resources which could be distributed to capital goods rather than to consumer goods necessary to subsistence. However, the increase in output from the initial allocation of resources would largely be saved and reinvested in more capital goods production. Over time, an increasing proportion of national output would be saved and invested and hence the rate of advance would accelerate. In this theory, as long as growth in output is to be maximized, it is important that growth in employment be minimized, since employment requires wage payments, which in turn add to consumption and divert resources from producing capital goods.

Mahalanobis' conceptualization was tied in with the tradition of economic growth theory developed in the context of western high-income countries by Roy Harrod and Evsey Domar, and by G. S. Fel'dman for the autarchical growth strategy of the Soviet Union.[4] There was no place in these theories for accelerating growth by mobilizing labor, and they led in practice to a capital intensive, low-employment strategy that had little role for investment in a dynamic agriculture. The bulk of resources were to be channeled into the set of large-scale industries—most notably steel and machine building—generally identified with modern world power. In India, the employment deficiencies of this strategy were explicitly recognized and were to be met by a set of policies for agricultural and cottage industry development that were parallel to, but not an integral part of, the strategy of growth.[5] The analogy to an element of current Maoist doctrine, "walking on two legs," is surprisingly close.[6]

The opponents of the Second Plan emphasized its failure to mobilize labor, the inefficiencies of centralized administration, the inadequate ef-

---

[4] A comparative analysis of the Mahalanobis model with Harrod-Domar and dualistic models and a statement of the conditions necessary for an alternative model providing a dynamic place for agriculture and employment are given in Mellor, "Models of Economic Growth and Land-Augmenting Technological Change in Foodgrain Production," in Nurul Islam, ed., Agricultural Policy in Developing Countries (London: Macmillan, 1974), pp. 3–30.

[5] Second Five-Year Plan (New Delhi: Government of India, Planning Commission, 1956), ch. xx.

[6] The Maoist position on this matter is discussed by Chalmers Johnson, "Building a Communist Nation in China," in Robert A. Scalapino, ed., The Communist Revolution in Asia (Englewood Cliffs, N.J.: Prentice-Hall, 1965), pp. 47–81, esp. p. 56.

forts toward developing private potentials to save and to manage, the neglect of agriculture, and a series of consequences of that neglect.[7] However, the final, determinative acceptability of the capital intensive Mahalanobis strategy lay with pressing features of the then current political scene. The employment-oriented theories dominating the contemporary development literature were not perceived as meeting the domestic political needs of a large, divided country in its early years of independence, nor as contributing to fulfillment of a major role in world affairs. The force of these considerations is too often understated by people from rich nations involved in advising poor nations.

Most important and unlike the implicit alternatives, Mahalanobis' was an action model. It set clearly defined goals and provided an explicit statement of the steps to be taken in moving toward those goals. The plan was, by its very nature, centralist. The emphasis on a few large-scale industries lent itself to administration from a highly centralized bureaucracy. Pulling power and channeling resources to a central government served both to meet the real economic needs of development and to counteract the centrifugal forces of diverse language, culture, and objectives on the Indian subcontinent.[8] Since much of the national government's resources were to come from aid, the plan provided an authoritative central power at little domestic cost. Of course, the eventual decline of foreign aid would bring the strategy more under question and require the central government to pay a domestic political price for obtaining control of resources, but that event was, in 1955, over a decade away.

The approach appealed to nationalist ambition. It not only involved import displacement of consumer goods but emphasized indigenous development of heavy industry. The planning model differed somewhat in this respect from the objective espoused for Latin America.[9] There it was im-

---

[7] Among the most vigorous critics of the Second Plan were C. N. Vakil and P. R. Brahmanand, *Planning for an Expanding Economy* (Bombay: Vora, 1956); B. R. Shenoy, *Indian Planning and Economic Development* (Bombay: Asia Publishing House, 1963); and Peter Tamas Bauer, *Indian Economic Policy and Development* (London: Allen & Unwin, 1961).

[8] See, for example, K. Santhanam, *Union-State Relations in India* (Bombay: Asia Publishing House, 1960), p. 56; Amal Ray, *Tension Areas in India's Federal System* (Calcutta: World Press, 1970), p. 9; and A. Krishnaswami, *The Indian Union and the States* (Oxford: Pergamon Press, 1965). The administrative dimensions of Indian planning are discussed by A. H. Hanson, *The Process of Planning* (London: Oxford University Press, 1966).

[9] See Raul Prebisch, *The Economic Development of Latin America and Its Principal Problems* (Lake Success: United Nations, Economic Commission for Latin America, 1950).

plicit, at least, that one moved first toward import displacement with respect to the consumer goods industries. One would then, eventually, trace back to displacing imports of basic capital goods. The Indian plan presented the logic for immediate development of large-scale capital goods industries followed by an eventual working forward to consumer goods.

Finally, the Second Plan, as formulated, was attractive to donors of foreign aid because of its conceptual simplicity, appearance of precision, and facility for specific statement of foreign aid needs.[10] In this strategy, a high proportion of capital goods would have to be imported, at least initially, from high-income nations. The resulting foreign exchange shortage or gap was then to provide an important economic rationale for foreign aid.[11] Massive foreign aid in the form of capital goods increased the feasibility of the capital intensive plan by providing investment in a form most necessary to the strategy and yet most difficult to generate within that strategy.

The Mahalanobis proposal left little direct place for the rural peasant, the petty industrialist, or the poor. The opposition to neglect of the poor was disarmed in the short run by the argument that a relatively costless, rural-community and cottage-industry development program would lift real incomes of the needy and produce the goods which they consumed.[12] Dealing with the impoverished in this way was thought to be consistent with Gandhian philosophy and was not expected to compete with resources for investment in heavy industry. It was argued that, in the long run, growth alone could bring about the basis for higher employment and higher income to the poor.[13]

[10] An example is provided by Joel Bergsman and Alan S. Manne, "An Almost Consistent Intertemporal Model for India's Fourth and Fifth Plans," in Irma Adelman and Erik Thorbecke, eds., *The Theory and Design of Economic Development* (Baltimore: Johns Hopkins University Press, 1966), pp. 239–56.

[11] H. B. Chenery and A. M. Strout, "Foreign Assistance and Economic Development," *American Economic Review*, 56:4 (September 1966), 679–733.

[12] Mahalanobis argued that "a comparatively small amount of capital (invested in small-scale and household industries) could generate a large volume of employment and could also supply much additional consumer goods for sale," op. cit., 1955, p. 15. See also *Second Five-Year Plan*, pp. 235–45.

[13] Note, for example, the similarity between Robert S. McNamara's statement of the "essential elements of any comprehensive program" for "increasing the productivity of smallholder agriculture" and those of the Second Plan in Robert S. McNamara, "Address to the Board of Governors," Nairobi, Kenya, September 24, 1974 (Washington, D.C.: International Bank for Reconstruction and Development, 1973), p. 17; and *Second Five-Year Plan*, p. 318.

With the largely political and administrative considerations receiving major weight, the Second Plan was supported, and the attention of the economics profession both in India and abroad turned to the practical and esoteric details of a capital-oriented pattern of growth. The labor-oriented approach, which had been in the vanguard of thought in the 1950s, became a dead end of academic curiosity, of little fashion in the economics profession and of even less impact on the policy of most developing countries and foreign aid donors.

Disappointing Growth

As for similar strategies in other countries, the Second Plan produced much slower growth than expected, and even that growth rate was substantially dependent on foreign aid. The poor did not benefit significantly from the ancillary development of rural areas and cottage industries. On the more positive side, a large infrastructure of growth institutions and a broad industrial sector were built which could, in the future, facilitate a more effective strategy of development. Most important, one of the world's largest, poorest, and most stagnant economies was thrust into a process of expansion which might later be steered in a more immediately productive direction. Although the overall rate of advance was slow, the structural changes within that advance were immense.

According to official Indian statistics, per capita national income, expressed in constant prices, grew at an annual rate of only 1.1 percent from 1955–56 to 1959–60 and 1.4 percent from 1960–61 to 1970–71—providing increases of 4 and 15 percent respectively (Table I-1). The rate of growth was faster during the Third Plan period (1960 to 1965), when foreign aid rose quickly, than in either the preceding decade or in the subsequent drought-afflicted years, when foreign aid declined rapidly. For the fifteen years from 1955–56 to 1970–71, foodgrain production increased at an annual rate of about 3 percent, with growth a little slower in the Third Plan period than in the Second, and then accelerated into the 1970s (see Chapter II). This compares with an average annual growth rate of foodgrain production of only 0.11 percent in the five decades preceding independence.[14] Industrial production rose at a rate of 6.5 percent during the 1955–56 to 1970–71 period, with somewhat faster growth in the Third Plan than in the preceding or subsequent five-year periods (see

[14] George Blyn, *Agricultural Trends in India, 1891–1947: Output, Availability, and Productivity* (Philadelphia: University of Pennsylvania Press, 1966), p. 96.

Table I-1. Indexes of net national income in constant prices, India, 1949–50 to 1973–74

Year	Net national income 1960–61 base *	
	Index	Index per capita †
1949–50	69.3	85.5
1950–51	69.5	84.4
1951–52	71.5	85.4
1952–53	74.3	87.2
1953–54	78.8	90.8
1954–55	80.7	91.3
1955–56	82.3	91.3
1956–57	86.4	94.0
1957–58	85.5	91.2
1958–59	91.5	95.5
1959–60	93.1	95.2
1960–61	100.0	100.0
1961–62	103.4	101.2
1962–63	105.5	100.8
1963–64	111.3	104.1
1964–65	119.7	109.6
1965–66	113.7	101.7
1966–67	115.0	100.8
1967–68	125.2	107.4
1968–69	129.5	108.5
1969–70	136.8	112.2
1970–71	143.5	115.1
1971–72	145.5	114.0
1972–73	144.2	110.4
1973–74	148.7	111.3

* Net national income in the base year was US$ 27,796 million at the current exchange rate.
† Per capita net national income in the base year was US$ 64.05 at the current exchange rate.

Sources: The single base series were constructed by connecting different base series presented in Government of India, Ministry of Finance, *Economic Survey, 1969–70* (New Delhi: Government of India Press, 1970); and Government of India, Central Statistical Organisation, *Monthly Abstract of Statistics,* 28:2 (February 1975).

Table I-2). The production of investment goods was particularly strengthened, rising to 21 percent of industrial value added in 1963 compared to less than 7 percent in 1951, while consumer goods' share of value added declined from 58 percent in 1951 to 38 percent in 1963.[15]

Slow growth in per capita national income under the capital intensive plan of the 1950s and 1960s was in part due to the basic strategy, in part to the pattern of administration, and in part to the initially low level of income.

[15] Jagdish N. Bhagwati and Padma Desai, *India, Planning for Industrialization* (London: Oxford University Press, 1970), pp. 106–7.

Table I-2. Indexes of industrial, agricultural, and foodgrain production, India, 1949–50 to 1973–74

	Indexes production		
	Industrial *	Agricultural †	Foodgrain †
Year	1960 Base	Triennium ending 1961–62 base	
1949–50	52.6	72.8	74.9
1950–51	52.0	68.9	67.4
1951–52	58.0	70.3	68.2
1952–53	60.0	74.1	75.4
1953–54	61.2	83.9	89.0
1954–55	65.4	84.8	85.7
1955–56	70.6	84.4	85.6
1956–57	76.9	89.5	89.5
1957–58	80.0	83.7	81.7
1958–59	82.8	96.6	97.0
1959–60	89.8	94.3	95.2
1960–61	100.0	102.7	102.1
1961–62	109.2	103.0	102.7
1962–63	119.8	101.4	99.4
1963–64	129.7	103.9	101.7
1964–65	140.8	115.0	112.0
1965–66	153.8	95.8	89.9
1966–67	152.7	95.9	91.9
1967–68	151.4	116.8	117.1
1968–69	161.1	114.8	115.7
1969–70	172.4	122.5	123.5
1970–71	184.3	131.4	133.9
1971–72	186.1	130.9	132.0
1972–73	199.5	120.6	121.2
1973–74	200.4	131.6	130.3

* Refers to calendar year.
† Refers to agricultural year ending in June.
Sources: Column 1: The single base series was computed by connecting four different published series, each based respectively in 1946, 1951, 1956, and 1960. The figures were taken from Reserve Bank of India, *Bulletin,* various issues; Reserve Bank of India, *Report on Currency and Finance* (Bombay: Reserve Bank of India), various issues; and Government of India, Central Statistical Organisation, *Monthly Abstract of Statistics,* 27:12 (December 1974). Columns 2 and 3: Government of India, Directorate of Economics and Statistics, *Agricultural Situation in India,* 29:9 (December 1974).

The Mahalanobis scheme contained, in practice, a potentially damaging inconsistency: it assumed that the ratio of capital to labor would remain constant over time—growth in capital allowing a proportionate mobilization of underemployed labor. However, since the vehicle of added investment was to be large-scale heavy industry, it was inevitable that the ratio of additional capital to additional labor employed would rise sharply, rather than decline (see Chapter V). As a result, as investment expanded, payments received per unit of capital would be expected to decline, with consequent loss of power to the system's basic engine of growth.

The chosen pattern of administration was to decrease further the short-run returns to capital. In the Indian approach to maximizing growth of the capital stock, the emphasis was not on concentrating wealth in the hands of private individuals who would be expected to save heavily—as in the private enterprise version of the strategy. Instead, for ideological reasons and because of uncertainty as to the will and capacity of the private sector to expand rapidly the predetermined sectors, the Indian emphasis was on the government itself directing the economy's resources to production of capital goods—in the style of the Soviet Union. The consequence of this attitude was insistence on types of production which could be managed by a government bureaucracy with a reinforcing impetus toward capital intensive, large-scale, public sector industry. In practice, the strategy led to low productivity of capital, at least in the short run, as the bureaucracy was exposed to difficult and unaccustomed tasks.

India commenced independence with one of the lowest per capita incomes in the world—Rs. 256, or about 54 dollars a year, in 1949–50 at the current exchange rate. In general, the lower the initial level of income, the more difficult it is to save and invest productively, and hence the slower the initial rate of economic growth. India faced additional immense problems of integrating a vast and diverse nation across strong regional and communal lines and of protecting itself against major external threats. The savings rate was an exceedingly low 5.0 percent of national income (at market prices) in 1951–52 and rose to a still modest 11.1 percent by 1965–66 (see Chapter VI). Nevertheless, India's growth rates were still faster than would be expected from intercountry comparisons of the relationship between per capita income and various elements of growth.[16]

Again, observers from already rich nations rather consistently underrate the extent of foundation-laying necessary to a high rate of growth, expect too much in the short-run and thereby become too pessimistic about the long-run prospects of developing nations—perhaps even drawing wrong conclusions as to the actual retardants of growth.

By current standards, the least satisfactory aspect of Indian economic

[16] Simon Kuznets, *Economic Growth of Nations* (Cambridge, Mass.: Harvard University Press, 1971).

performance was the degree of participation of the poor. In the fifteen years following inception of the Second Plan, total employment in the Indian economy probably grew no faster than population; per capita incomes of the lower third to half of the inhabitants certainly did not increase and may even have declined (see Chapters IV and X). Growth was slow, and participation in the benefits of growth exceedingly narrow. At least for the needy, the record had probably worsened by 1969–70 compared to 1955–56. Reflecting the pervasiveness of low-employment strategies, this lack of participation of the poor in growth was a world-wide phenomenon of economic developmment in the 1960s and was extensively noted in the increasing international concern for employment and income distribution.

The underlying consistency of the overall plan would, of course, make it difficult to improve the employment record without major structural changes. Given the actual deployment of investment toward capital goods, if employment were to rise substantially, there would be great inflationary pressures as increased demand for consumer goods, particularly agricultural commodities, pressed against a relatively static supply.

Need for a Change

By the early 1970s, political and economic evolution suggested the potential for a change in growth strategy. Most important, as India's problems of regional integration became less strident, the broadening of the political base encouraged and amplified demands of the poor for higher incomes. Concurrent with changing political pressures, major technological advances in agriculture were being demonstrated. Full realization of new agricultural potential would at once make a high-employment policy more necessary politically and at the same time facilitate the achievement of that very objective. The rapid decline in foreign aid, the achievement of a greatly diversified industrial structure, and an enlarged capacity to administer decentralized schemes of development in both the public and private sector all pointed toward a change in strategy. The timing of such change will of course vary among countries, not only in response to these factors but also in relation to varying development objectives and differences in the natural environment.

Finally, a number of inconsistencies in the Indian economic and political structure were becoming apparent (see Chapter VI). There was imbalance between agriculture and industry—an imbalance created by the increased demand arising from growing success in industry, masked by rapid growth in food aid during the 1960s and dramatized by the terrible droughts of 1965–66 and 1966–67. There was imbalance between investment in the public sector and the ability of the political system to create public sector resources or to draw them from the private sector. There was a general imbalance developing between growth in investment and growth in domestic savings as well as in the proportion of investment and savings originating in the private corporate sector. There was a growing imbalance between the demand of the industrial sector for import of machinery and raw materials and the ability to export, or to attract increasing foreign aid. Perhaps most important, there was an imbalance between the nascent power structure implicit in a broadening electorate and the actual power structure of the current political representation and of the government administrative services.

In retrospect, the decade of the 1950s can be seen as a period of political and economic foundation laying. The first half of the 1960s was a time of accelerated growth which would begin to bring the contradictions in the system to the surface. The drought and the decline of foreign aid in the last half of the 1960s would then emphasize the need for a choice either to reinforce the old strategy of development or embark on a new one.

Reinforcement of the old strategy would not be easy. The imbalances between demand and supply of agricultural commodities and between public sector savings and investment needs would both have to be met by tighter control of incomes and resources in order to decrease consumption, increase savings, and channel reserves more completely through government hands. These measures would entail greater control of the political as well as the economic system.

As will become clear in later chapters, the new strategy would involve considerable decentralization of government planning and administration of growth, and it would require major shifts in the structure of that growth. The complexity of these changes necessarily provides uncertainty as to the success to be achieved. Perhaps more important, the changes themselves involved shifts in the sources of power and could produce a feeling of despair for the future within a significant group of influential people. Nearly two decades of planning under the old strategy had given strength to substantial vested interests, and nearly a decade of relative stagnation had added an element of pessimism and cynicism inimical to the courage and self-confidence needed for an effective new thrust.

As for so many of the African and Asian nations, so in India, both economic and political factors make it unlikely that poverty will be substantially reduced by the introduction of measures for the redistribution of existing output. Initial levels of average per capita income are extremely low, and the consumption patterns of the poor differ substantially from those of the rest of society. Thus, for each unit of income transferred from the rich to the poor, there will be much less reduction in food expenditure by the rich than increase by the poor (see Chapter VII). Food rationing is politically difficult, even in the context of a major shuffling of power. In addition, redistribution of land and income will not help unless it deprives not just the top few rich landowners and capitalists but also vast numbers of politically potent middle-class peasants and factory workers and members of the urban middle class, particularly government civil servants (see Chapter IV). It seems unlikely that "relevant radicalism" will touch these groups. Nehru's statement as early as 1947 of the irrelevance of redistributing poverty is revealing of the political if not the economic realities.[17]

The New Strategy

The major theses of a consistent strategy of employment-oriented growth are conceptually simple. Income of the poor is determined by both the pace and the pattern of national production, which in turn determine the rate of growth of employment. It is through increased demand for labor that the poor participate actively in development. However, additionally employed labor must be productively used if it is to generate the income necessary for improved levels of living and the capital requisite for continued advance in employment. Economic progress may in practice be a necessary condition of increased income to the needy but it certainly is not a sufficient condition.

Substantially raising incomes of the poor necessarily increases their effective demand for food and, short of massive redistribution, requires rates of increase in food production far in excess of those achieved under previous strategies of growth. Increased food supply is thus the prime production component of increased welfare of the poor. Within the usual economic and political context, necessary increases in food supply can only occur through technological innovation which normally distributes

[17] Jawaharlal Nehru, *Independence and After: A Collection of Speeches, 1946–1949* (New York: Day, 1950), pp. 148–51.

the initial benefits largely to the already more prosperous rural people. This initial increase in rural income sets in motion a sequence of multiplier effects which can stimulate expanded production and employment in other sectors of the economy. These processes increase the relative importance of consumer goods industries and small-scale enterprises. Such industries tend to be less capital intensive than those emphasized in the earlier strategy and tap sources of savings not otherwise developed. They also require increased imports and facilitate increased exports. As an alternative to a capital intensive strategy, this employment-oriented approach has potential for a faster rate of growth in total income as well as for greater participation of the poor in the benefits.

The changes requisite to the employment-oriented strategy may be impeded or stopped at numerous points by difficulties in making the necessary institutional modifications and by political resistance from the vested interests in the old strategy. Success requires an altered approach to planning, setting of new investment priorities, and vigorous institutional change. None of this is particularly simple or more palatable than pursuit of the old strategy.

In practice, shift to an employment-oriented strategy for India as for other countries requires four substantive elements of change. *First,* it must give priority to increasing agricultural production through investment in new technology. *Second,* it must reduce the capital requirements per employee in the industrial sector and tap new sources of capital through decentralization of production. *Third,* to expedite the decrease in capital intensity, the growth rate of both exports and imports must increase. *Fourth,* planning and administrative procedures and institutions must also be decentralized and emphasis switched from regulatory to facilitatory procedures. These changes have profound implications for both domestic and international politics; as in the 1950s, the choice of strategy may depend primarily on these political considerations.

The Pivotal Role of Agriculture

The full role of agriculture in an employment-oriented strategy and the crucial conditions of its fulfilling that role are so little understood that they must be spelled out in some detail. Agriculture performs two key, related functions in the new approach. First, because foodgrains make up the bulk of marginal expenditures among the poorer classes, agriculture provides the physical goods to support increased employment and higher wage earnings. In other words, the agricultural sector is a crucial source of wage goods—the goods purchased with wages. And, it provides much of the increase in employment—directly through raising agricultural production, indirectly through the stimulus of increased income to the cultivator class and the demand effects of the consequent expenditure. Because of the conditions of agricultural production, these functions can be effectively fulfilled only if agrotechnical innovations are developed and applied.

Increased agricultural production, based on cost-decreasing technological change, can make large net additions to national income and place that income in the hands of the cultivator classes, who tend to spend a substantial proportion of it on nonagricultural commodities.[18] Agriculture may provide a demand drive for development similar to that often depicted for foreign markets in export-led growth (see Chapter VI).

In a peasant agriculture such as that dominating the bulk of Asia and Africa, the consumer goods industries, stimulated by increased rural incomes, are likely to be relatively labor intensive. The larger agricultural production by the wealthier landowning classes results in increased marketings of food and increased cash incomes to farmers from the marketings of that food. The bigger cash incomes provide a demand for increased nonagricultural production and a resultant rise in employment. The expanded employment of the lower-income laboring classes, who spend the bulk of increased income on food, provides the demand for additional food production. Indeed, if an increase in employment of lower-income people does not accompany the increased agricultural output, there will be inadequate demand, and agricultural prices may decline sufficiently to discourage continued growth of production. Accelerated growth of agriculture may be an important condition for a high-employment policy, but a high-employment policy is an important condition for continued rapid growth rates in the agricultural sector. This im-

---

[18] Theoretical and empirical expositions of this view are developed by Uma J. Lele and John W. Mellor in "Technological Change and Distributive Bias," Department of Agricultural Economics Occasional Paper No. 43 (revised), Cornell University USAID Employment and Income Distribution Project (October 1972). In subsequent references these publications will be identified as Cornell Agricultural Economics Occasional Papers, followed by the relevant number and date. Also see John W. Mellor and Uma J. Lele, "Growth Linkages of the New Foodgrain Technologies," *Indian Journal of Agricultural Economics,* 28:1 (January–March 1973), 35–55; and Uma J. Lele and John W. Mellor, "Jobs, Poverty and the 'Green Revolution,' " *International Affairs,* 48:1 (January 1972).

portant interrelationship requires the assistance of astute government policy if it is to work smoothly and effectively.

Unfortunately, agriculture has traditionally had difficulty in fulfilling either of its two roles in an employment-oriented strategy. Because of a relatively fixed land area and consequent diminishing returns to greater use of other production inputs, agriculture has tended to experience rising costs of production and decreasing productivity of labor and other non-land resources, as output rises. These increasing costs require that, over time, more and more capital and other resources be transferred to agriculture to achieve a given growth in production.[19] The mounting costs of production are likely to be reflected in relatively higher agricultural prices. Under these conditions, pyramiding agricultural prices have two deleterious effects. The upturn in food costs, and hence of wage goods, discourages labor intensive development. Similarly, growth in agricultural output through cost-increasing methods in the long run detracts from potential national income gains in other sectors by more than is added in agriculture. Thus the multiplier effects of increased agricultural income are unlikely to provide a net addition to development. It is this unfortunate and common state of affairs in agriculture which provides the most important justification of the Mahalanobis model of growth, and which dramatizes the key role of agricultural technology to an alternate, employment-oriented strategy.

As food prices rise, the politically potent urban middle classes and organized labor revolt and bring about policies which reduce the growth in employment and in the demand for food. More conservative monetary policy will restrict credit and squeeze those industries most dependent on working capital. It is the labor intensive industries that particularly need working capital not only to finance the labor force but also to finance the substantial quantity of raw materials which they inevitably process. Alternatively, inflation may be fought with a more conservative fiscal policy and a reduction in government spending. That burden, too, will most likely fall on shorter-term projects with a relatively high employment content. Thus, an employment policy without an accompanying increase in the supply of agricultural commodities at constant or decreasing cost will almost surely be defeated as inflation mounts and anti-inflationary measures are brought to bear.

[19] Mellor, in Islam, ed., op. cit.

There are three ways, other than massive redistribution of wealth and income, to deal with rising costs of production in the agricultural sector: imports of agricultural commodities, rationing, and cost-decreasing technological innovations.

The alternative of increasing imports is only marginally open to a large country, or for that matter the collectivity of small countries, whose aggregate demand might significantly raise world price levels. In addition, there is likely to be fear that imports will exacerbate an already difficult foreign exchange problem and make the country dependent on foreign sources for a critical element of survival.

Food rationing is an economically viable alternative, if increased quantities of manufactured consumer goods are more cheaply provided. Simplistically, rationing of food to the well-to-do releases supplies to be purchased by the poor, who then produce alternative, labor intensive consumer goods to absorb the pent-up purchasing power of the more wealthy. This result cannot be achieved by the price mechanism alone because the rich reduce their level of food consumption very little in response to higher prices; the adjustment thus is forced largely on the poor, whose income is sharply reduced by higher food prices. Unfortunately, the rationing approach is politically difficult because of the power of the middle- and upper-income classes, whose consumption must be constrained, and administratively difficult because of the large numbers of people to be reached.

Where feasible, the introduction of yield-increasing technological methods in agriculture can reduce costs of production, allowing increased demand to be met without increased prices, while real incomes of rural people rise. It is a superior alternative to imports and rationing, but it will cost money. Technological advance in agriculture requires research. There must be massive investment in the physical infrastructure of rural communication and irrigation systems as well as the institutional infrastructure for servicing agriculture with research, education, credit, input supply, and marketing systems. There must, in addition, be large expenditure on fertilizer and insecticides, in most cases requiring substantial allocation of foreign exchange. It may well be that, for technical reasons, success in the areas crucial to an employment-oriented strategy was not possible at the time of India's Second Plan and hence that the capital intensive approach was appropriate at that time. On the other hand, application of the plan's theory may have been self-fulfilling, as agriculture was deprived of the resources and attention necessary to the eventual success of technological development.

It is thus the dominance of agricultural commodities as wage goods and the large supply of labor available for mobilization which combine to make creation of a modern, technologically dynamic agriculture so important to economic growth and to the participation of the poor in that growth.

New Industrial Strategy

With success in agriculture, a new strategy for industry must conserve capital and tap new sources of savings. In the new approach, pressure on capital supplies arises from the additional needs for agricultural development combined with the large growth in employment. Compared to the capital intensive strategy, the new industrial plan will increase the relative importance of consumer goods and small-scale, decentralized industries, and will require larger imports of capital intensive products and enlarged exports of labor intensive products.

Consumer goods often offer a wider scope for labor intensive production than capital goods. This is particularly true, as in the Indian case, where the relevant comparison is between consumer goods purchased by peasant farmers in the new strategy with capital goods produced in large-scale modern industries under the old strategy. Increased demand for consumer goods is a material outgrowth of rising rural incomes associated with accelerated technological change in agricultural production. It is then the function of industrial policy to facilitate expansion of consumer goods production.

Rising rural incomes increase demand in rural areas and thereby encourage decentralization of production to those areas. Higher rural incomes and production encourage investment in the infrastructure of transportation, communication, and electrification, all of which are important to the development of small-scale industries. And, the higher incomes in rural areas provide a larger pool for investment in local, small-scale industries. The generality of this argument is perhaps most strikingly illustrated by its vigorous application in the People's Republic of China during the past decade.

Increased international trade is a crucial part of an employment-oriented industrial strategy. Both the agricultural and the industrial growth crucial to the employment-oriented strategy require large quantities of intermediate products produced with highly capital intensive processes—for example, fertilizer and pesticides for agriculture; and steel, petrochemicals, and synthetic fibers for industry. Domestic manufacture of these products will divert vital capital from agriculture as well as from the relatively labor intensive industries which must provide the bulk of employment. A substantial proportion of such products must be imported. Increased exports are then required to pay for the imports of capital intensive products. Fortunately, increased exports are expedited by the strategy, which raises the supply of wage goods and hence of relatively low-cost labor. It is in such labor intensive exports that India and other low-income nations have a potential, competitive advantage relative to high-income nations in the world markets. Increased domestic demand from the more prosperous rural areas will further speed the growth of labor intensive output and prepare more firms for export competition if their supplies of production resources are assured. The unfavorable trade record under the capital intensive approach does not indicate poor prospects under a labor intensive approach. Indeed, it is clear that, as has so often been the case, the prophecy of inferior export performance for India's Second Plan was self-fulfilling as resources were largely committed to capital intensive production, in which India was necessarily in an inadequate competitive position on world markets.

It should be remembered, however, that as the capacity to trade of low-income countries such as India increases, high-income countries will have to increase their imports as well as their exports, with consequent domestic adjustments. It seems hypocritical of spokesmen of developed nations to espouse high-employment policies and broad distribution of income within less-developed countries without the corollary actions directly under their own control.

Implementational Needs

Alternative strategies of growth pose different problems of implementation and therefore different personnel and institutional requirements. The emphasis, in India's capital intensive strategy, was on central determination of resource allocation and a system of restrictive licenses and controls to prevent distribution of resources to uses perceived as undesirable. But the plans failed to provide for detailed technical information necessary to guide controls and for technically competent personnel to operate the rapidly expanding assignments of large-scale industry.

The employment-oriented strategy will obviously demand even more trained personnel, and most important, the administrative structure will be much more decentralized. Agricultural development itself, because of the high degree of irregularity in the conditions of production, must be a considerably decentralized process. In addition, because of small-scale production and rapid growth in needs, agriculture requires an intricate set of public institutions to support its growth. Likewise, the development of consumer goods industries and small-scale enterprises is likely to prosper more under decentralized decision-making processes and a wide range of credit, transport, technical, and other facilitative institutions. This is because such industries operate under acutely variable production conditions, rapidly changing supply and demand situations, and a reduced ability to provide their own service needs, compared to large-scale capital intensive industries. Similarly, if export is to increase successfully, entrepreneurs must be free to take ready advantage of rapidly changing production and demand potentials.

The Prospects for Change in Strategy

In India, as in so many countries, the economic basis for an employment-oriented strategy of growth is more favorable now than in the 1950s. The potentials in agriculture and the means of reaching those potentials are larger. The industrial base has greatly broadened, increasing the domestic multiplier effects of rising rural incomes as well as providing a wider range of goods for export expansion. Perhaps most important, the public and private infrastructure of institutions and trained manpower has greatly increased. On the other hand, in 1975, ten years of near stagnation of the economy—due to droughts and the decline of foreign aid—had clearly created morale and even resource problems that were much more severe than in 1965. The droughts of 1972–73 and 1973–74 were particularly debilitating. Of course, optimism that the capital intensive strategy would provide high growth rates has diminished. Nevertheless, there remain uncertainties with respect to economic feasibility of the new strategy.

In general, the employment-oriented growth plan fails if major technological change in agriculture does not provide significant acceleration in production. Even though the means of achieving agrotechnical innovations are better understood now than a decade ago, and there have already been major breakthroughs in small regions, for India and most of the developing world acceleration in the overall growth rate in agriculture has still been modest at best. Similarly, there is likely to be lag in the promised export rise behind the immediately required import growth, with a consequent short-run increase in the trade deficit. Both alternatives—accumulated foreign borrowing and declining foreign exchange reserves— offer major political and economic risks. There is a related concern as to whether the trade policies of high-income countries will facilitate the necessary export expansion if the bulk of low-income nations becomes structured to produce relatively labor intensive exports. There may also be concern as to whether the necessary supportive structures, such as credit and communications, can be sufficiently developed to provide for rapid increases in employment in small-scale consumer-oriented industries and in agriculture.

But it is more likely that political factors, rather than these economic uncertainties, will retard a change in strategy. The problems and concerns with international power remain—and in the short run continue to be less effectively dealt with by the new strategy than by the old.

At least in the short run, the labor intensive strategy calls for relatively less investment in the large-scale industries that are associated with an industrial-military complex. A large country like India may well feel particularly ill-advised to follow such a course, given the current realities of world power politics. While it may seem unconscionable for a poor nation to turn away from an employment-oriented strategy which offers the major hope for quick alleviation of the poverty of its lower-income people, it seems equally unconscionable for the rich nations of the world to provide an environment of power politics which dissuades poor nations from that choice. As with development generally, so for national defense: the faster overall growth rates associated with the employment-oriented approach offer potential for a larger heavy industry complex in the long run—but Keynes' dictum that in the long run we are all dead may, in these circumstances, apply to nations, or at least to their rulers, as well.

It is also true that dependence on imports for capital intensive intermediate products presents a potential for uncertainty of supply from volatile international markets. This may, of course, be a no more serious problem than the normal vagaries of domestic supply in the face of small capacity relative to consumption, erratic power supplies, and frequent breakdown of domestic production, and may at least partially be met by long-term purchase contracts.

The old arguments of domestic political integration that supported the centralization of resources and political control which accompanied the capital intensive Second Plan are much less pressing now than in the first decade of independence. But meanwhile, application of the strategy that grew from those needs has now created its own set of vested interests. Farmers with large holdings have learned how to control the allocation of scarce supplies of fertilizer and other inputs of agricultural modernization, and politicians and bureaucrats enjoy the power and income which arises from continued scarcity of these elements.

More difficult to gauge, urban intellectuals of the political left tend to see their interests more in the old strategy of direct state control over allocation of resources than in the new approach, with its greater emphasis on the market. Defense of the old strategy by the left, undoubtedly of importance in many low-income nations, rises in part from an unrealistic view of the extent to which direct controls can be an effective tool to alleviate poverty without major redistribution of assets and related changes in institutions—in part from hope that radical redistribution of assets and income is indeed possible, and perhaps in part from desire to maintain the power and influence on the central planning mechanisms that are so important to the old strategy but which diminish in importance in the new. The dilemma for the left may increase as the new model tends to increase incomes of the small- and medium-scale businessman and large-scale farmers, as well as ameliorating the lot of the poor. Opposition to improved position for the businessmen and farmers may overbalance concern for improvement of the poor.

While understating the immensity of the adjustment process in moving from one type of plan to another, the succeeding chapters analyze the various components of an employment-oriented strategy of growth, emphasizing the role of agricultural development as a means of achieving the human objective of improved welfare.

II
The Agricultural Sector: Characteristics, Policy, and Achievement

Agriculture dominates change in essentially all low-income nations. In India it accounts directly for nearly half of the national product and provides a major portion of both raw materials and markets for the industrial sector. Agriculture will dominate an employment-oriented strategy of development because it contains over two-thirds of the labor force, including the bulk of the reserve army of low-productivity labor, produces the principal consumer goods needed to sustain rapid increase in incomes of the newly employed, and may provide a major net stimulus to demand for the output of other sectors.

The institutions and basic knowledge necessary for permanently accelerated growth in agricultural production are now largely in place as a result of the policy evolution of the past two decades. There has already been some increase in the output growth rate; very substantial change in the sources of growth promises faster development in the future. There must now be further refinement and expansion of the institutions and massive investment if the promise is to be realized.

The Dominant Size of the Agricultural Sector

It is the sheer massiveness of India's agricultural sector which dictates the large quantity of resources needed for its development and the substantial results possible from that development. Consequent to the economy's relatively rapid growth from 1960–61 to 1964–65, agriculture's share of the total net domestic product, measured in 1960–61 prices, declined from 51 percent to 47 percent and, by 1970–71, had fallen further, to 44 percent.[1] Nevertheless, in 1970–71, after two decades of

[1] Government of India, Central Statistical Organisation, *Statistical Abstract of India, 1970*, No. 18 (New Delhi: Government of India Press, 1972); Government of India, Min-

major emphasis on rapid growth in the industrial sector, agriculture was still nearly four and one-half times more important than industry as a proportion of net domestic product. Because of this continued agricultural dominance, it remains difficult for the industrial sector alone to provide high overall rates of economic growth. Similarly, major short-term, weather-induced changes in agricultural output contribute to a highly deceptive impression of current aggregate economic trends.

Since total national savings and investment are closely related to national income, agriculture-induced fluctuations in national income have a marked effect on the potential for investment in the industrial sector. This relationship was, of course, somewhat weakened in the decade from the mid-1950s to the mid-1960s by the availability of foreign aid as a major source of investment funds. In addition, many factors cause varying lags in adjustment between changes in savings, national income, and agricultural production. Nevertheless, sharp declines in domestic savings were associated with the three major setbacks in agricultural production of the post-independence period—1950–51, 1957–58, and 1965–66. The most dramatic cutback in savings was associated with the most dramatic decline in agriculture, in 1965–66, when production fell 17 percent from the previous year and total savings in current prices declined 27.5 percent from 1965–66 to 1966–67 (Figure II-1).

In each period of decline, the government, corporate, and household sectors participated in the decrease (and the subsequent sharp increase) in savings associated with the slump in (and recovery of) agriculture.[2] In the case of the government, it appears that a squeeze between increased wage expenditures, caused by higher food prices, and a decline in the tax base account for the drop in savings. In the household sector, savings are pressured by higher food prices and by less growth in employment. For the corporate sector, rising money wages and advancing agricultural raw material prices in the face of a downturn in production restrain both the abil-

istry of Finance, *Economic Survey, 1971–72* (New Delhi: Government of India Press, 1972). Subsequent references to these two serial publications, standard sources for data on the Indian economy, cite them as *Statistical Abstract of India* and *Economic Survey,* followed by the relevant year.

[2] These relationships are analyzed in detail in Ujagar S. Bawa, *Agricultural Production and Industrial Capital Formation, India, 1951–52 to 1964–65,* Cornell International Agricultural Development Bulletin No. 17 (March 1971), Cornell University, Ithaca, N.Y. In subsequent references, these publications will be identified as C.I.A.D. bulletins, followed by the relevant number and publication date.

Figure II-1. Indexes of agricultural production, industrial production, and savings, India, 1950–51 to 1971–72 *

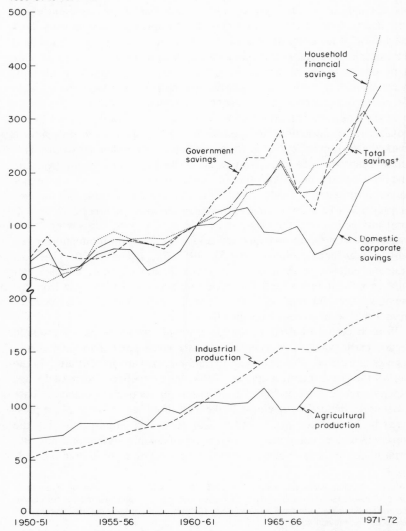

* Base year for the indices is 1960–61, except the index of agricultural production, for which the base is 1961–62.

† Excluding household physical assets.

Sources: Savings constructed from data in *Report on Currency and Finance* (Bombay: Reserve Bank of India, various issues); agricultural production and industrial production based on Table I-2.

ity and the incentives to save. It is noteworthy that in 1959, industries processing agricultural commodities still provided over 50 percent of industrial value added; for those industries, raw materials comprised over half of the total costs, with wages and salaries comprising an additional sixth of the total costs.[3]

In 1971, the total male labor force in India was on the order of 150 million people; it was growing by approximately 3 million persons per year, and over two-thirds of that labor force was occupied in agriculture.[4] Much of the rural labor force is exceedingly poor, only seasonally employed, and works at low productivity and low wages.[5] Any solution to the complex problem of poverty in India must provide additional employment sufficient to absorb both increments into the labor force and a substantial proportion of the man-year equivalent of the already seasonally unemployed. While, in the long run, increased employment will have to be found largely in the non-agricultural sector, greater productive employment in the agricultural sector will provide immediate improvement in incomes of the poor.

The Special Characteristics of Agricultural Production

Agriculture demands special attention in the development process not only because of its magnitude but also because of the peculiar nature of its production conditions.[6] Agricultural production in India takes place through the decisions of over 65 million farm families on a limited, heterogeneous land area. It is the paucity of knowledge and the immensity and

---

[3] See Bawa, pp. 9, 41.

[4] The estimate of annual additions to the labor force was derived by projecting age-specific population figures from the 1961 census (see Ansley J. Coale and Edgar M. Hoover, *Population Growth and Economic Development in Low-Income Countries: A Case Study of India's Prospects* [Princeton, N.J.: Princeton University Press, 1958]) and applying labor force participation rates from S. N. Agarwala, *Some Problems in India's Population* (Bombay: Vora, 1966). The estimate of the male labor force is from the 1971 census. The 1971 census uses such a restrictive definition of the labor force that women and agricultural laborers are substantially underestimated, compared to the 1961 census. The effect of change in definition is less marked with respect to the male labor force than for the female or total labor force. For a full discussion of the issues, see J. Krishnamurty, "Working Force in 1971 Census: Some Exercises on Provisional Results," *Economic and Political Weekly*, 7:3 (January 15, 1972), 115–18.

[5] For a detailed description of agricultural labor conditions in India, see *Agricultural Labour in India: Report on the Second Agricultural Labour Enquiry, 1956–57* (Delhi: Government of India, Ministry of Labour and Employment, 1961), Vol. I.

[6] The following review draws heavily on various chapters in John W. Mellor, *The Economics of Agricultural Development* (Ithaca, N.Y.: Cornell University Press, 1966).

complexity of the task of technological change for such a varied, diffuse sector that have baffled many development economists and administrators and often turned them away from agriculture as an engine of employment-oriented growth.

The human factor in agricultural development has always been a key consideration in Indian planning. Unfortunately, the view implicitly guiding the first two five-year plans, and one still surprisingly widespread with respect to other low income countries, was that the farmer was a tradition-bound, backward person who lacked the aspirations and the drive to respond to economic stimuli and who, in ignorance, rejected profitable opportunities to increase the nation's production and his income.[7] A primary effect of these assumptions was an underallocation of funds to research for providing new techniques of production (see Chapter III). The initial approach to community development was intended to change the attitudes of rural people toward the use of production-increasing technology and make possible their participation in rational decision making. In practice, there was little new, profitable technology for them to choose.

Misinterpretation of the human factor in rural development arose from failure to understand the complex economic relations between the farmer's business world and his household life, the economic implications of the high risks which farmers face, the effect of great heterogeneity of physical, economic, and institutional conditions on the applicability of innovations, and the burden which the limited land base places on technological change as the means of increasing agricultural production.

Farmers' decisions in allocating capital and labor between household and business uses may often entail the sacrifice of agricultural output in the future for the satisfaction of such immediate wants as improved health and better child care. In the complex decision-making environment of the farmer, innovation must allow for increases in the total welfare of the family if it is to raise output effectively.

Farmers appear conservative because agriculture has high risks. In India, only a small proportion of the land area is irrigated, and the mon-

---

[7] Sir Manilal Nanavati provides an early expression of awareness of this stereotype and its implications in "Problems of Indian Agriculture," *Proceedings of the Sixth International Conference of Agricultural Economists* (London: Oxford University Press, 1948), pp. 265–77.

soon is unreliable. Much of the small irrigated area depends on inadequate water storage capacity, with a consequent substantial reliance on short-run natural rainfall. Low-income farmers hesitate to invest in fertilizer and other inputs whose return depends on unpredictable weather. In addition, as long as the experiment stations and extension systems are rudimentary and farming conditions heterogeneous, there will be a high risk that recommendations concerning innovation will be incorrect. The apparent backwardness of farmers often reflects the actual backwardness of supporting organizations.

Severe pressure of population on the land conditions not only the decisions of individual farmers but the strategy of agricultural development as well. In India, this pressure on land is so great that returns to other resources have, under conventional conditions, already been driven to very low levels.[8] Thus, with traditional Indian foodgrain varieties, use of fertilizer beyond a modest initial amount causes returns from further increments to drop precipitously.[9] The same circumstance applies to labor and has already, in most of Indian agriculture, forced productivity to minimal levels.[10] Low returns to added inputs, under traditional agriculture, make aggregate production quite unresponsive to price and thereby largely rule out price policy alone as an effective direct means of increasing output.

In the early 1960s, as economists began to recognize the rationality behind the production methods of Indian farmers, there was a retreat from the desire to change their ways and attitudes. For a time, economists

[8] Land as a severe restraint on agricultural production is in India a phenomenon of the last century. The special incentives provided in the mid-eighteenth century to encourage land settlement and clearing in a new, densely populated district in central India are described in Thomas Weaver, "The Farmers of Raipur," in John W. Mellor et al., *Developing Rural India: Plan and Practice* (Ithaca, N.Y.: Cornell University Press, 1968). See also a description of the initial settlement, in the eighteenth century, of a village in Eastern Uttar Pradesh, now one of the most densely populated areas in India, in Sheldon Simon, "The Village of Senapur," ibid.

[9] Varietal comparisons between traditional and modern seed varieties are presented in Robert W. Herdt and John W. Mellor, "The Contrasting Response of Rice to Nitrogen: India and the United States," *Journal of Farm Economics*, 46:1 (February 1964), 150–60; and Gunvant M. Desai, *Growth of Fertilizer Use in Indian Agriculture: Past Trends and Future Demand*, C.I.A.D. Bulletin No. 18 (July 1969), 40–44.

[10] In a paper demonstrating the economic rationality of farmers, W. David Hopper shows a return to additional labor of about twenty-five cents per day, in 1954 prices: "Allocation Efficiency in a Traditional Indian Agriculture," *Journal of Farm Economics*, 47:3 (August 1965), 611–24.

stressed price policy as an alternative means of increasing production.[11] A number of studies demonstrated substantial potential for the effective use of varying relative prices to induce the shifting of acreage from one crop to another.[12] But in the context of stagnant technology and few purchased inputs, such shuffling cannot increase the aggregate foodgrain supply, as foodgrain crops already occupy the bulk of cultivable acreage. Empirical studies have shown that, in the past, the total supply of agricultural commodities in India has been quite unresponsive to shifts in relative agricultural prices.[13] (This, of course, does not mean that changes in relative agricultural prices cannot affect the composition of agricultural production and the employment content of that production [see Chapter IV].)

Relative agricultural prices indicate the balance between agricultural and industrial development and play an important role in distributing benefits or losses of a growth process.[14] When a growing population requires more agricultural production, at the cost of lower productivity and greater use of real resources, someone is getting poorer; relative price changes allocate the decline in per capita income between the farmer and the urban consumer. Similarly, when new technology increases production efficiency, someone is getting richer, and relative prices determine who he will be. Likewise, when nonagricultural employment grows rapidly, demanding more food production, rising agricultural prices signal the relative failure of the agricultural sector to play its supporting role and the need to increase production. If that production increase does not

[11] M. L. Dantwala presents a well-reasoned discussion of the various conflicting points of view on this matter in *Comparative Experience of Agricultural Development in Developing Countries of Asia and the South-East since World War II* (Bombay: Indian Society of Agricultural Economics, 1972), Preface.

[12] See, for example, Raj Krishna, "Farm Supply Response in India-Pakistan: A Case Study of the Punjab Region," *Economic Journal,* 73:291 (September 1963), 477–87; and L. S. Venkataramanan, "A Statistical Study of Indian Jute Production and Marketing with Special Reference to Foreign Demand" (Ph.D. dissertation, University of Chicago, 1958).

[13] For example, in one of the few such studies, Herdt shows the aggregate supply response for agriculture in the Punjab to range from −0.06 to 0.01 for the years 1951 to 1964, and from 0.21 to 0.22 for the years 1907 to 1946 (see Robert W. Herdt, "A Disaggregate Approach to Aggregate Supply," *American Journal of Agricultural Economics,* 52:4 [November 1970], 518–519).

[14] A more complete exposition appears in John W. Mellor, "The Functions of Agricultural Prices in Economic Development," *Indian Journal of Agricultural Economics,* 23:1 (January–March 1968), 23–37.

occur, agricultural prices may rise substantially, as the relatively inelastic demand presses against inelastic supply. The natural adjustment is then a reduced growth rate of industrial production and employment.

Technological change must be the keystone of policy by which aggregate agricultural production is increased in a manner to support economic development and transformation. In practice, as technological change increases the productivity of inputs, including fertilizer and labor, there will be not only an added incentive for increased use of such inputs, but an increase in price responsiveness and an enlarging role for price policy. But that result is an accompaniment of technological change, not a potential substitute for it.

The characteristics of agriculture just described are particularly applicable to the foodgrains sector. Many other commodities, such as fibers and oilseeds, are also major land users, but demand for them is quite responsive to changes in prices and income. Demand for vegetables, fruits, and livestock products is even more responsive to such changes. The relative importance of these commodities will grow rapidly as incomes rise. Because of their supply and demand characteristics and the interrelation of their own growth with growth in foodgrains, they are comparable with the small-scale dispersed elements of the industrial sector (see Chapter VII).

This chapter and the next emphasize foodgrains, which still dominate the agriculture of most developing nations. In India, they occupy 75 percent of the cultivated land area and carry a weight of 40 percent in total consumer expenditure. They account for about 75 percent of average spending on food and 54 percent of the total expenditure of low-income consumers.[15] Indian agricultural development policy of the last two decades has been largely a foodgrain-production strategy. As success is achieved, that strategy broadens to include a wider range of agricultural commodities.

---

[15] The figure for cultivated land is for 1969–70 and was calculated from Government of India, Directorate of Economics and Statistics, *Indian Agriculture in Brief*, 12th ed. (New Delhi: Government Printer, 1973). This official publication series will hereafter be referred to as *Indian Agriculture in Brief*, followed by the relevant date. The expenditure figures are for 1964–65 and were calculated from Government of India, National Council of Applied Economic Research, *All India Consumer Expenditure Survey, 1964–65*, Vol. II (New Delhi, 1967).

Rural Development Policy

Indian rural development policy has slowly evolved in both concept and practice.[16] The 1950s were dominated by emphasis on land reform, altering peoples' attitudes, and removing exploitation. There was also substantial investment in irrigation. It was a period of important social and political transformation but of relatively little change in the techniques of agricultural production. The first half of the 1960s focused on the Indian farmer as rational decision maker. New policies placed stress upon improving price incentives and making supplies of inputs, such as fertilizer, more readily available. In the last half of the 1960s, the role of new technologies paved the way for accelerated growth in agriculture and a consequent increasing contribution to overall economic activity. The 1970s would then logically have been a period for refining and expanding the basic agricultural production system, reaping the benefits of stepped-up growth, and adjusting the output structure to the changing demand associated with rising income.

The First Five-Year Plan

Motifs in the First Five-Year Plan approach to agriculture which dominated policy in the 1950s were the Community Development Program, later to blossom into the Panchayat movement toward local government; the furtherance of irrigation as a means of enlarging the productive capacity of the land area and increasing the certainty of crops; and the elimination of exploitation of farmers by landowners, moneylenders, and merchants. It was expected that expanding education, supplying water, and removing the dulling hand of exploitation would increase agricultural production.

Community Development Program

The Community Development Program launched on October 2, 1952, the eighty-third anniversary of Gandhi's birth, was the most ambitious and exciting feature of the First Five-Year Plan. There has been a tendency to judge the Community Development Program by its production failures. Prime Minister Nehru had a much broader concept of the program: "The community projects are of vital importance not only for the

---

[16] The following review of agricultural policy for the first three Five-Year Plans is largely digested from Mellor et al., *Developing Rural India*, pp. 31–93.

material achievements they will bring about, but much more so because they seek to build up the community and the individual, and to make the latter a builder not only of his own village center but in a larger sense of India." [17]

Community Development was a massive program commencing with 25,000 villages, expanding by the end of the First Plan to encompass 123,000 villages and 80 million people and, by the end of the Second Plan, providing coverage to nearly all of India's half-million villages and 300 million rural people. Although huge in coverage and in personnel requirements, it was, in a resource sense, a relatively low-cost program. The Indian education system had provided a general education to large numbers of people, although few had the specific scientific training necessary for assisting technological change in agriculture. The Community Development Program reflected these resource availabilities. It had a basic line organization—from the block development officer, to the assistant development officer, to the village-level worker. It was bureaucratized in the tradition of the Indian Civil Service. Promotion was gained by impressing distant administrators, with the consequent emphasis on skill in writing reports, and on careful but unimaginative administration. Gradually, if adaptation were to be made to heterogeneous local conditions, this initial organization would have to become more decentralized, more subject to local control, and more technical. In that sense, its political functions would evolve into the local governmental functions of the Panchayats, representing the locally elected village leadership system.

As the opportunity for genuine technological change in agriculture arose and as cultivators became more sophisticated in their demands, the scientific nature of the service would have to change. It would have to develop close ties with the research stations which would be the source of a continuing stream of new information. It would have to obtain technically competent personnel. This in turn would entail expansion and improvement of the system of higher education for the agricultural sector. These complex processes, even by the 1970s, were just under way.

Thus, the Community Development Program commenced with complex objectives, expanded rapidly, evidenced a number of errors, applied those errors broadly, and maintained, at best, a modest standard of tech-

[17] Statement at the First Development Commissioner's Conference, May 7, 1952; quoted in Government of India, Planning Commission, *The New India: Progress through Democracy* (New York: Macmillan, 1958), p. 169.

nical competence. The emphasis on political objectives and on changing rural attitudes may have been costly in directing attention away from the technical problems of agricultural development. On the other hand, its attention to agriculture eventually brought improved programs and initiated a continuous process of rural institutional development which would be necessary to later technological progress.

Expanding Irrigation

Expansion of the irrigated area alone accounted for some 20 percent of the increase in production during the First Five-Year Plan and more than 30 percent of the increase in production during the first two plans (Table II-1). The First Plan devoted over 16 percent of total expenditure to major irrigation projects. This was over twice the proportion to be allocated in the next two plans and was a continuation of the British policy emphasizing irrigation. Farmers clearly supported the policy as a means of ensuring crops against the vagaries of the monsoon. As yet, there was little understanding of the interaction between irrigation and technological change, a concept which was to come later and make much of the earlier investment in irrigation highly profitable.

Despite substantial investment, the proportion of acreage irrigated remained roughly constant during the first two plan periods. The pressures of population growth and the incentive effects of land reforms and other social changes resulted in new land coming into cultivation as rapidly as irrigation was expanded. This vast acreage of hitherto unirrigated land is estimated to have provided one-fifth of the production increase in the First Plan period and over one-sixth of the rise for the first two plan periods combined (Table II-1).

The initial impulse in irrigation projects was toward large-scale investments. This was dictated by the political need for grand, visible impact projects and, even more, by the administrative problems of developing management and supply systems for the many diffused, small-scale schemes. In addition, there was little knowledge of the interaction between careful water control and high-yield crop varieties. Because of the inapplicability to available crop varieties of the existing technology and the poor regulation of water, returns to use of irrigation were often low. This is clearly illustrated by Weaver's analysis in Raipur district, in which irrigation provided only a small physical increase in production,

Table II-1. Input estimates of change and sources of change in foodgrain production and marketings, India, 1949–50 to 1983–84 (in million metric tons)

| Year | Estimated production attributable to specific inputs | | | | Input estimate of total production | Domestic marketings from the foodgrain sector | Domestic marketings plus imports * |
| | Unirrigated land | Irrigated land | Intensification of labor | Fertilizer | | | |
	(Percent of increased production from previous period attributable to each input in parentheses)				(Rate of growth between periods in parentheses)		
1949–50	47.5	13.3	0.0	0.0	60.8 (2.4)	31.0 (2.3)	35.8 † (1.9)
1956–57	52.7 (46)	15.5 (20)	2.9 (26)	0.9 (8)	72.0 (2.8)	36.4 (2.4)	40.0 (2.1)
1960–61	54.4 (20)	16.7 (14)	7.6 (55)	1.8 (11)	80.5 (2.0)	40.0 (2.2)	43.5 (4.1)
1964–65	54.8 (6)	18.1 (21)	9.8 (34)	4.3 (38)	87.0 (3.5)	43.6 (4.5)	51.1 (2.3)
1970–71	53.9 (–5)	23.9 (29)	13.0 (16)	15.9 (59)	106.7 (2.5)	56.7 (2.9)	58.7 (4.3)
1973–74	53.5 (–5)	25.7 (22)	15.5 (30)	20.3 (53)	115.0 (5.1)	61.8 (6.8)	66.6 (5.2)
Future potentials							
1978–79	56.9 (10)	27.7 (6)	18.9 (10)	45.2 (76)	147.8 (4.7)	85.8 (5.8)	85.8 (5.8)
1983–84	56.9 (0)	31.6 (10)	22.2 (9)	74.8 (79)	185.5	113.8	113.8

* Assumes no imports for 1978–79 and 1983–84.
† Import figures for 1949–50 were unavailable. Therefore 1950–51 figures for production and imports were used. The growth rate given is for 1950–51 to 1956–57.

Sources: For foodgrain imports, see Appendix, Table 3. For all other figures, see Appendix, Table 9.

small return to the cultivator per acre irrigated, and low returns to the system.[18]

Over time, irrigation policy has gradually evolved toward greater emphasis on small-scale projects—particularly through ground water development—and the careful control of water which is necessary for the new high-yield technologies. As in the case of Community Development, these desirable shifts in emphasis move slowly as the bureaucracy resists change in an attempt to protect its vested interests in the procedures, investment patterns, and institutions of the past; as the new, requisite institutional structures are laboriously built and staffed; and, as the past physical infrastructure is gradually modified.

Eliminating Exploitation

In the initial years of independence, the popular view of the Indian farmer was of a man oppressed by ruthless landlords, grasping moneylenders, and greedy merchants. Under such circumstances, it would not be surprising if the cultivator was reluctant to make investments for increasing production and was unresponsive to the market signals of changing price relationships.

"Land to the tiller" was a popular slogan of the pre-independence period. With independence, the slogan was to be given effect by Zamindari abolition, a popular approach to land reform which was to remove the tax-collecting intermediaries interposed by the British over substantial areas of India and return that land to the tenants. Ali Khusro estimates that the land reforms instigated in the First Five-Year Plan probably increased the proportion of land in owner-operator systems from 40 percent to 75 percent; reduced the proportion in some form of tenancy from 60 percent to 25 percent; and lowered the proportion in undesirable forms of tenancy from 50 percent to 12 percent.[19] These reforms removed a major hindrance to improvement in cultivation. They may well have helped increase the rate of growth of foodgrains production from the 0.11

[18] Mellor et al., Ch. ix.

[19] A. M. Khusro, *An Analysis of Agricultural Land in India by Size of Holding and Land Tenure* (Delhi: Institute of Economic Growth, 1964). Dharm Narain and P. C. Joshi also show a decline in tenancy, in "Magnitude of Agricultural Tenancy," *Economic and Political Weekly,* 4:39 (September 27, 1969), A-139–42. Note, however, the contrary evidence of S. K. Sanyal, "Has There Been a Decline in Agricultural Tenancy?" *Economic and Political Weekly,* 7:19 (May 6, 1972), 943–45.

percent in the pre-independence decades to the 2.5 to 3.0 percent of the first two five-year plans.[20]

Because of the association of the system with the departed British, Zamindari abolition was, politically, relatively easy to achieve, thereby making the incentive system for the bulk of the land adequate for increasing agricultural production. Substantial inequalities in the countryside continued, but the remaining wealthier classes were large in number and a significant and growing part of the ruling political system. Although land reform continued to be a subject of controversy, little further action followed the initial Zamindari abolition.

Hand in hand with the landlords, it was believed, moneylenders and traders were exploiting cultivators. Beginning with the Cooperative Credit Societies Act of 1904, a steady progression of efforts had been made to displace the moneylenders with government-sponsored cooperative credit schemes. This effort was pursued vigorously in the First Five-Year Plan. By the end of the plan, there were 200,000 agricultural cooperatives in India, 80 percent of which were credit societies. These credit societies claimed 13 million members and an aggregate working capital of over one and a half billion rupees. But, at the beginning of the First Plan, only some 6 percent of borrowing by cultivators came from cooperatives and government sources. By the middle 1960s, this had expanded to 30 percent and by 1970–71, had reached 40 percent.[21] As in the case of irrigation, the great value of the credit programs was to come not at the time of their initiation but later, with the development of technological change in agriculture.[22]

In a traditional agriculture, credit is basically repressive, no matter who provides it. Borrowing is done not to increase production, for the land base and the technology provide little scope for that, but in order to maintain production and to meet pressing consumption needs (e.g., when in-

---

[20] George Blyn, *Agricultural Trends in India, 1891–1947: Output, Availability, and Productivity* (Philadelphia: University of Pennsylvania Press, 1966), pp. 94–97; and John W. Mellor and Uma J. Lele, "Alternative Estimates of the Trend in Indian Foodgrains Production during the First Two Plans," *Economic Development and Cultural Change,* 7:2 (January 1965), 232.

[21] Mellor et al., p. 62; H. C. Jain, "Growth and Recent Trends in the Institutional Credit in India," *Indian Journal of Agricultural Economics,* 26:4 (October–December 1971), 555.

[22] See the exposition on this point in Uma J. Lele, "The Roles of Credit and Marketing in Agricultural Development," in Nurul Islam, ed., *Agricultural Policy in Developing Countries* (London: Macmillan, 1974), pp. 413–41.

come declines owing to bad weather). It is difficult to repay loans from a stagnant, low income. The private moneylender guards against failure to pay by imposing high interest rates and exercising well-nigh ironbound supervision. Under these conditions, cooperatives tend to have low repayment rates and require government subsidization. In addition, the repayment problem is exacerbated by politically influential, wealthier cultivators, who control the cooperatives and use their influence to obtain loans for themselves and to evade repayment. It is revealing that repayment rates for cooperatives are lowest among the higher-income cultivators.[23]

The advent of recent agricultural technologies offers opportunity for increased production and income but requires substantial investment in new inputs such as fertilizer. Thus, while the need for production credit greatly increases, the capacity to pay debts increases as well so that concurrently the comparative advantage of the moneylender declines. The credit needs become large and too difficult for him to handle, the risks drop substantially, and repayment depends more on knowledge of the production possibilities than on the personal circumstances of the borrower. Of particular importance, new technology often causes large short-run increases in credit needs in the specific geographic areas where it is utilized, followed by a period of repayment in those areas, and then a sharp increase in credit needs elsewhere as a different region receives a new impetus. Such a wavelike spread of technology requires a system of credit institutions which integrates different areas as well as different sectors of the economy. Finally, technological innovations may require substantial intermediate-term credit for irrigation systems, simple machinery, and livestock, which overtax the traditional credit supply.

The conventional moneylender is often ill-equipped to satisfy these new needs, while commercial banks or the cooperatives are potentially suited to the coordinative task. The building of the credit societies during India's First and Second Five-Year Plan periods probably contributed little, at that time, to either the alleviation of social and economic inequity or the growth of production. An infrastructure, however, was being built which could be turned to useful purpose in the late 1960s and early

---

[23] For more information on the various points in this paragraph see Lele, in Islam, ed., op. cit.; N. S. Jodha, "Land-Based Credit Policies and Investment Prospects for Small Farmers," *Economic and Political Weekly*, 6:39 (September 25, 1971), A-143–48; and C. H. Hanumantha Rao, "Farm Size and Credit Policy," *Economic and Political Weekly*, 5:52 (December 26, 1970), A-157–62.

1970s. Improvement would then be needed to broaden access to the system in order to include small farmers and to increase repayment rates.

Marketing Policy

Policy with respect to the system of marketing agricultural commodities has been particularly complex and ambivalent. It was widely believed that the private trade was exploitative and discouraging to production; there was concern with the free market's inequity in allocating scarce food; and there was a stated belief in the social advantages of a cooperative structure. In her definitive work, Uma Lele shows that the shortcomings in the efficiency and productivity of the private marketing system stem largely from lack of transportation, communication, and information.[24] She concludes that these inadequacies are aggravated by haphazard government policies that tend to be short-term reactions to a series of successive crises rather than to be based on long-term production and welfare considerations. She also argues that the marketing problems are better dealt with by strong investment in infrastructure rather than by attempting to erect a costly parallel marketing system—she thus emphasizes the importance of substance rather than form in policy making.

It is difficult to argue the social advantages of cooperatives as long as cooperatives tend to be controlled by the wealthier rural people and there is scant participation by the smaller farmer. In periods of scarcity and rising prices, the market forces most of the reduction in consumption on the poor, whose low income and high proportion of expenditure on food offer little alternative. But it is doubtful that cooperative marketing can alleviate a problem rooted in income inequality and scarcity. Lacking viable alternatives for meeting a politically explosive problem, politicians usually resort to displacement of private trade as a palliative if not a solution—a procedure again fully documented by Uma Lele in the context of the broader questions of marketing efficiency. The periodic government takeovers of the grain trade dramatically illustrate how short-term political pressures force economic measures which do little to solve the immediate difficulty and may actually exacerbate the long-run problem.

The environment for effective development of cooperatives improves as technological change increases the demand for new forms of purchased

[24] Uma J. Lele, *Food Grain Marketing in India: Private Performance and Public Policy* (Ithaca, N.Y.: Cornell University Press, 1971). See also Uma J. Lele, "Agricultural Price Policy," *Economic and Political Weekly,* 4:35 (August 30, 1969), 1413–19.

inputs and markets outlets, and as the infrastructure develops.[25] In the longer run, cooperatively organized trade, with ready access to new technology and effective participation in management, may have a useful social and economic role to play. For the moment, the cooperative movement in India, as elsewhere in the developing world, must still be seen more as a means of dispensing political patronage than as a development institution.[26]

The efforts of the First Five-Year Plan were useful in providing institutions and resources which would later become important complements of change, with the introduction of yield-increasing innovations which were not yet available. Unfortunately, the plan failed to make a major effort to build rapidly the research structure necessary to mobilize and support such change.

The Second Five-Year Plan

The agricultural elements of the Second Five-Year Plan, occurring during the last half of the 1950s, were essentially a continuation of the First. Total expenditure on rural development increased by 30 percent, but declined from 30 to 20 percent of the expenditures in a greatly increased plan (Appendix, Table 2). The Community Development Program was evolving into a more decentralized system of local government; a higher proportion of expenditure on irrigation was being directed toward smaller-scale projects; and expansion of cooperatives in credit and marketing continued.

There were two major reasons for the continuation of what hindsight says were, at best, only moderately successful agricultural policies which still did not obtain the requisites of rapid technological change. First, the political environment demanded the development of a visible, modern industrial sector. By the mid-1950s, P. C. Mahalanobis had prepared the broad action plan for massive investment by the public sector in large-scale industry. Second, as the plan was being formulated, there was no visible upward pressure on food prices. The rural strategy of the First Plan appeared successful.

In the First Plan period, 1950–51 to 1955–56, foodgrain production rose at the compound rate of 4.8 percent per year (Table II-2), while rela-

---

[25] Lele, in Islam, op. cit., pp. 443–45.

[26] See, for example, Lele, "Agricultural Price Policy," and the *Economic Times* (Bombay, India), 12:287 (December 17, 1972).

Table II-2. Estimates of foodgrain production, India, 1949–50 to 1973–74 (in million metric tons)

Year	Official estimates of production	Percent change from previous year	Growth rate	Trend line of production	Input estimates of production	Percent change from previous year	Growth rate
1949–50	60.8	0.0		60.8	60.8	0.0	
1950–51	55.0	− 9.5	2.2	62.5	60.4	−0.7	2.6
1951–52	55.6	1.1		64.2	61.0	1.0	
1952–53	61.8	11.1	4.8	66.0	64.2	5.2	3.2
1953–54	72.4	17.1		67.8	68.6	6.8	
1954–55	70.8	− 2.2	2.8	69.7	68.7	0.1	2.6
1955–56	69.4	− 2.0		71.7	70.8	3.1	
1956–57	72.5	4.5	4.1	73.7	72.0	1.7	2.9
1957–58	66.7	− 8.0		75.7	73.6	2.2	
1958–59	78.9	18.3	3.4	77.8	76.9	4.5	2.6
1959–60	76.9	− 2.5		80.0	79.2	3.0	
1960–61	82.2	6.9		82.2	80.5	1.6	
1961–62	82.9	0.8	2.1	83.9	82.6	2.6	2.0
1962–63	80.3	− 3.1		85.7	84.4	2.2	
1963–64	80.7	0.5	2.1	87.5	85.7	1.5	2.4
1964–65	89.3	10.7		89.3	87.0	1.5	
1965–66	72.3	−19.0	2.1	90.8	88.0	1.1	2.9
1966–67	74.2	2.6		92.3	91.8	4.3	
1967–68	95.0	28.0	2.8	93.8	94.9	3.4	2.9
1968–69	94.0	− 1.0		95.4	100.1	5.5	
1969–70	99.5	5.8	1.8	97.0	104.7	4.6	2.8
1970–71	108.4	8.9	3.3	98.6	106.7	1.9	3.5
1971–72	104.7	− 3.4		100.2	110.8	3.8	
1972–73	97.0	− 7.4		101.9	111.8	0.9	
1973–74	103.6	6.8	1.7	103.6	115.0	2.9	3.1

Sources: Official estimates: 1949–50 through 1964–65 from Estimates of Area and Production of Principal Crops in India, 1970–71 (New Delhi: Government of India, Directorate of Economics and Statistics, 1971); 1965–66 through 1971–72 from Economic Survey: 1972–73 (New Delhi: Government of India, Ministry of Finance, 1973); 1972–73 and 1973–74 from Government of India, Directorate of Economics and Statistics, Agricultural Situation in India, 29: 8 (November 1974). Trend line: 1949–50, 1960–61, 1964–65, and 1973–74 are official estimates. The compound growth rate between the four years were used to compute the intermediate years. For input estimates, see Appendix, Table 9.

tive foodgrain prices actually declined (Figure II-2). It was logical to believe that Community Development, elimination of exploitation, and investment in irrigation had and would continue to succeed. Unfortunately, much of the success was an illusion derived from unusually good weather. For example, if the slightly better than average year 1949–50 is taken as a base, the rate of growth of foodgrain production to 1955–56 was not 4.8 percent but 2.2 percent—barely ahead of population growth.

Even if the Second Plan had given more expenditure to agriculture, it would likely, in the absence of new technology, have continued the old pattern of investment in large-scale irrigation and in community development programs with low current rates of return. What was needed was not so much an immediate increase in expenditure on agriculture as analysis of the sources of growth in the agricultural sector and the development of an improved strategy. That was to occur toward the middle of the Second Plan, when a basis was provided for a quite different orientation toward rural development for the Third and later plans.

Nevertheless, even in the 1950s, foodgrain production outpaced population growth. The compound growth rate of reported foodgrain production between the years 1949–50 and 1960–61 was 2.8 percent (Table II-2). (Detailed analysis of the use of four key inputs suggests a similar growth rate of 2.6 percent in foodgrain output [Table II-2]). During the same time, population advanced at a rate of 1.9 percent. For this period there was no upward or downward trend in relative foodgrain prices (Figure II-2) and imports of foodgrains (Appendix, Table 3). Indeed, it is indicative of the relative importance of agriculture in the economy that over one-third of the improvement in average per capita incomes during the 1950s came from the modest rate of growth in this sector.[27]

Agriculture was able, with only an unpretentious growth rate, to meet the small demands made on it in the 1950s. It was the much faster rise of population, per capita income, and employment in the first half of the sixties which would sorely tax its ability to produce and market, and which would require institution of a new strategy for more rapid growth.

Despite the apparently acceptable record of agriculture to date, in the late 1950s considerable doubt was arising concerning the success of the earlier policies. The poor crop year of 1957–58, when foodgrain produc-

[27] Calculated as the absolute increase in agricultural income from 1950–51 to 1960–61 as a percentage of the total absolute increase in national income from 1950–51 to 1960–61, all in current prices. The data are from *Statistical Abstract of India,* various issues.

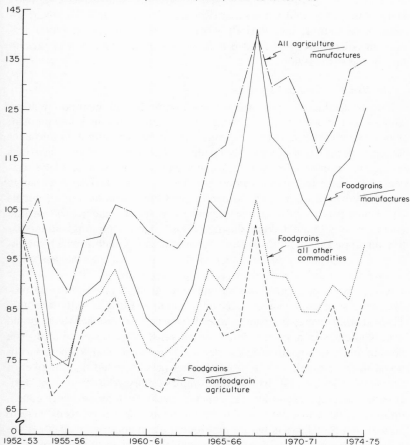

Figure II-2. Relative wholesale price ratios, India, 1952–53 to 1974–75

All agriculture
manufactures

Foodgrains
manufactures

Foodgrains
all other
commodities

Foodgrains
nonfoodgrain
agriculture

Note: The time series were constructed by connecting two wholesale price indices, for which the base years were 1952–53 and 1961–62. (The indices are not strictly comparable due to the use of different weights for the various commodity groups.)
Source: Reserve Bank of India, *Bulletin,* various issues.

tion declined 8 percent from the previous year, strengthened those doubts and led to a series of commissions and reports.[28] The most publicized of these was the Ford Foundation–sponsored joint Indo-American study team, which provided the leverage for instituting the Intensive Agricultural District Programme (IADP). That program dramatized the modifications in policy that were needed and epitomized the approach to agriculture of the early 1960s.

The Third Five-Year Plan

Two basic changes characterized agricultural development policy in the Third Plan period. First, the farmer was recognized as an economic man; policy shifted from attempting to alter his attitudes to attempting to alter the environment within which he made his decisions. Second, variations in regional productivity were acknowledged; resources were to be concentrated where the output response would be greatest. The first change paved the way for continuous diagnosis of farmers' production problems and hence provided the prime requisite for solving them. The second change greatly facilitated this diagnostic task by concentrating administrative attention on a few responsive geographic areas within which the interaction of needs could be understood and effected and the analytical approach then diffused to other areas when appropriate.

The package program made an intensive effort to raise foodgrain production in seventeen districts selected as the most likely to exhibit results. These districts were, in general, already prosperous, productive areas and were chosen with a special emphasis on satisfactory water control. The best of the administrative and extension personnel were to be concentrated in those districts. The program ostensibly assumed that the plan of action must include all the various complementary requirements of agricultural development—physical inputs, credit, marketing, and education—or none would pay off. All the important correlative needs were to be met in a few districts before proceeding to others.

If the program had indeed attempted to do everything at once, it would, on the one hand, have foundered on the immensity of the administrative problem and, on the other, spent too much time and effort on

---

[28] *Reports of the Team for the Study of Community Projects and National Extension Service* (New Delhi: Government of India, Central Government Publications, 1957); and Ford Foundation, *Report on India's Food Crisis and Steps to Meet It* (New Delhi: Government of India, Ministry of Food and Agriculture and Ministry of Community Development, 1959).

work which was already adequately handled as a result of past development efforts. In practice, the program was primarily a fertilizer scheme with substantial emphasis on demonstration, ensuring adequate supplies, and financing.[29] It neglected the exceedingly complex problem of water control and management, and adaptive research for providing new, high-yield varieties of crops and for improving production practices.

The question of water control was ignored, in part, because the districts chosen were presumed to have a well-administered supply; in part, because of the difficult political and administrative problems of improving its management; and, in part, because of failure to understand how water regulation interacted with new technology. The importance of adaptive research was still not generally recognized. It was assumed that there was a research backlog of several years, and that only when the results were applied would more research be needed.[30]

The statistical record of the IADP districts shows neither accelerated growth over time nor improvement in comparison with analogous non-IADP districts.[31] This outcome is ascribed to deficiencies in the IADP and the relatively easy spread of fertilizer, as the principal source of growth, into most of the comparable districts. The package program was, nevertheless, an important milestone in the evolution of thought toward an effective agricultural strategy.

The Changing Structure of Foodgrain Production

During the 1950s, foodgrain production and marketing in India grew steadily, each at about the same rate—somewhat faster than the population—and largely through the utilization of increased land area and labor intensive processes (Table II-1). Growth in acreage was the single major reason for increased output. Despite a high rate of gain, fertilizer is es-

---

[29] Mellor et al., pp. 83–86.

[30] For an exposition of this view see Douglas Ensminger, "Overcoming the Obstacles to Farm Economic Development in the Less-Developed Countries," *Journal of Farm Economics*, 44:5 (December 1962), 1367–87.

[31] Detailed data on this program are reported in annual reports and summarized in a perceptive analytical report of a committee chaired by S. R. Sen: *Modernising Indian Agriculture: Fourth Report on the Intensive Agricultural District Programme (1960–68)* (New Delhi: Government of India, Ministry of Food, Agriculture, Community Development and Cooperation, 1970). For a perceptive and well-documented highly critical analysis, see D. K. Desai, "Intensive Agricultural District Programme: Analysis of Results," *Economic and Political Weekly*, 4:26 (June 28, 1969), A-83–90. See also Dorris D. Brown, *Agricultural Development in India's Districts* (Cambridge, Mass.: Harvard University Press, 1971).

timated to have accounted for only 9 percent of the rise in production from 1949–50 to 1960–61.

Growth in output from 1960–61 to 1964–65 evidenced the development of new trends. Expansion in acreage of unirrigated land became insignificant as a source of additional output, while irrigated land increased both in absolute and in relative importance. Fertilizer rose from near insignificance to a position where it accounted for an estimated 38 percent of the gain in production. But the increase in fertilizer use was not sufficient to balance the decline in the growth rate for area of unirrigated land.

The change in the sources of growth was important because it removed the appropriate focus for production increase from natural-resource availability to one of policy determination. Both demand and supply for fertilizer are manipulated by public policy. By 1964–65, while the foundation was still being built for a sustained accelerated increase in foodgrain production, an agricultural crisis threatened to arise from a step-up in demand and an actual declining rate of growth of production. Three unsustainable forces precipitated the onset of an emergency.

First, relative foodgrain prices were rising rapidly from their low point of 1961–62 (Figure II-2). In the very good crop year 1964–65, they were at the highest level in over a decade. Rapidly rising farm prices, however, while shifting some demand to other commodities, had consistently brought strong political pressures for a change in economic plans.[32] Either foodgrain supplies had to be increased or the growth rate of consumption reduced.

Second, foodgrain imports rose rapidly, from 3.5 million tons in 1961 to 7.5 million tons in 1965 (Appendix, Table 3). For both political and economic reasons, that rate of growth could not be sustained. There was already fear of interference by the United States in India's domestic and foreign affairs, and the level of imports was approaching the limit of low-cost supplies from the principal exporting nations.

Third, and most unsettling, the rate of growth of fertilizer consumption in the mid-1960s could not long be maintained without substantial change in the structure of demand (see Chapter III). Much of the past growth had resulted from a process of diffusion of fertilizer use to situations in which it was profitable in conjunction with existing technology and resources.

[32] Norman K. Nicholson, "Political Aspects of Indian Food Policy," *Pacific Affairs*, 41:1 (Spring 1968), 34—50.

That spread was accelerated by increasingly favorable price relationships in the early 1960s. Continued advance in fertilizer consumption would require an agricultural research system that would provide a stream of new crop varieties responsive to higher levels of application per acre and a continued rapid expansion of irrigated area. The revolution in the wheat areas in the late 1960s indicated the potential; the stagnancy in most of the rice districts underlined the problems.

The early 1960s saw the conception and birth of agricultural development through technological change. The next step was to make the heavy investment in the organization of research and in the expansion of irrigation that was needed. The total process was dramatized by two events in the mid-1960s: the drought and the introduction of dwarf wheat varieties.

The Disastrous Drought of 1965 to 1967

The approaching difficulties within the agricultural sector and between agriculture and other sectors were brought to a climax by the disastrous drought of 1965–66 and 1966–67. In 1965–66 foodgrain production declined by 17 million tons and by 19 percent from the bumper crop of the previous year (Table II-2). That was by far the greatest yearly decrease during the fifteen years of planning and probably represented the most unfavorable monsoon of this century.

The problem was compounded the next year when the monsoon was again deficient. Production was still 15 million tons below that of 1964–65. Although the second drought year in itself was not as bad as the first, the cumulative effect was disastrous.

Analysis of foodgrain price behavior in the first three five-year plans suggests that farmers build stocks substantially in a period of heavy production and reduce them in a light year.[33] The 1964–65 bumper crop undoubtedly saw farm stocks built to unusually high levels. Those stocks were then depleted in 1965–66 and cushioned much of the shock of the poor production in that year. There was then no slack left in the system for the next harvest, so the second bad year bore terribly on the people and the economy.

Foodgrain imports rose from the already record level of 7.5 million tons in 1964–65 to 10.4 million tons in 1965–66. Even this sharp incre-

[33] John W. Mellor and Ashok K. Dar, "Determinants and Development Implications of Foodgrains Prices in India, 1949–1964," *American Journal of Agricultural Economics,* 50:4 (November 1968), 962–74.

ment of 2.9 million tons was equal to only one-sixth of the drop in production from the trend line for 1965–66 (see Table II-2). The result was not only extreme privation, due to a shortage of food, but a fall in demand for industrial goods as national income declined, purchasing power of farmers eroded, and tax revenues dropped. There was also a downturn in savings and investment both in government and business (see Chapter VI). This was in a situation that included substantial structural imbalance as a result of the rapid industrial growth in the preceding few years. India was entering a lengthy period of economic stagnation and adjustment.

The drought and the distortions caused agricultural prices to soar. Foodgrain prices relative to industrial prices rose approximately 30 percent from 1964–65 to 1967–68. Labor costs naturally increased, and the competitive export position deteriorated, nullifying much of the benefit to exports of the devaluation of 1966.

The large growth in Public Law 480 (the United States subsidized food aid program) foodgrain imports, though the result of a generous act by the government of the United States, placed greatly added power in its hands. That power was widely believed to have been used to influence India's domestic and foreign policy. The Johnson administration consistently delayed authorization of food shipments until a crisis was imminent, further strengthening the bargaining power of the United States.[34] It is not surprising that a widespread resolve developed in India not to be subject again to deficiencies in foodgrain supplies.

Thus, the drought was a catastrophe in four ways. It was, of course, a human disaster, bringing greater malnutrition and poverty to millions of people; it was an industrial disaster, halting economic growth; it was a trade disaster, driving up labor and other costs of export goods; and it was a disaster to aid programs, providing the opportunity for external

[34] See, for example, John W. Finney, "Stopgap U.S. Wheat Aid Is Annoying New Delhi," *New York Times,* 115:39, 330 (September 29, 1965), 1–2; also J. Anthony Lukas, "U.S.-Indian Discord: New Delhi Believes Stand on Food Has a Concealed Johnson Motive," *New York Times,* January 26, 1967, in which it is stated that the U.S. policy of very short-term agreements "has made it virtually impossible for the Government to make plans for feeding the people in the second consecutive year of severe shortages" and that "the United States has used its food and economic aid to press the Indian Government for some important policy changes . . . to grant concessions to foreign investors in the fertilizer industry . . . to liberalize imports and to devalue the rupee . . . [and] since the palmy days of the spring, Mr. Johnson seems to have become increasingly disillusioned with Mrs. Gandhi chiefly because of her stand on Vietnam."

pressures which made India less desirous of receiving assistance and inculcating a pessimism on the part of donors that lessened their desire to help.

There was one fortuitous element in the timing, however. It served to turn popular attention toward agriculture at precisely that moment in history when the biological scientists were providing the means for breaking major bottlenecks in agricultural growth. As a result, politicians and administrators quickly accepted policies for making the new technologies available for farmers; substantial additional resources were poured into research; a huge effort was made to increase fertilizer availability; resources were freed for rapid expansion of a complementary irrigation input; and a reshuffling of the whole development mechanism for agriculture was effected. The relatively high farm prices in this period undoubtedly gave an additional spur to the diffusion of the new high-yield varieties and the necessary accompanying inputs of fertilizer and water.

It can hardly be said that the drought and modifications in attitudes of the bureaucracy caused the green revolution. The green revolution was grounded in events of longer history and greater spirit and substance. But the drought and its concomitants did hasten the pace of governmental changes needed to take full advantage of the new possibilities.

The Foodgrain Revolution: Present Substance and Future Potential

An employment-oriented strategy of development will normally depend on the successful application of new agricultural technologies to the boosting of foodgrain production. This complex process involves major change in the structure of agricultural growth. It cannot be estimated by simple projections of the past, and can only be understood through a detailed analysis of specific crops, inputs, and regions. Accelerated growth in foodgrain production is generally possible, but its realization requires a major policy commitment, the allocation of a quantity of scarce resources which themselves will affect other elements of the strategy for economic development, and detailed knowledge as to how best to apply those resources. A substantial experience with respect to the new technologies has now accumulated which can be used to guide future accelerated effort. The very broad and extensive experience in India reflects rather accurately the results elsewhere, including the widely favorable record with wheat, the apparently discouraging but in practice very mixed record of rice, and, most important, the role of varying natural and institutional factors in determining the appropriate policy directives and the likely production response for a particular time and place.

The Foodgrain Record: 1964–65 to 1970–71

Both 1964–65 and 1970–71 witnessed favorable weather throughout most of India and excellent crop production. (Because annual fluctuations in production are large, relative to changes in trend, the most realistic analysis of the trend is made by comparing years of similar weather, such as 1964–65 and 1970–71.) In the six intervening years foodgrain production increased 19.1 million tons, a compound annual growth rate of 3.3 percent (Table II-2). (As a comparison, that is 18 percent higher than the growth rate shown by the same measures between the similar crop years 1949–50 to 1960–61.) The weather in 1964–65 was probably somewhat more favorable than in 1970–71, lending a slight downward bias to estimates of growth rates for the intervening years. The presence of such downward bias in the estimates is corroborated by the input analysis presented in Chapter II, which shows the rate of growth of foodgrain output increasing by 75 percent, from 2 percent per year during the period 1960–61 to 1964–65, to 3.5 percent per year from 1964–65 to 1970–71 (Table II-1). Even more striking, the analysis in Chapter II suggests that because of the change in the structure of production, the estimated rate of growth of marketings from domestic output may have accelerated even further, to 4.5 percent between 1964–65 and 1970–71.

That sharp gain is, of course, not reflected in expansion of the non-foodgrain sector or in declining relative agricultural prices during the same period, because it was substantially balanced by the rapid fall-off in foodgrain imports, a build-up of stocks, and a steep drop in foreign aid. The sum of estimates of marketings plus imports increased only 2.3 percent per year from 1964–65 to 1970–71, compared to 4.1 percent per year from 1960–61 to 1964–65, when imports grew rapidly. From 1964–65 to 1970–71, government stocks of foodgrains increased by 7.1 million tons, further reducing growth in supplies available to the market (Appendix, Table 3).

Production growth, of course, stagnated for several years subsequent to 1970–71 largely because of unfavorable weather, the worldwide fertilizer shortage, and sharply higher petroleum prices. Although it is clear that continued acceleration requires a number of important policy steps, the relatively poor performance in the years immediately subsequent to 1970–71 cannot be taken as an indication of the potential long-term growth rate.

The input analysis also emphasizes the dramatic change in the sources of growth. From 1949–50 to 1960–61, the use of additional fertilizer accounted for less than 10 percent of increased foodgrain output, while from 1960–61 to 1970–71, it was responsible for 53 percent (Table II-1). Although in the early 1960s fertilizer began to substitute for land as the primary basis of expansion, the first years of that change were marked by a decline in the growth rate of foodgrain production. Commencing in the late 1960s, the seed revolution greatly enhanced the absorptive capacity for fertilizer, causing further acceleration in its application and large increases in tonnage used. In the late 1960s fertilizer, as an input, became slightly more responsible for a much greater rate of growth in foodgrain output. The rising importance of fertilizer, very favorable to long-term growth, of course created greater vulnerability to the fertilizer shortage of the mid-1970s, thereby exacerbating the temporary downturn in foodgrain production.

Present Substance of the Green Revolution
The Wheat Drama

It is wheat that has dramatized the green revolution. The increase in wheat production illustrates the potentials of an outstanding research breakthrough applied in a locale with an impressive indigenous experimental system, with scope for rapid expansion of an effectively irrigated area, and with a well-developed set of institutions and physical facilities for the efficient transmission of knowledge, production inputs, and output.

Dwarf wheat varieties were introduced in large numbers to the experiment stations of India in the winter season of 1963–64; widespread trials on farmers' fields occurred the next year; substantial import of seed was made in 1965–66; and, by the 1968–69 crop year, seeds of the improved varieties had been multipled and were widely and amply available to farmers.[1] The 45 percent increase in wheat production from 1966–67 to 1967–68 signaled the beginning of the revolution (Appendix, Table 4). From 1964–65 to 1970–71, wheat production rose by more than 90 percent and 11.6 million tons, a rate of growth of more than 11 percent per year, well over three times the total long-term growth rate for foodgrains. Sixty percent of the rise in foodgrain production between 1964–65 and 1970–71 was from wheat, though this grain comprised only 14 percent of the total output in 1964–65. Because of the substantial quantities of purchased inputs used, the large share of incremental income received by landowners, and the relatively high incomes of producers, wheat provided an even higher proportion of the total increase in cash marketings.

The rapid growth in wheat production was primarily the result of a sharp rise in yields per acre consequent to widespread application of the

[1] For further discussion of the introduction and subsequent widespread use of the dwarf wheat and other improved varieties, see Carroll P. Streeter, *A Partnership to Improve Food Production in India*, a special report from the Rockefeller Foundation (New York: Rockefeller Foundation, December 1969), pp. 8–23.

new dwarf varieties. This growth then increased the profitability of irrigated production, which in turn accelerated investment in acreage expansion.

On a national basis, wheat yields per hectare were boosted by 43 percent from 1964–65 to 1970–71, while acreage increased by 36 percent. Thirty-eight percent of the gain in production in this period is attributable to increased acreage, and 62 percent to higher yields.[2] Some of the larger acreage planted to wheat was diverted from other crops. It is likely, however, that the bulk of the additional acreage was newly irrigated land which previously had at best very low yields for alternative crops.

The relatively homogeneous conditions for irrigated wheat production in India allowed a small number of dwarf varieties, initially developed in Mexico, to be highly successful over a large proportion of the growing area. The ability necessary to adapt the Mexican strains and to provide continuous further improvement arose from a well-advanced indigenous wheat research system.[3] Three major research centers of northwestern India (the Indian Agricultural Research Institute at New Delhi, Punjab Agricultural University, and the G. B. Pant University of Agriculture and Technology in Uttar Pradesh) comprised an experimental system considerably more effective than that available to any other Indian region or to any other food crop. This system could then obtain relatively heavier allocations for research and make expenditures more effective.

Expenditure for wheat research in 1968, though less in total than for rice, was, as a percent of commodity value, nearly two and a half times greater. Similarly, for the year 1968, crop-related research in the wheat-producing state of Punjab, expressed as expenditure per community-development block, was seven times as much as the amount spent in rice-producing West Bengal.[4] In addition, the Punjab could draw more heavily on the effective experimental work performed in the neighboring

[2] Calculated by multiplying the increase in area between 1964–65 and 1970–71 by the yield in 1964–65, and expressing that as a percentage of the total increase in production between 1964–65 and 1970–71, and attributing the rest of the increase in production to increased yield. The data used are from Appendix, Table 4.

[3] Analysis of relationships between agricultural research and output growth emphasizes the importance of indigenous research systems to "borrowing" of new technology. See Rakesh Mohan, D. Jha, and Robert Evenson, "The Indian Agricultural Research System," *Economic and Political Weekly*, 8:13 (March 31, 1973), A-21–26. For a general analysis of this set of problems, see Yujiro Hayami and Vernon W. Ruttan, *Agricultural Development: An International Perspective* (Baltimore: Johns Hopkins University Press, 1971).

[4] See Mohan et. al., pp. A-22 and A-23.

states, owing to a greater similarity of agricultural conditions. As a consequence, the original Mexican wheat varieties were quickly modified to make the quality more acceptable to Indian consumers, optimal cultivation practices were developed, and a start was made in raising yields further and assuring resistance to new strains of disease.

The large yield advantage of the new varieties when irrigated and the low cost of small-scale private systems resulted in a rapid expansion of irrigation. From 1960–61 to 1967–68, the irrigated area of wheat grew at a rate of 6.4 percent a year, compared to 2.4 percent for all crops (Table III-1). The percentage of wheat land irrigated increased only from 33 per-

Table III-1. Compound growth rates of total and irrigated areas under principal foodgrains, India, during the 1960s

Crop	Total area 1960–61 to 1969–70	Irrigated area 1960–61 to 1967–68
Rice	1.0	1.0
Wheat	2.3	6.4
Sorghum	0.6	1.6
Millet	1.6	3.5
Maize	2.7	6.9
Barley	−1.4	1.8
Other Cereals and Pulses	−0.5	1.2
All Foodgrains	1.3	3.3
All Crops	0.8	2.4

Note: The growth rates for the first seven items were computed by fitting a semi-log curve to the respective time series. The growth rates for the last two items were calculated between the first and the last years by using the formula:

$$\text{Growth rate} = \text{Anti-log} \left(\frac{\text{Log } (I_B/I_A)}{B - A} \right) - 1$$

where I_A and I_B are the official production data for years A and B.

Sources: Gunvant M. Desai, Nitrogen Use and Foodgrain Production, India, 1973–74, 1978–79, and 1983–84, Department of Agricultural Economics, Occasional Paper 55, Cornell University USAID Employment and Income Distribution Project (March 1973); also see Appendix, Table 4.

The data source used for column 1 was Estimates of Area and Production of Principal Crops in India, 1970–71 (New Delhi: Government of India, Directorate of Economics and Statistics, 1971); for column 2, Statistical Abstract of India, 1970 (New Delhi: Government of India, Central Statistical Organisation, 1971) and Agriculture in Brief, 12th edition (New Delhi: Government of India, Directorate of Economics and Statistics, 1973).

cent in 1960–61 to 37 percent in 1964–65, and then in the next two years spurted to 48 percent. This rate of growth for irrigated acreage is almost three times as rapid as the growth of the total wheat area (irrigated and unirrigated) during the comparable time span. The dramatic gain in irrigated wheat area is attributable to the fact that the large, cheaply developed ground water resources in the wheat areas facilitated development of private tube wells, which were made highly profitable by the new varieties.[5] The rapid expansion of rural electrification further aided this growth.

The wheat areas already had a much more fully developed infrastructure of public services than most other regions of India. Perhaps most important was the fertilizer distribution system. The northern region, comprised primarily of Punjab and Haryana, experienced extremely sharp growth in the use of fertilizer prior to the introduction of the new varieties, doubling its share of national nitrogen consumption between 1961–62 and 1964–65 (Table III-2). The adjacent central region, in which wheat is also important, increased its share of nitrogen consumption by 40 percent in the same period. The result was a widespread, efficient distribution system readily able to expand at a rapid rate as the new strains greatly increased the capacity to use fertilizer profitably. Also significant, the transportation and communication system was more highly developed in the northern wheat area than in many other parts of India.[6]

The extreme early success in wheat and the slackened growth subsequent to 1970–71 in themselves raise a question as to whether wheat can continue to carry such a disproportionate share of the growth in foodgrains. If it is to do so, there must be continued expansion in the traditional areas of wheat growing and rapid exploitation of the potential to increase production in the eastern Gangetic plain.

The well-developed research system in the established wheat-producing states argues for continued growth in yield per acre and further encour-

---

[5] Thus, on a typical four-hectare farm, the total investment in a private tube well was returned in less than two years. Because of the greater reliability of water supply incident to the reserve capacity, the returns on investment were 73 percent higher for private wells than for state wells. See T. V. Moorti, *A Comparative Study of Well Irrigation in Aligarh District, India,* C.I.A.D. Bulletin No. 19 (May 1971), ch. iii, pp. 15–18, 45, and 52. See also V. P. Shukla, *Interaction of Technological Change and Irrigation in Determining Farm Resource Use, Jabalpur District, India, 1967–68,* C.I.A.D. Bulletin No. 20 (July 1971).

[6] In corroboration, Uma Lele shows a higher correlation in prices among markets in the Punjab than in West Bengal, in *Food Grain Marketing in India: Private Performance and Public Policy* (Ithaca, N.Y.: Cornell University Press, 1971), ch. iv. See also S. S. Johl and Mohinder S. Mudahar, *The Dynamics of Institutional Change and Rural Development in Punjab, India,* Cornell University, Center for International Studies (November 1974); and Mohinder S. Mudahar, "Dynamic Analysis of Agricultural Revolution in Punjab, India," presented at the Annual Conference of the Western Agricultural Economics Association, University of Idaho, July, 1974.

Table III-2. Growth of nitrogen use and foodgrain production by regions, India, 1961–62 to 1973–74

Year	South	North	Central	West	East	All India
	Nitrogen consumption, in thousand metric tons (Percent of total in parentheses)					
1961–62	88	13	36	43	30	210
	(42)	(6)	(17)	(20)	(14)	(100)
1962–63	122	20	83	45	32	302
	(40)	(7)	(27)	(15)	(11)	(100)
1963–64	183	34	21	63	34	335
	(55)	(10)	(6)	(19)	(10)	(100)
1964–65	216	62	124	65	52	519
	(42)	(12)	(24)	(12)	(10)	(100)
1965–66	204	57	106	91	69	527
	(39)	(11)	(20)	(17)	(13)	(100)
1966–67	310	69	97	88	90	653
	(47)	(11)	(15)	(13)	(14)	(100)
1967–68	279	113	177	151	79	799
	(35)	(14)	(22)	(19)	(10)	(100)
1968–69	429	183	266	152	101	1,131
	(38)	(16)	(23)	(13)	(9)	(100)
1969–70	504	198	374	158	127	1,361
	(37)	(14)	(27)	(12)	(9)	(100)
1970–71	494	242	386	217	147	1,487
	(33)	(16)	(26)	(15)	(10)	(100)
1971–72	542	306	475	245	187	1,755
	(31)	(17)	(27)	(14)	(11)	(100)
1972–73	512	331	515	229	191	1,779
	(29)	(19)	(29)	(13)	(11)	(100)
1973–74	517	392	439	276	172	1,835
	(29)	(21)	(24)	(16)	(10)	(100)
	Foodgrain production, in thousand metric tons (Percent of total in parentheses)					
1961–62	18,461	7,293	29,043	9,025	18,884	82,706
	(22)	(9)	(35)	(11)	(23)	(100)
1964–65	19,437	8,155	30,868	9,696	21,150	89,356
	(22)	(9)	(35)	(11)	(24)	(100)
1970–71	21,736	13,952	39,471	10,080	23,111	108,422
	(20)	(13)	(36)	(9)	(22)	(100)
1973–74	23,142	13,507	32,976	10,978	22,820	103,611
	(22)	(13)	(32)	(11)	(22)	(100)

Note: Errors in summation due to rounding.

Sources: Estimates of nitrogen consumption: 1961–62 to 1966–67 were compiled from *Report of the Committee on Fertilisers, 1965* (Government of India) and *Report of the Fertiliser Credit Committee, 1968* (Fertiliser Association of India); 1967–68 to 1972–73 were taken from annual issues of *Fertiliser Statistics* (Fertiliser Association of India); 1973–74 was taken from *Production and Consumption of Fertiliser, Annual Review, 1973–74* (Fertiliser Association of India).

Estimates of foodgrain production: 1973–74 based on data in *Agricultural Situation in India* (Government of India, Directorate of Economics and Statistics) September, October, and November 1974; all other years taken from *Estimates of Area and Production of Principal Crops in India* (New Delhi: Government of India, Directorate of Economics and Statistics) various issues.

agement to expand irrigation and the use of fertilizer. The triple-gene dwarfs are a dramatic example of the continuing potential of research.[7] In 1969–70, over half of the national wheat acreage remained unirrigated; even in the Punjab, nearly 17 percent was still unirrigated. Expansion of the area under irrigation can be facilitated by future growth in rural electrification as it is consolidated in the Punjab and Haryana states and spreads actively into other wheat districts.[8]

The eastward spread of wheat has been dramatic. From 1964–65 to 1971–72, Bihar increased planted acreage by 120 percent, yields by 170 percent, and production by almost 500 percent, the largest percentage increase in the eight major wheat-producing states. Still, in 1971–72 only 13 percent of the gross acreage cropped in Bihar was planted to wheat. Rapid growth in wheat production is also occurring in eastern Uttar Pradesh (U.P.) and West Bengal.[9]

A generally weak infrastructure for agricultural development limits the potential for broader wheat farming in the eastern states. Research is needed to develop wheat varieties of short season and other characteristics suitable to the warmer climate in the eastern Gangetic plain. So far, this adaptation has been made largely by the experimental stations located in the northwest. In addition, the irrigated acreage is relatively small and water supplies poorly controlled, despite the huge potential of ground water sources. Large investment in irrigation is needed. Finally, the general infrastructure of transportation, fertilizer delivery, credit, and electrification is less developed in eastern U.P., Bihar, and West Bengal than in the principal wheat-growing states. The expansion of wheat production also depends on vigorous institutional development in areas with a poor history of such improvement. Success would provide the time needed for a solution of the immensely more complex problems of the rice revolu-

[7] See Streeter, pp. 20–23.

[8] For further discussion of rural electrification in the Punjab, see Mudahar, op. cit.; and Johl and Mudahar, pp. 36–40 and 60–61. See also Shanti S. Gupta, *Utilisation of Electricity in the Villages of the District of Aligarh* (Aligarh, India: Dharam Samaj College, Department of Economics, 1969); and S. M. Patel and K. V. Patel, *Studies on Economics of Rural Electrification and Lift Irrigation* (Ahmedabad, India: Indian Institute of Management, Centre for Management in Agriculture, 1969).

[9] Calculated from data in *Estimates of Area and Production of Principal Crops in India* (New Delhi: Government of India, Directorate of Economics and Stastistics), 1967–68 and 1972–73. This important source of primary data on Indian agriculture will hereafter be referred to as *Estimates of Area and Production of Principal Crops,* followed by the year of the issue.

tion that will eventually be necessary in order to sustain the accelerated growth of foodgrain production.

Rice: The Orphan of the Revolution

The view that India has *not* experienced a green revolution derives from the general failure to accelerate rice production and the dominance of this crop in the total output of foodgrains. From 1964–65 to 1970–71 rice production grew by less than 8 percent. The three-million-ton increase was merely 15 percent of the entire rise in foodgrain output during the period, while in 1964–65, rice comprised 44 percent of all foodgrains (Appendix, Table 4). The contrasts between wheat and rice in India reflect similar contrasts arising for similar reasons throughout Asia and Africa.

Because there was no widespread breakthrough in the development of high-yield rice varieties, yields did not increase appreciably, and there was no incentive to enlarge acreage and investment in irrigation. Thus, from 1964–65 to 1970–71, rice yields per hectare rose by only 4.2 percent, compared to 43 percent for wheat; area planted increased by only 3 percent, compared to 36 percent for wheat; and the proportion of land irrigated expanded only slightly, from 37 to 40 percent. A few states did, however, experience sharp increases in rice production—most notably Tamil Nadu, where yields and production rose respectively by 28 and 31 percent during the period. However, other important rice-producing states such as Bihar actually witnessed a decline in production during this period. In contrast, all the major wheat states sustained large increases in both yields and production.[10]

The lack of a green revolution in rice is due to the high proportion of acreage with poor control of water; an inadequate research system; and the wide dispersion of production over the country. The first circumstance sharply limits the total acreage of rice that can respond effectively to new technology; the second and third explain why practical technical innovation has been slow in forthcoming and will continue to be so.

There is a close relationship among the percentage of land that is irrigated, use of fertilizer, and increase in production.[11] Four states—Tamil Nadu, Andhra Pradesh, Mysore, and Kerala—which together produced

[10] Ibid., 1967–68 and 1972–73.

[11] See, for example, Gunvant M. Desai, *Growth of Fertilizer Use in Indian Agriculture: Past Trends and Future Demand,* C.I.A.D. Bulletin No. 18 (July 1969), Tables 29 and 31.

30 percent of India's rice in 1964–65, had a combined total of 85 percent of rice acreage irrigated in 1970–71. These four states increased the aggregate rice yield almost 10 percent between 1964–65 and 1970–71. The three adjacent states of West Bengal, Bihar, and Orissa, which produced 38 percent of India's rice in 1964–65, had irrigated one-third or less of their acreage. In these three states, the aggregate rice yield declined by 3 percent between 1964–65 and 1970–71.[12] Not only is a small proportion of the rice area irrigated in many states, but much of the irrigation system is dependent upon water diversion schemes which provide inadequate control for reaping the benefits of the high-yield varieties.[13]

It is the large, poorly irrigated eastern Gangetic plain, with its vast, readily tapped ground water reserves, which offers the most obvious potentials for a rapid increase in production on a pattern similar to that of the wheat areas. The potential is harder to achieve for rice because farms are smaller, creating more difficult risk and capital problems; the institutional infrastructure of the region is less widespread than in the wheat areas; a poor past history of fertilizer use has left a less developed set of distribution institutions; marketing operates imperfectly; and, most important, the research system is particularly weak, making experimentation with new varieties less likely. All these factors combine to provide less incentive to invest in irrigation. Yet if foodgrain production is to accelerate, it is essential that the priority decisions be made to make possible the necessary rapid growth in the water supply of this area.

It is much more difficult to develop a research system for rice than for wheat. Wheat production is concentrated in northwest India; the contiguous states of Uttar Pradesh, Punjab, and Haryana accounted for nearly 60 percent of production in 1971–72. In contrast, the rice production of five states, ranging from Uttar Pradesh in the north, to Tamil Nadu and Andhra Pradesh in the south, to West Bengal and Bihar in the east, was responsible for a similar proportion of total rice production in the same year. The vast range in temperature, moisture, and soil conditions within this broad rice region places a special burden on the research system to provide a large number of seed varieties to suit specific growing conditions. The problem is compounded because a high proportion of the production takes place in the monsoon season and, consequently, under

---

[12] *Estimates of Area and Production of Principal Crops,* 1967–68 and 1972–73.

[13] John W. Mellor et al., *Developing Rural India: Plan and Practice* (Ithaca, N.Y.: Cornell University Press, 1968), pp. 181–234.

variable, cloudy, low-sunlight conditions and with great difficulties in insect and disease management. These difficulties in turn call for a more complex breeding job in order to match the pest resistance of traditional varieties with high yields or expensive and, so far, largely unprofitable pest control programs. In addition, covering such a dispersed area is a strain on the institutional infrastructure.

Despite the importance of rice as an agricultural commodity and the complexity of the research task, allocation of funds has traditionally been meager compared to other crops, and integration of the experimental system has lagged. Even in 1968, the expenditure on research as a proportion of commodity value was from three to over six times as great for commercial crops such as sugar, jute, and cotton as it was for rice.[14]

Similarly, the All-India Coordinated Rice Research Scheme was the last scheme to be developed for the major food crops. Such a system was initiated for the minor crop of maize in 1957, for wheat in 1963, but for rice not until 1966.[15] Consequently, Indian rice farmers were not being provided with varieties which had potentials comparable to those of several other crops and most particularly wheat. A careful comparison of data from the 1950s shows that the best rice strains at the Indian experiment stations had yield ceilings less than half of those at American stations and lower response to fertilizer and other inputs at essentially all levels of input.[16] Despite this research lacuna, it is symptomatic of the perceptions of the period that in 1965, India employed nearly forty times as many man-years of extension workers as of scientific research personnel, in sharp contrast to nearly twice as many scientific man-years of research personnel as extension personnel in the United States.[17]

Although the effort to provide an adequate rice research system is well under way, the results are bound to come slowly, in the form of a series of innovations of modest individual impact rather than a dramatic breakthrough. Effective agricultural research requires a complex integration of scientists from several different fields, an interaction between the

[14] Mohan et al., p. A-22.

[15] Streeter, pp. 12, 26, and 39.

[16] Robert W. Herdt and John W. Mellor, "The Contrasting Response of Rice to Nitrogen: India and the United States," *Journal of Farm Economics*, 46:1 (February 1964), 152.

[17] Robert E. Evenson and Yoav Kislev, "Investment in Agricultural Research and Extension: A Survey of International Data," *Economic Development and Cultural Change*, 23:3 (April 1975), 521.

insights and systematics of basic research and the practicalities of applied investigation, and the exchange of questions, information, and materials across regions differing in problems and conditions. These functions require a large and intricate administrative and informational system. Concurrently with fulfilling an integrative function, the system must provide incentives for imaginative, creative effort by individual scientists. Given the substantial variation in rice production conditions, the research system must have a large number of field stations emphasizing adaptive research, which coordinate with each other, and central stations working on more basic questions. As a result, the number of stations must be large, the personnel requirements immense, and the complexity substantial.

The interacting needs for effective research and expanded irrigation are apparent in the very mixed record of new rice varieties under farm conditions. Gunvant M. Desai analyzed comparative cost and return data of strains of high-yield rice. From a large number of farm studies, he draws four key reasons to explain why farmers reject the new varieties despite their generally higher yields.[18] First, costs of the major variable costs of production (e.g., fertilizer and seed) are considerably greater for the high-yield varieties than for the traditional ones. Thus yields must be substantially larger to compensate for the added expense. Second, since cash expenditure is so much larger on the high-yield types, the farmer's exposure to risk is greater, particularly if he borrows money. The farmer will not grow these new varieties unless the profit margin is significantly higher than for less risky alternatives. He will also tend to restrict their use to fields with the best-controlled conditions; particularly important is water regulation to decrease the risks of crop failure and loss of the large cash expenditure.

Third, yields of the new varieties are highly irregular, not only for one strain in comparison to another but even for the same strain in dissimilar

---

[18] For the complete analysis, see Gunvant M. Desai, "Some Observations on Economics of Cultivating High-Yielding Varieties of Rice in India," *Artha-Vikas*, 7:2 (July 1971), 1–19. It is notable that there was ample evidence of farmers fully knowledgeable about new varieties, but reluctant to use them, and of farmers trying almost all currently available high-yield varieties but giving them up in the subsequent years. See also K. B. Kothari and A. G. K. Murty, *Rural Marketing Communications: Role of Opinion Leaders in Fertilizer Promotion* (Ahmedabad, India: Indian Institute of Management, 1969); and Gunvant M. Desai, P. N. Chary, and S. C. Bandyopadhyay, *Dynamics of Growth in Fertiliser Use at Micro Level* (Ahmedabad, India: Indian Institute of Management, Centre for Management in Agriculture, 1973).

growing areas. Fourth, the relative profitability of different types of rice varies greatly from one area to another and is a function not only of yields, but also of quality and of costs. Substantial growth in rice production can take place only with continuous attention to expanding the research system and relating it to the highly variable conditions, expansion of irrigation, and development of the infrastructure of rural facilities and institutions.

Other Foodgrains

Foodgrains other than wheat and rice comprise an important but declining proportion of foodgrain production. They are grown under largely unirrigated, high-risk conditions and substantially in areas of low income and low population density. Consequently, the infrastructure of institutions and physical facilities is poorly developed.

In 1959–60, foodgrains other than wheat and rice accounted for 45 percent of total production; by 1970–71 they had declined to 39 percent. From 1964–65 to 1970–71, aggregate production of the other foodgrains increased by 12 percent (Appendix, Table 4). Substantial success has been achieved in developing high-yield varieties of maize and distributing them to the limited irrigated areas of maize production. New varieties of millet have also been adopted, even in dry land areas. In contrast, sorghum production declined by 16 percent between 1964–65 and 1970–71, and dropped off by another 20 percent by 1972–73. Pulse production also fell, in part because of the diversion of acreage to wheat, but the decline was equal to only 8 percent of the increase in wheat output in the 1964–65 to 1970–71 period, and the decline in gram, which is particularly competitive with wheat for land, was only 5 percent of the increase in wheat production.[19]

Increasing the tonnage of other foodgrains is important and perhaps even more troublesome than for rice. The integrated research establishment has been longer in development—starting in 1956 for maize and 1957 for millet and sorghum. The first of the modern hybrid varieties of maize was released in 1961; hybrid strains of sorghum and millet followed in 1964 and 1965.[20] But the research on such other foodgrains is particu-

[19] *Estimates of Area and Production of Principal Crops*, 1970–71 and 1972–73.
[20] Daya Krishna and M. S. Swaminathan, *The New Agricultural Strategy* (Delhi: New Heights, 1971), ch. ii.

larly difficult because of greatly varying production conditions; the small proportion of area irrigated and the relatively slight potential for increasing it; the low current use of fertilizer; and especially poor fertilizer distribution facilities in the growing areas for these crops. In the short run, a major push is needed to exploit whatever irrigation potential there is, to expand fertilizer use, and to build a research system related to the special problems of unirrigated agriculture.

The Crucial Role of Fertilizer

Increased use of fertilizer is the single most important indicator of technological change in agriculture. It is an important source of growth in production and has even greater influence on the level of marketings. It reflects increases in irrigation and the development of new crop varieties, as each serves to provide its benefits in large part by raising the profitability of using greater quantities of fertilizer.

The rapid and accelerating growth in the use of fertilizer in the 1960s was comprised of sharply divergent trends among regions, which reflect differences in crop patterns and physical conditions. Analysis of these trends explains the sharp decline in the rate of growth of fertilizer consumption in the early 1970s and suggests measures needed for the rate to resume its steep rise.[21] This analysis again illuminates the role of research and irrigation in expanding the demand for fertilizer and the production of foodgrains.

The region of most rapid growth in the use of fertilizer has been the relatively small northern region. In 1961–62, that area provided 9 percent of the foodgrain production and used a disproportionately smaller 6 percent of nitrogen (Table III-2). By 1970–71 it was responsible for 16 percent of the national nitrogen consumption and produced 13 percent of the foodgrain output. During the period, it averaged a compound growth rate of 38 percent per year in the use of fertilizer. The rapid rise in fertilizer consumption in this region in the first years of the decade was due to a sharply improving price ratio between what farmers received for their wheat and what they paid for fertilizer. In addition, during the later years, the introduction of dwarf varieties more than doubled the quantity of fer-

---

[21] This discussion abstracts from the constraining effect of the worldwide fertilizer shortages in the mid-1970s caused by inadequate worldwide investment in the early 1970s and exacerbated by the oil crisis, but clearly on the way to solution in the mid-1970s.

tilizer per acre it was profitable to use.[22] Associated with these changes was an increase in the profitability of private tube-well irrigation and a large expansion in its use. The importance of wheat in the central region resulted in trends similar to those in the north.

The southern region accounted for 22 and 20 percent of foodgrain production in 1961–62 and 1970–71 respectively. Because of well-developed irrigation systems and a long history of aggressive selling, in 1961–62, 42 percent of all nitrogen consumption in the country was in this area. But gradual saturation of the existing market and limited applicability of new foodgrain varieties slowed the rate of growth in the use of fertilizer. By 1973–74, the region's share of total nitrogen consumption had declined to 29 percent.

The east is the area with strikingly low fertilizer consumption and a slow growth rate. In 1961–62 and in 1970–71 the region produced 23 and 22 percent, respectively, of all foodgrains, somewhat more than the south. Its consumption of nitrogen was only 14 percent in 1961–62, which dropped sharply to 10 percent in 1970–71. The eastern region is characterized by the dominance of rice, a low proportion of irrigated acreage, relatively poor water control, and an inadequate infrastructure of electrification, transportation, and institutions. The east uses only 30 to 40 percent as much fertilizer as the south and yet produces a higher proportion of the national foodgrain output. On the basis of these figures, the eastern region is a prime target for future increases in fertilizer use and production, again suggesting the need for major attention to irrigation and other requisites of growth for this area.

On a national level, the rate of growth of nitrogen use slackened sharply after 1969–70. In the four years 1969–70 through 1973–74, the average annual increment in consumption was 119 thousand tons compared to 209,000 tons for the average of the four preceding years, 1965–66 through 1969–70. Rapid increases in nitrogen use in the 1960s were largely due to the diffusion of fertilizer use to traditional crop varieties in areas in which application was already profitable but had not been widely adopted, to the introduction of the new high-yield types, and to an associated increase in irrigation. The diffusion of fertilizer use to traditional varieties, primarily on irrigated acreage, was largely accomplished

[22] Gunvant M. Desai, "Nitrogen Use and Foodgrain Production, India, 1973–74, 1978–79 and 1983–84," Cornell Agricultural Economics Occasional Paper No. 55 (March 1973).

by the late 1960s. Introduction of new varieties of dwarf wheat was dramatic but began tapering off in the late 1960s. Under these circumstances, a decline in the growth rate of nitrogen use was inevitable. Resumption of the earlier rates of increase requires diffusion of fertilizer consumption to traditional varieties in unirrigated areas, increased irrigation, and the development of more new high-yield strains.

The potentials for further diffusion of fertilizer use to the rain-fed areas, although difficult to realize, are substantial. In 1969–70, 72 and 77 percent of the rainfed area of wheat and rice, respectively, and 82 percent of the area growing other foodgrains were still not using fertilizer (Appendix, Table 7). Not all of this area is in regions with scanty and uncertain rainfall. What is needed is identification of the unexploited segments of the market for fertilizers and vigorous efforts to promote its use in this area. Similarly, nearly 80 percent of the total consumption of nitrogenous fertilizer has remained confined to about 100 of the 330 districts in the country.[23] This in turn implies that the organization for sale and distribution of fertilizers is virtually nonexistent in 60 percent of the districts in the nation. To exploit this market potential requires a vigorous selling effort, an effort which is unlikely to be made as long as supplies of fertilizer remain constricted to quantities easily sold in the already well-served districts.

Unfortunately, there are powerful forces restricting the expansion of fertilizer supply. Increasing domestic production requires large capital outlays and places a heavy burden on foreign-exchange supplies. Either considerable capital must be diverted to capital intensive fertilizer production—with a consequent large loss in aggregate employment potential—or substantial amounts of foreign exchange must be devoted to current imports. Annual increments of 200,000 tons of nitrogen, consistent with the short-term foodgrain needs and potentials outlined below, require annual increases of about 40 million dollars for imports or 150 million dollars in investment funds for the construction of new plants.[24] These

[23] Gunvant M. Desai and Gurdev Singh, *Growth of Fertiliser Use in Districts of India: Performance and Policy Implications* (Ahmedabad, India: Indian Institute of Management, Centre for Management in Agriculture, Monograph No. 41, 1973), p. 27.

[24] These figures provide the orders of magnitude for the 1960s. The cost of importing nitrogenous fertilizer into India was estimated to be twenty cents per kilogram. This figure was calculated from estimates given in S. K. Mukherjee, "Basic Problems for Increasing Fertiliser Production and Consumpton during Seventies," *Fertiliser News*, 15:7 (July 1970), 27. The cost of expanding plant capacity was based on data for the Gujarat State Fer-

are large magnitudes in comparison with the growth in foreign-exchange earnings, borrowing capacity, and savings rates. Therefore the pressures are great from the Ministry of Finance to accept conservative estimates of fertilizer needs, with the consequent danger that prophecies of low consumption levels may be self-fulfilling. It is too likely that the choice will result in little or no expansion of fertilizer supply to new areas and to small farmers and, consequently, in retarded overall rates of growth. Clearly, the public and private sector producers of fertilizer have a strong vested interest in a tight supply situation which ensures easy sales and favorable prices. The potential unity of interest between the manufacturers and a Ministry of Finance committed to the capital intensive strategy is all too clear.

The absolutely crucial role of fertilizer in the strategy of agricultural development emphasizes important interdependencies. The overexpansion of world capacity in the late 1960s and the consequent depression of world prices cut back the construction of new plant facilities in the early 1970s. This curtailment created an acute worldwide shortage of fertilizer, greatly exacerbated by the increase in world food prices and the heavy demand in high-income countries. During the three or more years required for the installation of new facilities to increase fertilizer plant capacity, Indian food production growth must mark time.

There are lessons to be learned from this experience: An input as crucial as fertilizer requires a world view of supplies. India must anticipate her requirements and arrange for long-term contracts. It may be that India should invest sufficiently in fertilizer production to ensure the fulfillment of a significant proportion of its needs, despite the economic arguments (presented in Chapter V) for emphasis on more labor-intensive industries, and should expend much greater effort in operating to a capacity well above the 65 percent rate that has been normal in the past.

---

tiliser Company, cited in *Fertiliser News,* 12:3 (March 1967), 6; and *Fertiliser News,* 12:8 (August 1967), 24–25. The figures given in the text assume production to be at 65 percent capacity. Note, however, the sharply contrasting view of Asoka Mehta, then deputy chairman of the Planning Commission: With 12 crores of rupees of foreign exchange, "it would be possible to import 100,000 tonnes of nitrogen equivalent of fertilisers. But with this 12 crores of foreign exchange, we will be able to put up one plant of fertiliser which will be capable of producing 200,000 tonnes of nitrogenous fertilisers for all years to come" (Inaugural Address, *National Seminar on Fertilisers: Proceedings* [New Delhi: The Fertiliser Association of India, June 1966], p. 20).

Potentials for the Future

The rate of growth of foodgrain production is determined by the basic structural forces of investment in irrigation systems, biological research, the diffusion of technical innovations to farmers, and their education for using new inputs intensively. The strength of each of these forces is the product of public policy. A simple projection of past production trends is unlikely to reveal either the potentials or the reality of future growth. Achieving high levels of production will require assigning top priority to each of these functions and engaging in vigorous action.

The preceding analysis of the contrasting conditions of wheat and rice production suggests the basic sources and determinants of growth in the output of foodgrains. Gunvant M. Desai has made a set of estimates consisting of crop-by-crop measures of the increase in irrigated and nonirrigated acreage, the increase in area planted to high-yield varieties, and the spread of the use of fertilizer and the rates of application. (See the Appendix, Tables 5–8, for details.) Each of these estimates is presented as a level which could be achieved under conditions of substantial government commitment to increasing agricultural production. The estimates provide a basis for judging the growth of foodgrain production and hence the extent of overall economic advancement. The components of the estimates supply a means of formulating the policies and strategies necessary for realizing the potentials set forth. These estimates are of course specific to India. They are discussed in detail to illustrate the nature of discussions which must characterize successful agricultural production policy in essentially all low-income nations.

The rate of growth of foodgrain production derived from Desai's assumptions is 4.9 percent per year for the period 1969–70 to 1983–84 (Table III-3). That is 40 to 50 percent higher than the rate apparently attained in the first period of accelerated technological change in agriculture, 1964–65 to 1970–71 (Table II-2). It is 88 percent higher than the rate achieved in the period 1949–50 to 1964–65. But it is only 88 percent of the 5.6 percent rate targeted for the Fourth Five-Year Plan. Although each individual goal represented by a component of these estimates appears attainable, it seems excessively optimistic to believe that all would be realized simultaneously. It will be shown in Chapter VII that growth rates of income and employment are extremely sensitive to the rate of

Table III-3. Estimated compound growth rates of production of various foodgrains, India, 1969–70 to 1983–84

Foodgrain	1969–70 to 1978–79	1978–79 to 1983–84	1969–70 to 1983–84
Rice	3.7	4.5	4.0
Wheat	8.1	6.8	7.6
Sorghum	5.0	4.8	4.9
Millet	5.2	5.8	5.4
Maize	8.1	7.5	7.9
Barley	0.9	0.7	0.9
Other cereals and pulses	1.4	2.1	1.6
All foodgrains	4.8	5.1	4.9

Sources: Calculated from Appendix, Table 8, and Gunvant M. Desai, *Nitrogen Use and Foodgrain Production, India, 1973–74, 1978–79 and 1983–84,* Department of Agricultural Economics, Occasional Paper 55, Cornell University USAID Employment and Income Distribution Project (March 1973).

growth of foodgrain production. An increase in foodgrain output of 2.5 or 3 percent per year provides little or no stimulus to income and employment, while a rise of 3.5 percent results in rapid growth. The estimates presented here allow for nonattainment by a margin of one quarter and still allow scope for the new strategy of growth. Of course, even a 3.5 percent rate of growth will require much realignment of priorities.

Irrigation

Increasing the acreage irrigated is crucial to a rapid growth in foodgrain output. The estimates of future potentials seem reasonable in terms both of irrigable area and past rates of gain. If the potentials are to be realized, massive investment will be required, together with a sense of priority that was not evident in the early 1970s.[25]

Government of India estimates indicate that only 44 percent of the nation's total potential for irrigation had been developed as of 1968–69. Almost half of the potential remaining is estimated to result from ground water and small-scale surface sources of water—each a system quite compatible with the employment-oriented strategy of growth.[26]

The growth rate assumed in these calculations for the area irrigated is that actually achieved in the period 1960–61 to 1967–68, which was one of particularly rapid development, as many of the large-scale projects ini-

[25] For a comprehensive and sensible analysis and diagnosis of the potentials and policy needs, see S. R. Sen, *Report of the Irrigation Commission* (New Delhi: Government of India, Ministry of Irrigation and Power, 1972).

[26] Government of India, Planning Commission, *Fourth Five-Year Plan, 1969–74,* draft (Delhi: Government of India Press), p. 184, Table 1.

tiated in the 1950s materialized and as the new high-yield crop varieties gave a particular spur to private investment in irrigation. During that period the gross area irrigated grew at a rate of 2.4 percent per year (Table III-1). Growth at that pace could continue for well over three decades before the presently estimated potential would be fully utilized. Maintaining the rapid earlier rates of increase of the wheat acreage irrigated will be difficult, while accelerating the earlier slow gains of rice may be even more troublesome.

The success of the new dwarf wheat varieties favored a very sharp growth rate in the acreage irrigated. Thus, projecting past trends, 68 percent of the increase in the foodgrain area irrigated from 1969–70 to 1983–84 would be in wheat, almost five times the increase expected in rice (Appendix, Table 5). Continuation of that growth pattern will probably have to result from rapid expansion into the eastern Gangetic plain. This would require the economic incentive to plant the high-yield varieties, rural electrification to facilitate private tube wells, quite possibly land consolidation to foster the necessary fixed investment on very small fragmented farms, and improvement in the currently poorly developed physical and institutional infrastructure—ranging from roads to credit facilities.

The previous rate of increase in irrigated rice acreage has been very slow. One would expect major improvements in rice varieties to increase the profitability of irrigation and so induce more rapid expansion, but much of the existing irrigated rice acreage has poor water control. The rapid spread of high-yield varieties to the acreage currently irrigated presumes improvement in water regulation that is not taken into account in this projection. Thus, the rate of growth of investment in irrigation projects for rice implied in these figures is considerable. It is greater than the expected rate of increase in the acreage to be irrigated.

It should be noted that the estimates of the area of future plantings of the nonfoodgrain crops, particularly cotton and oilseeds, are probably inconsistent with the fast rate of the growth of demand for these commodities which would accompany a 4 to 5 percent increase per year in the demand for foodgrains (See Chapter VII.) Technological advance could greatly increase yields for these crops. Substantial relative declines in foodgrain prices accompanying major technological breakthroughs could result in the transfer of acreage from the production of foodgrains to nonfoodgrains. Alternatively, a portion of the latter, such as cotton and oilseeds, which use a large land area, may be imported. Since, as will be clear later, even a 5 percent growth rate in foodgrain production could be effectively used in an employment-oriented strategy of growth, it may be prudent to assume large imports of other agricultural commodities, in which case the projection of past patterns of growth for these crops is reasonable.

High-Yield Varieties

Complementary to irrigation and equally crucial to the future sharp growth in foodgrain production is the increasingly widespread utilization of high-yield crop varieties. The estimates of potential require rapid progress in using such resources for enlarging the output of rice and the various dryland crops and for continued progress with wheat. That will entail priority attention to the presently developing experimental system, including rapid expansion of trained manpower and adequate individual and institutional incentives to encourage quality research.

Ministry of Agriculture estimates show that, for 1969–70, 85 percent of the irrigated acreage of wheat and 100 and 75 percent, respectively, of millet and sorghum are covered by high-yield varieties, while only 32 percent of the rice acreage irrigated is planted with these new types. Except for millet, negligible acreages of unirrigated crops are so occupied (Appendix, Table 5).

Realization of a high growth rate in foodgrain production assumes the rapid extension of coverage to 100 percent of all irrigated acreage and substantial coverage of the unirrigated acreage as well. The most pressing task is to evolve high-yield varieties of rice. Assuming that new strains will be developed to allow 80 percent and 100 percent coverage of the irrigated acreage by 1978–79 and 1983–84, respectively, and given the premises for the other crops, 47 percent of the total increase in production of foodgrains by 1983–84 is expected to come from high-yield varieties of rice, and over two-thirds of the increase will be on irrigated land (Appendix, Table 7). The high-yield rice varieties are depicted as somewhat more important in their contribution to future growth than high-yield wheat varieties—in very sharp contrast to the record for 1964–65 to 1970–71. Given the small success to date with rice, this is a very optimistic assumption—but it is so important to the overall success of agriculture and an employment-oriented strategy of growth that the stress must be on an allocation of resources that will ensure its fulfillment.

The research task for the unirrigated areas is also difficult. But extensive parts of these regions have assured rainfall. Given the current emphasis on problems of dry farming, it is likely that improved crop strains will be developed for many of them in the 1970s.[27] The future potentials stated assume that one-third to one-half the unirrigated areas will be covered by high-yield varieties by 1983–84.

Spread of the new types to the extent estimated requires the massive expansion of irrigation. It also requires the full contribution of small farmers whose special problems of capital-raising and risk-bearing may exclude them from participation. As is shown in Chapter IV, about one-quarter of the foodgrain production occurs on farms small enough to have special problems of using high-yield varieties. Therefore, the steep rates of increase in coverage assume detailed programs to meet these problems.

Fertilizer

Increased use of fertilizer is not only complementary to the development and spread of the new high-yield varieties, but it has a potential also for expanded application to existing crop types. The acute worldwide shortage of fertilizer of the mid-1970s worsened the prospects for the new strategy, of course, until the effects of massive further investment to increase the world's fertilizer capacity could be felt.

Rapid expansion in the use of fertilizer requires its spread to areas of currently low consumption and a large increase in the intensity of application where it is already used. Desai's analysis of a large number of farm studies suggests that the bulk of the irrigated acreage of foodgrains was, in 1969–70, already receiving at least some fertilizer (Appendix, Table 6). There is, however, still opportunity to increase its consumption—and foodgrain output—by the spread of the use of fertilizer to unirrigated areas. Many of these regions receive substantial rainfall and would, according to farm data, respond profitably to modest application.

Three circumstances impede extending the use of fertilizer to the unirrigated areas. First, the amount of fertilizer it pays to use on unirrigated land tends to be low, particularly on traditional varieties, so the individ-

---

[27] For a comprehensive review of dryland farming in India, see M. S. Krishnaswami and K. V. Patel, *Status of Dryland Agriculture* (Ahmedabad, India: Indian Institute of Management, Centre for Management in Agriculture, 1973). See also Prihar Singh and M. S. Randhawa, "Role of Research in Dryland Farming," *Fertiliser News*, 15:12 (December 1970), 39–42.

ual farmer forgoes relatively little income by not applying it. To overcome farmer apathy would require a substantial selling effort. Second, large portions of the unirrigated areas lie in the two-thirds of India's districts which used only 20 percent of all fertilizer consumed in 1968–69. In such low-intensity regions, the distribution networks are poorly developed. Finally, in the frequent periods in which there is a scarcity of fertilizer, little public incentive exists to market it in areas of poor distribution facilities and high cost.

Even with optimistic assumptions for the other elements, over onethird of the potential increase in foodgrain production between 1969–70 and 1983–84 is depicted as occurring in the unirrigated areas (Appendix, Table 7). The estimate of potentials is based largely on farm survey data of profitable levels of use, which implicitly include substantial discounts for risk and are, therefore, realistic measurements.

In the unirrigated areas that have little current demand for fertilizer, distribution costs are initially high and profit incentives low. The key to development of these areas is to ensure ample supplies and stocks of fertilizer so as to exert pressure on the distribution system to organize to sell fertilizer in the low-intensity areas. That requires the priority decision to allocate foreign exchange and capital resources to guarantee plentiful supplies.

Increased intensity of fertilizer use requires the development of new crop varieties and an expansion of irrigation that radically raises its profitability of application. Thus, estimates of future fertilizer consumption assume a gradual increase in use per acre under existing conditions as well as an increase in irrigation. The limitation posed by the restricted development of present varieties of rice is dramatically illustrated by rates of fetilizer use. The application of fertilizer by farmers on high-yield-variety rice in 1969–70 was half the rate of application on high-yield-variety wheat, reflecting the fact that a large proportion of rice acreage is planted to types and under conditions (particularly of water control) which are not nearly so responsive to its use as is typically the case for wheat (Appendix, Table 6). The rates assumed for the unirrigated crops are also very low, confirming the fact that the total income forgone by not using fertilizer is, under those circumstances, relatively small; consequently, there is little incentive for its use. The increase in the rate of fertilizer application for the *local* foodgrain varieties depends on a successful farmer-education effort and a vigorous selling and marketing program. The increase in rates of application on *high-yield* foodgrain varieties depends, additionally, on developing more fertilizer-responsive strains, particularly for the rain-fed rice regions. In the case of rice it is assumed that present low levels of fertilizer use, even on high-yield varieties, are the result of realizing relatively less of the basic potential than for wheat. Obviously, the rice-research system has a very crucial role to play in a successful foodgrain and employment strategy.

The above set of assumptions with respect to the use of fertilizer was employed to estimate the level of nitrogen consumption for 1969–70. The estimate is within 3 percent of the actual total utilization in that year (Table III-2 and Appendix, Table 6). Other combinations of assumptions could of course give the same total figure, but this test does support the consistency of the approach used.

The same estimating procedures are used to calculate nitrogen consumption for 1978–79 and 1983–84. The average annual increment in the level of nitrogen use is calculated to be about 273,000 tons between 1969–70 and 1978–79, and about 467,000 tons between 1978–79 and 1983–84 (Appendix, Table 6). These huge increases in fertilizer consumption, much greater than any ever achieved in the past, will of course occur only if the underlying assumptions about research, irrigation, and marketing prove to be correct because of a vigorous public policy that assigns the highest priority to expanding agricultural production.

Since data on fertilizer use by specific crops is not directly available from official Indian sources the breakdown given is of some interest. In addition, since the assumptions are based on a substantial number of observations of farmers' practices, they have some reliability. The data suggest that for 1969–70, 73 percent of the total amount of nitrogen was used on foodgrains. This compares with estimates in the late 1950s of 61 percent.[28] The difference seems reasonable in view of the large increase in the responsiveness of the high-yield foodgrain varieties to fertilizer. Half of all the nitrogen used on foodgrains in 1969–70 is depicted as applied to these high-yield types on irrigated land. In addition, 83 percent of all the nitrogen consumed in foodgrain production was on irrigated land, which comprised only 22 percent of the total foodgrain acreage (Appendix, Tables 5 and 6). The importance of developing new high-

[28] See Uma J. Lele and John W. Mellor, *Estimates of Change and Causes of Change in Foodgrains Production, India, 1949–50 to 1960–61*, C.I.A.D. Bulletin No. 2 (August 1964), 30.

yield crop varieties and expanding the irrigated acreage cannot be over-emphasized.

Wheat and rice are estimated to account for nearly 60 percent of the increment in nitrogen use in each of the future periods. Increased area, largely a function of expanded irrigation and the introduction of new crop strains, accounts for about one-third of the rise in each period. Diffusion of the use of nitrogen to previously nonusing areas continues as an important source of growth, accounting for about one-fifth of the total. Thus, for these growth rates to be achieved, success must be attained in each of the difficult tasks of developing new high-yield varieties, expanding the irrigated acreage, and marketing fertilizer effectively in low-consumption regions.

Foodgrain Production

For the period 1969–70 to 1983–84, a rate of growth in foodgrain production of about 4.9 percent per year follows from the preceding estimates. Growth rates for individual crops as well as the overall rates are shown in Table III-3. (The purpose of this calculation is more to show the nature of variation and to illustrate the diversity that may enter into an aggregate figure than to argue the specifics of the individual rates of growth.) The base used is 1969–70, as it appears to be a rather ordinary year with respect to weather. Because of the great difficulty of judging production trends over only a few years' time, it is not possible to judge whether the various components and totals are moving at the requisite pace or not.

According to these calculations, rice and wheat contribute nearly 70 percent of the rise in production during the period (Appendix, Table 7). Among all foodgrains, nearly 80 percent of the increment in output results from expansion in irrigation, increased use of fertilizer, and the planting of high-yield varieties. Again, on the basis of complex assumptions, the relative contribution of acreage and yield to increased production is calculated. Over 70 percent of the rise in production is due to increased yield (Appendix, Table 8). The most important factor in raising yields is the shift of acreage from low- to high-producing conditions of farming.

Priorities for Sustaining the Foodgrain Revolution

The immediate potential for accelerated growth in foodgrain production is the product of underlying physical conditions and past investment in infrastructure and rural institutions. Within this context, strategically placed public investment may stimulate additional private investment and thereby cause a large increase in foodgrain production. The preceding analysis both of past patterns of growth in foodgrains and of future potentials confirms that in the Indian context of the mid-1970s, the public priorities are: (1) to expand the capacity to carry on agricultural research; (2) to increase the area under well-controlled irrigation; (3) to increase the supplies of fertilizer; and (4) to extend participation in new technologies to poorer regions and smaller farms. Each of these priorities requires a major expansion in the number of trained agriculturalists. A vigorous thrust in agricultural development will place a heavy burden on educational resources.

The recent breakthroughs in research on crop varieties dramatized the potentials for yield increase and cost reduction; emphasized the need for experimentation and other essentials of technological change in agriculture; and raised immensely the morale and the will to produce of researchers and other technical personnel. Total expenditure on agricultural research rose almost three and a half times from 1950 to 1968, and the size of the expenditure as a proportion of agricultural production increased nearly two and a half times in that period.[29] The rate of gain accelerated greatly in the latter part of the decade. More important, the approach to research has been rapidly systematized. The basic outline of the coordinated research schemes is correct. The two key problems now are how to expand vigorously into those regions—such as eastern India—which have been historically weak in research and lack the traditions of state government or its resources for providing financial support; and how to increase rapidly the technical manpower supply so that it can encompass the full range of disciplines needed for a complete attack on production problems. These are the types of problems which appear simple, but which require the assignment of a priority which permits at least occasional access to the highest levels of decision making if they are to be resolved effectively.

Adequate rates of growth of irrigation not only require the stimulus of new crop varieties but may also entail major expenditure on electrification and other facilitative action. The needs are sufficiently complex to demand continued study, but they are clear enough now to test commitment to agricultural expansion. The necessity of a high growth rate in ir-

[29] See Mohan et al., Table 1.

rigation is adequate to justify the setting of well-defined policies in order to reach specific regional and crop potentials. A huge investment in electrification and private tube wells in the eastern Gangetic plain should probably receive priority.

A rapid increase in fertilizer supply is absolutely crucial to the whole strategy. This requires a massive worldwide investment in plant capacity, a priority for the use of resources to achieve that goal, and an equally strong commitment by India to the allocation of foreign exchange and domestic capital to fertilizer import and production.

The government must not only ensure vastly increased supplies of fertilizer but also provide the research, irrigation, and distribution policies needed for their productive use. India and other parts of the world failed in these respects in the late 1960s and early 1970s, bringing on the fertilizer crisis which then became exacerbated by the petroleum policies of 1973.

All aspects of agricultural growth through technological change are based on expanding the number of rural supporting institutions to benefit the small farmer, who is a crucial part of the overall high-growth strategy. Because of the agricultural sector's massive size, the intensity of use of trained manpower, and stress on broad participation in growth, an emphasis on rural development requires a huge expansion of education at all levels. Also, the broader the participation in rural development, the more intensive the requirement for trained manpower.[30]

It is important that the rates of growth of demand for educated persons not be underestimated by basing them on the demand that existed under the capital-intensive program of the recent past, or because of excessive aversion to increasing the length of time it takes graduates to find a job as increasing numbers force the educated to take lower-level jobs.[31] Even

[30] For a pre-green-revolution estimate of needs for agricultural graduates, which is large compared to enrollment in colleges of agriculture and yet is probably a gross underestimate of the needs for a dynamic agriculture, see Tyrrell Burgess, Richard Layard, and Pitambar Pant, *Manpower and Educational Development in India, 1961–1986* (Edinburgh: Oliver and Boyd, 1968), p. 25. See also *Report of the Education Commission 1964–66: Education and National Development* (New Delhi: Government of India, Ministry of Education and Youth Services, 1966), and Supplementary Vol. II (1970), p. 56, Table XV-A.

[31] It should be noted that the bulk of educated unemployed are those recently graduated and waiting for their first job. Mark Blaug, Richard Layard, and Maureen Woodhall show that the average wait by a 1954 "baccalaureate" graduate for a first job was six and one-half months (*The Causes of Graduate Unemployment in India* [London: Allen Lane, 1969], pp. 78–81). The waiting period for the first job appears shorter for the agricultural college

under past programs the rate of return to expenditure on education has been high.[32] Failure to expand education to upgrade its technical content and to furnish in-service training will provide a major constraint to rural development and particularly to the employment-oriented objective.

This chapter delineates a strategy of investment in irrigation, in agricultural research, in fertilizer, and in education which offers a possibility of an annual rate of growth in foodgrain production as high as 4.9 percent up to 1983–84. Even if discounted by the lower levels of efficiency of resource use assumed in the projections of Chapter II, such a record would still allow a growth rate of 3.9 percent to be reached, which Chapter VII shows to be sufficient to provide radical change in the structure and the progress of economic development. For each of the components of rapid growth there is a history which corroborates the feasibility of the rate of increase specified. It is essential, however, because of their complementarity, that success be achieved in each of the parts. The experience of the early 1970s suggests that these goals can be realized only if government focuses on irrigation investment, fertilizer supplies, and research establishments in a manner which consistently assigns them priority over all other concerns, at least until the levels of development and success delineated here are reached.

---

graduate. For graduates of the high-quality G. B. Pant University of Agriculture and Technology in Uttar Pradesh, the average waiting period between 1963 and 1971 for the first job was less than three months for all degree categories.

[32] Graduates (B.Sc.Agr.) of the G. B. Pant University earn high enough incomes on the average, compared to people with the next lower degree, to provide a 16 percent rate of return on their private investment in education and a 10 percent rate of return on society's total investment in that education. See Richard L. Shortlidge, Jr., "The Labor Market for Agricultural Graduates in India: A Benefit-Cost Case Study of G. B. Pant University of Agriculture and Technology," Cornell Agricultural Economics Occasional Paper No. 69 (April 1974), Tables 7 and 8. See also Richard L. Shortlidge, "University Training for Gramsevaks in India," *Economic Development and Cultural Change,* 24:1 (October 1975), 139–154.

IV

Agricultural Modernization and the Rural Poor

Technological change in agriculture is a necessary condition for the success of all other programs for the poor. Any definition of poverty is bound to be arbitrary, but Dandekar and Rath have set the poverty line, somewhat stringently, at Rs. 20, or $4.19 per person per month according to 1960–61 prices (and exchange rates), on the ground that persons with less than that income do not even obtain adequate calories for normal health and activity.[1] According to this definition, in 1960–61, 40 percent of India's rural population and 50 percent of the urban population were below the poverty line, and 44 percent of these poor were rural. Since urban employment growth has consistently been faster than the natural increase in urban population, poverty in the cities is largely a reflection of rural poverty and the consequent migration of the unemployed to the metropolitan areas. Although there is controversy on this point, real incomes of the people in the lower 40 percent of the income distribution scale probably have not increased in the past two decades.[2]

Categorizing population by the size of landholdings provides another measure of the extent of rural poverty and illustrates the political and economic constraints on policy making on this matter. About one-third of the rural householders are landless or almost landless (owning less than one

[1] See V. M. Dandekar and Nilakantha Rath, "Poverty in India," *Economic and Political Weekly*, 6:1 (January 1971), 30.

[2] This controversy is reflected in the following: Dandekar and Rath, op. cit.; Pranab K. Bardhan, "On the Minimum Level of Living and the Rural Poor," *Indian Economic Review*, N.S., 5:1 (April 1970), 129–36; B. S. Minhas, "Rural Poverty, Land Redistribution and Development Strategy: Facts and Policy," *Indian Economic Review*, 5:1 (April 1970), 97–128; and Wolf Ladejinsky, "Land Ceilings and Land Reform," *Economic and Political Weekly*, 7:5–7 (February 1972), 401–8. Because real incomes of the poor are so much a function of foodgrain production and prices, and these are so much a function of varying weather, choice of years of comparison is, in the short run, the principal determinant of change in numbers and average incomes of the poor.

acre) laborers (Appendix, Table 1). Their income depends on the demand for their labor by the owners of land and capital. Virtually all landless laborers fall into the Dandekar-Rath poverty class. Only a massive increase in employment can have an effect on this class.

Slightly more than one-third of the rural households have landholdings of between one and five acres and may be classified as small farmers.[3] About half of this group falls into the Dandekar-Rath poverty class; the rest are close to it. Since the small farmer earns over half of his income from labor on his own land or by working for others, his income is determined substantially by the same factors as that of the landless laborer.[4] More intensive land use would offer him the prospect of a significant increase in employment—and revenue. This potential—its relationship to new technology and patterns of demand—and the special production characteristics of small farms suggest programs different from those for landless laborers. Because small farmers and landless laborers are so numerous and the creation of a multitude of new jobs is so difficult, the landless laborer can benefit only if programs to aid impoverished small farmers succeed in keeping them on their farms by improving the use they make of their own farms. Thus, the problems of the small farmer and the landless laborer are closely related and require concurrent solutions.

The remainder of the rural population has farm holdings of over five acres.[5] Although the bulk of this class is not wealthy, it is safely above the Dandekar-Rath poverty line. Even though most of these owners also

[3] Here and elsewhere in this chapter, reference is to national averages, which necessarily cover large variability. Thus, in intensively irrigated areas, five acres may provide a high income, while in some dry areas, ten or more acres may qualify for the lowest decile in the income distribution. Since these variations do approximately cancel each other, acreage guidelines give a roughly correct impression of the proportions of the population falling in various resource categories.

[4] This statement accepts A. M. Khusro's rough approximation that, on an all-India average, five acres provide just sufficient family employment so that little work is sought away from that farm; and assumes that on the average, and in keeping with common practice, labor and land rent receive income equally ("Farm Size and Land Tenure in India," *Indian Economic Review,* N.S., 4:2 [October 1969], 133).

[5] This population includes tenants who, in terms of income determinants, should in substantial part be classified as landless laborers or small farmers. Using either the 1961 census or Khusro's estimates, such a correction would reduce the number of farm owners with over five acres, but would still leave from one-quarter to one-third of all rural households in this class. See *Census of India, 1961* (New Delhi: Government of India, Office of the Registrar General, 1961); and Khusro, "Farm Size and Land Tenure in India."

work on their farms, the main portion of their income is attributable to ownership of land rather than to labor. Changes in relative prices and in production technology are the prime determinants of increases or decreases in their land revenue. The earnings of the poor will not be raised by redistribution of income and of rights in land. The vast number of large landowners, and many small farmers as well, will oppose programs which potentially reduce existing rights in land.

The rural landless labor class is larger in India than in most other low-income countries, providing a more difficult economic and political problem. However, India again offers particularly timely and instructive lessons as population growth and diminishing availability of uncultivated lands bring a growing landless class to substantial numbers of Asian and African countries. The ineffectiveness of many apparently well-articulated efforts to improve conditions of the rural poor may be particularly instructive as an indication of the key role of the overall strategy as well as suggesting details of specific programs that may be effective, given a hospitable environment.

However ironical it is that the solution to the problem of rural poverty depends upon the spread of yield-increasing technological innovations that may markedly boost the incomes of the landowning classes, the increased food supplies are essential to the improved welfare of the poor. This is implicit in the Dandekar-Rath definition of poverty in terms of caloric deficiency and in the high proportion of additional income and expenditure allocated by the poor to food. The increased income resulting from the use of the high-yield foodgrain technology also provides the necessary incentive for small farmers to use the credit and production inputs which may be supplied to them in special programs. In addition, the larger income supports the expanded demand for labor intensive agricultural commodities on which the rest of the small-farmer programs must be based; the demand and potentially the financing for many of the rural public works programs; and the demand for labor intensive nonagricultural commodities which are very crucial to the success of employment programs for the landless laborer. Finally, the increase in direct demand for labor associated with the new technologies may be, in the short run, the largest single source of added employment.

Although the potential benefits to the poor from biological and other scientific advances are large, they may be inhibited by numerous economic and political factors. To prescribe appropriate programs requires knowledge of the technological basis of the initial distribution of benefits from the modernization of agriculture as well as the special characteristics of the small farmer and the landless laborer.

The Initial Benefits

The nature of new technology, the extent of its application, and the physical environment within which it is applied determine the increase in yield, the quantity of inputs purchased, and the amount of employment created. These forces, in combination with the distribution of production resources, are responsible for the initial allocation of benefits among different income classes. The effects vary greatly.

Typically, much of the increased income from the new high-yield varieties is a residual return to the landowners; only a small proportion derives from greater use of labor.[6] Even when, in specific geographic areas, there is a large percentage rise in production and hence in labor utilization and payments thereto, the proportion of total increased income paid to labor, relative to other inputs, is nevertheless small. This somewhat anomalous situation has confused many appraisals of the green revolution.

In a typical case of high-yield wheat varieties in Uttar Pradesh, actual and imputed payments to all labor, hired as well as family, absorbed only 10 percent of the increased income, while other inputs absorbed 23 percent, leaving 67 percent as reimbursement to the owners of land and capital (Table IV-1). Similarly, in twelve of the fifteen cases depicted in Table IV-2, the proportion of increased output attributable to labor was between 5 and 15 percent. In most cases, because of the large rise in production, the percentage gain in income to labor was also large— 59 percent in the U.P. case (Table IV-1), over 25 percent in seven of the fifteen cases in Table IV-2, and 20 percent or more in nine of the fifteen cases in the same table.

Expanding these examples reveals the implications of these changes for

---

[6] Michael G. G. Schluter shows returns to land per acre for unirrigated crops between 1966–67 and 1971–72 to range from one and one-half to three and one-half times more than the returns to labor per acre, depending on the crop planted. For irrigated crops in 1971–72, the respective returns to land per acre ranged from two to seven times more than the returns to labor per acre, again depending on the crop ("The Interaction of Credit and Uncertainty in Determining Resource Allocation and Incomes on Small Farms, Surat District, India," Cornell Agricultural Economics Occasional Paper No. 68 [February 1974], Table 7 and ch. iii).

Table IV-1. Division of the increased "payments" from a high-yield wheat variety, Aligarh district, Uttar Pradesh, India, 1967–68

Item	Traditional variety	High-yield variety	Percent increase
		(in quintals)	
1. Yield	7.5	14.8	96
		(in rupees)	
2. Gross value of production	653	1,115	71
3. Payments (costs) other than family labor, land, and capital	219	334	52
4. Payments for fertilizer (included in 3)	37	76	110
5. Payments (net return) to family labor, land, and capital	434	781	80
6. Payments (net return) to family land and capital	380	690	82
7. Payments to labor (cost or imputed value)	80	126	59
a. Family labor	54	91	68
b. Hired labor	26	35	35

	Increments in shift from traditional to high-yield variety	
	Rupees per acre	Percent of increment to gross production
8. Gross value of production (row 2)	462	100
9. Payments to labor (row 7)	46	10
10. Payments (returns) to all inputs, including land and capital, but excluding labor (row 2 minus row 7)	416	90
11. Payments (costs) other than labor (row 3 minus row 7b)	106	23
12. Payments for fertilizer (row 4) (included in 11)	39	8
13. Payments (net returns) to family land and capital (row 6)	310	67

Source: Adapted from R. S. Dixit and P. P. Singh, "Impact of High Yielding Varieties on Human Labor Inputs," *Agricultural Situation in India,* 24:12 (March 1970).

absolute income levels. In the case of the data from U.P., if a typical farm operator transfers ten acres of wheat from traditional to modern varieties, he increases returns to his land and capital by Rs. 3100. In contrast, if the 35 percent rise in payments to hired labor is applied to a typical laborer with a base income of Rs. 750 per year (an income consistent with the lower three deciles in the Indian distribution of family expenditure) his income increases by only Rs. 262. This is merely 8 percent as great as the gain received by the owner-cultivator. Even if all the additional labor is hired, instead of some being provided by the family, the cost of employment of laborers rises 177 percent, from Rs. 26 to Rs. 72

Table IV-2. Division of increased "payments" between labor and other inputs, various high-yield varieties, areas, and years

Area	Increase in gross value of output		Increase in labor "payments"		Percent of increased output to labor*	Percent of increased output to other inputs †	Percent increase in labor "payments" for 1 percent increase in gross value of output
	Rupees per acre	Percent increase	Rupees per acre	Percent increase			
Wheat							
Aligarh, Uttar Pradesh	462	71	46	58	10	90	0.8
Varanasi, Uttar Pradesh	620	65	11	15	2	98	0.2
Udaipur, Rajasthan	343	43	18	13	5	95	0.3
Punjab	450	100	56	42	12	88	0.4
Kharif Paddy							
West Godavari, Andhra Pradesh	269	38	32	17	12	88	0.4
East Godavari, Andhra Pradesh	216	33	20	13	10	90	0.4
Uttar Pradesh	1,100	200	67	92	6	94	0.5
Tamil Nadu	550	100	33	20	6	94	0.2
Laguna, Philippines	374	72	3	3	1	99	0.0
Sambalpur, Orissa	404	95	36	28	11	89	0.3
Rabi Paddy							
West Godavari, Andhra Pradesh	562	86	39	16	7	93	0.2
East Godavari, Andhra Pradesh	761	153	39	30	5	95	0.2
Tamil Nadu	625	100	46	21	7	93	0.2
Gumai Bil, Bangladesh	948	208	302	125	32	68	0.6
Millet							
Maira, Gujarat	300	85	39	27	13	87	0.3
Average	532	97	52	35	9	91	0.3

* Labor "payment" is defined as physical labor input (family and hired) in man-days at a constant wage.
† Other inputs "payments" defined as gross value of output minus share to labor.
Source: John W. Mellor and Uma J. Lele, "Growth Linkages of the New Foodgrain Technologies," *Indian Journal of Agricultural Economics*, 28:1 (January–March 1973), pp. 35–55, Table II.

per acre, and income increases by Rs. 1,327—still less than half as much as the gain in payment to the owners of land and capital. In such a situation, social discontent arises not because the incomes of the poor increase by such a small proportion, but because the absolute disparities widen so much. In this context, programs for alleviation of rural poverty logically emphasize assisting the low-income small farmer to participate in new production technology and turning the increased incomes of the landowning classes toward expenditures that stimulate the demand for labor.[7]

The Small Farmer

Small farmers cultivate roughly 15 to 20 percent of the total Indian harvested area, but by tilling very intensively, produce a consequential 26 percent of the value of agricultural output (Appendix, Table 1). Small farms can obtain higher incomes by using the new yield-increasing foodgrain varieties and by becoming more labor intensive. Both changes require facilitative programs to reduce the small farmer's special vulnerability to risk and uncertainty, to increase his access to capital, and to ensure his ability to acquire production inputs such as fertilizer. Special programs to assist the small farmer can be effective only in the context of a strategy which provides the essentials of production-increasing technological change in agriculture and growth in consumer demand for labor intensive commodities.

Foodgrain technology can result in a spectacular increase in the income of small farmers. Using input levels and responses from farm surveys, V. P. Shukla provides a dramatically instructive example of how the income from a two-acre farm in Madhya Pradesh is more than quadrupled, from Rs. 641 to Rs. 2775, by the addition of a tube well and the application of high-yield varieties of crops.[8] In this case, it was the combination of

---

[7] The complex cross-currents which confuse the policy issues with respect to new technology and income distribution are well illustrated in the context of a smallholder's agriculture in a statistical analysis for Taiwan reported by Yu and Lee. It was found that extension programs, carriers for technological change, served to widen income disparities among rural families; but the indirect effect of new technology, seen as increased farm and nonfarm employment, which particularly benefited small farmers, more than balanced the direct effect. The overall Gini coefficient, a measure of income inequality, declined from 0.36 in 1966 to 0.31 in 1970. See Terry Y. H. Yu and C. S. Lee, "Agricultural Technology and Income Distribution in Taiwan," paper presented at the Seminar on Agricultural Development, Joint Commission on Rural Reconstruction, Taipei, Taiwan, December 10–14, 1973.

[8] See V. P. Shukla, *Interaction of Technological Change and Irrigation in Determining Farm Resource Use, Jabalpur District, India, 1967–1968*, C.I.A.D. Bulletin No. 20 (July

technological change and irrigation which led to such startling results. Irrigation alone raised farm income by only Rs. 50 per year, or less than 10 percent, and provided a rate of return on the investment well below the normal costs of credit. It is the requirement that high-yield varieties must obtain an assured supply of water which makes the irrigation investment profitable. With new technology, even a two-acre farm, selling no water to other farms, returned 12 percent on the investment in tube-well irrigation, assuming the costs of a diesel engine in the operation of the system. The figure rises to 26 percent with the much lower costs of an electric engine.

The same example illustrates problems as well as potentials. Total cash needs to finance the additional annual resource requirements more than double, from Rs. 80 to Rs. 167. This increment is equal to nearly 14 percent of the previous level of net income. Furthermore, a diesel-driven tube well costs about Rs. 9000, or fourteen times the prior annual net receipts of the farmer with two acres. If electricity is available, the cost for the pump and well is nine times his annual earnings.

It is not surprising that small farms fall behind large ones in the application of high-yield varieties. That lag, however, differs considerably among regions and crops according to soil conditions and climate and capital requirements. It is due to economic forces, not ignorance, and suggests the basis for ameliorative programs.

The Agro-Economic Research Centres, associated with the Directorate of Economics and Statistics and the Programme Evaluation Organisation of the Planning Commission, have conducted numerous studies on the relationship between size of farm and adoption of innovation. Small farmers are slower than large cultivators to make use of technological advance when variation in yield is sizable (for example, millet grown in unirrigated areas compared to rice); or where the profitability is lower (for example, rice compared to wheat); or in unirrigated areas generally.[9] The inability of the small farmer to manage risk and uncertainty serves, in

---

1971), 63. For a comprehensive analysis of this question, see V. S. Vyas, D. S. Tyagi, and V. N. Misra, *Significance of the New Strategy of Agricultural Development for Small Farmers: A Cross-Sectional Study of Two Areas,* Agro-Economic Research Centre, Research Study No. 17 (Vallabh Vidyanagar, India: Sardar Patel University, 1968).

[9] Data on these relationships are carefully summarized in a comparative context in Michael G. G. Schluter, "Differential Rates of Adoption of the New Seed Varieties in India: The Problem of the Small Farm," Cornell Agricultural Economics Occasional Paper No. 47 (August 1971); see, in particular, ch. iii.

many sorts of situations, further to widen income disparities between small and large farmers.

Small farmers who adopt the new varieties finance far more of their cash expenditure through cooperative credit than those who do not; and a much smaller proportion of small than of large farmers borrow funds from cooperatives, while those small farmers who do raise money, borrow much more per acre of land.[10] The small farmer's special needs for credit are complicated by the problem of obtaining loans from cooperatives, which tend to be controlled by the larger farmers.[11]

An important positive finding from studies of adoption practice is the tendency, in the case of some crops, for small farmers to plant a higher proportion of their acreage to high-yield varieties than the larger farmer.[12] This is probably because of the great labor intensity of some of the yield-increasing strains. Lacking sufficient family help, large farmers may be reluctant to face the higher labor costs and management difficulties of large numbers of outside, paid workers. The labor restraint on adoption practices by large farmers may be of particular importance in the case of high-yield rice in a double-cropping context.[13] Adjusting programs to meet the need of small farmers to manage risk and uncertainty and obtain credit is not just a means of broadening income distribution, but may indeed raise productivity substantially.

Increased use of fertilizer and, to some extent, other purchased inputs

[10] Ibid., pp. 31–34.

[11] For further discussion of the small farmer's problems in obtaining credit, see Michael G. G. Schluter and Gokul O. Parikh, "The Interaction of Cooperative Credit and Uncertainty in Small Farmer Adoption of the New Cereal Varieties," *Artha-Vikas*, 11:2 (July 1974), 31–48; Uma J. Lele, "The Roles of Credit and Marketing in Agricultural Development," in Nurul Islam, ed., *Agricultural Policy in Developing Countries* (London: Macmillan, 1974), pp. 413–41; H. C. Jain, "Growth and Recent Trends in the Institutional Credit in India," *Indian Journal of Agricultural Economics*, 26:4 (October–December 1971), 555–56; G. Muttiah, "The Green Revolution—Participation by Small Versus Larger Farmers," *Rural Development for Weaker Sections*, Seminar Series XII (Bombay: Indian Society of Agricultural Economics, 1974); R. K. Sharma, *Co-operative Credit in the Package Programme: A Study in Aligarh District, Uttar Pradesh*, Agricultural Economics Research Centre, University of Delhi, 1966; and *Workshop on Small Farmers and Agricultural Labour* (New Delhi: Government of India, Planning Commission, 1970), pp. 171–74.

[12] See Schluter, "Differential Rates of Adoption of the New Seed Varieties in India," pp. 16–20.

[13] With respect to the labor restraint on adoption by large farmers for Mehsana district, see Michael G. G. Schluter and Richard W. Longhurst, "Some Aspects of the Suitability of High Yielding Rice and Bajra Varieties for the Small Farm, Thanjavur and Mehsana District, India," Cornell Agricultural Economics Occasional Paper No. 57 (October 1972), 13.

is essential to all successful small-farm programs. In periods of scarcity, the larger farmer will almost certainly corner the market—partly because he usually controls the cooperatives, partly because the quantities he uses are large enough to justify a special effort to obtain supplies. Government planning which results in a scarcity of fertilizer effectively nullifies all other programs for the small farmer. Given the political and economic realities, there is probably no way to ensure supplies for small farmers without guaranteeing ample supplies for all. That is a matter of higher priorities and a choice of growth strategy, and underlines the hypocrisy of talk about income distribution while a capital intensive program of growth is practiced.

The small farmer earns his income proportionately more from labor and less from land than the large farmer. Changing his combination of crops and livestock to more labor intensive alternatives may be an even more economic means of assisting the small farmer than helping him to grow high-yield varieties of foodgrains. Milk and vegetable production offer a major opportunity for intensification of production on small farms. As an example of the potential, Schluter finds from a study in Gujarat that "family income (returns to land and family labor) increases by Rs. 450 a year if a first buffalo is purchased, and by Rs. 700 if the herd size increases from one to two. In the context of returns from crop cultivation of Rs. 541 on farms of under 2 acres and Rs. 1,228 on 2 to 5 acre farms, this increase is substantial." [14]

More generally, the simulation analysis described in Chapter VII shows that in a consistent pattern of growth induced by accelerated foodgrain production, the nonfoodgrain agricultural sector soon becomes more important than the foodgrain sector as a source of increased employment. The effect of rising domestic demand on agricultural employment, as reflected in the simulation, may be reinforced by a change in agricultural trade, and a consequent change in the pattern of domestic production. Desai and Schluter provide an interesting case of cotton and groundnut oil, both of which are now imported and in Gujarat compete for the same land. Groundnut is the much more labor intensive of the two—requiring 23 more man-days of labor per acre. In Surat district, a transfer of 92.5 thousand acres of cotton to groundnut, equal to the total groundnut acreage and 28 percent of the total cotton acreage in the district in

[14] See Schluter, "The Interaction of Credit and Uncertainty in Determining Resource Allocation and Incomes on Small Farms, Surat District, India," p. 27.

1967–68, would add over 2.1 million man-days per year of employment which, valued at Rs. 3 per day, is equivalent to Rs. 6.3 million.[15] As a comparison, a normal expenditure per district of the crash scheme for rural employment is Rs. 1.25 million, of which no more than 70 percent is likely to go to wage payments for laborers.[16]

Two major problems must be solved if the potential for intensification is to be realized. First, consumer demand for labor intensive commodities must be enlarged. Fortunately, some of the most important of these commodities, such as milk and vegetables, experience a sharp increase in demand with rising incomes. A strategy which raises consumer incomes is an important condition for expanding labor intensive crops on small farms.

Second, since the labor-concentrated, high-income crops tend to have larger year-to-year price and yield fluctuations, means must be found to reduce or shift the high coefficient of risk and uncertainty involved.

Schluter finds in Surat district a high correlation among labor intensity, income per acre of land, capital requirements per acre, and uncertainty. A linear programming model showed that, on unirrigated land, for each Rs. 100 increase in income caused by a change to more concentrated cultivation, there is a Rs. 100 increase in the average deviation of income from the expected level.[17] A comparison of farmers' actual choice of harvesting practices with the alternatives from the programming model indicated that small farmers tend to choose the lower-income, more certain production pattern. In the same study, it is found that the amount of capital used per laborer and per acre rises rapidly with increased intensification of cultivation, especially for the high-yield crop varieties. The large capital requirements combined with the irregularity and uncertainty of production dissuade the small farmer from increased intensity.[18] Since

[15] See Gunvant M. Desai and Michael G. G. Schluter, "Generating Employment in Rural Areas," *Rural Development for Weaker Sections.*

[16] In the simplistic comparison, it must be recognized that the rural public works may be productive and generate future output, while the shift in cropping pattern itself may have a cost. See W. Graeme Donovan, "Rural Works and Employment: Description and Preliminary Analysis of a Land Army Project in Mysore State, India," Cornell Agricultural Economics Occasional Paper No. 60 (April 1973).

[17] See Michael G. G. Schluter, "The Role of Co-operative Credit in Small Farmer Adoption of the New Cereal Varieties in India," Cornell Agricultural Economics Occasional Paper No. 64 (May 1973), 33–39.

[18] Schluter shows that in the case of irrigated acreage, in contrast to unirrigated acreage, credit needs are large, and risk and uncertainty relatively less, in shifts to higher-income

traditional sources of credit are likely to be limited in supply, the small farmer will want to leave those sources intact for emergencies.[19]

Such political measures as tax rebates in poor crop years may shift some degree of uncertainty from the backs of small farmers. Price stabilization programs appear attractive, but cannot do very much for the farmer who sells only a small fraction of his produce.[20]

Indian policy has clearly recognized the need for special programs attuned to the different economic and political circumstances of small farmers. The two key programs, the Small Farmers Development Agency (SFDA) and the Marginal Farmers and Landless Laborers Agency (MFAL), have been initiated in a substantial number of pilot areas, 46 for the former and 41 for the latter.[21] Both programs are at once experimental and designed to work within existing political and institutional frameworks. They embrace both aspects of credit provision: on the one hand they assist small farmers to join the cooperative credit societies and to obtain priority for their borrowing needs; on the other hand, they provide subsidies to the cooperatives to cover the presumed higher risk and administrative costs of lending to small farmers. Thus, an attempt is made to meet the power of the larger farmers in the cooperatives by the stick of central authority and the carrot of subsidy.

The financing of fixed capital—such as tube wells—may pose an even greater problem for the small farmer than working capital and may be crucial to him if he is to intensify. For tube wells and other long-term investments the SFDA provides a subsidy of up to 25 percent. The SFDAs try to help small farmers participate in the green revolution by meeting their special problems of capital and risk. The MFALs deal with the even more complex problems of intensifying farming by the introduction of livestock and vegetable enterprises. They make specific efforts to

---

crops. The more intensive crops for irrigated areas are usually highly labor intensive, but utilize most of the additional labor at already peak seasons, such as harvesting, rather than year round, thus requiring that hired labor be financed to supplement family labor (ibid., pp. 39–45).

[19] See Schluter and Parikh, pp. 33–34.

[20] For an explanation of this complex point, see John W. Mellor, "The Functions of Agricultural Prices in Economic Development," *Indian Journal of Agricultural Economics,* 23:1 (January–March 1968), 23–37.

[21] See "Special Projects for Small Farmers, Marginal Farmers and Agricultural Labourers," a note from the Ministry of Agriculture, Government of India, *Rural Development for Weaker Sections.*

strengthen the marketing organizations and input-supply agencies for these activities.

The programs anticipate that the demand for more milk will make dairy enterprise a promising source of new jobs on small farms.[22] Similarly, they have recognized the special importance of rural electrification in connection with the use of the highly adaptable small engines, both for irrigation and for other purposes which are most important to the small farmer.[23]

It is clear that the economic rationale of the small- and marginal-farmer programs is correct. The politics may not be. The cooperatives have a major problem of nonrepayment of loans—probably because the larger farmers who control the cooperatives have an excessive tendency to default. (The record of repayment of small farmers is better.) [24] Default weakens the cooperative. If this essentially political problem cannot be solved, then the effort will have to be made to develop special integrated agencies designed to supply the full set of services required by small farmers.

Much more basic, the economic environment for these programs is still deficient in three crucial respects. First, the technology is largely missing that could bring to the bulk of small farmers the highly profitable production methods that have been dramatically effective in some areas.[25] Second, the capital-oriented strategy of growth has not raised incomes enough to accelerate the demand growth rate for labor intensive commodities, such as milk and vegetables. Third, continued pursuit of a capital intensive growth plan periodically results in insufficient resources for adequate supplies of fertilizer, irrigation, and other key inputs. The large

[22] See Schluter, "The Role of Co-operative Credit in Small Farmer Adoption of the New Cereal Varieties in India," and Milk Production through Small and Marginal Farmers and Agricultural Labourers, Interim Report of the National Commission on Agriculture (New Delhi: Government of India, Ministry of Agriculture, December 1971).

[23] See Shanti S. Gupta, Utilisation of Electricity in the Villages of the District of Aligarh (Aligarh, India: Dharam Samaj College, Department of Economics, 1969); K. S. Sonachalam, Electricity and Economic Development of Madras State (Delhi: Government of India, Planning Commission, Research Programmes Committee, 1968); and S. M. Patel and K. V. Patel, Studies on Economics of Rural Electrification and Lift Irrigation (Ahmedabad, India: Indian Institute of Management, Centre for Management in Agriculture, 1969).

[24] See Lele, in Islam, ed., op. cit., pp. 425–28; and C. H. Hanumantha Rao, "Farm Size and Credit Policy," Economic and Political Weekly, 5:52 (December 26, 1970), A-157–62.

[25] The importance of new technology is illustrated by Schluter and Parikh, who point out that without available innovation, small farmers make little demand on new credit institutions (p. 44).

farmers, with their greater economic resources and political power, continue to prosper relatively more than the small farmer despite the earnest efforts of these programs. It is unrealistic to think that this situation can be changed without a radical alteration in either the political system or the strategy of growth.

One other aspect of the small-farmer program deserves special notice. The intensive use of trained manpower requires the rapid expansion of agricultural education. Failure to expand agricultural education accordingly provides the basis for one more vicious circle of poverty: the Indian educational system has high per unit program costs, because salaries of personnel are maintained well above incomes of the poor; budgetary constraints on the programs slow their expansion and retard growth in demand for trained manpower; and to close the circle, that slow growth in demand justifies the slow expansion of educational facilities.

The Rural Landless Laborer

The most intractable component of rural poverty is the indigence of the landless laborer. He is the marginal member of the rural labor force whose employment is the residual between the total demand for labor and the labor performed by the landowning classes themselves, including the small farmer. Much of the employment necessary to lift the landless laborer from poverty will have to occur in the nonagricultural sector. Furthermore, four widely held myths of development must be exploded before realistic policies can be expected to succeed.

First is the myth that the amount of capital needed to provide a job is technically fixed and, therefore, the growth rate of the stock of capital (and the capital goods industries) alone sets the rate at which employment can rise. That myth has distracted attention from finding means of reallocating capital *between* agriculture and industry as well as *within* each of these sectors so as to increase the employment and the average productivity of the total labor force.

Second is the myth that increased wage goods are unnecessary for productive mobilization of additional labor. This myth distracts attention from agricultural development as the *first condition* of expanding labor utilization and production, and reducing poverty.

The second myth is closely related to the third, namely, that the low-income laboring classes are in substantial part idle and need only be provided jobs in order to be mobilized. This is the "underemployment" fable. It distracts attention from the need to increase the productivity of the labor force as well as from the social, political, economic, and institutional changes required if rural laborers are to obtain increased productive employment.[26]

Fourth is the myth that public works programs will provide a major part of the answer to rural poverty. Although such programs are of political and economic importance, the employment problem is so enormous that public works can do no more than supplement the underlying strategy. There is danger that their espousal will serve simply to hide the need for change in the basic strategy of growth.

The extent to which the income of the landless laborer can be raised within the agricultural sector depends on an intricate interplay of labor supply and demand factors: the size and composition of the rural labor force; its initial level and seasonal pattern of employment and productivity; the rate of population growth; the extent to which landowner family labor will displace the landless laborer; the increase in demand for labor due to yield-increasing agricultural technologies and change in the pattern of production; and the extent to which mechanization will reduce that demand for labor. Growth in employment for the landless laborer is diminished because he is already fully employed at seasonal peaks. The new crop varieties tend to encourage mechanization, which in addition to displacing hired labor directly, may facilitate further substitution of paid workers by the farmer's own family labor.

Nature of the Rural Labor Supply

Surprisingly little is known about the rural labor supply.[27] Characterized by highly seasonal employment, it includes a substantial proportion of women and children and a big owner-cultivator group which, at least according to the standards of high-income nations, tends to be un-

[26] For an early and perceptive view of these relations, see Gunnar Myrdal, *Asian Drama: An Inquiry into the Poverty of Nations* (New York: Pantheon, 1968).

[27] Microstudy of the economics of farm families has tended to emphasize those whose income is derived largely or even solely from farming rather than those whose income is derived from hired labor or a combination of the two. However, see M. Habibullah, *The Pattern of Agricultural Unemployment: A Case Study of an East Pakistan Village* (Dacca: Dacca University, Bureau of Economics Research, 1962); V. S. Vyas, ed., *Agricultural Labourers in Four Indian Villages,* Ad-hoc Research Studies, No. 4 (Vallabh Vidyanagar, India: Agro-Economic Research Centre, 1964); and Socio-Economic Research Board, *The Pattern of a Peasant Economy—Puthia: A Case Study* (Rajshahi, Bangladesh: Rajshahi University, 1963).

deremployed. Low-income households provide the disproportionately large number of women in the rural labor force (Appendix, Table 1). Among the landless and the nearly landless families, 43 percent of the workers are female, compared to 33 percent for families with holdings of over five acres. This suggests that women withdraw from the rural labor force as incomes rise.[28]

A similar phenomenon is observed among children. In Shortlidge's study of Badaun district of Uttar Pradesh, the preliminary findings indicate that in households with over fifteen acres of land, boys under the age of fifteen did not participate in the labor force at all. Among agricultural laborers and households owning less than fifteen acres of land, 45 to 49 percent of the boys between the ages of eleven and fifteen were working.[29]

Raising labor productivity and real wages will allow withdrawal of female and child labor and facilitate improved health and increased education. Of course, the effect of this will be to reduce the labor supply and further tighten the labor market.

The labor force in rural India is overemployed at seasonal peaks, and underemployed in slack seasons. The inelastic supply of labor at seasonal peaks creates economic pressures to mechanize as demand increases. The lack of demand for labor in slack seasons is a major cause of poverty.

The All-India Agricultural Labour Enquiry of 1956–57 shows that male agricultural laborers obtained an average of 222 days of employment per person per year. Sixty-eight of the days of unemployment were attributed to "want of work." Involuntary unemployment for this class can thus be said to represent 23 percent of the desired days of employment—a critical discrepancy for the low-income laborer. Seasonality of labor demand causes the periodic unemployment of males and the peak employment rate of low-income women and children, as well as cyclicality in wage rates for agricultural labor.

---

[28] This result is corroborated in Egypt; see Bent Hansen, "Employment and Wages in Rural Egypt," *American Economic Review*, 59:3 (June 1969), 298–313, esp. p. 311. In Bangladesh, where labor participation by women is generally lower than in India, Habibullah's study showed family labor to be inversely related to the size of the landholding (Appendix C-2.) Both the Egyptian data and those from Bangladesh suggest that labor by women and children tends to be concentrated in seasonal peaks.

[29] From unpublished data collected by Richard L. Shortlidge, Jr. For a description and analysis of these data, see "A Socioeconomic Model of School Attendance," Cornell Agricultural Economics Occasional Paper No. 86 (January 1976); see also Chapter X, below.

Even in the most densely populated areas there is full employment at seasonal peaks. The point is made dramatically by Habibullah about the extremely high-population-density village of Sabilpur, in Noakhali district, in Bangladesh.[30] Population density in the village is 3,354 per square mile, compared with an average density of 777 per square mile in the country as a whole. During the seasonal peak in labor requirements, the village labor supply increases by approximately 13 percent, as people return from urban areas for agricultural work. Nevertheless, because of the seasonality of demand in the village as a whole, more than 25 percent of the man-days available for work are unassigned during the full year. In the off-season for agriculture, work is performed at very low productivity and rates of pay in various supplementary activities.

Contrary to commonly held views of chronic surplus labor, it seems likely that there is an active and pervasive labor market which adjusts to complex interseasonal equilibria. During the seasonal trough, wages fall; women, children, the aged, and other marginal members of the labor force drop out; and men also work fewer days. With large seasonal differences in wage rates, the rational choice is to work more hours in the higher wage period and fewer in the lower. The labor market is probably in equilibrium at all seasons but with sharply different wage rates. A number of important points follow from this analysis.

First, although offering more employment at the off-season wage rate may not bring forth much supply even during low-demand periods, the supply may be so elastic that modest increases in wages will draw forth a large increase in supply—a supply which will, of course, melt away when peak seasons of demand arise, with higher wage rates. Thus, rural public works programs must offer wages somewhat above the seasonally low rate in order to meet their welfare and production goals, and that rate may vary considerably from place to place.[31]

[30] See Habibullah, pp. 5–23.

[31] Thus, in a study of a Crash Scheme project in Mysore state, Donovan found that the daily wage rate of Rs. 3 brought out large numbers of local laborers and small farmers. In some periods, more than 12 percent of the work force of the group of villages in which the project was located was employed in the task force. Sixty-one percent of the project workers were between the ages of eighteen and twenty-five ("Rural Works and Employment"). In contrast, a study in Maharashtra found that the scheme attracted largely women and older men, perhaps because nonagricultural employment was available at Rs. 4 per day for male workers. See D. P. Apte, "Crash Scheme for Rural Employment: Evaluation of the Programme in a District in Maharashtra," *Economic and Political Weekly*, 8:12 (March 24, 1973), 595–600.

Second, since the productivity of agriculutral labor is high at seasonal demand peaks, the wage rate may well be higher than in many types of urban employment, for example, in small-scale industry. The result is that nonagricultural employers in rural areas will have difficulty holding workers in peak seasons if they pay a steady wage at normal urban levels. The consequent unemployment of capital in the small-scale enterprises may then discourage development of such industry. To put it differently: it is expensive in annual wage costs to isolate nonagricultural activities from the agricultural cycle.

Third, the labor supply may be highly inelastic at seasonal peaks. This possibility is suggested by the sharply higher wage rates at such periods and by the high social costs of work by the marginal female and child members of the labor force. Farm operators will try to reduce peak requirements of labor by substituting more elastic supplies of capital (by mechanization), substituting their own family labor for hired labor, or changing their patterns of production. The last may, of course, include rejection of a high-yield crop variety which would also provide added slack season employment. Thus, a combination of inelastic supply of labor at seasonal peaks and an inability to mechanize may reduce employment in slack seasons. Most of the mechanization in India seems to have been suitable for resolving this problem.[32]

Households of landowners are about three times as numerous as households of landless laborers. While most landowners in India do farm work, little is known of the supply conditions of this major element of the labor force. It seems logical, given the low wage rate, that well-to-do landowners would hire much of the labor for the arduous physical work of farming, spending most of their own time on supervisory, managerial, and marketing activities. Farm survey data, though scant on this point, seem consistent with it.[33] On the other hand, it is entirely possible that

[32] See, for example, C. H. Hanumantha Rao, "Employment Implications of the Green Revolution and Mechanisation: A Case Study of the Punjab," in Islam, ed., op. cit., pp. 340–50; D. K. Desai and C. Gopinath, *Impact of Farm Tractorization on Productivity and Employment* (Ahmedabad, India: Indian Institute of Management, August 1973); and S. S. Johl, "Mechanisation, Labour Use and Productivity in Agriculture," *Agricultural Situation in India,* 28:1 (April 1973), 3–16.

[33] A study conducted by Rajshahi University in Bangladesh in 1963 indicated that among farmers who cultivate more than 1.5 acres, the number of unemployed days per head increases with an increase in holding per head (cited by Nural Islam, "Concepts and Measurement of Unemployment and Underemployment in Developing Economies," *International Labour Review,* 89:3 [March 1964], 248). Similarly, Habibullah found that family

the introduction of machinery, rising wage rates, and declining seasonality of employment will elicit higher direct labor-participation rates among the landowning classes. Budget data which show constant employment requirements where there is a combination of increased labor intensive commodities and mechanization may mask displacement of lower-income hired workers by higher-income landowner-operators.

The preceding set of labor supply crosscurrents can be summarized in a likely scenario: introduction of high-yield varieties and increased double-cropping demand considerably more labor, during both previously peak and slack periods; the peak season labor demands are met in substantial part by increased mechanization, which also makes performing the tasks less onerous; in an attempt to make yearly employment more uniform, and in reaction to higher wages in slack periods and the less onerous nature of the work, the landowning class assumes a higher proportion of the labor activities; in response to higher income, the withdrawal of women and children diminishes the landless-labor supply; other landless laborers transfer to nonagricultural occupations, which themselves expand in answer to the increased demand resulting from the higher incomes of the landowning classes; the landless laborers who remain in agriculture suffer fewer seasonal fluctuations in employment; wages during each season are higher than previously (it is this that induces the mechanization), but the seasonal differential in wage rates diminishes. It is significant that an increased proportion of the employment would be during the previously slack season, so that the average wage might not be any higher while annual income would be larger. Note that in this scenario, the real wage paid in the nonagricultural sector would not necessarily rise significantly. This sequence of events fits well with developments in the contemporary economic history of Japan and Taiwan.[34] It is, of course, not yet relevant to much of India and other developing nations because the necessary technological innovations in agriculture have not been sufficiently widespread.

labor use per acre declined from 160 man-days on farms of less than 0.5 acres to 71 man-days on farms larger than three acres (op. cit., Appendix C-2). From a survey of farms in an irrigated area of Mysore state, W. Graeme Donovan estimated that, as an average for all farms, as much as 69 percent of the labor used for direct crop activities came from outside the farm family ("Employment Generation in Agriculture: A Study in Mandya District, South India," Cornell Agricultural Economics Occasional Paper No. 71 [June 1974], 14).

[34] See T. H. Lee, *Intersectoral Capital Flows in the Economic Development of Taiwan, 1895–1960* (Ithaca, N.Y.: Cornell University Press, 1971), ch. iv; and Takeo Misawa, "Agricultural Development and Employment Expansion: A Case Study of Japan," in Islam, ed., op. cit., pp. 314–34.

Continued rapid population growth prevents increased demand for labor from tightening the labor market and thereby raising per capita employment. No group has a greater stake in reduced rates of population growth than the landless laborers, and, unfortunately, there is probably no better case of the divergence between individual and group interests. Population growth adds to the supply of unskilled labor, decreases the chances of any one person obtaining a job, and lengthens the time that is necessary for the economy to achieve full employment and rising real wage rates. But more children increase the number of wage earners in the individual poor family and provide greater security for the parents in old age. At the same time, the laborer incurs the added costs of child rearing when he is relatively young and at the height of his earning power. Children are a means of saving for a class that has few other opportunities or instruments for saving. In addition, the survival rate of children is sadly lower among the poor than the well-to-do.

If the poor participate in economic growth, these variables are apt to change: mortality rates decline, the potential to provide more than the bare necessities of life rises, and the opportunity to invest in education expands. Evidence increases that the poor respond to these phenomena with lower birth rates. (See Chapter X.) From the mid-1950s to the mid-1960s Taiwan cut its birth rate by about one-third, while South Korea reduced its by about one-fifth. Both countries are distinguished by low infant mortality and high rates of income growth for the impoverished and unskilled, in contrast to countries such as Mexico, Brazil, and the Philippines with comparable levels of income but little or no decline in birth rates.[35]

A strategy of growth that increases the demand for labor may have the significant side effect of reducing the long-run supply of labor through the effect on fertility, thereby further improving employment and wage rates of the laboring classes.

The Demand for Rural Labor

The major dynamics in the demand for agricultural labor are adoption of high-yield varieties, mechanization, and change in acreage and the pattern of cultivation. Again, surprisingly little is known about any of these

---

[35] See, for example, James E. Kocher, *Rural Development, Income Distribution, and Fertility Decline,* an occasional paper of The Population Council (New York: The Population Council, 1973); and William Rich, *Smaller Families through Social and Economic Progress* (Washington, D.C.: Overseas Development Council, 1973).

forces. In the few areas of major technological change, it is clear that wages, employment, and mechanization have all increased substantially.[36] These developments are, however, the product of a complex interaction of unusually successful geographically localized innovations.

In general, the new technologies require less increase in labor input for a given increase in additional output than traditional means of raising production, although labor coefficients do vary. A study of a cross section of farms by Hanumantha Rao, before the green revolution, shows that as land productivity rises, the proportion of output attributable to labor decreases—a 1 percent increase in output results in a .85 percent to .75 percent increase in implicit wage payments.[37] The data in Table IV-2 suggest an even lower figure of .31 percent, and that increase is under conditions with little mechanization. According to the latter data, a 4 percent per year increase in agricultural output provides a rise in the aggregate demand for labor of 1.2 percent per year, which is substantially less than the rate of population growth. That is, of course, consistent with the normal path of economic development in which the proportion of agricultural labor declines. Under these average conditions, one would not expect increasing wage rates, mechanization, or landowner family labor to displace landless laborers on the basis of growth in the foodgrain sector alone.

Although one of the greatest opportunities for increasing demand for agricultural labor is provided by the change to more intensive enterprise combinations, the division of the expanded labor requirement between the cultivator and the laboring classes has critical significance for the future of the landless laborer. The more intensive undertakings may well distribute much of the increased employment to the farm-owning classes, particularly the small farmers.

Farm Mechanization

It is the highly concentrated effect of yield-increasing innovation, which normally is not spread over a wide geographic area, and concurrent imperfections in the regional labor market that foster increased mechanization. If the migration of labor, for whatever reason, is not sufficient to

---

[36] See C. H. Hanumantha Rao, "Farm Mechanisation in a Labour-Abundant Economy," *Economic and Political Weekly,* 7:5–7 (February 1972), 393–400. See also Rao, in Islam, op. cit.

[37] See Rao, "Farm Mechanisation in a Labour-Abundant Economy," p. 397.

increase employment in a territory where the impact of technology is highly compressed, mechanization may occur to a greater extent than if the same results were dispersed over a larger area. The Punjab has become overmechanized, according to all-India standards, but, as can be seen, largely as a result of technical factors that would probably be uneconomic for policy to change—given the basic distribution of land.[38] The more yield-increasing innovation occurs in already labor-short areas, the more imperfections in the interregional labor markets; and the greater the concentration of labor requirements in periods of peak demand, the more mechanization will occur.

Billings and Singh examine a number of these interactions in the quite different states of Punjab and Maharashtra. They project to 1983–84 the spread of high-yield varieties and of various elements of mechanization, and their effects on the utilization of labor. For this exercise they used data from detailed farm survey reports. Their projections include labor market conditions, as well as a wide assortment of other circumstances. The exercise illustrates the complexities of the interaction of labor-saving and yield-increasing innovations and the great difficulties of setting fixed policies for protecting employment from mechanization.[39]

The Billings and Singh exercise for the Punjab depicts a substantial growth—of nearly 40 percent between 1968–69 and 1983–84—in human labor requirements resulting simply from continued expansion of irrigated and total cropped area at past rates. Those labor requirements are shown to exceed, without mechanization, the currently available labor supply at the seasonal peak, even in 1968–69, and to surpass the larger labor supply of 1983–84 by almost 50 percent. The new high-yield varieties were estimated to raise the demand for labor by 6 percent in 1968–69 and by 13 percent in 1983–84 over what it would have been with the projected acreages and traditional varieties. The exercise then presents the effects of various levels of mechanization on labor requirements. The authors argue that in the Punjab, by 1983–84, 60 percent of the irrigated

---

[38] In the Punjab, real wages of agricultural labor may not have exceeded previous peaks in the first few years of the wheat breakthrough, but they rose sharply after 1964–65, increasing by 85 percent in the next four years (ibid., p. 399).

[39] Arjan Singh and Martin H. Billings, "The Effect of Technology on Farm Employment in Two Indian States (Punjab and Maharashtra)," presented at the NESA Employment Conference, Kathmandu (July 1970); and Martin H. Billings and Arjan Singh, "Mechanisation and Rural Employment, with Some Implications for Rural Income Distribution," *Economic and Political Weekly*, 5:26 (June 27, 1970), A-61–72.

area will be covered by pump sets, 100 percent of the wheat crop will be threshed by power (compared to 50 percent in 1968–69), 50 percent of the grain will be harvested by power reapers, and 20 percent of the harvested area will be plowed by tractors. The result of this full set of changes, along with the introduction of high-yield varieties and growth in crop acreage, is a 14 percent larger input of labor in 1983–84, compared to that required for 1968–69 with entirely traditional crops and methods.

With a similar set of projections and judgments for Maharashtra, a state with proportionately much more landless labor and less potential for irrigation, the authors project considerably less mechanization and a net increase in labor requirements of 15 percent.

In a normative linear programming exercise for a group of villages in an irrigated rice and sugar cane area of Mysore State, Donovan shows the ability of mechanization (power tillers) to break labor bottlenecks and increase production.[40] In his study, labor supply is assumed to increase by 2.5 percent per year. Improved management and the introduction of multiple cropping, which together yield an increase of 152 percent in gross value of output over a ten-year period (a compound growth rate of 9.6 percent per year), are consistent with the realistic resource constraints imposed and no mechanization. The accompanying expansion in employment would be 76 percent (a compound growth rate of 5.8 percent per year over the ten-year period). Employment of the available labor supply, measured in man-days per year, would rise from 58 percent in the base period to 69 percent at the end of the period.

Within the same labor constraints, the introduction of mechanization allows the gross value of output to increase by 190 percent over what it was in the above base period. This further large jump in output relies on the success of the mechanization in loosening labor restraints in enough critical periods to increase significantly the proportion of the area under multiple cropping. But in the case of mechanization, the employment expansion is limited to 57 percent over the base period. Since the mechanization process is shown to be quite profitable, it is likely that it would be accepted under the circumstances postulated.

On the other hand, if the labor supply could be increased by a further 26 percent in three key specified monthly periods, say by migrant labor from nearby low-income dryland areas, an even greater expansion of

---

[40] See Donovan, "Employment Generation in Agriculture."

gross output value would be possible without machines: 196 percent over the base period. This would increase income to cultivators by *more* than the mechanization option, and would expand employment, compared with the rate in the base period, by over 116 percent.

This exercise demonstrates that in the presence of a tight labor supply situation with no relief from immigration, mechanization would be a profitable way to increase production. The form of mechanization which seems most likely to be adopted, however, results in less employment than other alternatives.

In their simplest terms, then, the model poses the following choices: (1) expand gross output by 190 percent and employment by 57 percent, using mechanization; (2) expand gross output by 152 percent and employment by 76 percent, without mechanization; (3) expand gross output by 196 percent and employment by 116 percent, using *immigration* instead of *mechanization* to break labor bottlenecks.

A concern for the laboring classes does not lead automatically to the simple solution of no mechanization. And there is not a dichotomy between labor-saving and land-saving mechanization. Pumps, thrashers, and tractors may all involve a reduction in costs leading to intensification which increases total labor use—or they may not. And mechanization which pays for itself in increased crop yields and a larger supply of the wage goods (food) necessary to increased employment may also displace labor which has little alternative use in agriculture and for which provision has not been made in the nonagricultural sector. Given the variability over time and region as to what is desirable, decisions about mechanization are necessarily best left to the marketplace. If they are, a few ancillary caveats are in order to avoid uneconomic mechanization.

First, do not subsidize machines more than labor. While there is little reason to think that market wage rates overstate the real costs of labor to society, development policies may favor excessive capital investment in machinery through effective import grants and reduced interest rates. In particular, credit may be subsidized for tractors and not for hiring labor.[41]

[41] But Rao argues that the effect of the subsidization in India has been slight. He points out that no more than 10 percent of the tractors purchased in India have been purchased with subsidized institutional credit, and even that amount at a 9 percent interest rate. The levy, in 1971, of a 30 percent import duty and 10 percent excise tax eliminated the tractor subsidy from overvalued currency, but black market prices had, in any case, previously removed much of that subsidy. Tractors were increasing because of rapidly rising food prices, which were pushing up labor costs, and, even more important, were raising bullock costs relative

Potential noneconomic rewards such as prestige may inflate further the economic returns to machinery.

Second, achieve as much as is politically possible by imposing land ceilings which keep the farm size small enough to avoid the management diseconomies of large labor forces. Since the need for mechanization in the short run arises in large part from regional inequalities in the application of yield-increasing technology, land reform which reduces the size of holdings in the areas of rapid technological change would obviate much of the immediate need for mechanization. Such a move is, of course, particularly unlikely in the present political context of most low-income nations.

A third need, whose fulfillment would be particularly productive, is to facilitate engineering research in order to develop machinery which meets specific labor problems inexpensively without displacing workers unnecessarily. For example, development of a small wheat reaper suited to Punjab conditions would prevent introduction of the much more capital intensive combine.

Rural Public Works Programs

The difficulty of the employment problem and the natural desire for simple answers have given rural public works programs undue weight. To raise the income of the 40 percent of the rural population in the Dandekar-Rath poverty group to the specified minimum level of Rs. 240 per capita (according to 1960–61 prices) would have required approximately Rs. 15 billion of annual additions to the aggregate income.[42] The current major schemes of rural public works envisage expenditure of about

---

to tractor costs, with bullock costs comprising over two-thirds of plowing cost. Rao also notes that less than 6 percent of 265 districts accounted for over one-third of all tractors; about 16 percent of the districts accounted for nearly 60 percent of the tractors. These were largely districts in which the rate of growth of agricultural output had been rapid, with particular emphasis on expansion of irrigated and total cropped area. Areas of substantial tractor use are areas in which total employment and real wages have been rising ("Farm Mechanisation in a Labour-Abundant Economy," pp. 395–99).

[42] This estimate was made by multiplying the number of people in each of the lowest four expenditure categories in the Dandekar-Rath study by the difference between the average income for the respective category and the Rs. 240 minimum. Since the number of people in these classes must have increased on the order of the annual population increase of 2.23 percent between 1961 and 1971, the number should be inflated by that amount and, of course, further inflated by price increases in order to obtain a current figure.

Rs. 700 million per year.[43] It will be a major organizational feat to expend that much, and certainly at most 70 percent will go to the laboring classes as wage payments. Therefore, less than 3 percent of a minimum poverty abatement program is to be met in this manner.

Rapid agricultural advancement requires vast improvement in roads, small-scale irrigation projects, rural electric distribution systems, land leveling, and other labor intensive public works. Where new agricultural technologies are appropriate, local people tend to demand the economic benefits of rural public works. This relationship creates a dilemma: once agricultural development gets well under way, further work programs are very much in order and easy to finance in the already rapidly developing areas; oppressive poverty remains in the regions in which new production technologies do not work and in which repayments to the public works projects are low. In some such cases, these projects may provide the infrastructure necessary for eventual success of the new technology. In others, they may help provide minimum levels of welfare while research on other potentials provides a longer-term basis for growth. The dilemma arises in those areas where there is little apparent prospect for future development; then the political question crops up as to whether to use public works as a means of distributing welfare to such regions, to choose other welfare devices, or to invest elsewhere and expect migration to solve the problem. The last is the most usual, but frequently not a particularly satisfactory, approach.

The first three Five-Year Plans devoted considerable lip service, but few resources, to rural public works. The First Plan was perhaps least ambivalent in its statements, but made no specific fund allocation for rural programs. The Second Plan had a euphoric tone with respect to the employment problem but still made no specific distribution of funds. The Third Plan allocated the substantial sum of Rs. 1.5 billion for five years, but only 10 percent of that was actually allotted to projects.[44]

By 1973, the "Garibi Hatao" (abolish poverty) election had brought

[43] *Crash Scheme for Rural Employment: Guidelines for 1972–73* (New Delhi: Government of India, Ministry of Agriculture, Dept. of Community Development, March 1972).

[44] *First Five-Year Plan* (New Delhi: Government of India, Planning Commission, 1952), p. 29; *Second Five-Year Plan* (New Delhi: Government of India, Planning Commission, 1956), p. 124; and V. S. Vyas and H. B. Shivamaggi, "Unpublished Review of Agricultural Labor Market Research," Sardar Patel University, Vallabh Vidyanagar, India, January 4, 1973.

three major rural employment programs: the Crash Scheme for Rural Employment (CSRE), the Drought Prone Areas Programs (DPAP), and the Pilot Intensive Rural Employment Project (PIREP).[45] The three together attempt to make an annual expenditure of about Rs. 700 million. Each of these experimental programs recognizes the current lack of knowledge about labor supply conditions, types of projects to institute, and administrative arrangements and capabilities. The PIREP is an intensive experiment attempting to reach all the underemployed in a single small area in each of fifteen states. The DPAP emphasizes productive projects in dry areas; the Crash Scheme is a massive attempt to reach significant numbers of people in every district. The various projects specify a large number of alternative rules for administrative arrangements, labor intensity of works, and systems of payment. The experimental, pragmatic approach is impressive.[46]

Commitment to rural public works schemes now appears more substantial than in previous plans. Certainly, the administrative capacity to develop and administer a large program has grown at both the local and the national levels. Its effectiveness depends on two major elements of the overall development plan: first, on an agricultural strategy that provides the food supplies to back increased incomes of the poor; and second, on an employment strategy in both the agricultural and nonagricultural sectors that meets the bulk of the labor problem and does not leave an unrealistically large residual for the public works programs. The necessary agricultural policy will, in addition, raise rates of return to rural public works projects and provide an extra incentive to engage in them.[47]

---

[45] *Crash Scheme for Rural Employment: Guidelines for 1972–73;* Government of India, Ministry of Agriculture, "Pilot Intensive Rural Employment Project," *Seminar on Rural Development for Weaker Sections;* "Special Projects for Small Farmers, Marginal Farmers and Agricultural Labourers"; and *Workshop on Small Farmers and Agricultural Labour.*

[46] For a description of one of the more successful efforts, see Donovan, "Rural Works and Employment."

[47] There is considerable cynicism as to whether rural public works funds can reach the poor when they are channeled through the agencies controlled by the wealthier elements of rural society. For example, Raj Krishna concludes that radical politicization of the poorest groups will be necessary if they are to obtain the share allocated for them ("Unemployment in India," *Indian Journal of Agricultural Economics,* 28:1 [January–March, 1973], 1–23). Rather than trying to obtain merely a larger share of the tiny allocation to public works, radical politicization of the poor might more logically have as its objective the much more effective radical redistribution of assets. Analysis of public works programs as the primary welfare device for the poor seems relevant only if one assumes that there will not be radical political change.

It is clear that as various presumably short-run factors created a tight food situation in the mid-1970s, the effort to expand rural public works programs slackened, particularly in comparison with the effort and sloganeering of the early 1970s period of large crops.

Not only is increased agricultural production essential to a rural public works program for the poor, but there is also a potent trade-off between employment and foodgrain prices. The most important single determinant of the level of real wages of the poor is the level of foodgrain prices. The poor spend one-third to two-thirds of their income on foodgrains alone. Since the prices of most other goods they consume are closely related to foodgrain prices, they experience a change in real income almost proportionate to the change in foodgrain prices.[48] Since the landowning classes spend little of their income increments on food, there is a natural mechanism that makes it possible for the poor to benefit from increased production. Either the expenditure of increased farm income, directly or through taxes, raises employment and hence the purchasing power of the poor for foodgrains, or foodgrain prices decline, providing direct benefits to the poor. Lower food costs and a more stable and possibly cheaper labor force may further encourage employment growth. If food production increases, the poor stand to benefit whether rural public works projects are effective or not, whereas if such projects are influential in raising employment but without increasing food production, the poor will lose in higher prices much of their gain from higher employment.

Unfortunately, not even the benefits of increased agricultural production are certain for the poor. The landowning classes may succeed in preventing a price decline by lobbying for reduced imports, subsidized exports, and price support programs. From 1964–65 to 1970–71, despite accelerated growth in production, foodgrain prices relative to industrial prices remained constant because the foodgrain production was used to reduce imports and increase public stocks (annual imports declined from 7.5 million tons in 1964–65 to 2.0 million in 1970–71). In the same period, 7.1 million tons were added to government warehouses (Appendix, Table 3).

---

[48] The distribution of this benefit is in proportion to market purchases, but even the rural landless laborers have shifted in substantial part to cash wages. See, for example, John W. Mellor et al., *Developing Rural India: Plan and Practice* (Ithaca, N.Y.: Cornell University Press, 1968), Part IV.

Land Reform and Redistribution of Rights in Land

In rural India, the disparities in land ownership direct the initial rewards of yield-increasing new technology to the higher-income rural landowners. But redistribution of land or some portion of the rights in land, however feasible economically, is politically improbable.[49] Indeed, given the present distribution of power, it is much more likely that substantial numbers of tenants will lose what land rights they have and revert to the landless labor class.

There is immense potential, at least in theory, for raising the incomes of the rural poor through a massive redistribution of land. A ten-acre land ceiling, well above Khusro's assumption of an adequate size unit for full use of bullocks and for other economies of scale, would provide a huge amount of land for redistribution.[50] The 1960–61 census showed 10 million families and 263 million acres in holdings of over 10 acres. With a 10-acre ceiling, that would have provided 163 million acres for redistribution. There were then 22 million households with holdings of between 1 and 5 acres, averaging 2 acres. To raise them all to 5 acres would have required 66 million acres. The remaining 97 million acres, distributed to the landless laborers in the form of, say, cooperatives of 10 to 15 acres, would have provided an average of 4.3 acres for each male landless agricultural laborer (see Appendix, Table 1). The economic implications of such a redistribution were not greatly different in 1970–71 or in 1960–61, for land productivity has increased in pace with population growth, and net cropped area has increased about 6 percent.

Such a massive redistribution of land is unlikely. The Zamindari abolition during the early independence period was substantial and effective, but its very success makes further reform unlikely.[51] Zamindars and other large landholders were few in number and at least somewhat identified

---

[49] See, for example, Wolf Ladejinsky, "Ironies of India's Green Revolution," *Foreign Affairs*, 48:4 (July 1970), 758–68; Uma J. Lele and John W. Mellor, "Jobs, Poverty and the 'Green Revolution,' " *International Affairs*, 48:1 (January 1972), 20–32; and Clifton R. Wharton, Jr., "The Green Revolution: Cornucopia or Pandora's Box?" *Foreign Affairs*, 47:3 (April 1969), 464–76.

[50] The productivity of cultivated land in India is highly variable. Ten acres in one area may be equivalent to only one in another. Khusro, in an attempt to generalize at the all-India level, suggested five acres as the minimum size farm providing basic economies of scale. In practice, some larger farms would not meet the criteria and some smaller ones would (Khusro, op. cit.).

[51] Mellor et al., p. 53.

with the departed colonial regime. Today landowners with over five acres of land comprise over one-third of the rural population and occupy over three-quarters of the land (Appendix, Table 1). Since, together with the upper half of the small-farmer group, they wield considerably more than half the provincial political power, they are in a strong position either to block or to evade effectively any change in rights to land. The political problems resulting from alienating the present landowners are compounded by the immense issues of defining units of land in terms of widely varying productivity and determining specifically who would obtain the newly available land. Given these pressures, the current probability of additional major reforms was already well stated in the First Plan: "The facts available at present suggest that these aims . . . are not likely to be achieved in any substantial measure." [52]

Although land ceiling legislation was accepted by most states in the 1950s, its history in India has been one of evasion. Restrictions on farm size were set according to the standards of ownership units in the respective states, and often applied to the individual rather than the family, allowing large farms to be divided among several family members (some even imaginary). Enforcement appears to have been lax. [53] Following Mrs. Gandhi's 1971 voter appeal to the poor and her subsequent election, a new wave of attention was given to ceiling legislation. In August of 1971, the Central Land Reforms Committee set guidelines for state government regulations: a limitation of 10 to 18 acres of irrigated land and 54 acres of unirrigated land—the ceiling to apply to the family, not the individual, with a high restriction for families of over five persons, but the ceiling still not to exceed twice the amount specified in the guidelines. Relatively high limits did not prevent the appearance of a full range of devices for minimizing the effect of land ceilings, and there was little expectation that substantial areas would be available for redistribution.

In this context it is of much greater practical benefit to the poor to protect existing rights of tenants than to attempt redistribution of land. The new, high-yield crop varieties greatly increase the value of land and payments to management—and the landowner's incentive to displace tenants and operate the land himself. Worse, if operation of a farm is

---

[52] *First Five-Year Plan*, p. 187.

[53] Ladejinsky, "Land Ceilings and Land Reform"; Khusro, op. cit.; and V. S. Vyas, "Institutional Change, Agricultural Production and Rural Poverty—the Experience of Two Decades," *Commerce*, 125:3198 (August 19, 1972), 40–44.

inefficient with hired labor, increased mechanization may solve the problem—thus completing the decline in status from tenant to landless laborer to unemployed landless laborer. Protection against the process is crucial in exactly those states, such as Bihar and West Bengal, which are priority targets for production-increasing technology.[54]

Such circumstances demand more innovative legislation for institutionalizing tenancy.[55] Such legislation should encourage landowners to share in the risk and the capital needs of an expanding agriculture. Registration of tenants would guarantee their security, assist them in obtaining loans, and increase the certainty that they would benefit from increased production. The longer the delay, the higher will new technology raise the payments to land, and the more resistance there will be to effective reform. However, even modest measures leading to change might, in the long run, result in a significantly greater share of income to tenants.

Increased agricultural production must form the cornerstone of a strategy for the relief of poverty. Agriculture must provide the food to back higher incomes and to improve health, and it must directly account for much of the rise in employment in the short and intermediate run. The agricultural revolution is essential to provide the wage goods and the purchasing power to sustain growth in the nonfarm labor force. And to be effective, the goals of agricultural policy must be supported by an employment-oriented, capital-conserving industrial policy.

[54] Wolf Ladejinsky, "Land Ceilings and Land Reform"; and "Green Revolution in Bihar, the Kosi Area: A Field Trip," *Economic and Political Weekly*, 4:39 (September 27, 1969), A-147–62.

[55] G. Parthasarathy and D. S. Prasad note that landowners in the Delta area of Andhra Pradesh already share the risk and capital needs for the adoption of new technology ("Response to and Impact of H.Y.V. Rice by Size and Tenure in a Delta Village, Andhra Pradesh, India," Department of Co-operation and Applied Economics, Andhra University, Waltair, December 1972). See also V. S. Vyas, "Tenancy in a Dynamic Setting," *Economic and Political Weekly*, 5:26 (June 27, 1970), A-73–80. However, for indication of the resistance to even modest reforms, see Ladejinsky, "Land Ceilings and Land Reform." Simplistic programs of giving land to the tiller ignore the fact that tenancy is often used by farmers with already substantial holdings; they often rent land from those with too small a holding to afford the fixed investment in bullocks. Schluter found in his sample in Surat district that essentially all land rented was by larger farmers from very small landholders ("The Interaction of Credit and Uncertainty in Determining Resource Allocation and Incomes on Small Farms, Surat District, India," p. 3).

V
Industrial Growth: The Changing Structure

Rapid industrial growth is necessary for the success of an employment-oriented strategy of development. Large interindustry differences in the capital intensity of production provide considerable scope for changing the composition of output in such a manner as to increase significantly the employment content of industrial growth.

From the inception of the Second Five-Year Plan, Indian industrial development has undergone major changes in the composition of output because of the rapid growth and evolution of a few previously minor industrial groups and the slow growth or stagnation of a few previously dominant ones. These overall structural changes have led to an increasingly capital intensive arrangement, a low employment content of growth, and slow overall expansion of output. This breadth of experience also makes India a particularly fertile field for examining the potentials and implications of structural change for broader application to a wide range of developing nations.

Indian economic development has often incurred criticism for putting industrial growth ahead of agricultural growth.[1] It is not this general emphasis which should be criticized, but rather the means by which the objective was to be achieved and the limited role agriculture was to play in that process. Instead of competing with industrialization, a rapid increase in agricultural production may be an important element of a strategy for accelerated industrial expansion.

In an employment-oriented development program, the primary reason for the relative growth of the industrial sector lies in the structure of

[1] See, for example, Edward S. Mason's unfavorable comparison of India with Pakistan in *Economic Development in India and Pakistan,* Center for International Affairs Occasional Paper No. 13 (Cambridge: Harvard University, 1966); and also Theodore W. Schultz, *Economic Crises in World Agriculture* (Ann Arbor: University of Michigan Press, 1965).

demand. As incomes rise, consumers spend an increasing proportion of added income on nonagricultural goods and services. As the pattern of production conforms to the changing pattern of demand, the nonagricultural sectors outpace the agricultural sector. Anomalously, accelerated growth in agriculture, by raising per capita incomes, hastens the decline in the relative size of the agricultural sector.

The effect of rising agricultural production on incomes and consequently on the composition of demand is modified by the characteristics of distribution. If the new agricultural technologies allocate the increased output largely to low-income laborers, the transformation to an industrial economy will proceed slowly. Low-income laboring classes spend more of their increased income on foodgrains and other agricultural commodities than on industrial goods.[2]

The high-yield crop varieties on which agricultural prosperity is now largely based distribute most of the benefits to higher-income rural people, who spend a substantial and growing proportion of their income increments on nonagricultural commodities. These expenditure patterns inevitably cause the nonagricultural sectors to grow at a much faster relative rate. Thus, in Chapter II, a 4 to 5 percent rate of growth in foodgrain production was depicted as impressive. A comparable measure of success for industry would be on the order of a 10 to 15 percent annual increase.[3] In accordance with these disparate rates of advancement, the industrial sector rapidly increases its weight in growth indices and thereby further accelerates the overall rise.

Variations in labor productivity reinforce the effect of changes in the structure of demand on relative industrial growth rates. That very aspect of agricultural technology which helps shift demand toward the nonagricultural sector also sharply raises labor productivity in agriculture. As a result, employment may veer toward the nonagricultural sector even more rapidly than the pattern of demand and output.

[2] For a rigorous exposition of the theory of these relationships in the form of a dualistic model, see Uma J. Lele and John W. Mellor, "Technological Change and Distributive Bias in a Dual Economy," Cornell Agricultural Economics Occasional Paper No. 43 (June 1971).

[3] See the comparative data for Taiwan in Chapter VI, below. For India, Ashok Rudra used a quite different approach to provide a set of consistency estimates which present agriculture as a major supplier of the goods on which rising incomes are spent, and rates of growth of the industrial sector on the order of twice that for the agricultural sector (*Relative Rates of Growth, Agriculture and Industry*, University of Bombay Series in Economics No. 14 [Bombay: University of Bombay, 1967]).

The generalization that the industrial sector grows faster than the agricultural sector does not apply to all branches of agriculture. Much of the large nonfoodgrain group of agricultural commodities is labor intensive in production and also has highly elastic demand. In particular, across nearly all income classes, a high proportion of additional consumer expenditure is allocated to potentially labor intensive commodities such as livestock products and vegetables. In this context, milk production and textile manufacture make an interesting comparison.

As a measure of their relative importance in the economy in 1965, milk and milk products represented about the same share of consumer expenditure as did textiles. But the proportion of increments to increased expenditure on milk and milk products is about 50 percent higher than the proportion spent on textiles in most income classes. And, in each case, increased labor input provides a high percentage of the value added in additional production—somewhat more so for milk than for textiles. Thus, although industrial development is necessary for the long-run solution of employment problems, important opportunities for growth and employment exist in parts of the rural sector which have development characteristics quite similar to those of manufacturing.

An industrial growth strategy that derives from accelerated agricultural production places a dual burden on a nation's financial resources that necessitates efforts to reduce capital requirements per worker and to find additional sources of savings. Stepped-up agricultural growth itself has large investment needs, and faster expansion of nonagricultural employment increases the demand for capital to combine with those new employees.

The primary device for reducing capital intensity in the industrial sector is a shift in the structure of output toward commodities produced with relatively labor intensive technology—and within that shift an emphasis on small-scale units which tend to have a comparative advantage. Increased trade and policies encouraging domestic consumption of labor intensive commodities may facilitate the necessary changes.

Concurrently with efforts to reduce capital requirements per worker, an attempt may be made to tap new sources of savings and investment, particularly the increased wealth of the rural classes benefiting from higher agricultural production. Emphasis on small-scale industry—especially the production of consumer goods—is likely to aid that effort as well as to lower average capital-labor ratios. Thus, *there is potential reinforcement*

*between strategies to diminish capital intensity and those to increase the
rate of savings and investment in industry.*

The Changing Structure of Indian Industry

Three major, mutually reinforcing changes occurred within the Indian
industrial sector from 1951 to 1965: [4] investment goods industries grew
more rapidly than the consumer goods industries; the public sector grew
more rapidly than the private sector; and large- and medium-scale firms
grew more rapidly than small-scale firms. These changes were all mani-
fested in rapidly rising capital-labor ratios in Indian industry. Such increase in capital intensity has been characteristic of most low-income
countries experiencing limited economic participation of low-income
people—even though the causes may differ from those in India. In India,
these tendencies were mainly an outgrowth of the Second Five-Year Plan
and happened largely between 1955–56 and 1965–66.

Bhagwati and Desai report that, in 1951, investment goods comprised
only 6 percent of industrial value added, a proportion that tripled to 18
percent in 1961, and rose further, to 21 percent, by 1963. The share of
consumer goods declined from 58 percent, to 48, to 38 in the same years,
respectively.[5] Raw materials and intermediate goods comprised the remainder of industrial value added. These differential growth rates reflect
the planned concentration of investment in capital goods industries during
this period.

In the Second Five-Year Plan, 56 percent of the aggregate investment
in organized industry and mining was placed in the public sector, and in
the Third Plan, 59 percent; 63 percent was allocated in the original draft
of the Fourth Plan.[6] Because of the low initial base of production and the
poor productivity of such investment, the proportion of value added and
even of additions to value added in the public sector is much lower than
the proportion of additional capital allocated to that sector.

---

[4] The effect of Indian industrial development policy on structure is best seen during the
ascendancy of central planning from the beginning of the First Five-Year Plan in 1950–51 to
the historic drought of 1965–66. After the drought and the accompanying drastic decline in
net foreign aid, industrial development and the planning process itself were in disarray for
several years; it is only in the mid-1970s that recovery and possibly the initial elements of a
new strategy of growth became possible.

[5] Jagdish N. Bhagwati and Padma Desai, *India: Planning for Industrialization* (London:
Oxford University Press, 1970), p. 107.

[6] Ibid., p. 137.

The growth of small-scale industry is measured by a complex set of estimates which give only a rough approximation of change over time. The government of India's *Estimates of National Product* seems to indicate that during the Plan periods, large- and medium-scale industrial firms grew much more rapidly than small-scale enterprises. From 1960–61 to 1965–66 (the Third Plan period of relatively rapid industrial growth), the proportion of production in the small-scale, unregistered sector declined from 40 percent to 36 percent, while the proportion in the large- and medium-scale registered sector rose from 60 to 64 percent. Similarly, large- and medium-scale businesses increased their share of the gross national product (GNP) by one-third, while that of small-scale firms rose by only 10 percent.[7]

Table V-1 dramatically illustrates the increasingly capital intensive structure of Indian industry. The nineteen major industry groups are arrayed in decreasing order of the amount of productive capital per employee in 1965. The data, from the *Annual Survey of Industries (A.S.I.)*, cover all firms within the registered sector (medium- and large-scale industries).

During the period 1951 to 1965, each of the four most capital intensive industry groups increased its proportion of capital investment, value added in production, and employment. Similarly, but with one exception, each of the four industry groups with the lowest capital intensity de-

---

[7] Indian industry consists of the registered sector, those industries with ten workers working with the aid of power or twenty or more workers without the aid of power; and the unregistered sector, those industries with less than ten workers with the aid of power or less than twenty without the aid of power. The registered sector is further divided into the census sector, which pertains to those industries with fifty or more workers with the aid of power or one hundred or more workers without the aid of power; and the sample sector, registered industries with less than fifty workers with the aid of power or less than one hundred without the aid of power. The *Annual Survey of Industries (A.S.I.)* collects data from all census sector firms and from a sample of sample sector firms. Most analyses use the term industrial sector synonymously with registered sector—e.g., Bhagwati and Desai, p. 84. The discussion of industrialization in India in this and following chapters uses the terms small-, medium-, and large-scale industry to refer to unregistered, sample, and census sector, respectively. Because of the scarcity of data on the small-scale industries, much of the analysis of the industrial sector will refer to the aggregate of the medium- and large-scale industries only. For a systematic description of the definitions and sources of industrial statistics, with particular emphasis on the small-scale sector, see Jan H. van der Veen, "Capital Intensity, Absolute Size and Growth Rate of the Small Industries Sector in India: A Critique of Official Estimates," Cornell Agricultural Economics Occasional Paper No. 56 (July 1972). See also van der Veen, "A Study of Small Industries in Gujarat State, India," Cornell Agricultural Economics Occasional Paper No. 65 (May 1973).

Table V-1. Industry groups ranked by degree of capital intensity, registered industrial sector, India, 1965

Industry group or manufacturer	Productive capital per employee	1965			Percent change between 1951 and 1965 in		
		Proportion of total value added	Proportion of total employment	Proportion of total productive capital	Proportion of total value added	Proportion of total employment	Proportion of total productive capital
	('000 Rs)	(%)	(%)	(%)			
Group 32 Products of petroleum & coal	121.9	1.0	0.4	3.1	33.7	601.9	2136.8
Group 51 Electricity, gas, & steam	68.6	7.4	6.0	28.4	203.2	512.6	224.6
Group 34 Basic metal products	35.7	10.9	7.6	18.7	134.1	241.9	473.8
Group 31 Chemicals & chemical products	25.2	8.9	4.3	7.5	54.3	27.2	46.2
Group 21 Beverage industries	16.6	0.6	0.3	0.3	28.7	-0.8	-24.3
Group 37 Electrical machinery, apparatus, appliances, & supplies	15.3	4.6	3.4	3.6	30.6	-7.6	-0.8
Group 30 Rubber products	11.5	2.0	1.1	0.9	145.3	106.1	27.1
Group 36 Machinery except electrical machinery	11.2	6.6	5.6	4.3	1497.6	1050.5	2327.9
Group 27 & 28 Paper & paper products; printing, publishing, & allied industries	10.4	4.4	4.4	3.2	3.3	26.4	-60.7

Industry							
Group 33 Nonmetallic mineral products except products of petroleum & coal	8.8	3.9	4.8	2.9	12.1	35.4	12.1
Group 35 Metal products except machinery & transport equipment	8.8	2.8	3.1	1.9	−26.4	−15.4	−50.8
Group 29 Leather & fur products except footwear & other wearing apparel	8.5	0.3	0.4	0.3	−52.3	−43.1	−59.3
Group 38 Transport equipment	8.3	9.4	9.5	5.5	246.7	240.3	67.6
Group 20 Food industries except beverage industries	8.0	9.8	12.7	7.0	−37.8	−20.5	−61.7
Group 39 Miscellaneous mfg. industries	6.6	1.5	1.9	0.9	−69.7	−75.4	−86.2
Group 25 & 26 Wood & cork; furniture & fixtures	5.7	1.1	1.7	0.7	40.5	100.1	36.2
Group 23 Textiles	4.9	22.5	29.5	10.0	−45.3	−33.3	−68.0
Group 24 Footwear, other wearing apparel, & made-up textile goods	4.0	0.3	0.5	0.1	−72.1	−46.9	−78.0
Group 22 Tobacco	3.5	1.9	2.8	0.7	−21.3	−40.0	−66.1
Total registered industries	14.5	100.0	100.0	100.0	−	−	−

Sources: Appendix, Table 10, which is based on data in Government of India, Cabinet Secretariat, *Sample Survey of Industry*, 1951 and 1957, National Sample Surveys Nos. 15 and 83 (Calcutta); Government of India, Cabinet Secretariat, Central Statistical Organization, *Annual Survey of Industries* (Census Sector) 1961 and 1965 (New Delhi); and Government of India, Cabinet Secretariat, *Annual Survey of Industries* (Sample Sector), 1961 and 1965 (Calcutta).

creased its share of the same three variables. All four of the low capital intensity categories are producers of final consumer goods; none of the top four is a manufacturer of such commodities.

If the *A.S.I.* industries are divided into 212 groups and then reassembled according to capital-labor ratios into 11 classes, all 5 of those classes with less than Rs. 15,000 productive capital per employee lost in relative position (in proportion of value added) from 1961 to 1965, while half of the 6 categories with more than Rs. 15,000 per employee gained (Table V-2). The 3 classes with plus signs include only 33 of the 212 industries. The increase in capital intensity was the product of concentration of investment in a small number of relatively capital intensive industries.

Table V-2. Proportion of value added, by capital intensity class, Indian manufacturing, 1961 and 1965

Class according to productive capital per employee, 1965 (in rupees)	Number of industries in group	Proportion of total value added, 1961	Proportion of total value added, 1965	Percent change in the proportion of total value added, 1961–1965
0–1,000	3	0.5	0.4	− 20.0
1,001–3,000	18	2.1	1.3	− 38.1
3,001–5,000	35	11.3	8.8	− 22.1
5,001–10,000	60	35.7	20.9	− 41.5
10,001–15,000	44	21.2	19.9	− 6.1
15,001–20,000	17	3.8	5.4	+ 42.1
20,001–30,000	17	10.7	9.9	− 7.5
30,001–40,000	8	2.2	17.7	+704.5
40,001–50,000	1	0.1	0.1	0.0
50,001–75,000	8	10.6	14.9	+ 40.6
Greater than 75,000	1	1.8	0.7	− 61.1
Total	212	100.0	100.0	—

Sources: Calculated from Government of India, Cabinet Secretariat, Central Statistical Organization, *Annual Survey of Industries* (Census Sector), Vol. I, 1961 and 1965 (Bombay); and *Annual Survey of Industries* (Sample Sector) 1961 and 1965 (Calcutta).

The rise in the proportion of investment in capital intensive industries has been much greater than the increase in either the share of value added or employment in these same industries. For example, from 1951 to 1965, basic metal industries, which include steel, enlarged their share of productive capital by more than five times—from 3.5 percent to 19 percent; but the proportion of value added was little more than doubled—from nearly 5 percent to 11 percent; and the participation of these industries in total employment rose only three and one-half times—from 2.2 percent to 7.6 percent (see Appendix, Table 10).

The disproportionate increase in capital relative to value added is in part due to the expected unfavorable investment returns in such industries in a low-wage country. The situation is aggravated because the complex problems of organization and management that arise during the rapid expansion of large-scale firms result in a low percentage of capacity utilization. These are, in essence, problems of time. Output, returns, and employment per unit of capital may all achieve greater relative growth in the long run. Nevertheless, the data do show the short- and intermediate-term employment cost of the Second and Third Plan investment patterns as compared to that of earlier periods.

The labor intensive industry groups lost relatively less position over time with respect to share of employment than they did with respect to share of capital (Table V-1). This reflects the fact that the capital intensive industries increased their intensity of investment relatively more than did the labor intensive industries. Thus, from 1951 to 1965, the ratio of productive capital to employment rose by only 54 percent and 53 percent, respectively, in food processing and in textile manufacture. In contrast, for the manufacture of petroleum and coal products the ratio increased nearly tenfold, and for basic metals it expanded over fivefold (see Appendix, Table 10).

Different rates of growth over time of the average capital intensity in Indian industry show the changing effect of industrial development policy. If the capital-labor ratio for each industry in 1965 is weighted by the value added in that industry in 1951, 1957, 1961, and 1965, a rough approximation is provided of the variation in capital intensity due to a change in industrial composition. From 1951 to 1957, there was only a slow increase in the weighted average capital-labor ratio—it rose at the rate of 1.25 percent per year. In contrast, in the three years 1957 to 1960, the ratio advanced at the rate of 6.7 percent per year. In the next period, 1960 to 1967, the ratio grew at the somewhat slower pace of 5.5 percent per year, despite a faster rate of inflation which would be expected to cause some upward bias in the calculation. The early results of the Second Plan very effectively increased the capital intensity of industry; in the Third Plan, various leakages (into increased employment and consumer income) were slowing this trend.

Structural change in industrial investment has had a critical impact on employment. If all the incremental investment between 1951 and 1965 had been distributed in the same proportions in each industry as in

1951—that is, if each industry had expanded by an equal percentage—employment in registered manufacturing would have been 2.3 times greater than the actual level in 1965.[8] The calculation assumes the much higher 1965 level of capital per employee in each industry and consequently reflects only the change in employment due to variation in the relative importance of the nineteen industry groups. This dramatic illustration of the significance of industrial structure in determining the employment content of growth argues against pessimism with respect to potentials for increasing employment through new growth strategy.

Two common assumptions have led many analysts to gloomy conclusions about the employment potentials of the industrial sector. The first is that cost-reducing technological change—rather than alterations in the relative composition of industry—have in the past caused low rates of employment growth.[9] The second is that, in any case, the structure of industrial production is determined by technical factors and by the pattern of demand, and therefore is not manipulable by public policy. Accelerated growth in employment then becomes possible only through the passage of time and the privations of a higher rate of savings and consequent reduced consumption in the short run. The data, with respect to the change in Indian industrial structure, are clearly counter to both these conjectures.

The calculations presented above actually understate the effect on employment of changing the composition of industrial growth. Each of the nineteen industrial groups is far from homogeneous. It is logical to expect the same factors which caused relatively more rapid growth of the most capital intensive industry groups also to cause similarly more rapid

[8] See Uttam Dabholkar and Arthur Goldsmith, "Changes in the Composition of Capital, Employment, and Value Added by Industry Group, India, 1951–1965," Cornell Agricultural Economics Occasional Paper No. 84 (October 1975).

[9] J. G. Williamson does not use data on capital in his analysis of balance in industrial development; he uses a labor-output coefficient as the variable reflecting technological change, and sectoral share in total manufacturing output (value added) as the variable reflecting balance or lack of balance in industrial development. Williamson's technological change variable, therefore, is effectively a measure of change in labor productivity while his notion of composition in terms of output (value added) may not faithfully reflect the allocation of investment resources within the industrial sector in the short run ("Capital Accumulation, Labor-Saving and Labor Absorption: A New Look at Some Contemporary Asian Experience," Social Systems Research Institute, Workshop on Economic Development and International Economics, Series No. 6932 [1970], pp. 1–51). See also H. B. Chenery, S. Shishido, and T. Watanabe, "The Pattern of Japanese Growth, 1914–1954," Econometrica, 30:1 (January 1962), 98–139.

growth of the more capital intensive industries within the groups. Accordingly, some of the large increases in capital intensity within each group come from compositional change and are therefore not entirely due to technological innovation. Moreover, because capital and, therefore, net income have in general been less productive in the capital intensive industries, the capital stock and, hence, employment have probably grown more slowly than if investment had been relatively greater in other types of industries.

The data as presented also include factors which may somewhat overstate the effect of structural change on employment. The capital-labor ratios for each year are based on the current book value of investment per employee. The less rapidly expanding industry groups will have acquired a higher proportion of their capital assets at an earlier date and therefore at lower market prices. Since these were, in practice, the less capital intensive groups, the data will somewhat understate the current capital requirements in these industries and overstate the potential increase in employment. But an attempt to measure this bias by estimating replacement values suggests that the bias does not, in this case, overestimate by more than 10 percent the actual reduction in employment that has occurred through structural change.[10]

It may also plausibly be argued that, as compared to the underlying pattern, new investment tends to go disproportionately to more capital intensive processes in all industries. This may be because the increased domestic demand would justify larger-scale, more capital intensive production; or because the expansion would require and contribute to a higher level of profits and hence of funds for investment; or because faster growth would bring a sector closer to an equilibrium which was itself more capital intensive. If such tendencies toward more capital intensive technologies exist, the rapid advancement of less capital intensive industries would have resulted in a somewhat steeper increase in overall capital intensity in those industries than actually occurred. Be that as it may, the four most capital intensive industry groups still have capital-labor ratios from four to thirty-five times those of the four lowest categories (Table V-1). This suggests that shifts in structure from the more to the less capital intensive industries may indeed be of greater im-

---

[10] For data and calculations, see Grace Horowitz, "Capital-Labor Ratios, Capital-Output Ratios, and Rates of Profit in Indian Industry," Cornell Agricultural Economics Occasional Paper No. 44 (February 1971).

portance than countervailing shifts due to technological change within the groups.

Including the small-scale industrial sector in the above calculations would have increased further the employment effect. Overall production in small-scale establishments, the textile subsector to the contrary, actually expanded less than proportionately to large firms and had lower capital intensity. An economic environment encouraging less capital intensive industries would have promoted faster expansion of textiles (somewhat less rapid in the unregistered enterprises) and various elements of unregistered industry. Given the relative sizes, the net effect of these forces would presumably have been a decline in capital intensity.

But all the preceding qualifications to the estimates of employment effects of structural change are minor compared to the absolutely crucial question about the composition of demand: *whether it can be consistent with a pattern of industrial output creating additional employment.* The capital intensive strategy of development assumes that demand will not constrain the planned output because investment goods comprise a substantial proportion of production. The pattern of investment is itself designed to absorb the output of capital goods; fiscal policy is to keep consumption on a par with the supply of consumer goods. The complex system of input-output tables and programming models was developed specifically to help achieve this balance. In practice, of course, plans do go awry—as occurred in the mid-1960s, when there was insufficient demand for the output of the capital goods industries. In addition, the demand for the more labor intensive consumer goods provided only a low rate of growth, because exports, as a proportion of the output of such goods, declined and consumer income was rising very slowly.

Clearly, if the old plans had at least a rough consistency between supply and demand, and if change in the structure of output is to be a major source of employment growth, there must be a similar alteration in the pattern of domestic consumption and foreign trade. In the exercise above, showing the effect of the proportionate expansion of Indian industry from the 1951 base, the consumer goods industries were, of course, presumed to grow much more rapidly than under actual plan conditions. Textiles may serve to exemplify a broad range of relatively labor intensive consumer goods, including electronics and fabricated plastic products. Nevertheless, foreign and domestic demand would have to rise much more sharply than thay did to achieve the employment advantages of this structure.

Exports of the more labor intensive industries would have performed better as more rapid expansion of the consumer goods industries increased efficiency, lowered costs, and improved competitive position in world markets. India need not have lost relative position in consumer goods exports to other low-income countries. To be competitive and, also, to reinforce the employment effect, expansion of exports would have required increased imports of capital intensive and resources-based intermediate products such as fibers, steel, aluminum, and plastics. Accordingly, it is clearly difficult to exclude a major trade component from the restructuring of industrial growth.

Rising incomes of the rural farm and urban laboring classes tend to promote more rapid expansion of demand for labor intensive consumer goods than occurred in the capital-oriented strategy of development. Thus, the supply and demand aspects of a production pattern favoring industries with a high labor content are at least partially reinforcing.

Key Industries in Structural Change

Although industrial expansion in India from 1951 to 1965 generally emphasized capital intensive investment, the change in structure was, in practice, heavily concentrated in four industries. According to information gathered by the *A.S.I.*, over 60 percent of the total increase in fixed capital in Indian manufacturing from 1951 to 1965 occurred in two industry groups—basic metals and power (electricity, gas, and steam). Investment in basic metals increased over thirtyfold and in power nearly fifteen fold. Similarly two industry groups, textiles and food manufacturing, suffered the bulk of the loss in relative position; they account for less than 10 percent of additional fixed capital between 1951 and 1965.

For the seven industries which lost in share of value added from 1951 to 1965, the total decline was 31 percent. Over three-quarters of that decrease was accounted for by food processing and textiles. Textiles plus food processing declined from 45 percent to 15 percent of fixed capital, 50 to 17 percent of productive capital, 60 to 42 percent of employment, and 57 to 32 percent of value added. Basic metals plus power rose from 20 to 55 percent, 12 to 47 percent, 3 to 14 percent, and 7 to 18 percent, respectively, of those same measures.

Basic metals (mainly steel) and textiles offer particularly interesting illustrations of industrial policy in action. The other sector with very rapid growth, manufacture of machinery other than electrical, is of only average capital intensity (Appendix, Table 10-2).

The Steel Industry

Investment in the Indian steel industry poses the classic development dilemma. Steel accounts for the sharp increase in capital intensity and the low content of employment in Indian economic growth since the beginning of the Second Five-Year Plan. Arguments for investment in the steel industry—that it would lead to higher rates of domestic savings and investment and to net savings in foreign exchange—did not hold up in the short run, although India has the basic raw materials to be a low-cost steel producer in the long run. Steel production also seems to be the *sine qua non* of the modern industrial state, a factor not without meaning in post-colonial India. The fundamental argument against steel is on the ground of its capital intensity, and there was then little basis to sustain the view that Indian agriculture of the 1950s or even early 1960s could have supported a much larger investment in a more labor-oriented strategy of growth.

In 1951, India produced 1.5 million tons of steel, entirely in the private sector. In 1956, production was only 1.7 million tons. The Second Plan raised it to 3.4 million tons in 1960–61, and the Third Plan increased it to 6.5 million tons in 1965–66. But steel production was only 6.1 million tons in 1970–71, and by then over half of it was in the public sector.[11] For the period 1963–64 to 1965–66, the steel industry averaged 44 percent of the total public sector industrial investment.[12]

A simplistic but rather revealing calculation indicates the number of jobs forgone by the pattern of investment in the basic metals industry. On the basis of estimates of productive capital and employment from the *A.S.I.*, the capital requirement per worker is calculated to be approximately Rs. 35,700 for large- and medium-scale basic metals firms in 1965. In contrast, in van der Veen's sample of unregistered industries for 1969–70, the total capital requirement per employee in the basic metals and metal products industry was Rs. 3,748.[13] To dramatize the issue,

[11] Calculated from Government of India, Ministry of Steel, Mines and Metals, *Iron and Steel Bulletin* (New Delhi), various issues; and Hindustan Steel Ltd., *Statistics for Iron and Steel Industry in India, 1966* (Ranchi, India, 1966).

[12] Bhagwati and Desai, Table 9.4.

[13] Figures were calculated from Appendix, Table 10, below, and van der Veen, "A Study of Small Industries in Gujarat State, India," Table 4.

one may say that the capital invested in the large- and medium-scale basic metals industry could have produced nearly ten times as many jobs in the corresponding small-scale industry. Investment of productive capital in the larger firms, from 1957 to 1965, may have led to a net loss of over 2.9 million potential jobs.[14]

The job loss may in fact be much greater than that. Inefficient operation of the public sector steel industry has provided a low rate of profit and capital formation and hence retarded growth in job opportunities. Even during the favorable period, from 1960–61 to 1964–65, the public sector Hindustan Steel showed a loss in three years, and only a 2.1 and 3.3 percent rate of gross profit on capital in the two years of profitable operation.[15]

The low return on steel investment in India traces from long delays in construction and from serious operational problems which depressed rates of capacity utilization. Delay in construction arises not only from the size and complexity of the industry but also from the reliance on foreign financing which was considered necessary to rapid expansion. Padma Desai's review of the experience with the Russian-financed Bokaro steel mill shows clearly how the vested interests of western and Russian donors may diverge widely not only from each other but from those of India as well, with resultant costs in efficiency.[16]

In capital intensive industry, efficient operation is basically a consequence of maintaining production close to capacity, and Indian steel mills have typically operated at low levels of capacity.[17] High utilization rates require technical skills in maintaining the plant, economic skills in gauging markets, and personnel skills in managing an extremely large labor force. Not surprisingly, the civil service type of management (initially imposed on the public sector steel industry) had difficulty in providing these necessary skills. The problem and its solution are clearly detailed in government reports.[18] The lesson is not so much that development of the Indian steel industry was badly handled or that operation by the public sector is

---

[14] Figures were calculated from Appendix, Table 10, below, and previous figures given.

[15] See Bhagwati and Desai, Table 9.6.

[16] See Padma Desai, *The Bokaro Steel Plant: A Study of Soviet Economic Assistance* (New York: American Elsevier, 1972).

[17] See *Economic Survey, 1970–71*, p. 17, for further discussion of the low levels of capacity utilization in the steel industry.

[18] Government of India, Ministry of Steel and Heavy Industries, Department of Iron and Steel, *Report* (New Delhi), 1961–62 through 1963–64; Ministry of Steel, Mines and Metals, *Iron and Steel Bulletin*, various issues.

in error, but rather that large-scale capital intensive industries are likely to have low rates of profit for a considerable period of time, thereby slowing, rather than accelerating, capital accumulation, with a consequent further depression of employment. A more pessimistic view is that years of inefficient management by the public sector may have created vested interests in the bases of that inefficiency and thus drastic action is required to bring improvement.

If India changes to an employment-oriented program of growth, a simple strategy for steel is apparent. The Second and subsequent plans did provide capacity to design and build steel plants, in large part with indigenous materials. Growth of steel mills within the limit set by this capacity, with minimal imports, would both reduce the capital costs of construction and slow the rate of expansion below that of the past peak periods, thereby releasing investment capital for more labor intensive purposes and providing more time for management to improve.

Other Capital Intensive Industries

Electric power generation is highly capital intensive, and massive investment in this industry is essential to an employment-oriented strategy of growth. Like steel, electric power is an important intermediate product, but unlike steel, it cannot be imported. One-third of the increase in book value of productive capital in the registered manufacturing sector from 1951 to 1965 was in electricity, gas, and steam—nearly 50 percent more than in basic metals. The growth rate of generated electricity, as estimated from the *Economic Survey,* was 12.3 percent from 1950–51 to 1960–61; 14.3 percent from 1960–61 to 1965–66; and 11.1 percent from 1965–66 to 1970–71. Despite this progress, in 1972 and 1973 severe power shortages impeded both agricultural and industrial expansion. For example, P. M. Agerwala, managing director of Tata Electric Companies, in a statement reported in the January 31, 1973, issue of the *Economic Times,* said: "The loss in [industrial production] during the [past] five to six months had been over Rs. 1,000 crores"; and "At a time when there was drought in several states and the need to operate the agricultural pumps was the maximum, power for even normal irrigation purposes was not available, thereby accentuating the seriousness of drought." Agerwala also pointed out that "power shortages seemed to have added a new dimension to the ideological differences over granting priorities to industry and agriculture. In one state, power supplies were being stopped specifically for providing interim relief either to industry or to agriculture at the cost of the other.''

It seems likely that an employment-oriented program of development will require a much faster growth rate of electric power. That accelerated growth will claim a substantial proportion of the investment resources available to the public sector, and make even more difficult the allocation of funds to other capital intensive industries. Indeed, the distribution of capital to those industries is likely to starve the power sector, ensure the failure of agricultural and labor intensive industries, and, as a result of that deficiency, guarantee a foreign-exchange gap. Similar points could be made about the transportation and communication systems.

The employment-oriented strategy of development requires substantial investment in certain capital intensive areas of the economy. It is this need which gives great urgency to choosing only those capital intensive investments for which there is no import alternative and which are necessary to complement employment intensive industries.

The Textile Industry

Unlike steel and other capital intensive enterprises, the textile industry was, in 1951, a large, internationally competitive business. Subsequently, the industry became inefficient and barely profitable. The decline of textiles is as much a product of the capital intensive strategy of growth as the rise of steel and also provides useful lessons for the future.

In 1951, the medium- and large-scale textile sectors produced 41 percent of all value added and included 26 percent of all fixed capital in Indian registered manufacturing. In 1952, an estimated 35 percent of textile output was sent abroad—38 percent of total Indian exports. Foreign shipments of cotton fabrics dropped continually from 1951, and in 1970–71 accounted for about 4.9 percent of all exports. Between 1951 and 1965, only 4.5 percent of the increase in productive capital in registered industry occurred in textiles (Appendix, Table 10). By 1965, the share of value added declined to 22 percent.[19]

The textile industry has suffered from rising raw material prices, rising wage rates, relatively dormant demand, and a government policy discouraging to investment.

Tight import controls and stagnant domestic cotton production caused

[19] The export figures were calculated from data in *Statistical Abstract of India, 1953–54*, and *Economic Survey, 1971–72*, pp. 140–41. Also see Chapter VIII, below.

raw cotton prices to more than double from 1961 to 1970, while the price of cotton manufactures rose between 13 and 38 percent. During the period, synthetic fiber imports were restrained, prejudicing the shift of exports to synthetics; cotton imports declined 23 percent; and production of cotton yarn and cloth increased by only 16 and 13 percent, respectively. Between 1961 and 1968, minimum wages in principal textile centers expanded by nearly 60 percent without any evidence of a substantial rise in labor productivity.[20] Concurrently, government policy tried to reduce capital requirements and increase employment by encouraging the cottage and small-scale sectors.

The rate of profits was low. A survey by the Reserve Bank of India of 276 textile firms showed average profits as a percentage of net worth at 4.5 percent in 1966–67 and 1.9 percent in 1967–68, hardly a level to encourage expansion.[21]

Textile industry management is said to be inefficient—but any industry with such a history of growth is bound to have a high proportion of antiquated equipment, to draw off profits to other enterprises, and to have a conservative attitude toward its affairs. The underlying reason for the poor performance of the textile business was the overall strategy of development, which starved it of capital, raised its raw material costs, and provided insufficient growth in demand. The result was not only inefficient production, but a rapid loss of foreign markets as well (see Chapter VIII).

The Special Role of Small- and Medium-Scale Industries

The small- and medium-scale sector of industry has a particularly important role to play in a rural employment-oriented strategy of growth.[22] It already produces a large share of aggregate industrial output. Despite its potentials, small-scale industry has advanced less rapidly than the rest of the industrial sector. If the sector is to prosper, the strategy of develop-

[20] Price data were calculated from *Statistical Abstract of India, 1970*, Table 163. Figures with respect to cotton imports and production were calculated from *Economic Survey, 1971–72*, pp. 94–95 and 138–39. Figures with respect to wages were calculated from *Statistical Abstract of India, 1970*, Table 149.

[21] See "Finances of Public Limited Companies, 1967–68," Reserve Bank of India, *Bulletin* (Bombay), 24:10 (October 1970), 1617–1708.

[22] For a highly documented and detailed analysis of the favorable relationship between various Hindu social customs, including the joint family, and the development of industry, particularly small-scale industry, see Milton Singer, *When a Great Tradition Modernizes* (New York: Praeger, 1972).

ment must be consistent with its demand and input requirements. In addition, the very fact that operations are on a small scale places a greater responsibility upon the authorities to design public policies and institutions to meet the sector's special problems.

The desirable characteristics of small-scale enterprise were clearly recognized in the second Industrial Policy Resolution of 1956: "Then, as now, the government pursued the development of this [small-industries] subsector on the basis of its capacity for creating considerable employment per unit of capital investment, its potential for reducing inequalities in existing personal and regional income distribution patterns, and its ability to mobilize otherwise underutilized scarce resources." [23] The subsequent plan documents continued and expanded this rationale. [24] But in 1970, the report of the Administrative Reforms Commission, chaired by K. Hanumanthaiya, drew attention to the failure to meet the objectives, stating that this subsector "has not been given the position of high priority which should be its due." [25]

Indian planning had a tendency to assign a priority to a particular effort in the context of an overall plan which simply does not allow the policy to succeed. The problem is not necessarily that the overall strategy was wrong, and certainly not that the administration of the strategy was inept, but simply that some efforts were inconsistent with the strategy and hence could not be successfully pursued. There is, of course, an inefficiency in the allocation of administrative resources to an effort that can hardly succeed.

There are two general reasons for the past failure of small-scale in-

[23] As quoted in van der Veen, "A Study of Small Industries in Gujarat State, India," p. 1.

[24] See, for example, Second Five-Year Plan (New Delhi: Government of India, Planning Commission, 1956), p. 32; and Third Five-Year Plan, 1961, p. 42. See also Ford Foundation, International Planning Team, Report on Small Industries in India (Delhi: Government of India, 1954); P. N. Dhar, Small Scale Industries in Delhi (Bombay: Asia Publishing House, 1958); P. N. Dhar and H. F. Lydall, The Role of Small Enterprises in Indian Economic Development, (New York: Asia Publishing House, 1961); D. T. Kakdawala and J. C. Sandesara, "Small Industries in a Big City," University of Bombay, Series in Economics No. 10 (Bombay, 1960); Ford Foundation, International Perspective Planning Team, Development of Small Scale Industries in India (Delhi: Government of India, 1963); M. C. Shetty, Small-Scale and Household Industries in a Developing Economy (New York: Asia Publishing House, 1963); and H. Banerji, Survey of Small Engineering Units in Howrah (Bombay: Reserve Bank of India, 1964).

[25] See K. Hanumanthaiya, chairman, Administrative Reforms Commission, Report on Small-Scale Sector (Delhi: Government of India, 1970), p. 8.

dustry to achieve vigorous growth. First, the general economic environment was no more favorable for small-scale firms than for the consumer goods industries generally. The lack of demand for consumer goods, a scarcity of raw materials, and a paucity of investment in infrastructure all strike particularly hard at the small firm which may itself be short of capital, lack political power to obtain scarce resources, and be located disadvantageously in outlying areas.[26] While the government's right hand was encouraging the development of small-scale industries, its more powerful left hand was channeling a high proportion of both imported and domestic resources to the large-scale (primarily public) sector.

Second, a major portion of small-scale business has needs for assistance with respect to the form of capital and credit requirements, infrastructure, and input supplies which differ from those of larger firms, yet public policies have not been keyed to those problems. At such a time as the growth strategy changes, these specific questions must be understood and acted upon.

For purposes of planning assistance, the Government of India defines a small-scale firm as any enterprise with plant and machinery investment of not more than .75 million rupees or, if it is an ancillary firm, less than 1 million rupees. In practice, the upper size limit is interpreted liberally. This definition includes the lower end of registered industry, which in turn includes perhaps half of the value added in the total small-scale sector as defined for public assistance programs.[27]

The small- and medium-scale sector can usefully be divided into three different size groups. The medium-scale firms receive the bulk of government help.[28] That aid has been based on the implicit assumption that the problem of small- and medium-scale industries is in essence the same as that of large-scale industries. Therefore, past policy has emphasized easier access to credit for fixed investment and easier access to modern machinery, technical skills, and improved management practices. To some extent, infrastructure is provided through the establishment of industrial estates. The policies do improve the competitive position of the smaller

---

[26] See, for example, van der Veen, "Capital Intensity, Absolute Size and Growth Rate of the Small Industries Sector in India," and "A Study of Small Industries in Gujarat State, India."

[27] Van der Veen, "Capital Intensity, Absolute Size and Growth Rate of the Small Industries Sector in India," Tables 2, 3, and 6.

[28] Ibid., pp. 5–6.

firm vis-à-vis the large firms in the same industry, but they are of little assistance to the very small firms.

Perhaps half of the gross production in the small-scale—i.e., unregistered—sector is provided by minute firms whose labor force comes largely from the owners' households.[29] These businesses are substantially in service trades and have very low value added per worker and probably only a small proportion have potential for substantial growth.

Much more interesting in the current context than either the medium-scale firms or the minute "household" firms is that group of firms which are unregistered—but which are large enough to employ workers outside the family. Van der Veen's study of a random sample of 206 such firms in Gujarat provides a basis for understanding their growth potentials and problems. The analysis covers unregistered firms with five or more employees in "urban" areas (essentially all centers with a population of over 5,000) in Gujarat. The sector accounts for about 10 percent of the gross production in the industrial part of the state, or almost one-third of the total output of the unregistered subsector.

These firms epitomize the attractive features of small-scale enterprise. They make efficient use of resources, utilize little capital per worker, have a potential for tapping substantial new sources of savings and entrepreneurship, and lend themselves to location in rural market towns. In addition, they are growing as a result of increased consumer expenditure and rural savings associated with the new agricultural technologies.

Such firms are not marginal businesses. Even in the relatively unfavorable business environment prevailing in 1969–70, they averaged a net return on capital of 13.5 percent.[30] Their ratios of productive capital—excluding land and buildings—to gross output of 0.33, and to value added of 1.64, are both low and suggest that the small amount of investment used per worker is in fact extremely fruitful. Even if the value of land and buildings were included in the capital costs—a somewhat misleading assumption since most of the small-scale firms rent these inputs—the ratios of capital to output and value added in the unregistered industrial sector would compare favorably with those in the large-scale industrial sector (Table V-3).

High labor intensity in the small-scale sector occurs in part because it pays lower wages than the large-scale firms. But the small-scale sector

[29] Ibid., Table 7.
[30] Van der Veen, "A Study of Small Industries in Gujarat State, India," Table 4.

Table V-3. Comparison of key ratios for small- and large-scale industries, Gujarat State, India, 1969–70
(in Rs. 1,000)

Item	Small-scale industry (urban unregistered industrial subsector) *	Large-scale industry (registered census sector)
Gross output	1,506,226	8,468,500
Gross output/unit	146	7,164
Productive capital/gross output	0.49 (0.33)	0.73
Productive capital/value added	2.40 (1.64)	3.07
Productive capital/employment	6.97 (4.76)	17.91
Employment/gross output	0.07	0.04
Emoluments/employment	1.83	3.15
Value added/employment	2.90	5.82
Value added/fixed capital	0.76 (1.83)	0.41
Working capital/fixed capital	0.84 (2.01)	0.27
Gross input/gross output	0.80	0.71

* Figures in parentheses are for productive capital, excluding the value of land and buildings.
Sources: Column 1: Jan H. van der Veen, "A Study of Small Industries in Gujarat State India," Department of Agricultural Economics, Occasional Paper 65, Cornell University USAID Employment and Income Distribution Project (May 1973); column 2: Government of India, Central Statistical Organisation, Annual Survey of Industries, Census Sector (Provisional Results), Calcutta, 1969.

does appear to make as large wage payments relative to output and larger wage payments relative to capital, as well as spreading those wage payments over a larger population.

The high degree of labor intensity in small firms is both the product and the cause of its capital structure. The different parts of the capital structure have different resource components with quite dissimilar social costs. The small-scale sector does use a substantial amount of capital for its land and buildings. But this capital is almost universally rented, tapping many financial and physical resources that would otherwise not enter into productive use. Thus the opportunity cost of employing these inputs in the small-scale sector would appear to be quite low. Of the remaining capital, a high proportion is working capital used for financing the labor force itself and for purchasing the large quantity of inputs that are processed. One may argue that the form of capital for which there is the greatest social need to economize is productive capital, and the small-scale sector has a low ratio of this input relative to employment and value added.

There are two very closely related features which are evident from the Gujarat study that are of critical importance to public policy for encouraging small industries. First, as indicated by the large working capital requirement, the labor intensive small-scale sector processes a heavy volume of purchased inputs. Second, it has very important interactions with the large-scale sector.

Ensuring an adequate supply of purchased inputs is the most crucial element for the success of the small-scale sector. And that is the greatest problem. Sizable market imperfections in the supply of inputs cause excessive price fluctuations. Firms may be closed over long periods for lack of supplies or in anticipation of purchasing at a more favorable price.[31] Moreover, entrepreneurial talent will concentrate more on trading activities and less on improving production methods. Several authors have commented unfavorably on the trading orientation of small businessmen.[32] But trading is where the profits are, given existing market imperfections. Indeed, until circumstances change, trading will continue to be a socially desirable use of the entrepreneur's time.[33]

Public policy can lessen the uncertainty of input supplies and thereby increase the small businessman's attention to production efficiency. A relative increase in public expenditure on transportation and communication would facilitate better operating markets, in which prices would be more predictable. The general shortage of raw materials which arises from overvalued foreign exchange and the attempts to channel resources to specific large-scale industries produce black markets and implicit high values for licenses. These conditions force the small businessmen to spend disproportionate effort to obtain import quotas and licenses or to try to profit from sudden price changes in response to the rapidly fluctuating supply-demand environment. Unfortunately the conflicts in policy are large. Strong vested interests—including the bureaucracy that administers the regulations and the large business interests that are in a privileged

---

[31] See the statement of this for rice milling in ibid., p. 42; and in Uma J. Lele, "Modernization of the Rice Milling Industry," *Economic and Political Weekly*, 5:28 (July 11, 1970); for oil goods, see A. G. K. Murty and D. K. Desai, *A Study on Solvent Extraction and Expeller Oil Industries* (Ahmedabad: Indian Institute Management, 1968), p. 21.

[32] See, for example, J. T. McCrory, *Small Industry in a North Indian Town: Case Studies in Latent Industrial Potential* (New Delhi: Government of India, 1956); and J. J. Berna, *Industrial Entrepreneurship in Madras State* (New York: Asia Publishing House, 1960); and the critique of their position in Jan H. van der Veen, "Small Industries in India: The Case of Gujarat State," Ph.D. dissertation, Cornell University, December 1972, pp. 137–44.

[33] See, for example, the situation of small rice mills in Uma J. Lele, *Food Grain Marketing in India: Private Performance and Public Policy* (Ithaca, N.Y.: Cornell University Press, 1971), p. 191.

position vis-à-vis the authorities—oppose a freer market. Bhagwati and Desai have commented at length on the inefficient resource allocation of poorly working markets caused by government regulation.[34]

The misallocation of entrepreneurial effort and talent may be even more serious. Both the weak infrastructure and the insufficient raw materials are the offspring of a strategy of development which allocates most of these resources to other uses and leaves little available for the small-scale sector.

The second feature of the Gujarat study that is important for public policy is the substantial interaction of small industries with large. Van der Veen shows that linkages are primarily on the input side. Small firms buy great quantities of intermediate products from large firms which may themselves be highly capital intensive. Consequently, in a closed economy, it is difficult for small-scale industry to grow without a complement of large firms, and therefore it is hard for the average capital intensity of the economy to decline through such a process. Van der Veen quantifies these interindustry dependencies in an aggregate input-output analysis.[35] The solution to the dilemma is to import more of the capital intensive intermediate products. Steel is an important product of this type; so are plastics and synthetic fibers. Similarly, small-scale firms may do well in exporting their products because of comparatively cheap labor, but if they must pay a high price for raw materials, they lose that advantage. The rapid, related growth of exports and imports in Taiwan is a case in point.

Accordingly, the small-scale industry sector requires a ready availability of inputs. Achieving this availability may entail substantial investment in transport and electric power infrastructure, credit for working rather than fixed capital, and imports of raw materials and intermediate products. Rapidly expanding markets are also necessary. Growth may come from an increase in exports, but failing that, domestic consumption must be developed as a consequence of greater employment and rising rural incomes. Therefore, in the small-scale sector as in the consumer goods industries generally, fulfilling a high employment potential can only occur as a complement to other policies, and consequently is a function of the broad overall strategy of growth.

[34] Bhagwati and Desai, pp. 335–67.
[35] Van der Veen, "A Study of Small Industries in Gujarat State, India," ch. vi.

VI

Industrial Growth: The Pace and the Constraints

Industrial Growth—1950 to 1960

Complex crosscurrents in Indian industrial growth offer opportunity for a particularly wide range of both positive and negative lessons to other developing countries. India's long and distinguished record of organized trade and manufacture predates the British colonial period by many centuries.[1] Development of a vigorous textile industry and a small and efficient iron and steel industry under the British at least partially maintained the tradition. India entered its First Five-Year Plan with a significant foundation of industrial institutions and an entrepreneurial class. In 1951, the registered, or large- and medium-scale industrial sector, accounted for less than 6 percent of the net domestic product, utilized only 2 percent of the total labor force, and was weighted heavily toward textiles. But the industrial sector as a whole, including small-scale enterprises, accounted for over 16 percent of the net domestic product in 1951—a large percentage relative to per capita national income. For example, Kuznets' data for contemporary developing nations show that 14.3 percent of the gross domestic product in manufacturing is consistent with a per capita income over three times greater than India's at that time.[2]

Accordingly, the industrial base in the early 1950s seems to have been broad enough to support a plausible alternative to the capital intensive, public sector–oriented strategy of growth actually chosen. In fact, the industrial growth rate in the years immediately preceding the Second Plan was only moderately lower than the highest rate of growth achived during

[1] For a brief interpretative history of that period, see Jagdish Bhagwati and Padma Desai, *India: Planning for Industrialization* (London: Oxford University Press, 1970), ch. ii.
[2] Simon Kuznets, *Economic Growth of Nations* (Cambridge, Mass.: Harvard University Press, 1971), Table 26.

the Second and Third Plan periods of extensive foreign aid (Table I-2). Greater emphasis on agriculture, increased rural incomes, larger demand for industrial consumer goods, and fewer restrictions on investment in their production and on the importation of capital intensive intermediate products might have provided vigorous expansion of the private industrial sector to serve both domestic and foreign markets.

A great debate emerged between the advocates of the capital intensive, Mahalanobis-type plan of development and such opponents as P. V. Shenoy, C. N. Vakil, and P. R. Brahmananda, who stressed high employment growth. Policy went with Mahalanobis. Paradoxically enough, the consequent broadening of the industrial base to include many relatively labor intensive industries—such as machine tools—would further strengthen the argument for a later change in strategy.

Agricultural processing and the consumer goods industries dominated the industrial sector in the 1950s. Since output was particularly sensitive to changes in the weather and the production of agricultural raw materials, it is difficult to determine the effect of developmental policy on industrial growth rates. It appears that industrial production lagged in the early 1950s as a consequence of unfavorable harvests, recovered to average a 7.9 percent growth rate for the three years from 1953 to 1956, then slowed to 3.8 percent for the two years 1956 to 1958. The reduced rate of growth is, in part, explained by poor weather, but perhaps also by the initiation of Second Plan efforts to divert resources away from the traditional consumer goods industries and toward new, more capital intensive enterprises. Following 1958, industrial production advanced rapidly, averaging 9.9 percent per year for the remaining two years of the Second Plan and continuing at 9.0 percent through 1965. For the nine years 1951 to 1960, industrial production grew at an average rate of 6.2 percent per year (Table I-2).

The substantial growth of the industrial sector during the 1950s was fueled by a rapid expansion in domestic savings and in foreign aid and accompanied by a decline in foreign exchange reserves (Figures VI-1a, VI-1b). Domestic savings as a percentage of national income (at market prices) increased from 5.0 percent in 1951–52 to 8.9 percent in 1960–61—an annual compound rate of growth of 6.6 percent (Figure VI-2). Savings of increments to income averaged 19 percent during this period.[3]

[3]. Ujagar S. Bawa, *Agricultural Production and Industrial Capital Formation, India, 1951–52 to 1964–65*, C.I.A.D. Bulletin No. 17 (March 1971), Table 8.

1950–51 to 1971–72

Figure VI-1b (right). Foreign exchange reserves and net foreign resource transfer,* India, 1950–51 to 1974–75

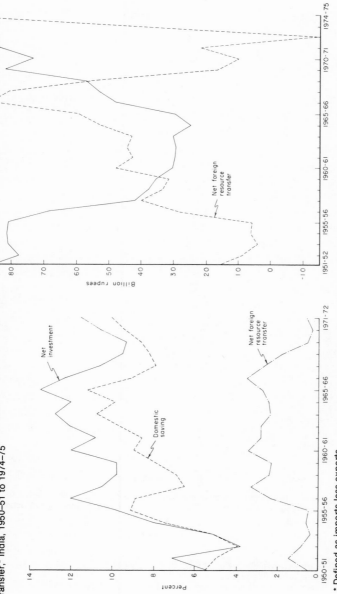

* Defined as imports less exports.

Sources: Domestic saving and net investment taken from data in Reserve Bank of India, *Bulletin* (March 1965); Government of India, Planning Commission, *The Fourth Plan Mid-Term Appraisal*, Vol. I (December 1971); Reserve Bank of India, *Report on Currency and Finance, 1971/72*; and Government of India, Central Statistical Organisation, *Estimates of National Income, 1948/49 to 1960/61*. Foreign resource transfer taken from data on imports and exports in R. P. Yadev, "An Econometric Model for the Foreign Trade Sector of India, 1960-61–1971-72," unpublished Ph.D. diss., Cornell University, January 1975; and Reserve Bank of India, *Report on Currency and Finance*, various issues. Net foreign resource transfer as a percentage of national income (at market prices) was computed on the basis of information in Government of India, Central Statistical Organisation, *Estimates of National Income*, various issues. Foreign exchange reserves taken from Government of India, Ministry of Finance, *Economic Survey*, various issues.

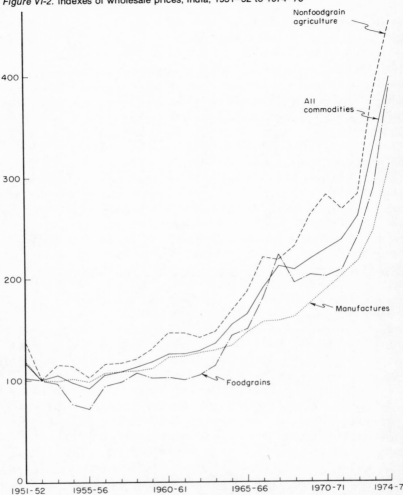

Figure VI-2. Indexes of wholesale prices, India, 1951–52 to 1974–75

Note: The single base series were calculated by connecting two published series, based in 1952–53 and 1961–62 respectively. The nonfoodgrain agriculture index was derived using the formula:

$$I_{NA} = \frac{(I_A \cdot W_A) - (I_F \cdot W_F)}{W_A - W_F}$$

where I = index, W = weight given to each category, NA = nonfoodgrain agriculture, A = agriculture, and F = foodgrains.
Source: Developed from Reserve Bank of India, *Bulletin,* various issues.

The Mahalanobis theory of growth emphasized a high rate of savings from increments to income as a means of increasing the capital stock and releasing the nation from dependence on foreign aid. At least until 1960–61, a rising savings rate, a crucial condition of the plan, was being fulfilled. The relative importance of government, corporate, and household sectors in contribution to savings remained almost constant during the period 1951–61, although within the household sector the urban portion gained relative to the rural, and the significance of financial instruments increased in comparison with physical assets—both good omens for continued industrial growth.[4]

Strongly reinforcing the expansion of domestic savings, foreign resource transfers to India rose even more rapidly, from an average of 269 million dollars per year during the period 1951–52 through 1954–55 to an average of 687 million during the period 1955–56 through 1960–61. Foreign exchange reserves had been built to a total of 1,703 million dollars by 1954–55, then reduced to 623 million by 1961–62, adding further to foreign aid as a source of net foreign resource transfers. Excluding food aid, foreign resource transfers were equal in value to 25 percent of total domestic savings in the period 1951–52 to 1960–61.[5]

Agricultural growth, too, was in rough balance with industrial growth in the First Plan period, and relative agricultural prices in general increased but slowly. The index of wholesale prices for all commodities rose by 25 percent from 1952–53 to 1960–61, a compound rate of increase of 2.8 percent per year (Figure VI-2). From the same base year, prices of agricultural and manufactured commodities increased by virtually the same amount, 24 percent. And the prices of foodgrains—most vital to the poor and most likely to provide a wage goods constraint—went up a total of only 2 percent from the 1952–53 base, representing a decline of 17 percent relative to the price of industrial commodities and 22 percent relative to all nonfoodgrain commodities (Figures VI-2 and II-2).

But the creditable record of industrial growth was, in this period, hardly a test of economic consistency, since it was from a small base, with a small employment content. Consequently, the pressure on resources was slight.

[4] Ibid., ch. ii, particularly Tables 6 and 7.
[5] Figures in this paragraph were calculated from data in Reserve Bank of India (Bombay), *Bulletin,* various issues, and converted to dollars, using the current exchange rate for the period.

In the period 1952–53 to 1960–61, foodgrain prices relative to other prices declined in a context of very slow growth in demand. Employment in registered industry grew at only 2 percent per year from 1951 to 1961; the overall population increased merely 1.98 percent per annum; and real per capita incomes were rising at an annual rate of only 1.1 percent. Low-income persons, with a most elastic demand for food, probably participated little or not at all in that growth. Thus, hardly any demand pressure was placed on a scant 2.5 to 2.75 percent rate of increase in foodgrain production. Similarly, the sizable jumps in the savings and investment rates had started from very low bases (Figure VI-1a). And foreign aid, which accounted for a very large percentage of total investment, would, even if maintained in an absolute amount, rapidly diminish in proportion as the size of the economy grew. Accelerated or even continued growth of the industrial sector would increase its relative size and begin to illuminate underlying inconsistencies and tensions which would either restrain expansion in the early 1960s or introduce distortions sufficiently serious to cut back the rate of advance in the late 1960s.

Accelerated Industrial Growth and Increasing Distortion—1961 to 1965

Despite mounting signs of difficulty, the first four years of the Third Five-Year Plan formed a period of unprecedented advancement, the pace of which is often not recognized because of the disastrous effects of the catastrophic drought in the last year of the Plan. Notwithstanding the crucial role of foreign aid, this period demonstrates the potentials for high employment growth and the conditions which must be met if such growth is to be sustained.

From 1960–61 to 1964–65, industrial production in the larger-scale sector rose at a compound rate of 9.6 percent per year; small-scale industry, too, made rapid strides—at a 6.4 percent annual rate.[6] The progress of industrial employment was also impressive. For the four years from 1961 to 1965, the rate of increase of employment in registered industries averaged 6 percent (Appendix, Table 10). These rates are high relative to international standards for low-income countries and to the growth rate of India's own industrial output.[7]

---

[6] Government of India, Central Statistical Organisation, *Estimates of National Product (Revised Series), 1960–61 to 1968–69* (New Delhi, 1970).

[7] For comparative data, see David Turnham, *The Employment Problem in Less Developed Countries* (Paris: Organisation for Economic Co-operation and Development, 1971).

In view of the widespread pessimism regarding the employment potentials of industrial growth, it is useful to note just how rapid that expansion was in the Third Plan period; how it developed despite an industrial investment pattern basically inimical to its progress; and the nature of the distortions that were soon to follow and terminate it.

Thus, while overall manufacturing production was rising at a rate of 8.9 percent per year, from 1961 to 1965 (Table I-2), output in relatively labor intensive consumer goods industries was increasing much less rapidly, and production of intermediate materials and capital goods was growing much more quickly than the average.

If the growth structure had been more heavily weighted toward consumer goods, employment would have risen even more. The consumer goods industries presumably pay for the use of funds faster than the capital goods industries, thereby hastening the availability of money for investment. They also provide more jobs for a given amount of investment. Also, if rapid agricultural growth had enabled the consumer goods sector to accelerate expansion without a fully commensurate decline in the availability of capital to the other industrial sectors, the net accretion to overall development would have been very dramatic.

But three distorting tendencies were soon to slow the pace of industrial growth. First, deficiences in the agricultural sector were not only to produce a wage goods squeeze (paucity of food and other goods on which added wages are spent), in the face of a rapid increase in employment, but were to create one of the several sources of a capital constraint. Second, the capital constraint was to become increasingly restrictive because of an inconsistency between the means of growth and the sources of finance. And third, unrealistic and inconsistent aspects of the Second and Third Five-Year Plans resulted in administrative failings of far-reaching significance.

The Agricultural Production Constraint

Despite its small role in the overall strategy for economic development, the agricultural sector bulked large in accounting both for the periods of accelerated industrial expansion and the contradiction which led to the eventual slowdown. The magnitude of annual fluctuations in agricultural output (induced by the weather) caused large changes in national income and in the savings and investment rate. Growing urban employment increased the demand for food in the Third Plan period. This circumstance, in conjunction with the continued large role of the private industrial consumer goods sector, permitted changes in agricultural production, both cylical and secular, to have a major effect on overall output and investment rates. Analysis of this record not only helps explain the past, but also gives a particularly useful perspective on the significance of the relationship between agricultural and industry in an employment-oriented strategy of growth.

Shifts in relative agricultural prices affect real wages, money wages, and the demand for nonagricultural commodities—all factors that influence production, profit rates, and investment in the industrial sector. The jump in industrial investment and production in the early 1960s was facilitated by a short-term upsurge in agricultural production cased by good weather and relatively low prices. It was sustained for a while by a subsequent rapid growth in food imports. An increase in demand resulting from higher incomes and the lack of wage goods constraint to employment served both to accelerate expansion of output and to boost profit levels. As these forces gained momentum, demand outpaced supply, despite the rapid growth in imports, and foodgrain prices rose sharply.

While foodgrain production advanced at a rate of 5.6 percent per year from the drought period of 1957–58 to 1961–62, demand did not keep up (Table II-2). Consequently, prices of foodgrains—relative to those of manufactured goods—declined by 10 percent during that period (Figure II-2). At the same time, the rate of profits in the private industrial sector rose 50 percent, while retained profits as a percentage of capital formation seem also to have increased (Table VI-1). The combination of low and stable prices of wage goods and high rates of profit is particularly conducive to investment in relatively labor intensive industries.

Then, from the low of 1961–62 to 1964–65, foodgrain prices soared relative to prices of manufactures by nearly one-third, or about 10 percent per year, exceeding the previous record high of 1952–53 (Figure II-2).[8] They climbed 3 percent from 1961–62 to 1962–63, another 8 percent by 1963–64, and leaped 21 percent by 1964–65. While the money supply was rising by about one-third, foodgrain prices leaped 45 percent (Figure VI-2).

[8] For a careful and perceptive analysis of relative price movements, see R. Thamarajakshi, "Intersectoral Terms of Trade and Marketed Surplus of Agricultural Produce, 1951–52 to 1965–66," *Economic and Political Weekly,* 4:26 (June 28, 1969), A-91–102.

Table VI-1. Sources of investment resources, private industrial sector, India, 1951–52 to 1964–65

		Percent of resources available for investment		
Year	Profits after tax as percentage of net worth	Retained profits	Depreciation allowance	Borrowings
1951–52	9.6	28	31	41
1952–53	5.7	30	111	−41
1953–54	6.8	30	67	3
1954–55	7.8	22	38	40
1955–56	9.1	30	37	33
1956–57	8.8	17	25	58
1957–58	6.5	8	29	63
1958–59	7.1	16	46	38
1959–60	10.5	39	57	4
1960–61	11.0	22	44	32
1961–62	10.0	22	48	30
1962–63	8.7	16	46	38
1963–64	9.5	19	45	36
1964–65	9.3	17	45	38

Sources: Column 1: Reserve Bank of India, Bulletin, various issues; columns 2–4: Ujagar S. Bawa, Agricultural Production and Industrial Capital Formation, India, 1951–52 to 1964–65, Cornell International Agricultural Development Bulletin No. 17, Cornell University, March 1971, Table 11, for which the source was Reserve Bank of India, Bulletin, September 1957, June 1962, and November 1966.

The inadequate growth in foodgrain production restrained industrial expansion, which was also suffering from a similar lag in the production of industrial raw material crops, such as cotton and oilseed, and other food commodities—for example, livestock products and fruits and vegetables. In 1957, 46 percent of the value added in registered Indian industry occurred in the industries processing such materials (Appendix, Table 11). The prices of agricultural raw materials other than foodgrains had fluctuated within a narrow range between 1956–57 and 1963–64 and then jumped by almost 50 percent in three years.

Change in relative agricultural prices indicates an underlying shift in the availability of resources to various groups in a society. Thus, the rise in agricultural production from 1957–58 to 1960–61 increased the national income significantly. Such an increase is initially distributed in much the same way as the benefits from technological change. A large proportion of the agricultural production increase is marketed and thereby creates purchasing power for nonagricultural commodities. If agricultural prices are maintained, the additional purchasing power emanates from farmers. If, as is more likely in the short run, relative agricultural prices decline, that same purchasing power and demand transfer to the nonagricultural sector. Provided that the supply of nonagricultural commodities is highly responsive to price, growth in nonagricultural production is commensurate with increasing demand. If, however, production is not responsive, the price of the unyielding factor of production—for example, capital—rises. The very fact that the food supply increases at a steady or declining price will ensure that the labor supply will not be a constraint to growth. In this situation, the gain in employment is not so much a result of the decline in the cost of labor due to lower prices of wage goods, but rather of an increase in the demand for nonagricultural commodities due to higher national income. If a capital shortage restrains an increase in output, industrial prices will rise relative to the prices of agricultural commodities and of labor; the increased profits should then help relax the capital restraint.

Thus, from 1957–58 to 1960–61, industrial profits rose as a result of a buoyant demand and a ready supply of labor. The more jobholders, the greater the demand for agricultural commodities, so agricultural prices and money wages went up. But once bad weather had ended the stimulation to agricultural production, industrial demand stopped growing, and yet agricultural prices still increased, now due to the drop in agricultural production. Industrial profits were therefore squeezed between rising costs and stagnant demand. The import of food under aid terms postponed the adjustment, as it substituted for domestic production by providing an addition of real goods (hence, creating income and demand) while ensuring support for a further enlargement of the labor supply. Clearly, domestic agricultural production was a weak element of the industrial growth effort of the early 1960s. Three courses of action were open if the rate of employment increase was to be sustained: technological change in agriculture, even more importation of foodgrains, and rationing of foodgrains.

Increased imports of foodgrains were unlikely to result from foreign aid—first, because of a growing reluctance on the part of the United States to continue to supply food aid at high levels; second, because India was discovering that such massive assistance was furnishing increased political leverage to the contributors. Nor could increased food imports be financed commercially without a major change in industrial policy leading to a much more successful export record. Foodgrain imports in 1964–65, prior to the drought, were already equal in value to one-quarter of the total exports in that year (Appendix, Tables 11 and 12).

An alternative to further imports would have been the mandatory reduction of food consumption (rationing) by upper-income purchasers in order to release food for the newly employed lower-income people and to transfer the demand of upper-income people from agricultural to industrial commodities. Higher food prices are not effective for this purpose because the well-to-do have an inelastic demand for food, and the demand of the poor is elastic. But in any case, production of alternative consumer goods was constrained by the planning emphasis on allocating resources to the output of capital goods. In the absence of equivalent consumer goods, rationing would have had to be accompanied by a commensurate level of taxation—or forced savings—to mop up the additional purchasing power. Accordingly, the growth strategy and the political penalties of taxation both stood in the way of the option of rationing.

Without increased domestic production, imports, or rationing, political pressures from the middle classes forcing either monetary or fiscal restraint would shortly contain the rate of employment growth. Over the long term, rising relative prices would increase money wages, decrease demand for industrial goods, and therefore squeeze profit margins and reduce business expansion. The more labor intensive businesses would, of course, be most sensitive to these developments.

The success of the early 1960s demonstrates that industrial employment growth rates in India can surpass the record of many other low-income countries, but also that supporting such rapid employment growth rates requires much more food than a traditional agriculture normally supplies.

The Capital and Savings Constraint

A high rate of capital formation was necessary to the sharp growth of industrial production attained in the early 1960s. But the capital intensive strategy of investment restricted retained profits, and limited the attractions for private savings. At the same time, the political system seemed ill-designed for the accumulation of public savings in quantity. Therefore, India looked to a large increase in foreign aid to pay the costs of accelerated expansion.

Savings data vary substantially, depending on the calculating procedures. The *Fourth Plan Mid-Term Appraisal* estimated that domestic savings amounted to 8.9 percent of national income (at market prices) in 1960–61 and only 9.8 percent in 1964–65 (Figure VI-1a). That is a compound growth rate of 2.4 percent for the four years, compared to a rate of 5.1 percent for 1950–51 to 1960–61. A rise in the savings rate to 11.1 percent in 1965–66 is accounted for by a small increase in savings and a sharp drop in national income; subsequently the domestic savings rate declined to as low as 7.9 percent in 1967–68, before starting gradually to recover.

From 1960–61 to 1964–65, the growth in savings in the government sector increased one-third, from 2.1 to 2.8 percent of national income. But this proportion had peaked in 1963–64, and it seems likely that political pressures and the economic effects of wage goods inflation would have prevented a further rise. The household savings rate went up from 6.1 to 6.5 percent of national income during the same period. That level would be difficult to maintain, too, given the wage goods inflation.

Most disturbing, however, was the fact that savings in the corporate sector as a percentage of national income rose slightly until 1961–62 and then dropped by nearly half by 1964–65. The absolute quantity of such savings in constant prices fell by over one-quarter in this period. Although growth in the private sector can be sustained, in substantial part, through loans from the banking system and from the government, it probably requires, under present circumstances, some balance between its own retained savings and borrowings. Consequently, the decline in savings in the corporate sector was likely to presage a drop in investment and, later, in the expansion of employment.

During the period 1961–62 to 1964–65, total investment in the Indian economy was, of course, growing faster than savings because of large net foreign resource transfers, mainly the product of foreign aid. These averaged 1,019 million dollars per year in the Third Plan period, compared to 624 million in the Second Plan period, and 269 million in the First Plan period. Accordingly, even though domestic savings and investment rose during this period, net foreign resource transfers, as a proportion of total investment, increased from 17.2 percent in the First Plan period to 23.1 percent in the Second Plan period, before slipping to 21.2 percent in the Third Plan period.

Industrial expansion from 1960–61 to 1965–66 depended heavily upon the large increase in foreign aid during the preceding period. Continuing the Third Plan pace would require (1) reduction in the capital content of growth, (2) still more foreign aid, or (3) an increased rate of domestic savings. Each would be difficult to achieve.

The capital constraint could have been relieved by a basic change in strategy toward a more employment-oriented structure, but India already faced a major agricultural constraint from the insufficient growth in agriculture to provide the wage goods necessary to back increased employment and wage payments. Shifting the strategy toward employment would have required more food. Importing food would have depended upon greater exports of other commodities or larger foreign food aid. The alternatives involved domestic changes, including rigorous rationing of food and fiscal restraint, or accelerated technological change in foodgrain production.

Ex post, a continued increase in foreign aid seems an unreasonable expectation, given its subsequent rapid decline. But India has consistently received only very small amounts of aid per capita. It is quite possible that a quantum of assistance per person, maintained for a decade at the levels received by Taiwan, South Korea, Chile, Israel, or even West Pakistan would have moved India into a period of self-sustaining growth within the context of the capital intensive strategy and without the privation implicit in providing the bulk of savings domestically.

While the burden of meeting the rapidly growing need for capital was to fall heavily on the capacity for domestic saving, public policies were at odds with the practical aspects of meeting that need.

According to the Plan theory, public sector enterprises, particularly those in heavy industry, would, through a high profit rate, provide a large portion of the resources for their own accelerated expansion. The practice was sharply counter to the theory. Indeed, the public corporate sector, while accounting for a bigger and bigger portion of total industrial activity, was to a much smaller extent self-financed from ''profits'' than the private sector, thereby increasing the strain on alternative sources of equity. During the Second Plan, capital resources were heavily invested in enterprises which would not show a profit for a very long time. According to Bhagwati and Desai, public sector concerns had more than Rs. 2.4 billion of invested capital in 1965–66; of eleven such firms whose employed capital exceeded Rs. 100 million by 1964, only five showed a positive gross profit on capital in 1960–61; and none had a level of profits as high as the average of 10.1 percent exhibited in the Reserve Bank of India's analysis of 1,333 public limited companies.[9] As of March 31,

[9] Bhagwati and Desai, ch. ix, particularly Tables 9.4, 9.5, and 9.6.

1972, central government industrial undertakings disclosed a net loss of Rs. 1,173 million.[10] In fact, a number of public sector concerns did make acceptable profits, but they were relatively small firms.[11] The total public sector results were, of course, dominated by Hindustan Steel, which still claimed nearly 40 percent of all government industrial investment in 1965–66 and was showing substantial losses even through the late 1960s.

The low profits of public sector steel, in some years, may have been due to pricing policies which transferred benefits to steel users, but in general they were the result, first, of long construction delays and, subsequently, of a low utilization of capacity.[12] Poor performance at the outset may simply be the cost of learning to operate a large-scale industry in the public sector with the possibility of making future political and economic gains. In the short run, it created a major problem for further investment.

Although the private area of the economy relied much more heavily than the public segment on retained earnings as a source of investment capital, it too used a high proportion of borrowed funds and, as time went on, depended on them for an increasing share of its expansion requirements. Consequently, in 1960–61, retained earnings of the private corporate sector comprised 23 percent of gross capital formation, compared to 3 percent for the public sector in the same year. In the period 1951–52 to 1960–61, the private segment drew 41 percent of its investable resources from depreciation allowances, 36 percent from borrowings, and 23 percent from retained profits (Table VI-1). The small proportion of investment accounted for by retained earnings and depreciation was less ominous than their decline over time. Borrowings increased rela-

---

[10] This figure refers to net loss after prior period adjustment. See Government of India, Ministry of Finance, Bureau of Public Enterprises (Finance Division), *Annual Report of the Working of Industrial and Commercial Undertakings of the Central Government, 1971–72* (New Delhi), Table II-B.

[11] Bhagwati and Desai, Table 9.6.

[12] The March 9, 1968, issue of *Commerce* reported: "It is well known that a majority of public sector projects have taken a longer time to complete than was initially estimated, the benefits from them have come much later than expected, their capital costs have been higher than originally planned and consequently the returns from them have been smaller than anticipated" (p. 645). "Utilisation of installed capacity in steel during 1970–71 has been of the order of only 67 percent as against 71 percent in the previous year. In the case of the public sector steel plants, utilisation was as low as 59 percent." (*Economic Survey, 1970–71*, p. 17).

ive to retained earnings—a trend to become much more marked in the Third Plan period. As a result, in the 1961–62 to 1963–64 period, retained profits made up an average of 18.5 percent of investment resources, compared to 27.5 percent in the 1951–52 to 1953–54 period. This drop occurred despite the fact that the average profit rate had increased by 25 percent in the later period. More and more, the private sector would be competing directly with the public sector for financial resources.

At the same time that the household sector was to be particularly hard-pressed for capital, the strategy of development discouraged growth of those small-scale industries which could best attract savings; private industrial profits were in decline; and political exigencies hindered raising taxes.

The level of taxes on urban incomes by 1965 seemed to have reached the point of diminishing collections. Essentially all tax commissions, both foreign and domestic, had recommended a large increase in agricultural taxes as the best way to relax the capital constraint.[13]

The desirability of a net transfer of resources from agriculture to other sectors depends on the objectives and means of economic development. The Second Plan's emphasis on increasing capital goods production would have been assisted by a net transfer of resources from agriculture if that could have been achieved without reducing the rate of growth. Taxing higher-income farmers more heavily would also have forwarded the equity objective of the plan.

Ved Gandhi estimates that from 1951 to 1961, agriculture's share of taxes paid was considerably less than its share of public expenditures. Agriculture was responsible for a net drain of the public finances of other sectors despite the fact that production was growing slowly, primarily through the traditional means of expanded acreage, irrigation, and intensified use of labor. Ved Gandhi calculates that the share of the central and state governments' expenditures on current account allocated to agriculture increased from Rs. 2,860 million to Rs. 7,210 million between 1950–51 and 1960–61, while revenue increased from Rs. 1,860 million

---

[13] See I. M. D. Little, "Tax Policy and the Third Plan," in P. N. Rosenstein-Rodan, ed., *Pricing and Fiscal Policies: A Study in Method,* (Cambridge, Mass.: M.I.T. Press, 1964), pp. 30–76; Nicholas Kaldor, *Indian Tax Reform: Report of a Survey* (New Delhi: Government of India, Ministry of Finance, Department of Economic Affairs, 1956); and Government of India, Ministry of Finance, *Report of the Committee on Taxation of Agricultural Wealth and Income* (Raj Committee) (New Delhi, October 1972).

to Rs. 3,990 million in the same period.[14] The balance on capital account is even more heavily weighted toward agriculture.

In agriculture, the proportion of taxes paid to income rose between 1950–51 and 1960–61 from 3.6 to 5.6 percent, while in the nonagricultural sector it increased from 8.8 to 13.1 percent; the proportion of nonagricultural income paid in taxes was consistently two and one-third times higher than that for agriculture. Only 7.5 percent of additional income was paid in taxes by agriculture, compared to 44 percent for the nonagricultural sector in the period 1950–51 to 1964–65.[15] More striking from an equity point of view is the fact that in 1960–61, the agricultural upper-income class, owning 50 acres or more, paid only 6.6 percent of their income in taxes, contrasted to 18 percent in the comparable nonagricultural income class.[16]

Without tax reform, agriculture would provide little additional revenue. Similarly, the slowly growing agricultural sector had little scope for contributing to the accumulation of capital, either through a decline in relative prices or direct investment of increased rural incomes in small industries.

Thus, at a time when both large-scale public and private corporate enterprises were forced increasingly to seek investment funds from the household sector, the largest element of that sector, agriculture, was not managed in a manner adequate for providing those funds out of current income; nor was a strategy followed to raise the rural tax base through rapid technological change.

The inevitability of a retardation of industrial expansion in the mid-1960s is evident from the alternatives available for obtaining financial resources. Increased public revenues from the private household or corporate sector would have further restrained the growth of the more efficient and profitable private sector. Under the conditions of the 1960s, for each rupee transferred from the private to the public sector, there

[14] These data are drawn from Tables 15, 16, and 25 of Ved P. Gandhi, *Tax Burden on Indian Agriculture* (Cambridge, Mass.: The Law School of Harvard University, 1966). One crore equals ten million.

[15] Bawa, pp. 32–33, particularly Table 17.

[16] Gandhi, Tables 30 and 32. Note in this respect the much higher tax burden on agriculture shown by Mahesh T. Pathak and Arun S. Patel, *Agricultural Taxation in Gujarat* (New York: Asia Publishing House, 1970), as compared with the data of Ved Gandhi. Their results follow from a study of Gujarat State at a later time; both influences were associated with higher farm incomes, a higher degree of commercialization of agriculture, and a higher proportion of expenditure on purchased consumer items.

would have been a net reduction in the advance of industrial output and an even greater decline in the growth of employment.

The Administrative Constraint

The development strategy of the Second and Third Five-Year Plans placed a decision-making burden on a bureaucracy that had little technical competence for those types of allocative decisions. The resulting low level of economic efficiency included the poor use of resources, unfavorable rates of return, and retarded growth. Increased bureaucratic control of the economy intensified the problems.

The Second Plan's strategy of development emphasized growth of the capital stock as the basic engine of expansion and mandated direct administrative allocation of resources, rather than the operation of "imperfect" market forces, as the means of driving the engine. The emphasis on capital formation, in effect, favored the large-scale capital goods industries which were most logically located in the public sector. The emphasis on direct allocation of resources contributed to an intricate system of licensing for regulating the growth of industry throughout the economy and for governing imports. These controls were thought necessary to direct resources into the capital goods industries. Administration of both the public sector industries and the licensing systems fell largely into the hands of the government bureaucracy.

Since the political ideology of the time emphasized socialism over private enterprise and served to reinforce the economic strategy, the responsibilities of the bureaucracy multiplied.[17] The fact that India had inherited from the British a large, disciplined administrative organization undoubtedly also encouraged the allocation of tasks to public officials. But the colonial staff had had little experience with technology or, more important, with growth. Thus, in the postcolonial period administrative performance was poor. Not only were the public sector enterprises generally inefficient and unprofitable, but the regulatory function of licensing industrial capacity was also badly performed. This is voluminously documented by Bhagwati and Desai and numerous study groups such as the

---

[17] For example, with regard to the agricultural sector, see the recurrent history of public takeover of the grain trade in Uma J. Lele, *Food Grain Marketing in India: Private Performance and Public Policy* (Ithaca, N.Y.: Cornell University Press, 1971), Appendix 1: "Official Policy on Food Grain Prices and Marketing," pp. 225–37.

Hazari commission.[18] The consequence of the weaknesses has been a substantial misallocation of existing resources and a failure to realize potentials for mobilizing additional means of production.

In principle, the bureaucracy faltered because of an inadequately detailed set of guidelines. The initial plan had divided the economy into sectors and specified the allocation of resources to each sector. Over time, new tools of aggregate input-output systems and, eventually, multisectoral dynamic programming models, were developed to obtain for any given objective the precise distribution of resources to each industry. By 1965, quite detailed models of the economy had been constructed.[19] Ideally, the function of the bureaucracy was to see that the resources were allocated as stated in the system. The authorities would then have had a rather straightforward administrative task, not unlike that imposed by the demands of a colonial government. The approach was workable as long as the economy and the operational rules were simple or the planning models commensurately complex. The first conditions largely held in the Second Plan period. The allocational decisions were in effect made mainly within the context of restraining the growth of consumption goods industries and involved allotting resources principally to steel and, to a certain extent, heavy machinery production. Exports were to receive little attention. As a result, licensing for both domestic production and imports could follow relatively simple rules.

But even this uncomplicated approach presented problems. First, consumer goods can be converted to capital goods through trade, and consumer goods provided some of India's most promising export potential. If exports of such goods were to succeed, the products might often require imported components. The planning models gave few answers to the problem of obtaining such components. The resulting arbitrary bureaucratic decisions bore little relationship to economic efficiency. Second, increasing employment requires a large production of labor intensive consumer goods, unless accompanied by a tight income policy. Without

---

[18] "The licensing authority and the departments which service it are loaded at any one time with hundreds or thousands of proposals, without clear and definite criteria to appraise their worth in terms of relative costs and the attainment of targets in related, particularly basic, industries/projects" (R. K. Hazari, *Industrial Planning and Licensing Policy*, Final Report, Vol. I (New Delhi: Government of India, Planning Commission, 1967), p. 20.

[19] See the input/output table constructed by the Government of India, Planning Commission, entitled "Structure of the Indian Economy: Inter-Industrial Flows and Pattern of Final Demand."

restraint on income, resources leak into consumer goods production, confounding the plans and placing allocational demands on the bureaucracy for which the planning models provided no solutions.

During the Third Plan period, the complexity of the decisions about the distribution of resources became greater as diverse industries expanded, consumer incomes rose, and exports began to be encouraged. The difficulty of these decisions then completely outran the capacity of the economic models.

Lacking adequate analytical tools, the bureaucracy would have to turn to technical knowledge of the matters which required decisions. But the administrative structure inherited from the British was perhaps even more backward than that of Britain itself in recognizing the importance of technical knowledge in terms of salary and promotional advances. D. R. Gadgil, then deputy chairman of the Planning Commission, put it clearly: "The 'generalist,' i.e., the Indian civil servant and his successor, the I.A.S. [Indian Administrative Services], still completely dominates the scene. There is an enormous concentration of power on top in this strata and new elements of specialists or managers of business still rank low in prestige and authority." [20]

In the public sector firms, where management was largely in the hands of the civil service, the consequences were disastrous. As commission after commission reported on just this problem, the civil service fought vigorously and largely successfully to prevent reform.[21] Furthermore, decisions on licensing were made by civil servants who regularly changed jobs and therefore lacked experience and technical knowledge. Administrative procedures and organizational structures impeded the entrance of persons with the necessary professional talent. Also, the policy of frequent transfer prevented those already in the system from acquiring and employing the appropriate knowledge.[22] These tendencies were rein-

[20] Quoted in Bhagwati and Desai, p. 131.

[21] Bhagwati and Desai, pp. 164–95; H. K. Paranjape, *The Industrial Management Pool: An Administrative Experiment* (New Delhi: Indian Institute of Public Administration, 1962); H. K. Paranjape, *The Flight of Technical Personnel in Public Undertakings* (New Delhi: Indian Institute of Public Administration, 1964); and A. H. Hanson, *The Process of Planning* (London: Oxford University Press, 1966), ch. viii.

[22] "Numerous studies have shown that the task of management was seriously underestimated by the traditional civil service, who proceeded to assume most of the managerial functions in these complex, industrial enterprises in the assured belief that their general, nonspecialized expertise would be adequate to the job. The effect of this was not merely general incompetence but rapid turnover of people in important roles. . . . At the same

forced by the "club" atmosphere of the civil service, which can apply group pressure to prevent change from within the system.[23]

If the capital intensive, import displacement strategy was to be continued, major administrative reform was necessary. The operation of the public sector would have to improve sufficiently to provide a primary source of capital, consistent with the underlying objective. And, given the inadequacy of the planning models, the administrative services would have to substitute experiential knowledge for instruction from the programmed systems.

An alternative strategy of rapid growth of agriculture, consumer goods industries, small-scale industry, and exports calls for even more radical administrative reform. The basic operating scheme of favoring capital over consumer goods is abandoned. At the same time, expansion of the agricultural and smaller-scale industrial sectors demands a reservoir of scientific knowledge for the development of facilitating institutions. Such circumstances cry out for a professionally competent administrative service that will petition the free market for assistance in resolving problems. Some movement in this direction can be detected: many civil servants now specialize by remaining in at least technically related posts over time and by studying scientific subjects, while more and more are technicians rising to administrative posts. Only official support over time will enable these changes to bear fruit.

Drought, Declining Aid, and Industrial Stagnation—1965 to 1973

India entered what was to have been the Fourth Five-Year Plan with a rate of growth that was to be severely reduced: inadequate expansion in agricultural production retarded advancement in demand, employment, and savings; insufficient increase in the savings rate slowed capital formation; and an administrative service ineffective for the circumstances was generally debilitating. What would, in any case, have been a difficult and uncertain period of adjustment in 1965–66 was turned into a disaster by

---

time it has meant that . . . these officials have inevitably tended to act with bureaucratic caution and unimaginativeness rather than in bold and inventive ways. While efforts to move towards more efficient and stable management . . . have been made, they have proved only a little better than abortive" (Bhagwati and Desai, pp. 164–65).

[23] "The I.C.S. and the I.A.S. function as an exclusive club and it is openly alleged that you cannot function effectively in top positions in administration unless you belong to this group" (D. R. Gadgil, then chairman of the Planning Commission, New Delhi, India, 1953, as quoted in Bhagwati and Desai, p. 131).

the worst drought on record, which shrank the supply of wage goods and greatly reduced industrial demand and domestic savings. A sudden decline in net foreign aid further cut demand for industrial output as well as the supply of capital goods. Then came a second drought, exacerbated by a worldwide fertilizer shortage in 1972–73 and 1973–74. Political instability added to the difficulty initially, but in the latter part of the period it was more the result of the faltering economy.

Industrial production, which grew at the rate of 8.9 percent per year from 1960 to 1964, advanced at only 3.4 percent per annum from 1964 to 1968. In 1965 to 1967, the actual drought period, industrial output did not grow at all. The following year saw recovery: output increased by 6.4 percent, rose to 7.0 percent the year after that, then slid back, and rose at a rate of only 3.8 percent from 1969 to 1973 (Figure VI-1). In the 1965 to 1973 period as a whole, the industrial sector lagged behind the agricultural sector in output growth rate (Table I-2).

Domestic savings as a proportion of national income dropped sharply, from 11.1 percent in 1965–66 to 9.0 percent in 1966–67, and declined further, to 7.9 percent in 1967–68, before making a partial recovery in 1968–69 (Figure VI-1a). The plunge in industrial profits because costs were up and demand was down, the rapid fall in real government expenditure due to a reduction in foreign aid receipts and lowered budget deficits, and the decline in household income all served to diminish both the incentive and the ability to save and invest.

The industrial recession struck particularly hard at the capital goods industries. The *Economic Times* Index showed output in this sector growing at a 28.8 percent rate from 1960 to 1965 and at a minus 5.1 percent rate from 1965 to 1970.[24] The reasons are probably related, first, to the drought and the decline in foreign aid, and second, to the structural imbalance of excessive capacity relative to demand in this period of economic stagnation. The government's dwindling ability to finance capital expenditure produced a dramatic cutback. Output of railroad equipment virtually evaporated to nearly a third of its 1965 level by 1970; meanwhile shortages of railcars were inhibiting the movement of grain from the Punjab, fertilizer from the ports, and coal from Bihar.[25]

Of greater long-run concern, the structure of the capital goods indus-

[24] See the *Economic Times*, 11:156 (Sunday, August 8, 1971), 7.
[25] See, for example, K. S. Gill, *Wheat Marketing Behavior in Punjab and Haryana: Post Harvest Period, 1968–69—1970–71,* Punjab Agricultural University Bulletin, 1971.

tries was based on assumptions about the planned growth rate. Errors or changes in these assumptions, plus inevitable miscalculations in the planning process itself, were bound to result in overcapacity in some of these industries.

Government expenditures and deficits rose substantially subsequent to 1964–65, but it seems likely that the structure of those expenditures was different from that of the earlier period and may have simply aggravated inflationary pressures by increasing requirements in sectors for which physical resources were not available for expansion, while leaving other sectors with insufficient demand (Table VI-2).

Table VI-2. Combined receipts and disbursements of central and state governments, India 1960–61 through 1972–73 *
(in ten million rupees)

Year	Revenue account			Capital account		Total surplus (+) or deficit (−)
	Revenue receipts	Tax revenue	Revenue expenditure	Capital receipts	Capital disbursements	
1960–61	1,710	1,355	1,634	1,266	1,283	+ 59
1961–62	1,846	1,537	1,769	1,122	1,351	−152
1962–63	2,424	1,855	2,287	1,319	1,584	−128
1963–64	2,999	2,313	2,734	1,469	1,906	−172
1964–65	3,330	2,585	3,006	1,850	2,307	−133
1965–66	3,689	2,902	3,411	1,801	2,431	−352
1966–67	4,026	3,240	3,856	2,485	2,956	−301
1967–68	4,361	3,423	4,264	2,369	2,710	−244
1968–69	4,846	3,727	4,742	2,145	2,631	−382
1969–70	5,392	4,182	5,318	2,836	2,898	+ 12
1970–71	5,958	4,735	5,812	2,611	3,183	−426
1971–72	7,043	5,516	7,178	3,089	3,585	−631
1972–73	7,842	6,322	7,413	2,739	3,410	−242

* 1971–72 is a revised estimate; 1972–73 is a budget estimate.
Source: Reserve Bank of India, Report on Currency and Finance, Bombay, various issues.

As late as 1974, industry showed little evidence of recovery from the preceding decade of reduced growth, but several circumstances did suggest the basis for a vigorous revival. First, although the drought of 1972–73 to 1973–74 and the worldwide fertilizer shortage darkened the prospects for agriculture, both those situations were temporary, and food-grain production was definitely established at a higher growth rate than in the past, with a consequently relaxed wage goods constraint and expanded demand for consumer goods. Second, foreign resource transfers had stopped declining and may indeed have been ready for a significant increase, which would relax the capital constraint—although not by as much as in the early 1960s. Third, the structural imbalances resulting from errors in planning might have worked themselves out by that time, eliminating the drag of a decline in several industrial subsectors. Indeed, although the data are too fragmentary to provide complete support, it seems likely that by the mid-1970s the small-scale industrial sector was already evidencing greatly accelerated growth.

Comparative Industrial Growth in Taiwan and India

India may now have the opportunity for a period of accelerated development based on the stimulation of rapid technological change and growth in the agricultural sector. Such a pattern of expansion has few historical precedents. The details of the pace and the pattern of economic development of each nation represent a unique adaptation to physical, technological, political, and social environments. Although one can take detailed lessons neither from the central tendency of many countries nor from the specifics of one, Taiwan is of particular interest because of its recent history of rural-led, employment-oriented growth.

In 1971, India's population was thirty-six times that of Taiwan, although its national income was only ten times larger (Table VI-3). India's greater size and broader endowment of resources facilitate greater diversification in the economy. Its economic environment is particularly conducive to entry into large-scale, capital intensive industries. The comparison with Taiwan is made in order to illustrate the effects of a more labor intensive approach to development based substantially on growth in agriculture and a derived expansion in domestic demand. India's size may be of some advantage in this approach, but certainly not as much as it would be in a capital intensive strategy.

Size does affect a country's involvement in foreign trade. It may be argued that a nation of India's size, with a broad market and large industrial base, has more limited opportunities in exports—because of its impact on aggregate world trade and relative prices—than a smaller country. However, even in 1971, Taiwan's total exports were only 2 percent smaller than India's, and the increment to exports over the preceding decade was 2.6 times larger, equal to 89 percent of India's foreign shipments in 1971. Of course, Taiwan industrialists can now export a much higher proportion of output than Indian manufacturers, with consequently less dependence on the domestic market.

Taiwan's record of economic growth in the 1950s and early 1960s indicates that its technological possibilities in agriculture and other sectors were similar to those now available to India. Population growth rates during this period are roughly comparable to those facing contemporary India. Indeed, population growth in Taiwan in the early 1950s and 1960s was, owing to a high rate of natural increase and immigration, much faster than India's even in the 1970s. While in many respects Taiwan had not already progressed further in economic development in 1951 than India had in 1971, the comparison must be carefully qualified. In 1951, Taiwan's national income per capita was one-fourth smaller than India's in 1971, and the structure of the economy had not yet become radically different from India's. Sixty-two percent of Taiwan's labor force was still in agriculture in 1951, compared to 72 percent in India in 1971; net domestic product in agriculture was 34 percent in 1951 in Taiwan, compared to 45 percent in India in 1971. The percentage of net domestic product in manufacturing was 20 percent in Taiwan in 1951 and 23 percent in India in 1971. A comparison of the two countries indicates that in 1951 Taiwan had a more diverse industrial structure than India had in the same year. For example, Taiwan had only 17 percent of manufacturing production in textiles, compared to 27 percent for India.[26] But by 1971, India's industrial composition had broadened considerably and was, in its diversity, perhaps more comparable with Taiwan in 1951. Domestic savings rates were significantly higher in India in 1971 than in Taiwan in 1952 (Table VI-3).

Perhaps surprisingly, Taiwan's industry in 1951 was more heavily in the public sector than India's in 1961, but by 1971 the proportion in Taiwan had dropped by almost half. Taiwan's agricultural output, from 1952 to 1961, grew 20 percent more quickly than India's during the same period. (India's rate was substantially influenced by the poor weather at the beginning of the period and good weather at the end, and should perhaps be more realistically depicted as less than 3 percent, thereby increasing further the margin in Taiwan's favor.) Perhaps more revealing is the fact that Taiwan's rate of agricultural growth was one-third faster than

[26] Kou-shu Liang and T. H. Lee, "Process and Pattern of Economic Development in Taiwan," unpublished paper, Joint Committee on Rural Reconstruction, Taipei, Taiwan, 1972, Table 7, for which the source was Directorate-General of Budgets, Accounts and Statistics, Executive Yuan, *National Income of the Republic of China,* October 1971, pp. 86–89, Table II.

India's from 1961 to 1971 (Table VI-3), but was nevertheless actually slower than the rate suggested as a realistic potential for India in Chapter III and the rate used in the calculations of Chapter VII.

A matter for contrast is defense expenditure, which for Taiwan averaged 12 percent of the gross national product from 1955 to 1965, and accounted for nearly 60 percent of all government expenditure.[27] For India, the comparable figures would be about 3 percent of GNP and one-third of government expenditure. The effect of the difference is difficult to assess. If such expenditure is entirely unproductive of growth, it would represent a large offset to Taiwan's foreign aid.

Three features of Taiwan's record of growth in the 1950s and 1960s are particularly relevant to India. First, although Taiwan's economy grew relatively rapidly in the 1950s, the period of explosive advance did not basically occur until the 1960s. Accordingly, the rate of growth of national income increased 42 percent from the 1950s to the 1960s. This was largely owing to great acceleration in the pace of expansion of industry, from 12 percent in the earlier period to 17 percent in the 1960s. Savings, as a percentage of national income (at market prices), progressed from 4.3 percent in 1952 to 7.1 percent in 1961, and climbed to 23.3 percent in 1971, while the rate of net capital formation jumped from 11.1 percent to 20.8 percent. Similarly, the rate of increase of exports was 7.7 percent in the 1950s and 27 percent from 1961 to 1971 (Table VI-3).

The base figures for Taiwan in 1951 and the growth achieved from then to 1961 are not sharply different from India's record of development in the early 1960s. India's domestic savings rate alone has almost touched the rate of capital formation on which Taiwan's growth in the early 1950s was based (Table VI-3). It is this potential comparability which makes the overall correspondence interesting.

The calculations in Chapter III suggest the potential for India to achieve a comparable or higher rate of growth in the agricultural sector than did Taiwan in the 1950s and 1960s. The agricultural expansion may, however, require more capital investment than was needed in Taiwan in the 1950s. In 1951, over half of the cultivated area of Taiwan was already irrigated, compared to about one-fifth in 1970 in India. Thus, while Taiwan was able to draw heavily on agriculture for resources to develop

---

[27] Calculated from Council for International Economic Co-operation and Development, Executive Yuan, Republic of China, *Taiwan Statistical Data Book, 1972,* June 1972.

Table VI-3. India and Taiwan: A comparison

Item	Units	India	Taiwan
Area	Thousand square km.	3,268.1 (1) *	35.9 (2)
Population	Million persons		
1951		356.8 (3)	7.9 (2)
1961		441.6	11.1
1971		548.0	15.0
National income	Million U.S.$		
1951	(current prices)	20,937 (4)	573 (2)
1961		29,366	1,407
1971		49,554	4,851
Per capita national income	U.S.$ (current prices)		
1951		57.6 (4)	68.1 (2)
1961		66.2	122.3
1971		89.5	325.1
Industry as percent of national income			
1951		16 (4)	20 (2)
1961		24	25
1971		23	35
Agriculture as percent of national income			
1951		50 (4)	34 (2)
1961		44	31
1971		45	17
Growth rate of agricultural output			
1952–1961		3.4 (4)	4.1 (2)
1961–1971		2.7	3.6
Percent of employment in agriculture			
1951		69.7 (5)	62.0 (2)
1961		69.5	55.8
1971		71.6 †	42.3
Percent of cultivated land irrigated			
1951		17.6 (1)	55.6 (6)
1961		18.4	56.0
1970		22.2 (7)	51.8
Percent of industry in public sector			
1951		1.5 (8)	61.9 (2)
1961		8.4	43.9
1971		n.a.	26.7
Exports	Million U.S.$		
1951	(current prices)	1,503 (9)	93 (2)
1961		1,387	195
1971		2,092	2,060

Item	Units	India	Taiwan
Imports	Million U.S.$		
1951	(current prices)	1,838 (10)	144 (2)
1961		2,290	322
1971		2,416	1,844
Net foreign resource transfer as percent of national income ‡			
1951		1.6	8.9
1961		3.1	9.0
1971		0.7	−4.5
Net domestic saving as percent of national income (at market prices) §			
1952		3.9 (11)	4.3 (2)
1961		8.6 (12)	7.1
1971		10.0 (13)	23.3
Net investment as percent of national income (at market prices) §			
1952		3.8 (11)	11.1 (2)
1961		10.8 (12)	14.6
1971		11.5 (13)	20.8

* Numbers in parentheses refer to the sources listed below. All figures converted to U.S. dollars at official current exchange rates.
† Estimate. ‡ Net foreign resource transfer is defined as imports less exports.
§ National income at market prices for Taiwan computed by adding indirect taxes, less subsidies, to national income.

Sources:

(1) *Statistical Abstract of India* (New Delhi: Government of India, Directorate of Economics and Statistics), various issues.

(2) *Taiwan Statistical Data Book* (Council for International Economic Co-operation and Development, Executive Yuan, Republic of China), various issues.

(3) *United Nations Statistical Yearbook* (New York: United Nations, Statistical Office, Department of Economic and Social Affairs), various issues.

(4) *Economic Survey* (New Delhi: Government of India, Ministry of Finance), various issues.

(5) *Census of India* (New Delhi: Government of India, Office of the Registrar General), various issues.

(6) *Taiwan Statistical Abstract, 1972* (Provincial Government of Taiwan, China, Bureau of Accounting and Statistics).

(7) *Agriculture in Brief,* 13th ed. (New Delhi: Government of India, Directorate of Economics and Statistics, 1974).

(8) Ishrat H. Farooqi, *Macro Structure of Public Enterprise in India* (Aligarh: Aligarh Muslim University Press, 1968).

(9) Appendix, Table 12. (10) Appendix, Table 11.

(11) Reserve Bank of India, *Bulletin,* March 1965.

(12) Government of India, Planning Commission, *The Fourth Plan Mid-Term Appraisal,* Vol. I (December 1971).

(13) Reserve Bank of India, *Report on Currency and Finance, 1971/72.*

other sectors, India, for both political and economic reasons, may be less able to do so. On the other hand, because the technological state of Indian agriculture is initially very far behind that of Taiwan in 1951, there is a potential for a sharper increase in production and net income and hence for the self-financing of agriculture's investment needs.[28]

Nevertheless, the current potentials for India's growth in both the agricultural and the industrial sectors are surprisingly comparable with those for Taiwan in the late 1950s or early 1960s. However, since the agricultural segment still represents a larger proportion of the total economy in India than in Taiwan in 1951, similar rates of increase for the sectors would translate into somewhat lower overall rates of gain for India.

Agriculture played a very important role in the evolution of Taiwan's economy, influencing the structure and rate of advancement of both industry and trade. Greater agricultural production financed growth through major net transfers of resources out of the sector; it stimulated economic activity by providing a rapidly growing market for industrial goods; and most important of all, it assured the supply of wage goods necessary for a labor intensive approach to development which would conserve the scarce capital resources.[29] In Taiwan, a scarcity of capital produced a labor intensive strategy of capital accumulation. Agriculture produced the wage goods that the newly employed workers wanted to purchase and thereby facilitated rapid, noninflationary, growth in employment and output.

Real wages in Taiwan stayed roughly constant until the early 1960s, favoring both domestic production and, of course, exports.[30] In the 1960s, real wages rose more rapidly, climbing 50 percent in ten years—but by then savings rates had risen sharply, and a more capital intensive strategy was in order. As a result, labor productivity was able almost to double in the same period. For India, probably facing a larger pool of underemployed labor, the time for increasing real wages and more capital intensive growth would be somewhat further in the future than it was for Taiwan in 1951.

The second relevant feature of the Taiwan record of economic achievement is the substantial growth in exports in the 1950s and the explosive

[28] As a simplistic example, in 1970, rice yields in India averaged 1,209 kg. per hectare, compared to an average of 3,173 kg. per hectare for Taiwan, nearly three times higher than India. See Appendix Table 4, below, and *Taiwan Statistical Data Book, 1974*, Table 4-6a.

[29] See T. H. Lee, *Intersectoral Capital Flows in the Economic Development of Taiwan, 1895–1960* (Ithaca, N.Y.: Cornell University Press, 1971).

[30] See Liang and Lee, Table 10, p. 14.

rise in the 1960s, starting from a foundation even less promising than India's and advancing on the basis of production originally intended for the domestic market. The key role of the domestic market needs emphasizing in view of the common tendency to view Taiwan's development as principally export-led and therefore not reproducible in large countries. Exports did facilitate overall expansion of the economy, but they did not become dominant in the mix of things until after Taiwan attained a solid period of overall growth.

In Taiwan, even in the case of nondurable consumer goods, the proportion of exports to total domestic production was only 11 percent in 1960, rising to 21 percent in 1965, and to 55 percent in 1970. Metals and machinery exports have been a large component of foreign shipments, yet as a percent of total demand were only 1 percent in 1955 and 3 percent in 1960, but 8 percent in 1965 and 19 percent in 1970.[31] For consumer durables as well as metals and machinery, it appears that a dynamic domestic market permitted an expansion of production, which then favored exports. Government policy actively encouraged this process through subsidies of various types and technical assistance.

Taiwan's record seems to indicate that a policy of developing the domestic markets will also facilitate increased exports. India's export achievement may be creditable—given its previous level of development—but a vigorous promotion might hasten the growth rate substantially in the future.

The third noteworthy feature about Taiwan's development is the large net inflow of foreign resources (primarily in grant form) through 1965. However, India's domestic savings rates alone, at their maximum, have exceeded the level of Taiwan's domestic savings plus foreign aid in the early to mid-1950s. The extent of the privation of consumption that these higher savings rates caused, given the considerably lower per capita national income of India, was substantial. For Taiwan, net resource transfers came largely from American aid up to 1965; 82 percent of that was in the form of grants. Taiwan thus avoided the immense repayment problems India now faces, as a result of past assistance in loan form.[32] Any chance of India's emulating Taiwan's growth of the 1950s depends on India rescheduling her debt in order to reduce its burden. Net foreign resource transfers to Taiwan in the 1966 to 1970 period were only about

[31] Ibid., Table 22, p. 43.   [32] Ibid., pp. 20, 35–36.

one-quarter the average for the years 1953 to 1960, and by the later period most of the transfer was in the form of loans, and largely on private account.[33]

Foreign aid to Taiwan was employed largely on private imports of raw materials. India initially used the aid it received to purchase capital equipment. Currently, if India were to follow an employment-oriented strategy of growth it could use aid of the type received by Taiwan in the 1950s. The result of Taiwan's use of aid to purchase raw materials was to facilitate the expansion of labor intensive industries, which, as noted previously, are also large consumers of raw materials. In contrast, the earlier use of foreign aid in India to promote capital goods imports resulted in a capital intensive structure of production.

Foreign aid to both India and Taiwan, during the 1950s and early 1960s, probably served to reduce the short-run growth of exports. It did so by meeting import needs without the necessity of compensating exports. For India, the effect was to divert resources to capital intensive investment which had potential only in the distant future. For Taiwan, foreign aid probably helped sustain a level of domestic consumption which helped create a market for, and aided the additional expansion of, labor intensive industries which eventually found a strong export market. The decline in foreign aid to India may reduce the allocation of resources to capital goods, and the growth of income from agriculture may encourage industries with an eventual export potential. Renewed large-scale foreign aid for India could now reduce the constraints on raw material imports as well as the extremely heavy reliance on domestic savings, and encourage a rapid, labor intensive expansion of the industrial sector. Without such aid, economic development can be substantial, but it will probably be restricted by shortages of imported materials and, possibly, by the low level of domestic savings as well.

[33] Ibid., Table 19, p. 32.

VII | Rural Growth Linkages

Poor performance in agriculture is widely cited as a retardant to economic growth, but the potentially stimulating role of the rural sector is rarely recognized. Hirschman states, "Agriculture certainly stands convicted on the count of its lack of direct stimulus to the setting up of new activities through linkage effects—the superiority of manufacturing in this respect is crushing." [1]

But while traditional agriculture may well be a sector of diminishing returns and increasing costs, the conclusion that increased agricultural production must eventually become a net drain on the productivity of other sectors ignores the potentials and implications of rapid modernization of agriculture through technological change.

Lack of capital is normally seen to be the basic restraint to growth. This view finds increased consumption in conflict with development and incapable of providing positive multiplier effects. Hirschman defines linkage from the standpoint of supply of output to other production sectors and demand for input from other sectors. [2] The demand agriculture furnishes for consumption goods is not usually regarded as a positive force because it is believed to divert resources from the production of capital goods to the production of consumption goods. This is not an unrealistic view in the context of a technologically stagnant farm economy in which increases in output occur through higher relative agricultural prices which simply transfer purchasing power from one sector to another with an associated decline in productivity. [3] But the increased efficiency of techno-

[1] See A. O. Hirschman, *The Strategy of Economic Development* (New Haven, Conn.: Yale University Press, 1958), pp. 109–10.

[2] Ibid. See also Benjamin Higgins, *Economic Development—Principles, Problems, and Policies* (New York: Norton, 1959).

[3] For an exposition of this point, see John W. Mellor, "The Functions of Agricultural Prices in Economic Development," *Indian Journal of Agricultural Economics*, 23:1 (January–March 1968), 23–28.

logically advanced farming allows a large net increase in national income, which provides the dynamics of growth led by the agricultural sector.

Thus, for India, rate of growth of foodgrain output of 5 percent would currently provide an annual increment of about five million tons per year to national output. At a market price of Rs. 750 per ton, the value of this added output is Rs. 3,750 million, or 500 million dollars. It is the immensity of the annual additions of real resources which makes this output such a dynamic element in overall growth. In comparison, net foreign resource transfer for the high-aid period, 1957–58 to 1968–69, averaged 937 million dollars per year, and increased by 677 million from 1956–57 to 1965–66, an average annual increase of 75 million per year (see Table IX-1). It may be said—as a rough approximation—that for India a technologically induced addition of one percentage point to the growth rate for foodgrain production provides a stimulus greater than the average annual increase of foreign aid during its period of most rapid expansion.

It is common to think of the pattern of demand as either fixed or as malleable only as a welfare measure. The contrasting view here is of demand as manipulable for production purposes: to reduce capital and other bottlenecks to expansion, to raise the productive use of land, and concurrently to obtain a sufficient increase in the consumption of foodgrains to sustain the agricultural production revolution. Crucial to this view of growth is the potential for a major advancement in national income as a result of efficiency-increasing technological change in agriculture and the mobilization of underutilized labor resources for productive purposes by the expansion of real demand.

The Changing Structure of Demand

Effective planning both to meet increased demand and to prescribe correctives for incipient imbalances between the production and consumption of various goods requires knowledge of patterns of expenditure of additional incomes. With rising rural incomes, expenditure may increase for both capital and consumer goods. However, larger expenditure for capital goods may be determined technologically by the nature of innovation, thereby leaving the structure of consumer goods production as offering the only major scope for manipulation of the expenditure pattern.

To the extent that the new agricultural technologies are highly profitable, only a small proportion of increased income is allocated, in the longer run, to the purchase of capital goods for agricultural production; a large proportion is available for consumption or for investment in the output of other goods. In the short run, however, with rapid diffusion of innovations, total expenditure on capital goods for increased agricultural production may be substantial. Current expenditure on fertilizer and other production inputs is generally much more important than fixed investment, although that relationship will vary with the nature of the technology and the environment within which it is applied. The size of increments to fixed investment may fluctuate considerably over time.

Purchased producers' goods may themselves be capital and import intensive and therefore have only weak employment multiplier effects on the domestic economy.[4] To the extent that such tendencies are determined technologically, they reinforce the desirability of allocating remaining expenditure to employment intensive activities. In such circumstances, the more profitable the innovation, the more flexibility there will be in the patterns of expenditure of the resultant income.

In a low-income country, fertilizer, for example, has basically poor domestic multiplier effects, particularly on employment. Fertilizer and chemical inputs, in general, are either imported and consequently have little domestic growth linkage, or are produced at home with highly capital intensive production techniques. The capital equipment for chemical fertilizer and pesticide production is likely to be largely imported, and the low employment content allows little increase in demand for domestically produced consumer goods.

In contrast, increased expenditure on intermediate- and long-term capital goods for agriculture may have strong domestic growth linkages. In India, such investments are largely for irrigation works and labor-saving machinery, including engines and pumps for lifting water, mechanical thrashers, and a wide range of farm implements. Many of these mechanical items could be produced in small-scale rural enterprises with low capital-labor ratios. Demand for such capital goods may be highly volatile. The rapid growth and subsequent decline of the diesel engine and pump industry in Gujarat illustrate the problems of such uneven expan-

---

[4] To the extent that capital or other factors do not constrain growth of other sectors, the size of the multiplier effect from release of the agricultural wage goods constraint will be inversely related to the share of incremental income expended on agricultural commodities (or more narrowly, foodgrains), which in turn is in substantial part a function of the labor share in production and, hence, of the distribution of added income.

sion.[5] Accordingly, for the potential to be fully realized, public policy should facilitate using this industry as an entry point for a wider range of metal-working industry products.

In the long run, the purchase of consumer goods absorbs most of the increased rural incomes. The nature of the new foodgrain technologies, along with the availability of resources, determines the distribution of the additional income. Data about those determinants indicate that on the order of 60 to 80 percent might be expected to be expended on consumer goods.

Consumption expenditures allocated to foodgrains, other agricultural commodities, and nonagricultural commodities, each differ in their demand and in their production characteristics and hence are analyzed separately.

Demand for Foodgrains

Agricultural laborers in India, represented mainly by landless workers (the bottom two deciles of expenditure classes) spend over three-quarters of increments to consumption on agricultural commodities and 59 percent on foodgrains alone (Table VII-1). Therefore, increasing foodgrain production through labor-using methods is substantially a self-balancing process. More labor is employed in foodgrain production; much of the increased output is paid to the laborers who will directly consume a substantial proportion of the payments; and there is small effect on cash flows or stimulus to other sectors of the economy. In contrast, agricultural technology which distributes benefits to higher-income rural people provides much more complex linkages.

In successively higher expenditure classes, the proportion of increments to expenditure spent on foodgrains declines rapidly. For the sixth, seventh, and eighth deciles (representative of farmers producing a major portion of the national agricultural output), only 16 percent is allocated to foodgrains. Thus, these income groups market foodgrains to the equivalent of about 84 percent of the value of increments to expenditure. These marketings provide the food supplies to sustain an increase in the labor force in the nonfoodgrain sectors; these sales supply the cash incomes to purchase the goods and services which the added labor can produce. The

---

[5] Jan H. van der Veen, "Small Industries in India: The Case of Gujarat State," Ph.D. dissertation, Cornell University, 1972, Appendix II, pp. 124–26.

nature of the various equilibria and of the resultant policy needs is determined by the composition of the remaining consumption allocation.

Demand for Nonfoodgrain Agricultural Commodities

Nonfoodgrain agricultural commodities as a broad class comprise roughly 35 percent of incremental expenditure in all income classes except the lowest. Even in the sixth, seventh, and eighth deciles, these commodities are two-thirds as important as the total of all nonagricultural commodities. Consequently the linkage effects of increased rural incomes are particularly strong with the nonfoodgrain sectors of agriculture itself. This important point—rarely recognized in the growth literature—has critical significance for public policy because of the urgent need of this small-scale sector for supporting institutions and facilities. This sector is of relatively even greater importance in the many countries of Asia, Africa, and Latin America with a higher average per capita income than India's. Thus the common neglect of this subsector of agriculture is even more unfortunate in those other countries.

In India, milk and milk products are the most important of the nonfoodgrain agricultural commodities. They take roughly 12 percent of incremental expenditure in all but the highest- and lowest-income classes. For the upper middle expenditure group (sixth, seventh, and eighth deciles), milk and milk products are nearly twice as important as cotton textiles, a third more important than all textiles, and over six times as important as consumer durables. In other low-income countries other livestock products, such as poultry or pork, may have similar production characteristics to dairy products but be of greater importance in consumption than dairy products.

Demand for Nonagricultural Commodities

In India only 21 percent of incremental expenditure is allocated to nonagricultural commodities in the lowest two income deciles, while 48 percent is so distributed in an average of the sixth, seventh, and eighth deciles (Table VII-1). Textiles comprise the largest single component of expenditure on nonagricultural commodities and remain relatively constant in proportion to incremental expenditure. However, as expenditure increases, the proportion spent on cotton textiles declines relative to woolens and synthetics.

The share allocated to consumer durables and semidurables is low in

Table VII-1. Division of incremental expenditure among expenditure categories, by rural expenditure class, India, 1964–65

Decile: (rough correspondence to agricultural holdings of:)	Bottom two (landless)	Third (under 1 acre)	Fourth & fifth (1–5 acres)	Sixth, seventh, & eighth (5–10 acres)	Ninth (10–15 acres)	Lower one-half of tenth (15–30 acres)	Upper one-half of tenth (30+ acres)
Mean per capita monthly expenditure (Rs.)	8.93	13.14	17.80	24.13	30.71	41.89	85.84
Allocation of an additional rupee of expenditure							
Agricultural commodities	0.79	0.69	0.59	0.52	0.46	0.40	0.33
Foodgrains	0.59	0.38	0.25	0.16	0.11	0.06	0.02
Nonfoodgrains	0.20	0.31	0.34	0.36	0.35	0.34	0.31
Milk & milk products	0.07	0.11	0.12	0.13	0.13	0.12	0.09
Meat, eggs & fish	0.02	0.03	0.03	0.03	0.03	0.03	0.02
Other foods	0.01	0.05	0.07	0.09	0.10	0.12	0.16
Tobacco	0.01	0.01	0.01	0.01	0.01	0.01	0.01
Vanaspati	–	0.01	0.02	0.02	0.02	0.02	0.01
Other oils	0.05	0.05	0.04	0.04	0.03	0.02	0.01
Sweeteners	0.04	0.05	0.05	0.04	0.03	0.02	0.01
Nonagricultural commodities	0.21	0.31	0.41	0.48	0.54	0.60	0.67
Textiles	0.09	0.08	0.07	0.08	0.07	0.06	0.07
Cotton textiles	0.09	0.08	0.07	0.06	0.06	0.05	0.03
Woolen textiles	–	–	–	0.01	0.01	0.01	0.02
Other textiles	–	–	–	0.01	–	–	0.02
Nontextiles	0.12	0.23	0.34	0.40	0.47	0.54	0.60
Footwear	–	0.01	0.01	0.01	0.01	0.01	0.01
Durables & semi-durables	0.01	0.01	0.01	0.02	0.02	0.03	0.05
Conveyance	0.01	0.01	0.02	0.02	0.03	0.05	0.10
Consumer services	0.02	0.02	0.02	0.03	0.03	0.04	0.06
Education	0.01	0.01	0.02	0.03	0.03	0.05	0.11
Fuel & light	0.07	0.07	0.06	0.05	0.05	0.04	0.03
House rent	–	0.01	0.01	0.02	0.03	0.04	0.08
Miscellaneous	–	0.09	0.16	0.22	0.27	0.28	0.16
Total	1.00	1.00	1.00	1.00	1.00	1.00	1.00

Sources: The table is from John W. Mellor and Uma J. Lele, "Growth Linkages of the New Foodgrain Technologies, Indian Journal of Agricultural Economics, 28:1 (January–March 1973), 35–55. The data are reported in B. M. Desai, "Analysis of Consumption Expenditure Patterns in India," Occasional Paper No. 54, Department of Agricultural Economics, Cornell University USAID Employment and Income Distribution Research Project, August 1972. The source for the data is National Council of Applied Research, All-India Consumer Expenditure Survey, 1964–65, Vol. II (New Delhi, 1967).

all income classes, but does show a large percentage increase as total expenditure rises. Incremental spending on these items may be significantly understated because the period to which the data refer was one in which such goods were not widely and readily available.

Additional expenditure on consumer services and education rises sharply with increased income and attains major importance in the higher deciles. These two catagories are comprised largely of labor with various levels of training and offer an excellent opportunity for public policy to be influential, particularly by enlarging the educational system and reducing costs.

The considerable size of the miscellaneous group dramatizes the paucity of expenditure data on nonagricultural commodities. A fuller understanding of the growth linkages of increased foodgrain production must commence with more detailed knowledge of expenditure patterns.

Rural-Urban Contrasts in Demand

Sharp contrasts between rural and urban people (Table VII-2) suggest a dissimilarity in short-run development patterns between the sectors and, for the rural segment, a potential for sharp changes in the future. The expenditure elasticity for foodgrains is higher in all deciles in the rural areas. Most notably, the elasticity drops much less in conjunction with rising expenditure in the rural than in the urban areas. Expenditure elasticities for milk and milk products are also consistently somewhat greater in rural than in urban areas. For clothing, they are smaller in the low-expenditure groups, then fall much less rapidly, then end up higher in the upper-expenditure groups.

Hanumantha Rao shows that foodgrains may be as much as 19 percent cheaper and urban goods 34 percent more expensive in rural than in urban areas.[6] Apparent elasticities may change substantially as rural markets are more fully integrated into the national centers. Consumer tastes may also alter over time, especially in the dynamic context of rapid increase in income, enlargement and integration of markets, and change in income distribution.

Furthermore, Simon found a strong tendency for lower-income members of a particular socioeconomic group to emulate several aspects of consumption of higher-income members of the same group, with resultant contrasts among different social classes within the same income

[6] See C. H. Hanumantha Rao, "Resource Prospects from the Rural Sector: The Case of Indirect Taxes," *Economic and Political Weekly*, 4:13 (March 29, 1969), A-53–58.

Table VII-2. Comparison of rural and urban expenditure elasticities for three commodity groups, by expenditure class, India, 1963–64

Per capita monthly expenditure class * (rupees)	Rural			Urban		
	Foodgrains	Milk and milk products	Clothing	Foodgrains	Milk and milk products	Clothing
Lower expenditure						
0–8	1.2	3.4	2.8	1.2	2.8	5.6
8–11	0.9	2.7	2.4	0.8	2.2	4.1
11–13	0.8	2.3	2.2	0.7	1.9	3.5
13–15	0.7	2.1	2.1	0.6	1.8	3.1
Lower middle expenditure						
15–18	0.6	1.9	2.0	0.5	1.6	2.8
18–21	0.6	1.8	2.0	0.4	1.5	2.5
Upper middle expenditure						
21–24	0.5	1.7	1.9	0.3	1.4	2.2
24–28	0.5	1.6	1.9	0.3	1.3	2.0
High expenditure						
28–34	0.5	1.4	1.8	0.2	1.3	1.9
34–43	0.4	1.3	1.7	0.2	1.2	1.7
43–55	0.4	1.2	1.7	0.1	1.1	1.5
55–75	0.4	1.2	1.7	0.1	1.1	1.3
75 & above	0.3	1.0	1.6	0.1	1.0	1.1
Mean elasticity	0.5	1.6	1.9	0.2	1.2	1.8

* The expenditure classes refer to the following deciles: Lower expenditure to bottom three deciles, lower middle expenditure to fourth and fifth deciles, upper middle expenditure to sixth, seventh, and eighth deciles, high expenditure to top two deciles.

Source: John W. Mellor and Uma J. Lele, "Growth Linkages of the New Foodgrain Technologies," *Indian Journal of Agricultural Economics,* 27:1 (January–March 1973), 35–55, Table IV.

group.[7] Past consumer survey data are an important source of information but can be no more than broadly indicative of changes in consumption.

The complexities of predicting expenditure patterns and the consequent adjustments of production afford a substantial and multifaceted opportunity for public policy. In a rural-oriented growth strategy, the rewards of a highly pragmatic and flexible planning program are much greater than in the capital intensive approach.

The Effect of Alternative Distribution of Income on Demand Structure

The profound differences in consumer demand and linkage effects deriving from alternative income distributions are summarized for two

[7] See Sheldon R. Simon, "The Village of Senapur," Part IV of John W. Mellor et al., *Developing Rural India: Plan and Practice* (Ithaca, N.Y.: Cornell University Press, 1968), particularly pp. 319–28.

different examples in Table VII-3. In each case, a total sum of Rs. 2,400 million is allocated among consumption expenditure categories. Rs. 2, 400 million is approximately equal to the value of a 4 percent increment to foodgrain production, minus about 20 percent of the gross income for production expenditures.

In one case, characteristic of many of the new high-yield foodgrain varieties, 10 percent of the Rs. 2,400 million is expended by the laboring classes (the lower three deciles in expenditure patterns), and 90 percent is spent by the dominant owner-cultivator class (the sixth, seventh, and eighth deciles). In the alternative case, 80 percent of the income is expended by the laboring classes and 20 percent by the owner-cultivator class. The latter division is analogous to the division of expenditure in the case of traditional, labor intensive increases in agricultural production.

In the first case, only about 19 percent of the added expenditure is allocated to foodgrains and therefore is not sold out of the foodgrains sector. In the second case, 39 percent is consumed as foodgrains. Presumably, in both cases, all the foodgrains produced will be utilized. The first involves much more complex production and trading relations.

The composition of the increment in demand for nonfoodgrain agricultural commodities depends on the distribution of income. For milk and milk products, it is about 20 percent greater in the distribution that favors the upper-income groups. The increment in demand for other foods, including fruits and vegetables, is 50 percent greater in the distribution toward the landowning classes than for that toward the laboring classes. In contrast, among the laboring classes, the additional consumption is relatively larger for edible oils and sweeteners.

Striking differences occur in demand for nonagricultural commodities. While the increment in demand for cotton textiles actually is 16 percent less in the distribution toward the rich, as compared to the distribution toward the poor, the increment in demand for woolen and other textiles is more than four times larger in the "rich" case. The increase in consumption of miscellaneous goods, largely consumer nondurables, is twice as great for the rich as compared to the poor.

These are, of course, the consumption patterns that would occur if the underlying demand functions did not change and if adequate planning allowed the desired quantities to be produced and supplied without relative price changes. Careful study of all the various implications, facilitative actions, alternative influences, and policy needs to realize those alternatives can contribute to a favorable climate for growth.

Table VII-3. Distribution of Rs. 2,400 million expenditure assuming two different distributions of income (in million rupees)

Item	10 percent of expenditure by landless laborers and 90 percent by owner-cultivators for*:			80 percent of expenditure by landless laborers and 20 percent by owner-cultivators for*:		
	Laborers	Cultivators	Total	Laborers	Cultivators	Total
Foodgrains	101	324	425	806	72	878
Milk & milk products	24	281	305	192	62	254
Meat, eggs, & fish	8	65	72	58	14	72
Tobacco	2	43	45	19	10	29
Vanaspati	2	43	45	19	10	29
Other edible oils	12	64	77	96	14	110
Sweeteners	12	86	98	96	19	115
Other foods	12	194	206	96	43	139
Cotton textiles	22	151	173	173	34	206
Woolen textiles	-	22	22	-	5	5
Other textiles	-	22	22	-	5	5
Footwear	-	22	22	-	5	5
Conveyance	2	43	46	19	10	29
Consumer services	5	65	70	39	14	53
Education	2	65	67	19	14	34
Fuel & light	17	130	146	135	29	163
House rent	-	43	43	-	10	10
Durables & semi-durables	2	43	46	19	9	29
Miscellaneous	17	454	470	134	101	235
Total	240	2,160	2,400	1,920	480	2,400

* Landless laborers are defined as the lowest three expenditure deciles, and owner-cultivator as the sixth, seventh, and eighth expenditure deciles.

Sources: Based on the data in Table VII-1; see John W. Mellor and Uma J. Lele, "Growth Linkages of the New Foodgrain Technologies," *Indian Journal of Agricultural Economics*, 28:1 (January–March 1973).

Policies to Influence Consumption Patterns

It should be apparent that expenditure patterns for the additional income generated by technological change in foodgrain production do not necessarily create sufficient domestic employment to meet the society's income distribution objectives or sufficient derived demand for foodgrains to maintain relative prices at a level to sustain the incentive for increasing foodgrain production. To shift the structure of domestic production toward greater employment, taxes and subsidies may be used to channel consumption toward more labor intensive commodities; change in trade patterns may allow a relative expansion of industries with a comparatively high labor content; taxation of the well-to-do rural population may provide revenues for expenditure on labor intensive public works projects.

Correct policy choice rests on knowing how much increased employment can be supported by food supplies, the employment content of alternative production structures, and the effect of various policies on both demand and production. Because of its size, the agricultural sector itself offers particular opportunity for a net increase in employment through change in the pattern of consumption and production. Similarly, rural public works provide a promising potential for expanding the employment content of expenditure. All public programs intended to increase employment should focus on the net increase from the given set of prerequisites, such as wage goods and administrative talent. For example, directing public works programs requires administrative resources which might also be used promptly to increase foodgrain production so as to further relax the wage goods constraint. Likewise, the levying of taxes to pay for public works projects may reduce expenditure on similar labor intensive consumer goods and services. Deriving policy to maximize employment is thus an economic exercise in optimal allocation of the various resources requisite to increased employment.

Those rural public works projects should be emphasized which contribute to increased foodgrain production, thereby further relaxing the wage goods constraint, rather than schemes with a possibly higher short-run employment content but less agricultural productivity. Closely connected is the question of the extent to which the works created contribute to a growing number of jobs—as, for example, through the increased labor intensity of farming associated with irrigation provided by public works—

or simply provide employment in the projects themselves. These issues may relate to an important element of regional development, an aspect illustrated and explored by Donovan in the context of alternative uses of resources in irrigated and dry areas of Kanartaka state.[8] According to his study, the irrigated area is already provided with a well-developed infrastructure of roads, electricity, and irrigation canals. In that environment, investment in credit programs to support a considerable intensification of agriculture yields as much—or more—additional employment as the same sum spent on rural works in a nearby dryland area. In addition, the heightened investment in the irrigated area yields much more aggregate income because the area is on the threshold of being able to support the use of high-performance agricultural activities. A dilemma may then emerge: whether to invest in the regions already somewhat advanced technologically, with the expectation that dryland regions will become servicing areas for irrigated agriculture (via labor migration); or whether to invest directly in employment-creating programs in dryland regions, even though their prospects for further advances may be small. The former alternative raises the tax base and may appear more desirable on grounds of increased production; the latter preserves existing communities and may be required on social and political grounds.

The answers to the questions of where, when, and how much to spend on rural public works projects may become most relevant in the context of a broad, employment-oriented strategy of development, particularly if foodgrain production is increasing faster than employment. Thus, rural public works may occasionally, as in the case of small irrigation projects and sometimes roads, provide the basis for an increased supply of the wage goods needed to support the greater number of jobholders. They may also distribute income toward small, especially vulnerable, target groups in the context of a low-employment strategy of growth. Unfortunately, rural public works schemes are all too often regarded solely as sources of employment, without the necessary concern for the resources they use and the supply of those resources. In such cases, they may easily result in a net decline in employment.

[8] See W. Graeme Donovan, "Employment Generation in Agriculture: A Study in Mandya District, South India," Cornell Agricultural Economics Occasional Paper No. 71 (June 1974).

Expanding Nonfoodgrain Production in Response to Increased Demand

The linkages arising from increased foodgrain production cannot have their full stimulative effect on growth unless restraints on expanded production in the domestic consumer goods sector are removed. In the agricultural sector, where the greatest short-run potentials for increased employment lie, it is institutional deficiencies which are most likely to restrain development. Growth in industrial production may face a constraint from institutional barriers particularly with respect to capital, input, and output markets. Public policy must diagnose the bottlenecks and make appropriate adjustments.

The nonfoodgrain agricultural sector is the most important recipient of increased demand resulting from rising incomes and is, in many respects, the most attractive for expansion because of its labor intensity and the wide geographic dispersion of its pattern of demand and production. In recent decades, supply has, in general, lagged somewhat behind demand in this sector, primarily because of the lack of a broad infrastructure of rural development.

In India, dairy production epitomizes the opportunities and the development needs of the labor intensive nonfoodgrain area. In other countries poultry, pork, or fisheries may play a similar role—with a similar set of problems. India's dairy sector is large: in 1968–69, milk and milk product production, estimated in terms of rupee value, was nearly one-quarter as great as foodgrain production. And, as is shown in Table VII-1, all but the lowest-income class spent 50 percent more of increments to income on milk and milk products than they did on textiles. The incremental demand for dairy products over the next ten years could well support an additional 4.5 million full-time jobs.[9] The relatively poor supply response of milk to even the slow growth in demand in the 1950s and 1960s un-

[9] This calculation uses the following assumptions: (1) population grows at an annual rate of 2.5 percent from 1971 to 1981, on a base of 355 million; (2) real national income per capita grows at 2.5 percent per annum from 1971 to 1981, on a base of Rs. 355 in 1971 (at 1960–61 prices); (3) marginal propensity to expend on dairy products is 0.13; (4) dairying expansion takes place in small, family units whose managers do their own local marketing, receiving all of the gross value of sales and having 25 percent of the gross left over as return to their labor and management; and (5) each worker in the family earns Rs. 800 per annum, in 1960–61 prices (equivalent to Rs. 1,480 per annum in 1971 prices).

derlines the difficulty of realizing these substantial potentials. During that period, prices of dairy products consistently rose faster than foodgrain prices. Presumably, the supply inelasticity would be even more binding in the context of greatly accelerated expansion.

Milk production must cope with at least three restraints to growth. Most important is marketing. Highly perishable dairy products present technical problems of distribution, particularly if they are to be produced mainly on small farms. Second is the matter of credit. Dairy animals are expensive and, equally important, animal mortality imposes a heavy financial burden on small farmers.[10] As a result, credit institutions need to be molded to these special risk factors and to the problem of intermediate-term credit. Third, the research and extension infrastructure for milk farming is particularly weak. Expansion of production can be stimulated in part by higher relative prices financed by the advance in foodgrain technology, and in part by cost-reducing technological improvements. Both the research and the educational establishments for these purposes are understandably less developed than for foodgrains.

A basis for meeting these needs can be provided by the current Dairy Development Schemes, the Marginal Farmers and Landless Laborers Agencies, and the general credit, research, and educational institutions. Of course, these institutions cannot have a major impact without a strongly accelerated growth in demand for dairy products. Once that occurs, a vigorous impetus is required to realize the potentials through rapid expansion of the necessary organizations.

Vegetable production is also a labor intensive system with a similar set of institutional requirements. As a matter of fact, any labor intensive and demand elastic agricultural product faces problems of expanding marketing facilities, large credit requirements, substantial risk and uncertainty, and poorly developed research and educational facilities. And each product requires separate diagnosis of its specific problems and the development of programs to overcome them.

Although institutional development is the key to labor intensive growth within a rural-led strategy of expansion, capital is also significant. Increased foodgrain production not only relaxes the wage goods constraint,

[10] See Michael G. G. Schluter, "The Role of Co-operative Credit in Small Farmer Adoption of the New Cereal Varieties in India," Cornell Agricultural Economics Occasional Paper No. 64 (May 1973), for a discussion of the special problem of credit and uncertainty for small farmers in purchasing improved dairy animals.

enlarging the potential need for capital in expanding employment, but may itself require substantial additional investment. The capital constraint may be eased by the foodgrain technological advances themselves, if either the resultant increase in demand is for commodities with relatively low capital-labor ratios (thereby reducing resources requirements per worker) or if the consequent structure of income, demand, and production stimulates a higher rate of capital formation.

The past planning emphasis on capital goods industries has yielded a poor quality and quantity of data on consumer goods industries. Nevertheless, the statistics do suggest that the capital used per employee is comparatively less in the consumer goods industries experiencing the largest rise in demand resulting from increased rural incomes (Table V-2). It also appears that, while capital intensity within these industries varies considerably, industries with relatively high capital-labor ratios are primarily those catering to demand from high-income urban consumers (Table VII-4).

Accordingly, the capital-labor ratio for urban milk processing is high and is comparable to that of the chemical industry. The ratio for the cigarette industry is somewhat lower than for milk and milk products, but is much above that for several other major consumer goods industries, especially the traditional types of tobacco products. Under small-town and rural conditions, these products, or their close substitutes, are consumed in a form requiring much less capital intensity in their production.[11] Thus, if the structure of demand does not change drastically to conform to high-income urban consumption patterns, it may influence the choice of techniques as well as the scale of production of many of these goods. By means of both of these factors, the demand structure associated with rising rural incomes can encourage a more decentralized and labor-using pattern of industrialization. To achieve that pattern may, however, require considerable investment in the rural infrastructure.

From 1961 to 1965, the industries which experienced a sharp rise in demand resulting from increased rural incomes actually showed a relative decline in importance. Noteworthy large decreases occurred in the low-capital intensive consumer goods industries. Major increases in rural income may help to reverse this tendency and change the structure of growth of demand and output toward more labor intensive industries.

[11] See Ray W. Nightingale, *The Modernization Decision in Indian Urban Fluid Milk Markets*, C.I.A.D. Bulletin No. 15 (August 1969).

Table VII-4. Capital-labor ratios and value added for various consumer goods industries, India, 1960 to 1964

Consumer goods industry	Productive capital per employer	Plant machinery and tools per employee	Percent of all industrial value added	
			1960	1964
Milk foods & malt foods	26,446	12,949	0.1	0.1
Other foods				
Processed fish & seafood	6,498	4,249	–	–
Processed fruits & vegetables	5,871	1,678	–	0.1
Tobacco				
Biri	816	33	0.2	0.0
Cigarette	17,798	2,056	1.2	1.2
Snuff	10,754	1,267	–	–
Jerda	3,658	476	0.1	–
Other Tobacco	1,653	135	(not comparable)	
Edible oils	7,635	2,380	0.6	0.4
Other oils				
Vanaspati	14,010	4,299	0.9	0.4
Sweeteners				
Sugar	12,107	6,113	4.4	3.0
Gur	1,961	976	–	–
Cotton textiles	4,843	2,382	23.7	17.7
Other textiles				
Wool	9,259	2,729	0.7	0.8
Art silk	11,427	5,274	1.3	2.2
Footwear	4,821	610	–	0.1

Source: John W. Mellor and Uma J. Lele, "Growth Linkages of the New Foodgrain Technologies," Indian Journal of Agricultural Economics, 28:1 (January–March 1973), 35–55, Table VII.

While demand generated by agricultural expansion allows shifts in the composition of industry which reduce capital requirements per employee, other elements of the process offer a potential for greatly increased savings and investment. Added savings may not only finance much of agriculture's larger capital needs, but may also partially finance expansion of the nonagricultural sector.[12] The extent to which agriculture supports investment in other sectors depends on (1) the net capital requirements for agriculture's own increase; (2) the development of institutions for transferring savings within agriculture itself as well as for moving them to other sectors; (3) the returns to capital in other sectors; and (4) the form of institutional growth in other sectors of the economy.

[12] See John W. Mellor, "Accelerated Growth in Agricultural Production and the Intersectoral Transfer of Resources," Economic Development and Cultural Change, 22:1 (October 1973), 1–16, for a review of this controversy and elaboration of the basic case for net resource transfers from agriculture.

A rural-led strategy of development is likely to produce high average rates of returns to investment in agriculture; rapid growth of small-scale rural industry receiving direct capital from cultivators; price relationships for industrial consumer goods which facilitate high profits and reinvestment; and an income base in agriculture sufficient to support taxes to self-finance much of the infrastructure requirements. The resulting substantial net outflow of resources from agriculture will spur growth in other sectors of the economy even while agriculture itself is expanding rapidly and profitably.

Since these relations are difficult to grasp and widely disputed, it is useful to summarize the experience of Taiwan as a nation which followed such a pattern vigorously and successfully over a substantial period of time and under varying conditions of rural development.

Two elements of the Taiwan experience are particularly relevant even to a large country like India. First, continuously from 1895 to 1960, through several major periods of agricultural expansion, there were large net resource transfers out of agriculture. Second, several quite different devices were used for such transfers, each appropriate to the economic and political conditions of the respective periods.

The period from 1911 to 1920 witnessed rapid growth in irrigation projects but, in other technological respects, was stagnant. In that decade, the net resource transfer from the agricultural sector was equal to over half the value of its sales and 30 percent of the value of its production.[13]

In the technologically dynamic period of the 1920s when, for example, the new Ponlai rice varieties were introduced and fertilizer use was accelerating, purchases of nonagricultural commodities by the agricultural sector more than doubled. Nevertheless, the net outflow of resources rose and was maintained at a high level. The value of net resource transfers, as a percentage of production and sales, declined from the earlier period, but increased production allowed larger absolute totals. At the same time, agriculture was making greater use of industrially produced capital and consumer goods.

In the 1950 to 1955 period of extraordinarily rapid population growth, economic development, and technological change in agriculture, the net

[13] These and the following data on Taiwan are from T. H. Lee, *Intersectoral Capital Flows in the Economic Development of Taiwan, 1895–1960* (Ithaca, N.Y.: Cornell University Press; 1971), Table 2, and are compared with India and other countries in Mellor, "Accelerated Growth in Agricultural Production and the Intersectoral Transfer of Resources."

real resource transfer from agriculture hit a new high. In this period, such transfer recovered to nearly 40 percent of agricultural sales and over 20 percent of total agricultural production.

It was only in the next period, 1956 to 1960, after the economic transformation to a substantially industrial economy had been largely completed, that the net transfer began to decrease slightly in real, absolute terms to equal only 15 percent of production and 25 percent of sales of agricultural products. The decline in net resource transfers from agriculture continued after 1960. Thus, agriculture made a major contribution during the critical period in development of a rapidly growing labor intensive nonagricultural sector.

Just as revealing as the large net transfers from Taiwan's agriculture were the dramatically changing roles of various transfer mechanisms. In the post–World War II period, the transfer of resources was achieved primarily by a sharp turn in relative prices against the agricultural sector so that invisible items represented over 40 percent of the transfer from 1950 to 1955. The most important mechanisms of this shift were a barter exchange of rice for fertilizer and the compulsory purchase programs. In addition, technological change provided more than compensating production incentives in agriculture through greatly improved physical input-output relationships.

In the pre–World War II period, fiscal measures and land rent payments were vital in the transfer. In the latter part of the prewar period and in the postwar period, outflow through financial institutions was also significant. The importance of particular methods and institutions for financing resource flows changed substantially from time to time, in accordance with economic and political factors. The choice was not necessarily the most efficient according to economic criteria. For example, the heavy reliance in the postwar period on what was, in effect, a tax on fertilizer presented to farmers one of the most unfavorable fertilizer-rice price ratios in the world. However, the proceeds were used in a total context favorable to cost-reducing technological change in agriculture and to rapid overall economic growth and demand for agricultural commodities.

In contrast to Taiwan, India has, since independence, continually transferred resources into a generally technologically stagnant agricultural sector.[14] Government expenditures on agriculture have consistently exceeded

[14] For a full comparative exposition, see Mellor, "Accelerated Growth in Agricultural Production and the Intersectoral Transfer of Resources."

tax revenues from agriculture. Relative prices have, with a few brief exceptions, moved in favor of the sector; credit institutions have transferred funds into it; and the nature of industrial growth has encouraged little net investment by rural people, while urban workers have made net remittances back to the agricultural sector.

The economic changes associated with rural development could alter these relationships in the future. High rates of return provided by the new technologies in irrigated areas could supply the basis for recovering investment in a few years and therefore the potential for placing money outside agriculture, for paying increased taxes, or for absorbing lower relative agricultural prices.

Only 20 percent of India's cultivated acreage was irrigated in 1967–68 as compared to 41 percent in Taiwan in 1921.[15] A low percentage irrigated reduces the rate of growth of agricultural production and of income, and diminishes the potential for net transfer of resources to other sectors. To the extent that the requirements of investment in irrigation are high, it becomes even more important to a rural-led strategy of growth to restrain the capital intensity of nonagricultural advancement. Fortunately, in India, because of the great possibility of very high rates of return for small-scale irrigation, the period of large net investment by agriculture in other sectors need be only briefly delayed.

A wide variety of means is at hand for tapping the savings potential arising from a dynamic agriculture. Continued growth of a nationally integrated system of rural credit, including the credit cooperatives and rural branches of banks, is necessary to move financial resources from regions in repayment stages of the technological investment cycle to those in the net borrowing stage, as well as to make timely net transfers of resources out of agriculture. Development of the infrastructure for small-scale rural industry can encourage agricultural savings and direct investment in industry. Indeed, if political factors remove the other means of capital transfer from agriculture, the potential for direct investment by agriculturalists in industry becomes a strong argument for fostering country-based, small-scale industries as major means of extracting resources. Stimulation of small-scale industry itself requires large investment in

[15] This raises the question as to why India did not have net resource transfers out of agriculture in recent decades, since Taiwan had such transfers when irrigation investment was large and technology relatively stagnant. The explanation of the contrast probably lies with the orientation of India's investment pattern toward heavy industry with a large import content; the capital needs were necessarily met largely from foreign resource transfers.

communication and power. Thus, tapping rural sources of savings may demand a shift in the strategy of growth toward rural areas generally.

In nearly all low-income countries, rural taxation has been singularly unproductive. The economically preferred levy, the land tax, has declined to the point of insignificance as a source of revenue. Charges for water and electricity have tended to contain a subsidy element. The hope must be that in a technologically dynamic agriculture, allocation of taxes for local purposes and an increasing role for local government will reverse the past trends. As rural consumption patterns shift toward nonagricultural goods, the incidence of indirect taxes on agriculture can rise rapidly.[16]

Sharp increases in rural incomes can, of course, raise relative prices of industrially produced consumer goods and hence provide an effective transfer of resources to consumer goods industries. The more capital limits this growth, the greater the price increase in response to greater demand, and the higher the profits; therefore the incentive and the means to invest will be greater. The very increase in rural demand and the improvement in rural roads needed to encourage rural industry may also provide a relatively painless additional boost to the industrial sector through their effect on relative prices.[17] High costs of transportation, the reinforcing effect of small markets, and consequently high distribution costs have resulted in rural consumption patterns in which agricultural commodities predominate over manufactured goods (Table VII-2). High returns to investment in rural infrastructure and the economies of scale resulting from the broadening of markets, in effect, allow changes in relative prices which act as a source of capital for growth of consumer goods produced in the industrial sector.

Agriculture's capital contribution to other sectors does not require that any particular mechanism be used for tapping agricultural income, but policy should not eliminate all possible devices. There is a genuine

---

[16] For example, Ved P. Gandhi shows indirect taxes as a percentage of income in urban households to be nearly twice as high as for rural households in the higher-income groups and approximately 50 percent higher in the low income groups (*Tax Burden on Indian Agriculture* [Cambridge, Mass.: The Law School of Harvard University, 1966], Table 26), whereas in a study done in more prosperous Gujarat, at a later period, Mahesh I. Pathak and Arun S. Patel show the incidence to be approximately the same for the agricultural and nonagricultural sectors (*Agricultural Taxation in Gujarat* [New York: Asia Publishing House, 1970], Table 1.3).

[17] See Rao, "Resource Prospects from the Rural Sector," p. A-54.

danger that this will happen. Strong farmers' lobbies may prevent land or other taxes on agriculturalists from being raised or may obtain farm price supports and subsidies on inputs. If, in addition, small-scale industry is not supported by investment in infrastructure and supply of raw materials, and if middle-class urban consumers lobby successfully to prevent a rise in prices of major industrial consumer goods, agriculture will lose all the means and sources contributing to capital formation. If lack of government revenues then prevents even the rural investment necessary for a continuation of expansion in agricultural output, there may be a return to a low-level equilibrium among scant development in agriculture, slight employment increase, moderate rise in demand for agricultural output, and reversion to a capital intensive, slow-growth industrial strategy.

It has been implicit throughout this discussion that the bulk of increased demand for consumer goods will be met by expanded domestic production. Leakages into imports, of course, reduce the employment multiplier effects. Leakages are likely to be small in India because the expenditure patterns are toward the relatively labor intensive kinds of goods in which India has a comparative advantage in production; and because the basic industrialization effort has provided a production base of capital and entrepreneurship suitable for expansion to meet domestic demand and for exports to pay for required capital intensive intermediate products. If ownership of land were concentrated in large holdings providing the bulk of income to families consuming predominantly capital intensive imported goods, the strategy would not succeed. In addition, if the existing industrial production base encompasses a much narrower range of commodities, an active import-displacement policy would be required, with consequent lags in the response to increased demand.

A Test of Key Quantitative Relationships in Rural-Led Growth

Now that the basic components of the rural-led employment-oriented strategy of growth have been presented, it is appropriate to quantify those key interrelationships and thereby to test the foundation upon which the details of the argument necessarily rest.

The most important principle in the argument is that the supply of foodgrains as wage goods is a major binding constraint to employment growth, but that attainable levels of foodgrain production can relieve that constraint sufficiently to allow employment growth that is significantly faster than in the past. Previous rates of increase of foodgrain production in the 2.5 to 3 percent range, given the old political construct, cannot sustain a rate of employment growth significantly faster than the unsatisfactory pace of the past; conversely, acceleration to an achievable range of 4 to 5 percent will materially advance employment growth.

The second principle is that more rapid expansion of foodgrain production alone will not directly increase employment enough either to stabilize the foodgrain production growth rate itself or to provide sufficient overall advancement in the number of jobholders. Faster foodgrain production must be associated with accelerated growth in employment in other sectors; therefore, many elements of the development strategy must change in consort.

The third principle is that increase in income in a foodgrain-employment strategy will generate substantially more jobs in the non-foodgrain part of the agricultural sector, so that a high proportion of the accelerated employment growth will occur in the agricultural sector. This principle shows the importance of increased demand in the strategy of development and further justifies a major allocation of resources to the agricultural sector. It also suggests the potential for a less binding capital constraint to growth than in other conceptualizations of economic evolution, partly because agriculture will create so much employment and partly because of the potential for reduced capital intensity in consumer goods industries within the industrial sector.

The analytical framework for testing these principles was provided first by a mathematical model of the key elements in the relationship, and then by a simulation model in which was entered the empirical evidence from the preceding investigation.

The mathematical model examines the relationships between increased foodgrain production achieved through alternative technologies and the rates of growth of nonagricultural employment, nonagricultural sector capital-labor ratios, relative price relationships between agricultural and nonagricultural commodities, and the course of per capita incomes of the labor force.[18] That analysis confirms the theory that a shift in the income distribution attendant on technological change in agriculture has a pronounced impact on increasing marketings and employment and empha-

---

[18] The mathematical model is reported fully in Uma J. Lele and John W. Mellor, "Technological Change and Distributive Bias in a Dual Economy," Cornell Agricultural Economics Occasional Paper No. 43 (revised; October 1972).

sizes the need for empirical data if the true relationships are to be understood.

The simulation model which develops from the mathematical relationships deals with a sequence of questions through a set of simultaneous equations.[19] The model shows, first, for any given rate of growth of foodgrain production and a given initial distribution of income, how much employment will have to increase—assuming the propensity to spend wage income on foodgrains—in order to create exactly enough added demand to consume the extra supply of foodgrains. That increase indicates the extent to which accelerated foodgrain production will relax a wage goods constraint on employment growth.

Next, given the total increase in employment, the model specifies the division of employment among economic sectors. Employment in the foodgrain sector is determined by the initial assumptions with respect to the nature of the technology. Employment in the nonfoodgrain agricultural sector is determined by the demand for production from that sector generated by the previously determined increase in income. The employment-to-output ratio in that sector is taken as given. Employment in the nonagricultural sector is then the difference between the total employment and the sum of that in the two agricultural sectors. The growth of national income is consequently the sum of the technology-determined rate of increase for foodgrains; the demand-determined rate of growth of nonfoodgrain agricultural production; and the residual expansion in the rate of employment growth in the nonagricultural sector, multiplied by the output-labor ratio of that sector. The latter is not determined in the model, but is presumably a function of the savings rate, and therefore of the rate of capital formation, as well as of institutional factors determining efficiency.

The model uses assumptions drawn from the consumption data presented in this chapter, employment data such as those reported in Chapter IV, and data on structure of the economy from the Indian Planning Commission's input-output tables, to test the effect on employment of chang-

[19] A full statement of the assumptions and the findings of the simulation model are in John W. Mellor and Mohinder S. Mudahar, "Modernizing Agriculture, Employment and Economic Growth: A Simulation Model," Cornell Agricultural Economics Occasional Paper No. 75 (June 1974); and John W. Mellor and Mohinder S. Mudahar, "Simulating an Economy with Modernizing Agricultural Sector: Implications for Employment and Economic Growth in India," Cornell Agricultural Economics Occasional Paper No. 76 (June 1974).

ing assumptions with respect to the growth rate for foodgrain production, the nature of the technology used, and population growth.

Table VII-5 shows for seven different sets of assumptions the rate of growth of foodgrain output and of employment. Each simulation was continued for a period long enough to absorb unemployment equal to 30 percent of the initial-period agricultural labor force. The end of the period is stated as the point of "full employment" or, perhaps more accurately, the point at which real wage rates might begin to increase at an accelerating rate.

The first three sets of assumptions in effect compare a 2.75 percent, a 3.0 percent, and a 3.9 percent rate of growth in foodgrain production. The initial rates of growth of employment are respectively 2.7 percent, 3.0 percent, and 4.0 percent. More strikingly, it takes 39 years to reach "full employment" in the first case, 27 years in the second, and only 12 in the third. Thus, the difference in employment effect between a 2.75 percent and a 3.9 percent rate of growth in foodgrain production is dramatic.

Comparison of assumption sets 4 and 5 (Table VII-5) shows the significant effect of type of agricultural technology on employment growth. In each case, the initial rate of production growth is about the same at 4.0 and 3.8 percent. But in the low labor productivity case, foodgrain supply restrains employment growth to an initial level of 3.7 percent, compared to 4.4 percent for the alternative technology.

Comparison of assumption sets 6 and 7 shows the striking effect of the difference between a 2 percent and a 3 percent population growth rate. For the former, nine years are required to move to full employment compared to nineteen years for the latter, if the other assumptions are kept the same in each case.

The technological assumptions which provide the 3.9 percent rate of growth of foodgrain production, in assumption set 3, are responsible for a 2.9 percent rate of growth of employment in foodgrain production, enough to absorb only 22 percent of the total increase that can be supported by the foodgrain supply (Appendix, Table 15). In fact, this is a somewhat higher employment elasticity with respect to output than that shown in most studies cited in this chapter. However, the demand generated by the increased incomes furnishes the basis for the nonfoodgrain agricultural sector to expand at an initial rate of 5.7 percent per year. Since that sector initially supplies about half as much employment as the

Alternative foodgrain growth rates

Assumption set 1

$g_m = 2.75$
$g_d = 1.75$
$g_p = 2.50$
$t = 0.60$

Year	Foodgrains	Total employment
2	2.7	2.7
5	2.8	2.8
10	2.9	2.9
15	2.9	2.9
20	3.0	3.0
25	3.0	3.0
30	3.0	3.1
35	3.1	3.1
39	3.1	3.1

Assumption set 2

$g_m = 3.00$
$g_d = 2.00$
$g_p = 2.50$
$t = 0.60$

Year	Foodgrains	Total employment
2	3.0	3.0
5	3.0	3.0
10	3.1	3.1
15	3.2	3.2
20	3.2	3.3
25	3.2	3.4
27	3.3	3.4

Assumption set 3

$g_m = 3.00$
$g_d = 2.00$
$g_p = 2.50$
$t = 1.25$

Year	Foodgrains	Total employment
2	3.9	4.0
5	3.9	4.0
10	3.9	4.0
12	3.9	4.0

Alternative technologies

Assumption set 4

$g_m = 3.00$
$g_d = 0.75$
$g_p = 2.50$
$t = 2.00$

Year	Foodgrains	Total employment
2	4.0	4.4
5	4.1	4.3
10	4.2	4.2

Assumption set 5

$g_m = 3.00$
$g_d = 2.80$
$g_p = 2.50$
$t = 0.70$

Year	Foodgrains	Total employment
2	3.8	3.7
5	3.8	3.8
10	3.8	3.9
14	3.7	4.0

Alternative population growth rates

Assumption set 6

$g_m = 3.00$
$g_d = 2.00$
$g_p = 2.00$
$t = 1.25$

Year	Foodgrains	Total employment
2	3.9	4.0
5	3.9	4.1
9	3.9	4.1

Assumption set 7

$g_m = 3.00$
$g_d = 2.00$
$g_p = 3.00$
$t = 1.25$

Year	Foodgrains	Total employment
2	3.9	4.0
5	3.9	4.0
10	3.9	4.0
15	3.9	4.0
19	3.9	3.9

The g_m = yield growth rate in modern foodgrains sector; g_d = yield growth rate in traditional foodgrains sector; t = rate of transfer of land from the traditional to the modern sector.

Note: This table shows, under various assumptions, the growth rates of foodgrain production and agricultural employment, at 5-year intervals, and at the final year in which full employment is reached.

Source: John W. Mellor and Mohinder S. Mudahar, "Simulating a Developing Economy with Modernizing Agricultural Sector—Implications for Employment and Growth," Cornell Agricultural Economics Occasional Paper No. 76 (June 1974), Table 21.

foodgrain sector, and since its employment grows at nearly twice the rate of employment in the foodgrain sector, it provides as much added employment as foodgrain production does. Thus, in this case, agriculture in total accounts for 43 percent of the increased employment. The remainder of 57 percent is to be accounted for in the nonagricultural sector, which requires a rate of employment growth of about 4 percent per year. That is a slow rate compared to the first half of the 1960s. Accordingly, the burden on capital supplies would be smaller than in that earlier period, allowing either the capital intensity to increase or a relative transfer of resources to the agricultural sector. In this context a greater increase in capital intensity might be absorbed in agriculture and a lesser increase in the nonagricultural sector.

The rate of output growth in the nonagricultural sector would depend on the rate of investment in that area, as well as the efficiency of investment, and the consequent increase in labor productivity. It would perhaps be reasonable to expect output in the nonagricultural sector to rise at a rate twice that of employment—i.e., 8.0 percent per year if employment were growing at 4.0 percent. That would probably be reasonably consistent with the implications with respect to demand elasticities. With that assumption and the growth of other sectors as above, and the initial sectoral weights in the model, the overall rate of increase of national output would be 5.4 percent per year. Assuming a 2.5 percent rate of growth of population, per capita income would rise 2.9 percent per year.[20] If income of the laboring class were only a function of the growth rate of employment, their income would increase at a 1.5 percent rate on a per capita basis. However, in the model it is assumed that the real wage rate also rises as a function of the degree of unemployment in the agricultural sector, which in this simulation increases the growth of laborers' per capita income to about 3.0 percent per year. What happens in practice, of course, depends on the operation not only of the labor market, but of the capital market as well.

A very striking contrast appears in a comparison of the achievement of similar rates of foodgrain production growth from very low-productivity and very high-productivity technologies (assumption sets 4 and 5, respectively). In the high-productivity case, a negligible proportion of increased employment occurs in foodgrain production, while the bulk, initially 78

[20] See Mellor and Mudahar, "Simulating an Economy with Modernizing Agricultural Sector," esp. p. 51.

percent, must be absorbed in the nonagricultural sector—requiring rates of growth that may be difficult to manage, and certainly placing a heavy burden on capital formation potentials. In contrast, the low-productivity case absorbs a high proportion of increased employment in foodgrain production—with an easier but much slower growth in other sectors and in the aggregate.

The simulation thus confirms the concepts of a binding constraint on employment from foodgrain production, the importance of a demand-derived expansion of the nonfoodgrain agricultural sector, and the significant role that choice of technology has in determining these forces.

Integrated Rural Development

Growth led by increased incomes in the dominant foodgrain sector has many features which recommend a broad, integrated approach to rural development. First, increments to income from the high-yield foodgrain varieties are broadly diffused in rural areas. Second, a substantial portion of increased demand is for nonfoodgrain agricultural commodities. Third, the agricultural growth, in both its production and consumption aspects, increases the effective demand for infrastructure such as roads, electricity, and communications, which can, in combination with other reinforcing elements of rural development, support such improvement. Fourth, there is important mutual reinforcement between the infrastructure of roads, electrification, and communication and the attraction to rural areas of the trained personnel who are very essential to the development of provincial institutions but who may be reluctant to serve in outlying areas without the minimal amenities of a modern society. Fifth, the increased infrastructure reduces disparities in rural-urban price relationships, thereby stimulating greater exchange of goods between the two sectors. Sixth, the nature of the new foodgrain technologies widens income inequalities and demands rapid growth in employment, while rural industries tend to be labor intensive. Seventh, the increased rural incomes offer a source of savings that can be readily tapped by taxes for local infrastructure and for industrial investment in small-scale firms. Eighth, widened rural income disparities create a need for a broader range of provincial-based public health and education facilities, while the higher incomes provide an effective demand for at least a portion of such services.

Taking advantage of these rural-based potentials for accelerated growth requires massive development of institutions, the personnel to staff them, and the physical infrastructure of transportation, communication, and electric power. Thus, at least in its early stages, such a structure of development requires a major redirection of resources from the pattern of the Second and Third Plans. After some time, growth may increase sufficiently to allow savings rates to support the rural-oriented strategy *and* a high level of investment in capital intensive industry. In the short run, however, the two approaches are bound to conflict.

A broad, integrated plan of rural development requires mechanisms for raising resources locally for particular purposes, for setting priorities as to the type and timing of physical infrastructure, institutions, and social services, and for marshaling local administrative capabilities. In the early stages of rural development, it may be necessary to limit priorities within a relatively narrow range of complements. However, India has made substantial progress in many states in evolving the organizational structure for effective local initiation and administration of development efforts. As provincial bodies expand, the growing complexity of the tasks undertaken may require increasing decentralization of the decision-making and resource-mobilization processes; the specific choices will depend on past institutional history as well as current power structures. Decentralization will encourage a more pragmatic response to events as they occur.

Within the context of integrated rural development, the market town could be the focal point for organization and decision making. It is a logical center for analysis of infrastructure needs and communication; it facilitates a means of balancing agricultural, small-manufacturing, and trading interests; it fosters a commercial orientation favorable to increasing productivity; and it is a large enough unit to promote the coordination of a wide range of activities. The market town approach has, of course, been long recognized as a means of taking jobs to the rural labor force and consequently reducing social overhead investment in urban centers, as well as of tapping provincial sources of capital.[21]

Despite its intellectual appeal, the market town concept has, in general, failed because the basic strategy of growth did not provide the essential foundation for raising rural incomes. With change in the strategy, the market town can become the cornerstone of the development effort.

Unfortunately, however, the very features that recommend integrated

[21] See in particular John P. Lewis, *Quiet Crisis in India* (Washington, D.C.: Brookings Institution, 1962).

rural development and the market town as means of accelerating and broadening participation in growth across socioeconomic classes pose serious problems of widened income disparities between areas. The foundation of the development effort described herein is technological change in the dominant agricultural sector. Since, empirically, it is the already lower-income areas which are least inclined to respond to new technology, the rural-led process of growth is apt to widen regional income disparities further.

Appropriate policy can correct a lack of infrastructure investment.[22] Unfortunately, where backwardness is a result of unproductive physical resources, little is known about an appropriate investment policy except that education is needed to assist the labor force in migrating to other areas.[23] This is hardly an argument against the rural strategy, since alternative approaches essentially leave provincial areas out of the growth process and fail to provide either the wage goods or employment basis for improvement of the laboring classes. The argument does suggest that rural-led growth is not a panacea for all problems of inequity and shows the need for attention to regional disparities as possibly the most intractable of all problems. Noteworthy is the extent to which regional disparities are receiving increasing attention in China as other disparities have been reduced and rural development accelerated.

Future Policy Needs and Effects

The period of India's green revolution, from 1964–65 to 1971–72, was not accompanied on a national basis by rapid rural development as described in this chapter. The apparent failure of such a process may be as revealing of the requisites to success as success itself would be. There was a marked acceleration in the rate of increase of foodgrain production from 1964–65 to 1971–72. Three forces nullified the potential multiplier effects of that growth. Most important was the extraordinary drought of 1965 to 1967, which reduced stocks, and the subsequent decline in imports, which were largely in the form of foreign aid. Consequently, in

[22] For example, see the potentials suggested for dry farming areas in N. S. Jodha and V. S. Vyas, *Conditions of Stability Growth in Arid Agriculture* (Vallabh Vidyanagar, India: Agro-Economic Research Council, Sardar Patel University, 1969).

[23] For example, note literature on the backward rural areas of the U.S.: *The People Left Behind*, Report of the National Advisory Commission on Rural Poverty (Washington, D.C.: U.S. Government Printing Office, September 1967); *Rural Poverty in the United States* (Washington, D.C.: U.S. Government Printing Office, May 1968).

this period (1964–65 to 1971–72) there was neither a net increase in the growth rate of the total consumable supply of foodgrains nor in their contribution to net national product. Second, the decline in foreign aid markedly reduced the investment rate in the Fourth Five-Year Plan period. Third, the rigid plan structure of investment and resource allocation probably inhibited expansion of alternative industrial sectors. In 1972–73 and 1973–74, the drought, the worldwide shortage of fertilizer, and the lingering effects of supporting the Bangladesh refugees further postponed realization of the opportunities in rural development.

From these circumstances follow the necessary elements of a policy for the future pursuit of a rural-led strategy of growth. First, adhere to the basic steps for accelerated expansion in foodgrain production. Second, make massive public investments in transportation, communication, and electrification, including feeder lines into rural areas. This second point is, of course, a part of the foodgrain objective, but it is equally part of the nonfoodgrain agricultural and industrial strategy. Third, facilitate change in the structure of industrial production toward consumer goods, and encourage the establishment of small-scale enterprise, especially those that can be located in provincial areas. The latter requires modification in import and export policy as well as change in general guidelines for industrial development. In the short run, such an approach would probably require so much capital for rural infrastructure and the reorientation of industry as to be inconsistent with the direction of a high proportion of capital to the large-scale, heavy-industry sector. In the long run, a significantly faster rate of growth might soon allow a greater absolute level of investment in those sectors than would the present plan. It is, however, just this part of the strategy which runs most directly counter to the vested interests of the controlling bureaucracy, the big industrialists, the managers of the public sector heavy industry, and the politicians who are comfortable with the existing structure of the patronage system.

The effect of the new strategy on the distribution of income is complex. On a comparative basis, one might expect it to be similar to that in Japan or Taiwan, which have followed analogous tactics. Their Gini coefficients, measures of income distribution, of about .35 are not markedly different from India's estimated coefficient in the .35 to .40 range.[24] The

[24] See Terry Y. H. Yu and C. S. Lee, "Agricultural Technology and Income Distribution in Taiwan," paper presented at the Seminar on Agricultural Development, Joint Commission on Rural Reconstruction, Taipei, Taiwan, December 10–14, 1973.

rural-led strategy of development increases incomes of the poor, laboring class markedly. It probably does not increase incomes of the very rich significantly. The rise in earnings of the laboring class would be smaller, however, than the increase for the peasant cultivator and small-scale industrialist. The division between the last two groups depends upon the elasticity of supply of consumer goods purchased by the peasant cultivator classes. If a capital constraint retards output, employment will grow more slowly, foodgrain prices will fall, and the prices of consumer goods will rise, transferring income from the peasant class to the petty-capitalist class. If supply of capital is not limiting or increases rapidly through higher savings of industrialists or peasants, employment expands sharply and relative foodgrain prices are maintained. Of course, of the alternatives described, the latter provides maximum growth in national income. In each case, incomes of the poor increase quickly through some combination of lower foodgrain prices and more employment.

Finally, the process of rural-led growth is in many ways consistent with the objective of self-reliance, heavily stressed in the *Approach to the Fifth Plan*, particularly with respect to generating the savings necessary to development.[25] The need to contain increases in capital intensity of domestic production will require accelerated growth of imports, particularly of capital intensive intermediate products. That may occur without foreign aid as the domestic industries, stimulated by the new strategy, offer increased opportunity for relatively labor intensive exports.

[25] See *Approach to the Fifth Plan, 1974–79* (Delhi: Government of India, Planning Commission, January 1973).

VIII The Changing Pattern of Foreign Trade

The Indian economy, like that of a bare handful of other nations, is so vast, its resources so diverse, and its current level of trade so low that foreign trade will never account for a major portion of the national product. But exports can make a significant contribution to the Indian economy in an employment-oriented strategy of development; and they may play a critical role in the necessary reduction of the capital intensity of the industrial sector. On the one hand, growth in employment can be accelerated by the export of relatively labor intensive commodities, while the import of capital intensive commodities frees domestic capital for more employment-oriented production. On the other hand, release of the wage goods constraint through increased agricultural production allows greater employment without rising money wages and thereby facilitates increased production of the labor intensive products which are most competitive in foreign markets. Concurrently, a larger and more rapidly expanding domestic market for commodities with a high labor content promotes lower-cost production, which further strengthens competitive positions in foreign markets. In these respects trade may play a role in accelerating growth in India similar to its potentially positive role in the bulk of smaller low-income nations. Similarly, export growth has been retarded in India for reasons familiar in a wide range of countries.

Export growth was particularly slow in the Indian Second Plan period because of the choice of development strategy, the nature and conditions of foreign aid, and the initial composition of exports. The program of development diverted resources from the more labor intensive industries in which a low-income country might expect to find a comparative export advantage, while it failed to increase foodgrain production adequately to support a high level of employment. Foreign aid then financed a substantial proportion of the imports necessary to investment in large-scale capital intensive industries. Strengthening these forces, the strategy fostered bureaucratic regulation, which was itself inimical to the expansion of exports. The composition of India's exports in the 1950s was weighted heavily toward agricultural commodities, such as jute and tea, which were believed to have particularly poor growth prospects. That belief reinforced the policy of pursuing import displacement in spite of the rising capital intensity of such efforts. Initially imports displaced may be produced domestically by labor intensive methods, confirming the policy recommended for so much of Latin America by Raul Prebisch, but over time the imported goods to be displaced prove to be increasingly capital intensive. India, with an already broad industrial base, found itself in this position even in the 1950s. The import displacement policy, then, helped fulfill the prophecy of poor export performance. This set of forces is reflected in the 1.2 percent rate of decline in exports from 1951–52 to 1960–61 (Table VIII-1).

In contrast to the first two Plans, the Third and subsequent Plans did explicitly emphasize exports.[1] They recognized that substantial import demand for raw materials and capital goods was continuing and that foreign aid could not be relied on indefinitely to finance the bulk of the growth in imports. This new concern was mirrored in a growing host of export subsidies and licensing preferences, the eventual complexity and inefficiency of which precipitated the 1966 devaluation. Exports reversed the declining trend of the 1950s and accelerated to a 6.2 percent rate of growth from 1960–61 to the predrought year 1964–65. This performance, probably impressive at India's stage of development, was soon dulled by the effects of drought and economic distortion and stagnation. Exports declined to a 1.9 percent rate of increase from 1964–65 to 1969–70, and overall, for the period 1960–61 to 1971–72, averaged a rise of 4.1 percent per year (Table VIII-1). The sharply improved record subsequent to 1971–72, though substantially due to accelerated worldwide inflation, still gives some portent of future potential, and reflects underlying structural changes in production and policy.

The Changing Growth and Structure of Imports

The capital intensive theory of growth postulates large-scale importation of capital goods at the outset; imports will decline gradually as the

[1] See *Third Five-Year Plan* (New Delhi: Government of India, Planning Commission, 1961); *Fourth Five-Year Plan* (New Delhi: Government of India, Planning Commission, n.d.); and Jagdish N. Bhagwati and Padma Desai, *India: Planning for Industrialization* (London: Oxford University Press, 1970).

Table VIII-1. Indian exports, 1951–52 to 1973–74

Year	Total exports		Traditional exports			Nontraditional exports		
	Million U.S.$ (current)	Percent growth rate	Million U.S.$ (current)	Percent of total	Percent growth rate	Million U.S.$ (current)	Percent of total	Percent growth rate
1951–52	1,503		1,332	88.6		172	11.4	
1955–56	1,242	– 4.7	1,081	87.2	–5.1	159	12.8	– 1.9
1960–61	1,349	– 1.2	1,120	82.8	–1.9	232	17.2	+ 3.4
1961–62	1,387	+ 1.7	1,153	83.1	+0.7	235	16.9	+ 7.8
1962–63	1,440		1,223	84.9		217	15.1	
1963–64	1,666	+ 4.6	1,350	81.0	+4.1	316	19.0	+ 7.0
1964–65	1,715		1,446	84.3		269	15.7	
1965–66	1,692	+ 3.2	1,368	80.8	+1.4	325	19.2	+ 9.3
1966–67	1,542		1,217	79.1		322	20.9	
1967–68	1,598	+ 3.9	1,214	76.0	–0.6	384	24.0	+17.1
1968–69	1,810		1,242	68.6		569	31.4	
1969–70	1,884	+ 3.6	1,219	64.6	+0.7	668	35.4	+12.6
1970–71	2,047		1,330	65.0		716	35.0	
1971–72	2,091	+12.5	1,430	68.3	+8.3	663	31.7	+16.0
1972–73	2,431		1,466	60.3		971	39.9	
1973–74	3,021		1,812	60.3		1,208	40.0	

Note: Errors in summation are due to rounding.
Definitions: Traditional exports: food, beverages and tobacco, crude materials, mineral fuels, animal and vegetable oils and fats, and cotton textiles and jute manufactures. Nontraditional exports: chemicals, manufactured goods other than cotton textiles and jute manufactures, machinery and transport equipment, miscellaneous manufactured goods, and others.
Source: Appendix, Table 12.

country becomes more self-sufficient. India's import record was initially consistent with the theory. From 1951–52 to 1955–56, imports decreased sharply because a succession of good crop years drastically reduced the need to import food. Then, as the capital-oriented strategy was applied, imports increased at a rate of 11.5 percent per year from 1955–56 to 1960–61 and dropped subsequently to a 4.7 percent growth rate in the 1960–61 to 1964–65 predrought period of rapid industrial expansion (Table VIII-2). In the next period, 1964–65 to 1970–71, imports actually fell by nearly a quarter, but that was owing to the industrial recession, to the great drought of 1965–1967, and to the concurrent sharp decline in foreign aid, rather than to the further success of the development strategy.

India's imports from 1950 to 1960 grew at a rate of 5.5 percent per year—comparable to the rate of mature economies such as the United States, 4.6 percent, and the United Kingdom, 3.3 percent; more rapid than Singapore's 0.35 percent, and comparable, among developing countries, to Taiwan's 6.4 percent, the Philippines' 4.5 percent, and Hong Kong's 5.7 percent.[2]

The sharp contrast between India and the other countries occurred in the 1960s. While most nations rapidly increased the growth rate of their imports—particularly of manufactured commodities—in this period, India actually experienced a decline (Table VIII-3). It is noteworthy that those countries which achieved accelerated rates of increase in exports and in national income, such as Japan, Taiwan, Hong Kong, and Singapore, also experienced a concurrent accelerated expansion in imports.[3]

The composition of India's imports was changing quickly. Thus, consistent with the capital intensive strategy, machinery and transport equipment comprised more and more of India's imports, increasing by almost 50 percent in the rapid growth period between 1960–61 and 1965–66—though dropping by 25 percent in the period of slow industrial development, between 1964–65 and 1973–74.

Machinery and transport equipment comprised over one-third of all imports in 1965–66, and in 1973–74 still accounted for over one-fifth of the total (Appendix, Table 11). In changing to an employment-oriented strat-

[2] These data and much of the analysis in this chapter are drawn from John W. Mellor and Uma Lele, "The Interaction of Growth Strategy, Agriculture and Foreign Trade—The Case of India," in George S. Tolley and Peter A. Zadrozny, eds., *Trade, Agriculture and Development* (Cambridge, Mass.: Ballinger, 1975), pp. 93–113.

[3] Ibid., pp. 97–99.

Table VIII-2. Indian imports, 1951–52 to 1973–74

	Total imports		Traditional imports			Nontraditional imports		
	Million U.S.$ (current)	Percent growth rate	Million U.S.$ (current)	Percent of total	Percent growth rate	Million U.S.$ (current)	Percent of total	Percent growth rate
1951–52	1,838		1,526	83.0		312	17.0	
1955–56	1,365	− 7.2	1,082	79.3	− 8.2	280	20.5	− 2.7
		+ 2.8			+ 2.9			+ 2.3
1960–61	2,356	+11.5	1,976	83.9	+12.8	382	16.2	+ 6.4
1961–62	2,290		1,864	81.4		427	18.6	
1962–63	2,377		1,956	82.3		423	17.8	
1963–64	2,569	+ 4.7	2,104	81.9	+ 5.3	464	18.1	+ 1.1
1964–65	2,834	+ 3.0	2,445	86.3	+ 2.3	390	13.8	+ 5.6
1965–66	2,959		2,557	86.4		403	13.6	
1966–67	2,771		2,403	86.7		368	13.3	
1967–68	2,677	− 5.9	2,303	86.0	− 7.5	372	13.9	+ 2.0
1968–69	2,545		2,118	83.2		427	16.8	
1969–70	2,109	− 3.3	1,681	79.7	− 5.0	429	20.3	+ 5.1
1970–71	2,179		1,732	79.5		445	20.4	
1971–72	2,416	+13.9	1,874	77.6	+10.6	542	22.4	+24.7
1972–73	2,311		1,779	77.0		532	23.0	
1973–74	3,555		2,517	70.8		1,038	29.2	

Note: Errors in summation are due to rounding.
Definitions: Traditional imports: cereal and cereal preparations, raw cotton other than linters, chemicals, manufactured goods, machinery and transport equipment, miscellaneous manufactured goods, and residual imports. Nontraditional imports: food other than cereal and cereal preparations, beverages and tobacco, crude materials other than raw cotton, mineral fuels, lubricants, animal and vegetable oils and fats.
Source: Appendix, Table 11.

Table VIII-3. Growth rates of trade by commodity groups, India and world total, 1960 to 1969 (percent per year)

Commodity group	World	Industrial areas	Eastern trading bloc	Developing areas	India
Exports					
Total primary goods	5.6	5.8	4.9	4.9	1.2
Food	5.6	6.7	5.5	4.1	0.6
Agricultural raw materials	2.7	3.5	2.6	-3.3	1.4
Crude minerals and ores	6.3	6.5	5.1	6.4	3.2
Mineral fuels	7.8	6.6	5.9	8.7	-1.0
Total manufactured goods	10.8	10.9	8.7	13.2	6.0
Chemicals	11.0	11.2	8.9	12.0	10.6
Basic metals	8.6	8.2	8.5	11.3	19.8 *
Machinery and transport equipment	12.0	12.2	9.9	21.3	26.7
Textiles and clothing	9.4	9.0 †	8.5	11.2	0.5 ‡
Other manufactured goods	10.4	10.5	6.0	16.0	15.3
Total exports	8.8	9.5	7.9	6.8	3.6
Imports					
Total primary goods	5.6	6.1	3.5	4.1	-1.2
Food	5.6	5.9	5.5	4.6	0.6
Agricultural raw materials	2.7	3.0	0.0	3.6	-3.8
Crude minerals and ores	6.3	6.6	4.5	8.9	6.6
Mineral fuels	7.8	9.3	4.0	4.6	1.0 §
Total manufactured goods	10.8	12.7	8.5	7.7	-1.1
Chemicals	11.0	12.2	12.1	8.6	3.9
Basic metals	8.6	9.7	5.4	6.2	-7.4
Machinery and transport equipment	12.0	14.5	9.9	8.9	-2.4
Other manufactured goods ‖	10.0	12.2	6.9	6.1	6.9
Total imports	8.8	9.7	7.1	6.6	-1.2

* Iron and Steel only.   † Excluding Australia, New Zealand, and South Africa.
‡ Textiles only.   § Growth rate to 1970.   ‖ Including Textiles and Clothing.
Definitions: Industrial areas: North America, Western Europe, Japan, South Africa, Australia, and New Zealand. Eastern trading bloc: Eastern Europe, Soviet Union, China, North Vietnam, North Korea, and Mongolia. Developing areas: Latin America, South and East Asia, Middle East, Africa, and other parts of the world.
Sources: Columns 1–4: United Nations Conference on Trade and Development, *Handbook of International Trade and Development Statistics, 1972;* except for exports of textiles and clothing, for which the source was General Agreement on Tariffs and Trade, *International Trade* (Geneva), 1963 and 1971. Column 5: United Nations Department of Economics and Social Affairs, Statistical Office, *Yearbook of International Trade Statistics,* various issues.

egy, a higher proportion of the capital goods requirements needed by small-scale, labor intensive industries could probably be met by domestic production, compared to the capital goods needed by large-scale, heavy industry emphasized in the capital intensive approach. Nevertheless, the faster overall growth rate could well result in accelerated machinery imports, though possibly with compensating greater exports of more labor intensive types of equipment. In this context, the Japanese example is instructive. Despite development of a broad base of domestic industrial capacity, Japan's imports of machinery and transport equipment grew at a rate of 20 percent per year from 1950 to 1960; even from 1961 to 1969, such imports advanced at a rate of 9 percent per year. However, Japan's machinery exports expanded even faster.[4]

During the period of rapid industrial growth in the early 1960s, India required additional large imports of natural-resource-based commodities. The vagaries of the monsoon and the failure to constrain consumer incomes resulted in large foodgrain imports. And, despite the strategy, capital intensive intermediate products, such as fertilizer, continued to be important. Since the shift to an employment-oriented program of development may substantially accelerate the growth of imports in each of these categories, the expansion of exports is imperative if the new approach is to succeed.

The future course of foodgrain imports is particularly difficult to determine. It is in part a function of the pace of technological change in agriculture. It is, however, also affected, on the one hand, by the extent to which a demand-increasing, employment-oriented strategy is pursued and, on the other, by the extent to which demand is contained by fiscal policy and the availability of foreign exchange from exports or aid. In individual years weather is, of course, the primary determinant of foodgrain imports. In the longer term, imports would probably be at a minimum with either a high or low foodgrain production growth rate, and at a maximum in association with an intermediate level of output growth.

Thus, a 4 to 5 percent rate of increase in foodgrain production might result in a low level of imports, as a relatively high growth rate of employment could be sustained with domestic production, while a slow rate of production growth, say lower than 3 percent, would also be accompanied by minimum growth in foodgrain imports as political concern about sustaining a high level of such imports argued for a low-employment strategy of development. At the same time, a moderate increase in foodgrain production of 3 to 4 percent per year might provide sufficient confidence for an expansionary employment policy and an economic base for accelerated export growth and might furnish, therefore, both the necessity and the means for obtaining large foodgrain imports in

[4] Ibid., p. 100.

years of poor weather and low production. Further complicating the prospects, especially within the context of stepped-up production and a high-employment strategy, foodgrain-exporting nations could foster increased Indian imports through bilateral concessionary trade agreements. Thus, with both demand and domestic supply of foodgrains subject to wide variations in growth, the difference between the two is particularly subject to error in estimates.

It seems virtually certain, however, that an employment-oriented strategy of development would require swift expansion in imports of non-foodgrain agricultural commodities. Vegetable oils and cotton already comprise a significant portion of India's imports—despite the slow growth of consumer income and of exports such as textiles. To avoid accelerated growth rates of such imports in the context of increasing demand patterns and in an environment of improved exports would require a vastly greater relative output of these commodities than of foodgrains. That, in turn, would demand a faster rate of technological change or a considerable shift of acreage (induced by a relative decline in foodgrain prices)—neither of which seems likely to occur in the near term.

In the favorable years of industrial growth, such as 1963–64 and 1964–65, the capital intensive intermediate products, iron and steel plus fertilizers, accounted for over 10 percent of India's import bill.[5] In a labor intensive strategy of development, demand for these commodities and others of similar characteristics, such as aluminum and synthetic fibers, will swell, not only in response to increasing national income, but also to growth of the highly labor intensive industries which process these commodities for the foreign market. At the same time, the new strategy will allocate capital supplies principally to more labor intensive industries. Accordingly, imports of this already large category of commodities must necessarily increase. That will be a general characteristic of low-income countries following an employment-oriented strategy with important implications not only to their export requirements, but to the trade *and* production patterns of the rich countries as well.

The very sharp rise in mineral fuel prices in 1973–74 dramatized this element of the longer-term problems of imports. As is the case with capital intensive intermediate products, demand for mineral fuels and their derivatives will grow at an accelerated pace with an employment-oriented

[5] See *Fourth Five-Year Plan: A Draft Outline* (New Delhi: Government of India, Planning Commission, 1966), Table 3, p. 102.

strategy of development. Insofar as such natural-resource-based commodities are not produced domestically, or are exploited through highly capital intensive processes for which foreign exchange is not readily and specifically available, imports will grow rapidly. Because of the inefficiency with which the capital intensive approach provides the larger requirement of foreign exchange, a general upward shift in relative primary product prices, as for petroleum in 1973–74, serves to buttress the logic of a change to an employment-oriented growth strategy with its greater export potentials. The rapid growth of exports from India to the OPEC nations following the oil price changes is consistent with this view. The changes in Indian policy with respect to use of foreign firms in exploration, undoubtedly inspired by the radical price changes and the prospects for large additions to domestic production by 1985, suggest how ephemeral are estimates of future imports.

The *Approach to the Fifth Plan* is basically at variance with the import analysis set forth here.[6] The *Approach* document is in roughly the same conceptual mold as the Second Plan. It is based on an input-output model, assuming a fixed, slow rate of export growth at 7 percent, and argues that imports must be constrained to that rate—or lower—by reducing "luxury" consumption and expanding the capital intensive sector to displace imports. Such a plan is hardly feasible, at least at the targeted level, without either the resumption of large-scale net foreign aid on a long-term basis or a domestic effort to achieve resource mobilization much greater than ever before attempted. It is certainly inconsistent with an employment-oriented strategy of development.

Although the capital intensive program has actually been prejudicial to exports, the *Approach* document argues that it *facilitates* exports.[7] Since the total quantity of imports is considered to be relatively fixed, increased domestic production of capital intensive intermediate products allows greater production of export goods for which they are raw materials. Similarly, "the exercise [in the planning model for the Fifth Plan] indicates that progress towards self-reliance will be significantly accelerated if higher levels of production can be achieved in a few sectors such as steel, non-ferrous metals, fertilisers and crude oil. All efforts should be concentrated on expanding production at a fast rate in these sectors."

---

[6] See *Approach to the Fifth Plan, 1974–79* (Delhi: Government of India, Planning Commission, January 1973).

[7] Ibid., p. 14.

Likewise, "it may be possible to improve the projected rate of growth of output of fertilisers. Since in the accepted variant, fertilisers continue to be imported in substantial quantities in the terminal year, any increase in production above the estimated level will be desirable from the balance of payments angle." [8] Indeed, so much weight is placed on the capital intensive intermediate sectors that expansion of electric power, clearly nonimportable, seems to have been slowed dangerously, even according to the standards of the *Approach* document, let alone the standards of the agriculture and employment-oriented strategy: "Rate of growth of electricity [for the Fifth Plan] is appreciably lower compared to the rate postulated by the Fuel Policy Committee. This is partly attributed to the same factors as mentioned for coal [slower than expected economic growth] and partly on account of restriction implied on the rate of growth of domestic demand for electricity as a result of reduced inequality." [9]

If the employment-oriented approach is followed, the consequent substantial increase in imports will necessitate finding means of ensuring vital supplies and protecting against sharp jumps in relative prices. An effective planning mechanism would provide estimates of future needs and use those as a basis for long-term contracts with foreign suppliers prudently dispersed among political and economic blocs. Although certainly not without risks, such a process may involve no greater peril to supplies than reliance on domestic production in circumstances of severe capital constraint, apparently poor ability to estimate future demand, and uncertain management and technology. It must be remembered that the fertilizer crisis of 1972 to 1974 occurred in the context of an effort to achieve substantial self-sufficiency and was certainly aggravated by miscalculations of future domestic production, based, in particular, on overly optimistic estimates of capacity utilization. [10]

The level and composition of India's imports have been and presumably will continue to be influenced by the countries it trades with and by the availability of foreign exchange. Past growth strategy emphasized imported machinery and foreign aid. The end of colonial control diminished the role of the United Kingdom while a desire for diversity in national origin of trade, the demand for heavy capital equipment, the attractions to the bureaucracy of trade with a centrally planned economy, and even

---

[8] Ibid., pp. 21–22.   [9] Ibid., p. 22.

[10] See, for example, "Demand for Fertilisers in India and Supply Prospects," *Fertiliser News,* 19:1 (January 1974), 58–65; and Satya Nand, "Prospects for an Adequate Fertiliser Supply to Developing Countries, *Fertiliser News,* 18:7 (July 1973), 11–17.

direct political sympathies enhanced the significance of the Soviet Union as a trading partner.

The United States provided only 14 percent of India's imports in 1955–56. The figure rose to 29 percent in 1960–61 and 39 percent in 1967–68, before declining to 17 percent in 1973–74 (Appendix, Table 13). Trade with the United States has been most dependent on aid. In 1969–70, only 17 percent of India's exports went to the United States, with a resultant balance of trade deficit of over 300 million dollars (Appendix, Table 14). In that same year, India maintained a modest balance of trade surplus with the Soviet Union, a large surplus with the rest of Asia and Oceania (approximately 150 million dollars with Japan), a small deficit with Western Europe, and a deficit of 70 million dollars with Africa. In 1969–70, India's trade deficiency was primarily with the United States, mainly because most of the foodgrain imports, which in 1969–70 totaled 348 million dollars, had come from America.

Imports from the United Kingdom have gradually declined from 19 percent of the total in 1951–52 and 1960–61 to 8.4 percent in 1973–74 (Appendix, Table 13). This change in trading relations is typical of former colonial countries.

The Export Performance and Its Determinants

Exports—to provide the means of payment for imports—must form the core of a strategy to support a policy of increased employment with importation of necessary capital intensive commodities. In India, one of the prime arguments for the capital intensive approach to development is based on pessimism with respect to export prospects—itself usually grounded in the expectation of poor growth in demand for primary commodities and of rising protectionism against manufactured goods by high-income countries.[11]

The evidence, particularly in the 1960s, does not support the gloomy view of exports either with respect to low-income countries generally or to India specifically. Total exports from less developed countries grew at a rate of 6.8 percent from 1960 to 1969 (Table VIII-3). This is more than two-thirds the rate of growth of exports from the developed countries for the same period, and 85 percent as fast as growth in exports from the Eastern bloc countries. More important, in all the classifications in which

[11] See Bhagwati and Desai, p. 369.

developed countries' exports grew rapidly, less developed countries' exports grew even more quickly. Worldwide, food, agricultural raw materials, and crude minerals and ores showed the smallest increases. It is only in these classifications that less developed countries have performed poorly compared to high-income nations. These commodities have, in the past, constituted the bulk of the less developed countries' exports; their heavy weight explains the overall slower growth rate. It is particularly noteworthy that imports of the various categories of manufactured goods to the developing areas expanded much less rapidly than exports of the same categories of commodities. Most striking, exports of machinery and transport equipment from developing areas increased 21 percent per year during the period 1960 to 1969, while their imports of these commodities grew at only 9 percent per year.

Accordingly, the efforts of less developed countries to industrialize seem to have paid off in the form of rapid advancement of exports in those categories experiencing the fastest rise in overall world trade. Less developed countries have learned to manufacture products which have quickly become competitive with those of the more developed nations. The more these items proliferate, the greater their importance, and the faster the overall rate of export growth. Relatively slow advances in food and raw materials and ores may, in part, derive from mushrooming domestic demand for these commodities as manufacturing increases, and from rigidities of supply due to natural resource constraints. The emphasis on developing manufacturing may also have resulted in some temporary neglect of the primary commodity categories, and consequent loss of productive output and export potentials. This neglect has probably been most substantial in agriculture and has taken the form of underinvestment in cost-reducing technological change.

India's export performance has been an exaggerated version of the pattern of achievement of less developed countries. Exports of the various classes of manufactured goods—except textiles and clothing—have grown at least as rapidly as those of other less developed countries. The front runners in exports from less developed countries were machinery and transport equipment—for which India's rate of expansion, in the period 1960 to 1969, was nearly 25 percent faster (Table VIII-3). India's generally good export performance in general manufacturing overcame the depressing effect of textiles. However, in most of the primary commodity areas, her export level was considerably inferior to that of the other less developed countries. An unfavorable geographic composition of markets, which traced from the colonial period, reinforced the pessimistic view of export prospects.

Thus, in 1955–56, the United Kingdom received 28 percent of India's exports, a share which had declined to 9 percent by 1972–73 (Appendix, Table 14). The value of India's exports to the United Kingdom declined by nearly 39 percent during this period. The uneconomic elements of colonial trading relationships tend to disappear with the loss of imperial power, resulting in rapid decline in exports from the ex-colony to the ex-imperial power. For example, from 1952 to 1969, Japan's share of South Korea's and Taiwan's exports declined from 54 and 53 percent to 22 and 15 percent, respectively, while the United States increased its share from 33 to 56 percent for South Korea, and from 6 percent to 43 percent for Taiwan. In the case of India, there was the additional liability of reducing a tie with a relatively stagnant trading partner. Thus, from 1960 to 1969, total imports into the United Kingdom increased by 5.8 percent per year—in sharp contrast to worldwide imports, which rose by 8.8 percent per year; United States imports, which expanded annually by 11.8 percent; and Japanese imports, which grew by 12.6 percent per annum.[12]

The Eastern bloc countries—the Soviet Union plus East European countries—began to replace the United Kingdom as a market for India's exports. Exports to the Eastern bloc region were less than 1 percent of India's total in 1955–56. From 1960–61 to 1973–74, the share had tripled, increasing from 8 percent to 24 percent of all exports (Appendix, Table 14). The ability of the Eastern bloc countries and India to manage their large trade agreements through state trading agencies facilitated the rise.[13] India's other important trading partner during this period was Japan. Indian exports to that country rose more than 14 percent per year from 1960–61 to 1973–74, largely because of iron ore.

Geographic patterns of trade for successful Asian exporters have been highly varied. Taiwan, South Korea, the Philippines, and Singapore essentially do not trade with the Eastern bloc countries. Japan's exports to those countries grew even faster than India's, while Hong Kong's declined. Taiwan owed her vigorous export growth chiefly to her market in the United States.[14]

[12] Mellor and Lele, in Tolley and Zadrozny, eds., op. cit., p. 107.

[13] See Bhagwati and Desai, pp. 429–31.

[14] Data are from United Nations, Department of Economic and Social Affairs, Statistical Office, *Yearbook of International Trade Statistics* (New York), various issues.

By 1973–74, India had achieved a balanced geographic composition of trade, with 25, 8, and 11 percent of exports respectively to Western Europe, the East European countries, and the U.S.S.R., and 15 percent each to North America, Japan, and other Asian countries (Appendix, Table 14). A similar balance in commodity composition had also developed. In 1951–52, tea, jute manufactures, and cotton textiles comprised 59 percent of all exports, a proportion which declined to 24 percent in 1973–74 (Appendix, Table 12). The dollar value of these traditional exports alone dropped 27 percent in this period, while exports of all other commodities rose over three and one-half times. These various adjustments in export performance had not, of course, been as striking as the success stories of some countries, for example, Taiwan. Nevertheless, they do suggest a much more favorable base for the future growth of exports, and therefore a more promising environment for an export-oriented strategy of development than prevailed at independence. The lessons from India on exports are similar to those of the bulk of Asian, African, and Latin American countries for which trading relations substantially influenced by a richer and more powerful partner had to be laboriously changed before trade could play the vigorous role delineated in this chapter.

The Policy Constraints on Export Performance

India's failure to realize the nascent export potentials during the past two decades of development stems primarily from the capital intensive growth strategy and secondarily from the bureaucratic restraints that were, at least initially, a product of that strategy. The result was failure to exploit India's two principal potential sources of increased trade. The first source was low-cost workers producing labor intensive commodities for export to high-wage countries; the other, closely interacting with the first, was a large, growing domestic market to foster the efficient manufacture of consumer goods with a high labor content.

Trade between countries with unlike proportions of factors of production reflects one of the more plausible theories of exchange.[15] According to this view, India would produce labor intensive commodities. As a variation on that theme, India, with its relatively large expenditure on higher

[15] See E. Hecksher, "The Effect of Foreign Trade on the Distribution of Income," in *Readings in the Theory of International Trade* (Philadelphia: American Economic Association, 1949); and Bertil Ohlin, *Interregional and International Trade* (Cambridge, Mass.: Harvard University Press, 1933).

education, might give particular emphasis to commodities low in capital intensity but high in requirements of both skilled and unskilled manpower. In practice, however, India's pattern of industrial growth has been highly capital intensive. Thus, during the period 1951 to 1965, of nineteen major industry categories the four most capital intensive increased their proportion of capital investment, value added in production, and employment, while, with one exception, the four industry groups with the lowest capital intensity decreased their share of each of the three measures. All four of the low capital intensive industries are producers of final consumer goods, and none of the top four falls in that category. And, even if the structure of capital investment had been more labor intensive, the slow growth in agriculture would have created a wage goods constraint to increased employment. Reinforcing the underlying problem was the lack of foreign exchange for the importation of heavy industrial machinery and intermediate products required to produce labor intensive value added. An 18 percent rise in the capital intensity of exports from 1964 to 1969 reflected the increased capital intensity of production.[16] In four of eight industrial trade categories, the weighted average capital intensity of exports increased during the period. There is also a tendency for the industries with greater capital intensity to have the fastest growth in exports, although the weighted average increase in capital intensity of exports was somewhat less than that for the economy as a whole.[17]

India could have produced inexpensive, low-quality consumer and capital goods for the home market, thereby achieving efficiency in production and providing competitive exports to similar markets elsewhere, particularly in other poor countries. This theory of building exports from industries meant to serve domestic markets is somewhat complementary to the resource endowment theory, in that poor countries would, in practice, consume lower-quality goods which were labor intensive in production and maintenance; the same would apply to capital goods.[18] The In-

[16] Mellor and Lele, in Tolley and Zadrozny, eds., op. cit., p. 108. See also the analysis of Ranganath Bharadwaj confirming a rise in the capital intensity of exports vis-à-vis imports replacement in 1958–59 compared to 1953–54, in *Structural Basis of India's Foreign Trade*, University of Bombay Series in Monetary and International Economics, No. 6, (Bombay, 1962).

[17] Rank correlation coefficients between capital intensity and export growth from 1964 and 1969 were statistically significant at the 90 percent level. See Mellor and Lele, in Tolley and Zadrozny, eds., op. cit., n. 34.

[18] This is, in essence, S. B. Linder's hypothesis that countries with similar per capita incomes and hence similar consumption patterns will trade with each other (*An Essay on Trade and Transformation* [New York: Wiley, 1961]). In a test of Linder's hypothesis, Lele

dian growth strategy militated against this approach to exports. Most important, consumer income, particularly of the poor, was stagnant; without growth the aggregate of consumer goods industries could not expand and increase in efficiency. In this respect, the experience of India is in sharp contrast to events in Taiwan, where a rapidly growing domestic market was used effectively to develop industries which later seized the export potential.[19]

It is sometimes argued that Indian export performance has been poor because the large domestic market draws off all production for its own use. While the argument is clearly specious, its refutation helps to clarify the problem. Under the capital intensive strategy of development, there was, of course, little expansion of consumer goods industries. Nevertheless, some increased income payments leaked into consumption channels and consequently raised domestic prices of the small quantity of consumer goods, the production of which could not be expanded commensurately because of restraints on resources resulting from the strategy. Exports could occur if domestic income was closely contained. In the labor intensive approach, consumer incomes may rise, but with the availability of resources for consumer goods production, that demand will stimulate the growth of consumer goods industries. The increased demand may initially cause higher prices, but these will provide the basis for the required investment in capital goods, even while the higher prices themselves temporarily contain domestic consumption (see Chapter VI).

The deleterious implications to trade of the theoretical model behind the Second and Third Plans drew strength from the simplifying assumptions of the planning models, which—in the context of the theory—appeared reasonable. The early planning models ignored trade and exports. The later, more sophisticated versions, such as Chakravarty's, incorporated trade in the model, but with the rate of growth of exports still set at a fixed percentage of domestic production, imports then being determined by the low level of exports and by foreign aid.[20] Capital goods received priority for the available foreign exchange. Such models permitted little foreign exchange for the imports necessary to efficient export.

found no correlation between propensities to import and income differences between India and pairs of regions (see Mellor and Lele, in Tolley and Zadrozny, eds., op. cit., n. 36).

[19] Kou-shu Liang and T. H. Lee, "Process and Pattern of Economic Development in Taiwan," unpublished paper, Joint Committee on Rural Reconstruction, Taipei, Taiwan, 1972.

[20] See S. Chakravarty, *Capital and Development Planning* (Cambridge, Mass.: M.I.T. Press, 1969).

Within both a theory of growth and a set of planning models inimical to the expansion of exports, a bureaucracy inept for this task further prejudiced the export effort.[21] Since foreign markets tend to be residual and, therefore, more competitive and volatile than domestic markets, bureaucratic delays and ineptitude particularly inhibit exports. Development of exports requires removal of controls on capital intensive imports. (It seems unlikely that such imports could be isolated from the domestic market; in any case, growth in the domestic market may be necessary to facilitate the economic expansion of export industries.)

Even in the context of reduced regulation, the public sector can play a vital, positive role in expanding exports—first, by taking risks to develop markets, and second, by ensuring adequate supplies of raw materials through the execution of long-term buying agreements. To fulfill this positive role requires technical specialization which is contrary to the generalist philosophy of the traditional Indian civil service.[22] It also requires a change from the stultifying emphasis on preventing leakages of foreign exchange and compressing growth into a plan framework toward an open, helpful, confident viewpoint about the advancement of exports. For this to happen, the strategy of growth must be changed and the bureaucracy must perform a different set of tasks with increased efficiency. By the mid-1970s some progress was taking place on these matters.

In the context of a new strategy, the role of the State Trading Corporation might well expand in two directions. First, if there is an increasing volume of imports of easily graded raw materials and capital intensive intermediate products, a case can be made for carefully estimating future needs and using these requirements as a basis for establishing market power through large-scale buying in advance of needs. Second, public investment in market analysis, development, and promotion, including risk absorption, could foster exports in new, promising lines.

Finally, it must be recognized that the regulatory bureaucracy is powerfully entrenched and can be expected to fight vigorously and effectively to maintain its power. In doing so, it may ally itself with politicians who themselves have much to gain from the distribution of patronage and windfall profit inherent in such a system of control. A substantial threat to the new approach may well lie in the combined opposition of the old-line bureaucrats and politicians.

[21] See Bhagwati and Desai, pp. 130–34.
[22] For a discussion of the civil service in India, see Chapter VI, pp. 147–50, above.

Lessons from the Textile Record

Probably textiles, better than any other set of commodities, illustrate the manner in which India's chosen growth strategy has penalized exports and made the assumption of poor performance self-fulfilling.

In 1953, subsequent to the Korean War boom, foreign shipments of all textiles and clothing (excluding jute) totaled 153 million dollars, or 15 percent of Indian exports (Table VIII-4). India, at that time, provided

Table VIII-4. Exports of clothing and textiles (excluding jute manufactures) from selected countries, 1953 to 1970 (in million U.S. dollars)

Year	India *	Pakistan	South Korea	Taiwan	Total less developed countries †	India's share of less developed countries' total (percent)	Japan
1953	153	–	–	–	398	38	413
1955	187	11	–	1	499	37	693
1957	200	7	–	3	612	33	869
1959	194	50	1	12	609	32	936
1961	182	13	1	28	743	24	1,069
1962	170	24	2	39	805	21	1,143
1963	185	48	12	45	946	20	1,126
1964	242	67	26	61	1,162	21	1,290
1965	211	62	47	65	1,255	17	1,427
1966	188	78	68	82	1,394	14	1,611
1967	181	116	108	121	1,608	11	1,565
1968	188	136	173	183	2,029	9	1,822
1969	236	143	226	266	2,420	10	2,097
1970	199	182	299	427	2,827	7	2,206

* Figures not exact due to use of financial year for jute manufactures and calender year for total textile and clothing exports, i.e. including jute.

† Estimated by deducting Indian and Pakistani exports of jute manufactures from total clothing and textile exports of less developed countries (excluding communist countries). Figures for 1953 to 1957 are approximations.

Note: Figures are not strictly comparable due to use of both calender and financial years.

Sources: Column 1: Computed from data in United Nations, Department of Economics and Social Affairs, Statistical Office, Yearbook of International Trade Statistics, various issues; Government of India, Central Statistical Organisation, Statistical Abstract India, various issues; and Government of India, Economic Survey, various issues. Column 2: Government of Pakistan, Central Statistical Office, Twenty-five Years of Pakistan in Statistics, 1947–1972 (Karachi: Manager of Publications, 1972). Column 3: Republic of Korea, Bank of Korea, Economic Statistical Yearbook, various issues. Column 4: Council for International Economic Co-operation and Development, Executive Yuan, Republic of China, Taiwan Statistical Data Book, various issues. Column 5: 1953 to 1957 estimated on the basis of data in United Nations, Yearbook of International Trade Statistics, various issues; 1959 to 1970 based on data in General Agreement on Trade and Tariff, International Trade, various issues. Column 7: General Agreement on Trade and Tariff, International Trade, various issues.

38 percent of all exports of these commodities by less developed countries. By 1970 India's exports of the textile group had increased by only 46 *million* dollars, while such exports by the total of less developed countries had risen by 2.4 *billion*. Pakistan had increased from zero to an amount 90 percent as large as India's, South Korea from zero to a total 50 percent greater, Taiwan from zero to an amount over twice as large. India's share of the less developed countries' exports of textiles declined from 38 percent to 7 percent between 1953 and 1970. If India had maintained her proportion during the period, textile exports would, in 1970, have totaled 1.1 billion dollars, a net addition of over 40 percent to total exports and a sum comparable in size to the largest annual net aid received by India. If India's share of the less developed countries' exports of textiles had dropped only by half in this period, exports would still have been larger by 340 million dollars.

It may be argued that India so dominated world textile trade in 1953 that it could not expect a dynamic performance in the future. In answer to that argument, it is sufficient to point out that in 1953 Japan's textile exports were nearly 2.7 times larger than India's and then increased over fivefold by 1970 for an addition to textile exports of 1.8 billion dollars—an increase almost exactly equal to India's foreign shipments of all commodities in 1968–69. Similarly, the sum of the increase in textile exports from Taiwan and South Korea in the two years 1968 to 1970 was nearly twice as large as India's total textile exports in 1970 (Table VIII-4).

India's problem was not an early saturation of markets or a lack of foreign outlets. She simply failed to produce, owing to inadequate market orientation, antiquated techniques, and inability to import raw materials. These insufficiencies trace from the development strategy and its implementation and suggest the basis for future failure in other export lines if the strategy does not change.

While India maintained the composition of its textile exports along traditional, historical lines, other countries were making dynamic adaptations to changing market conditions.[23] From 1953 to 1968, Japan's exports of cotton fabrics increased by only 30 percent and 60 million dol-

[23] See Manmohan Singh, *India's Export Trends and the Prospects for Self-Sustained Growth* (Oxford: Clarendon Press, 1964), pp. 50–55; Bhagwati and Desai, pp. 385–88; Vadilal Dagli, ed., *A Profile of Indian Industry* (Bombay: Vora, 1970), pp. 169–213; D. C. Barjatiya, *Current Economic & Commercial Problems* (3d. ed.; Agra: Navyug Sahitya Sadan, 1968), pp. 164–77; and Asoka Mehta, *Economic Planning in India* (New Delhi: Young India Publications, 1970), pp. 150–52.

lars.[24] Fabrics of other materials, dominated by synthetics, expanded over seven times and added 560 million dollars to exports. Even more spectacular, clothing exports rose tenfold, or by 350 million dollars. For India, clothing exports increased to only 20 million dollars in 1968; regenerated and synthetic fabric exports were actually lower in 1968 than in 1953. Clothing also dominated South Korean export growth, rising from 7 million dollars in 1964 to 112 million in 1968. Taiwan, too, experienced rapid expansion; clothing exports accounted for nearly half of her textile exports in 1968; but Taiwan also produced much more cotton fabric for export—her production rose from 9 million dollars in 1959 to 43 million in 1968.

As an exception to this pattern, Pakistan further emphasizes the cost to India of not adapting to new market potentials. Textile exports (excluding jute) grew from essentially nothing in 1953 to 182 million dollars in 1970. Over 80 percent consisted of cotton yarn and fabrics, almost exactly the same percentage in these two categories as India had. Thus, Pakistan's increase in textile exports, which accounted for about a third of total export growth from 1953 to 1968, was largely of the traditional type and probably in significant competition with India. India, failing to take advantage of its early start to move on to more promising product lines, stayed to compete with latecomers who may have had few alternatives.

Technological stagnation in India's textile industry also resulted in high-cost production and a consequent poor competitive position. Since the relatively dormant domestic demand required little expansion of the industry, the average age of equipment increased as new capacity comprised only a small proportion of the total. In addition, the capital intensive policies in the capital goods sector left few funds and little foreign exchange available for the textile industry. Importing special machinery to facilitate exploitation of new markets was simply impossible.[25]

The decision to emphasize the small-scale sector of the textile industry furnished the coup de grace. As a result, from 1951 to 1969, the mill sector stagnated while the small-scale sector nearly quadrupled its output. During that period, the physical volume of cotton fabric exports declined 30 percent. Small-scale firms were favored in recognition of the generally detrimental effects on welfare of the capital intensive approach to devel-

[24] See Mellor and Lele, in Tolley and Zadrozny, eds., op. cit., p. 111.
[25] See Barjatiya, p. 165, and Mehta, p. 152.

opment. The result may well have been the worst of both worlds: inefficient production in the privileged sectors, caused by stressing overly capital intensive production; and inefficient production in other sectors such as textiles, caused by emphasizing excessively labor intensive methods.

The technological problems of the textile industry also illustrate some of the genuine dilemmas of development. Efforts to expand the production of textile machinery rather than to increase imports may well have been a sensible policy, for India may require only a modest amount of time to develop the essential skills for establishing a competitive position in the industry. But during the period of protection, the domestic textile industry suffers from high-cost machinery and probably from technological backwardness as well. In the vigorous expansion incident to an employment-oriented strategy, this interim period would be very brief. Under India's capital intensive strategy, it has continued for a long time.

Additional difficulties of India's textile industry are high cost and an unreliable supply of basic fibers, which comprise over 50 percent of the total cost of the industry.[26] Exports require imports. Cotton production has grown very slowly in India; even with moderately rising demand, cotton prices have gone up relative to other prices. Accordingly, in the last half of the 1950s, while the United States subsidized cotton exports to the benefit of Japan and many other textile exporters, Indian producers encountered rising fiber prices. India's potential comparative advantage in providing value added in the textile industry was, in effect, sacrificed to her comparative disadvantage in producing cotton.

Similarly, the effort to restrict imports to capital goods prevented the importation of synthetic fibers—themselves the product of a highly capital intensive industry. And as synthetics became more acceptable in the framework of the overall plan of development, the emphasis shifted to domestic production of this extraordinarily capital intensive product. Further concentration of capital in a few industries diminished capital availability to other users, including the more labor intensive textile industry.

Hence, exports of textiles have shown no significant upward trend from 1951–52 to 1973–74 (Appendix, Table 12). Indeed, the growth of the major traditional exports—including jute and tea—has been sluggish. Expansion in exports has taken place in the nontraditional commodities,

[26] See Indian Cotton Mills' Federation, "The Indian Cotton Textile Industry," *Cotton and Allied Textile Industries,* 8 (1967), 21–24.

which rose in that period from about 172 million dollars to about 1200 million—a rate of increase of 9.3 percent per year (Table VIII-1). It is common to talk of the faster growing items of export as representing modern, manufactured goods. In fact, the dynamic export elements for India, as for most low-income countries, are a mixed lot. Increase in exports of metalliferous crude materials, in which iron ore is included, was equal to 10 percent of the total rise in exports from 1951–52 to 1973–74. The gains in exports of leather and leather goods, fruits and vegetables, and foods other than tea and mate were equal to over 37 percent of the increase in the period. Cashew nuts, fish and fish products, and vegetable oil cake are the most important constituents of the last category.

Cashew nuts are produced in India, but imports from East Africa represent a major portion of the raw material. Cashews are thus a prime example of a high-labor-using commodity whose production process adds considerable value to an imported raw material. Presumably, policy favored cashews but not textiles because cashew nuts are more easily isolated from the rest of the economy to ensure that the imports are almost certainly re-exported. Similarly, fish and fish products, substantially consisting of shrimp, are partly a natural resource with a high labor intensive value added. Fodder is composed primarily of oil cake, a livestock feed which remains after the crushing of oilseeds such as groundnuts and cottonseed for the oil. India's traditional vegetable oil exports were lost as domestic demand increased more rapidly than supply (Appendix, Table 12). Accelerating income growth in an agriculture- and employment-oriented approach to development will probably boost the demand for livestock products; the oil cake exports may be diverted to the domestic dairy and poultry industry, illustrating how fragile the export trade may be. Not only do international markets fluctuate considerably, with exporters the marginal suppliers, but domestic markets also change over time and may quickly wipe out a natural resource or an export surplus based on agriculture. Other exports must then be sufficiently dynamic to counterbalance such losses.

Manufactured goods generally, and machinery and transport equipment specifically, offered major scope for labor intensive exports. India's rate of growth in exports of machinery and transport equipment was 27 percent in the 1960s (Table VIII-3). This compares favorably with Japan's rate of increase in this category of 26 percent in the 1950s and 28 percent in the 1960s. But even in 1953, Japan was exporting 189 million dollars' worth of this equipment, contrasted with India's 60 million in 1967–68, while Japan's exports of this group had grown to 4.9 billion by 1968. Taiwan's exports of machines and transport equipment had increased to 104 million by 1968, more than two-thirds more than India's, and were rising in the 1960s at a rate of 55 percent per year.[27]

From 1960 to 1969, exports of machinery and transport equipment from developing nations were advancing at an average compound rate of over 20 percent (Table VIII-3). Therefore, despite the emphasis on industrialization, India's exports in this key category were only moderately better than the average of the world's less developed countries. Furthermore, the high rates of growth have occurred notwithstanding the unfavorable development strategy, because the small size of the industry requires only a small quantity of resources for rapid expansion. Now that machinery manufacture and exports are significant aggregates, they could well suffer the same fate as textiles if the underlying strategy of the allocation of capital, domestic demand, and imports does not change.

Export Prospects

The record of other low-income countries, the substantial change in both the composition of commodities and the geographic pattern of India's exports, and the broadening of India's manufacturing sector all suggest current potential for greatly improved export performance. Rapid growth in certain commodity categories, such as machinery, suggests the potentials under a new approach and warns of problems that imperil that sector's future achievement in the context of the old strategy.

The requirements for improving the record of exports illustrate clearly the interworkings of development strategy. To achieve a long-term major acceleration in export growth requires marked expansion of those types of industries which are relatively labor intensive. The greater number of jobholders makes necessary a faster rate of growth for agriculture as the chief producer of wage goods to back the increased wage payments; a change in investment patterns toward smaller-scale, more labor intensive industry; a change in the structure of imports and their magnitude, favoring more natural-resource-based and capital intensive raw materials and intermediate products; and, perhaps most important of all, a change in

---

[27] Figures were computed on the basis of data in United Nations, Department of Economic and Social Affairs, Statistical Office, *Yearbook of International Trade Statistics*, various issues.

planning and execution procedures to facilitate the new strategy generally and the new import and export potentials specifically.

Effective pursuit of expanded trade makes highly technical demands on institutions and personnel. On the import side, the preparation of estimates of future requirements would aid the timely buying of types of commodities with standard specifications. At least, economic analyses should be made independent of political pressures, and technically knowledgeable buyers must be able to operate in a stable institutional framework. On the export side, there is need for skillful promotion and the offer of credit arrangements in a climate of cooperation and division of effort between public agencies and the private trade. At the outset, complex measures may be necessary to ensure the supply of key raw materials for export industries as export development trails behind the increased requirements for imports and further tightens the foreign exchange constraint. In the longer run, the growth strategy itself should lessen this constraint.

Most important, a successful approach to exports is obliged to recognize that expansion is an opportunistic process that must be conducted in a flexible, pragmatic manner. Although facilitative policies and progress are essential, it is even more essential that existing bureaucratic controls be reduced rapidly.

Because exports are so volatile, they cannot be projected except in the broadest of terms. But if India achieved no more than the 7 percent growth rate indicated in the *Approach to the Fifth Plan,* her performance would compare poorly with the achievements of other low income countries.

For example, following the arbitrary classification of Table VIII-1, assume that traditional and nontraditional exports comprised 65 percent and 35 percent of total exports, respectively; if India experienced a rate of increase of 15 percent for nontraditional items, and traditional commodities grew at 6 percent, the average rate of growth of exports would be 9.6 percent for the first six years, accelerating to 10.1 percent for the next six years as the weight of the nontraditional items increased. For comparison, from 1960 to 1969 world exports of textiles and clothing, major traditional exports for India, grew at a 9.3 percent clip; and less developed country (LDC) exports of these items advanced at a rate of 10.6 percent. Worldwide exports of machinery and transport equipment, which comprises 15 percent of India's nontraditional exports, averaged a 12.0

percent growth per year; LDC exports of this item rose at an annual rate of 21.3 percent during the 1960 to 1969 period (Table VIII-3). India's nontraditional class of exports grew at a rate of almost 20 percent per year from 1964–65 to 1969–70 and of more than 18 percent per year from 1964–65 to 1973–74. In both the traditional and nontraditional categories, India is a major element in world markets only for jute and tea, which, however, in 1971–72 comprised over one-quarter of all India's exports.

It should be noted that a 15 percent rate of expansion for the nontraditional items accelerates the overall pace of the rate of increase even if traditional exports grow very slowly. Accordingly, with only a 2 percent annual increment for traditional exports and 15 percent for nontraditional items, under the previous assumptions, the overall growth rate jumps from 7.5 percent to 8.6 percent in the second six-year period, as compared to the first. It should also be pointed out that the traditional commodities include iron ore, fish (including shrimp), and vegetable oil cake, all of which are important and have been experiencing high rates of increase.

The appropriate question about the attainments of future Indian exports is not about the basic long-run feasibility of accelerated growth but about the impact of short-run deficits in the balance of payments arising from a lag in export performance and from the continuing burden of repayment of past debt. The imports needed to facilitate export expansion are largely in the nature of raw materials and intermediate products. Relatively rapid turnover makes short-term financing appropriate.

IX

The Legacy of Foreign Aid

Foreign aid to India, though insignificant in per capita terms, was crucial to the capital intensive strategy pursued in the Second and Third Plan periods. Indeed, in view of the political and economic constraints at that evolutionary stage of Indian development, neither the domestic nor the foreign exchange resources could otherwise have been provided in the form and quantity needed. The present slow pace of growth may still require large net foreign assistance for continuation of the old approach within the current political system.[1] And foreign loans in the past have created a body of massive repayments that were due long before the investments made from the loans could provide the growth in national income and exports required for reimbursement. Change in the function of foreign assistance could provide a favorable basis for new foreign aid programs, different from the old forms yet appropriate to the new needs.

The Amount of Foreign Assistance

"Foreign assistance" is itself an imprecise term. Official figures reflect commitments rather than actual dispersals, lumping together grants with loans (a substantial proportion of which may be at interest rates comparable to prime commercial rates), and failing to reflect various arrangements that diminish the value of assistance by tying purchases to higher-priced sources of supply.[2] In this discussion, the amount of foreign assistance is defined as the difference between imports and exports. Although

---

[1] This was in essence the position in B. S. Minhas' resignation from the Planning Commission. Minhas argued that the size and shape of the Fifth Plan was inconsistent with the emphasis on "self-reliance" and small foreign aid and that therefore one or the other had to be changed. See *Economic Times*, 13:272 (December 8, 1973).

[2] See, for example, the OECD definition in Organisation for Economic Co-operation and Development, Development Assistance Committee, *Development Assistance, 1970 Review*, December 1970, p. 30.

this measure, too, fails to separate loans from grants, it is an uncomplicated, readily obtainable figure which is roughly indicative of the extent to which resources are being made available to a nation in a quantity greater than that generated from current domestic sources.

Foreign aid to India in the form of gifts and loans was insignificant during the First Five-Year Plan, foreign exchange deficits being financed largely from the large reserves built during World War II. The era of "aid" began with a distinct jump at the beginning of the Second Plan, grew rapidly to a peak at the end of the Third Plan, held that peak briefly with the drought-induced increase in food aid, and then declined rapidly (Table IX-1). Thus, large-scale foreign aid as development assistance was concentrated largely within the ten years of the Second and Third Five-Year Plans. Concurrent with the large increase in oil prices in the early 1970s foreign assistance once again began to grow rapidly.

In the euphoric years of foreign aid, India in some respects dominated the scene. From 1951–52 to 1969–70, she was the single most important aid recipient, receiving over 13 billion dollars in net resource transfers (Table IX-1). This is nearly 50 percent more than the amount received by South Korea, the next highest recipient, and over three times that of Pakistan, the third largest aid donee. Nevertheless, during the period 1955–56 to 1969–70, India's total aid was equal to only 8 percent of Development Assistance Committee (DAC) official and private financial assistance to all less developed countries.[3]

In any case, aid to India is quickly placed in less impressive perspective when expressed in per capita terms. For the period 1951–52 to 1969–70, the net annual inflow of foreign resources to India averaged only $1.61 per capita and 2.3 percent of national income. The highest level of aid per capita for India was $2.63, achieved in 1965–66, and the highest percentage of national income was 3.9 percent, in 1966–67 (Table IX-1). In contrast, from 1952 to 1970, South Korea averaged $18.80 in per capita aid, or 12.7 percent of national income; Taiwan, $7.46 per capita, or 4.4 percent; and Pakistan $2.39 per capita, or 2.8

[3] Net foreign resource transfer during 1955–56 to 1969–70 for India was 12 billion dollars. The net flow of official and private financial resources from Development Assistance Committee (DAC) countries to less developed countries and multilateral agencies from 1956 to 1970 was 147 billion dollars (Organisation for Economic Co-operation and Development, Development Assistance Committee, *Development Assistance, 1968 Review,* December 1968, p. 257; and *Development Assistance, 1971 Review,* December 1971, p. 164.

Table IX-1. The relative importance of foreign resource transfer, India, 1951–52 to 1973–74

Year	Net foreign resource transfer *		Net foreign resource transfer as percent of			
	Total (million U.S.$)	Per capita (U.S.$)	National income †	Gross investment	Central government expenditures	Imports
1951–52	335	0.92	1.6	16.1	23.7	18.2
1952–53	193	0.52	0.9	18.0	16.6	13.7
1953–54	87	0.23	0.4	5.6	5.8	7.2
1954–55	132	0.34	0.7	5.9	7.2	9.6
1955–56	123	0.32	0.6	4.3	6.0	9.0
1956–57	590	1.48	2.4	14.9	26.0	31.3
1957–58	841	2.08	3.5	23.8	27.2	38.7
1958–59	692	1.68	2.6	18.9	22.3	36.6
1959–60	675	1.59	2.5	18.1	18.0	33.4
1960–61	1,007	2.33	3.6	22.9	26.6	42.7
1961–62	903	2.04	3.1	20.5	21.1	39.4
1962–63	937	2.07	3.0	17.0	17.7	39.4
1963–64	903	1.96	2.5	13.9	13.5	35.1
1964–65	1,119	2.37	2.7	14.9	15.4	39.5
1965–66	1,267	2.63	2.9	14.7	15.4	42.8
1966–67	1,229	2.49	3.9	20.8	20.8	44.4
1967–68	1,079	2.14	2.9	16.5	18.0	40.3
1968–69	735	1.43	1.9	10.8	12.3	28.9
1969–70	225	0.43	0.5	3.1	3.4	10.7
1970–71	132	0.25	0.3	1.7	1.9	6.1
1971–72	325	0.59	0.7	n.a.	3.5	13.5
1972–73	−120	−0.21	‡	‡	‡	‡
1973–74	534	0.92	0.9	n.a.	5.7	15.0

* Defined as imports less exports.   † At factor cost.   ‡ No net foreign resource transfer.
Sources: Columns 1 and 6: 1951–52, 1955–56, and 1960–61 to 1973–74, Appendix, Tables 11 and 12; all other years based on import and export figures in Reserve Bank of India, *Report on Currency and Finance,* various issues. Column 2: Based on population figures published in *Economic Survey* (New Delhi: Government of India, Ministry of Finance), various issues. Column 3: Based on data in *Estimates of National Product* (Government of India, Central Statistical Organisation), various issues; and Reserve Bank of India, *Bulletin,* various issues. Column 4: Based on data in Reserve Bank of India, *Bulletin,* various issues. (Gross investment for 1951–52 to 1959–60 was estimated by assuming that the average ratio of net investment to gross investment was the same in that period as in 1960–61 to 1970–71. Column 5: Based on data in *Economic Survey,* various issues; and *Report on Currency and Finance,* various issues.

percent.[4] West Pakistan (considered separately from the region which became Bangladesh) received an annual average of $3.92 per capita, or 4.1

[4] Data on exports, imports, national income, and population for South Korea for the period 1952 to 1970 are from Republic of Korea, Bank of Korea, *Economic Statistical Yearbook,* various issues. For Taiwan, data are from Council for International Economic Co-operation and Development, Executive Yuan, Republic of China, *Taiwan Statistical Data Book, 1974.* For Pakistan, data are from Government of Pakistan, Central Statistical

percent of national income.[5] This represented over two and a half times as much aid per capita as India received, and it was nearly twice as large a percentage of national income.

Because incomes and, therefore, investment rates in India are so low, the modest amount of aid relative to national income did comprise a substantial proportion of capital formation. For the period 1951–52 to 1969–70, net resource transfer averaged 16 percent of gross investment (Table IX-1). This figure was still topped by a number of countries with successful records of growth. The comparable statistic for West Pakistan is 29 percent; for South Korea, it averaged 69 percent from 1953 to 1970; Taiwan averaged 17 percent from 1952 to 1970, a figure similar to India's, but for the high-aid period 1952 to 1961, the net inflow of foreign resources to Taiwan was equal to 36 percent of gross investment, over twice the percentage for India.

Foreign assistance was also important relative to government expenditure and the total import bill. Thus, during the period 1951–52 to 1969–70, the net transfer of foreign resources to India equaled 18 percent of the total government expenditure on current and capital account, reaching a peak of 27 percent in 1957–58. Foreign resource transfer as a proportion of India's imports averaged 31 percent from 1951–52 to 1969–70, 36 percent in the Second Plan period, and 39 percent in the Third Plan period.

The form of foreign resource transfers reinforced the development strategy. Aid placed large additional assets in the public sector in the shape of foreign exchange, in a manner often requiring, or at least permitting, investment in capital goods. Without the foreign assistance programs, pursuit of the strategy of the earlier plans would have necessitated commensurately higher domestic taxes to provide funds for the public sector and reductions in domestic consumption of imported or exportable goods. An import reduction of this nature, given the import composition

---

Office, *Twenty-Five Years of Pakistan in Statistics, 1947–1972* (Karachi: Manager of Publications, 1972); and M. Haq, *The Strategy of Economic Planning* (Karachi: Oxford University Press, 1963). The figures in the domestic currencies have been converted to U.S. dollars, using current exchange rates.

[5] Exports and imports of West Pakistan include trade with East Pakistan. The data on exports, imports, national income, and population are from Government of Pakistan, Central Statistical Office, *Monthly Statistical Bulletin* (Karachi), various issues; and Government of Pakistan, Planning Commission, *Reports of Advisory Panel for the Fourth Five-Year Plan, 1970–75*, Vol. I (Islamabad), 1970; and M. Haq, op. cit.

and the program of growth, must fall heavily on foodgrain imports and agricultural exports, such as vegetable oils. In the existing political framework, changes of this kind were highly improbable.

Government revenues did, in fact, rise at the rapid rate of 8.8 percent per year from 1955–56 to 1965–66, by which time they comprised 11 percent of net domestic product. In the political and economic atmosphere of the 1950s and 1960s, taxes could hardly have been increased much faster. Indeed, the rate and means of tax increase caused widespread evasion and discouraged the incentive to generate the high private incomes that were very necessary for a future rise in the tax base.[6] The one clearly undertaxed group, the wealthier rural income classes, seems to be favored in nearly all contemporary low-income countries, indicating a widespread political problem.[7] Even recently, when agricultural incomes have advanced rapidly and foreign aid has declined sharply, there seems little likelihood of a substantial increase in land taxes or in agricultural income taxes.[8] Boosting sales taxes is a politically more practical means of increasing agricultural taxation, as increased rural incomes are spent on purchased consumer goods.[9] But, the strategy of the Second and Third Plans did not facilitate such a move.

Imports were largely confined to the capital goods and raw materials necessary for the fulfillment of the industrial program of development—except for foodgrains—and again political considerations prohibited a significant reduction in the substantial foodgrains imports. Incomes of the poor were already tightly restrained by the strategy of growth. Even so, when foodgrain supply declined as a result of poor weather, political efforts were made to curb the consequent price increases, including desperate and admittedly futile attempts at taking over the grain trade.[10] In such circumstances, reducing foodgrain imports

[6] Nicholas Kaldor, *Essays on Economic Policy,* Vol. I (London: Duckworth, 1964), pp. 216–24.

[7] See Chapter VI, below; Ved P. Gandhi, *Tax Burden on Indian Agriculture* (Cambridge, Mass.: The Law School of Harvard University, 1966), p. 135; John W. Mellor, *The Economics of Agricultural Development* (Ithaca, N.Y.: Cornell University Press, 1966), ch. v; and Kaldor, pp. 256–58.

[8] See Kaldor, pp. 230–41 and 258–60; and *Economic Times* (Bombay) 14:64 (May 17, 1974).

[9] John W. Mellor, "Accelerated Growth in Agricultural Production and the Intersectoral Transfer of Resources," *Economic Development and Cultural Change,* 22:1 (October 1973), 1–16.

[10] See, for example, Uma J. Lele, *Food Grain Marketing in India: Private Performance and Public Policy* (Ithaca, N.Y.: Cornell University Press, 1971), Appendix 1, pp. 225–37.

seems an improbable tactic. Similarly, in the low-aid period of 1973–74, imports of foodgrains were increased in response to a short crop, despite heavy foreign exchange expenditure.[11] At the same time, vegetable oil exports, a major item in the early 1950s, declined rapidly because there was little other basis for cushioning the effect of rapidly rising vegetable oil prices.

Choice of an alternative political balance or growth strategy also appears difficult, even in retrospect. If the capital intensive approach had remained but was to be based entirely on the use of domestic resources, the burden would surely have fallen more heavily on the prosperous rural people—exactly the group which the strategy of the Community Development Program and Panchayati Raj (as a system of local government) was attempting to integrate more fully into the national political system. Accordingly, the political tactics of broadening participation to include the prosperous rural landowners would have had to be reversed. Such a reversal would not necessarily have significantly reduced disparities in rural income. It could have resulted in more repressive rule by the bureaucracy without displacing the landed peasantry.

Choice of a different growth strategy would not have been simple either. It would have required resources for short-term acceleration in agricultural production at the time of the Second and Third Plans. And, since the Plan had invested very heavily in the steel industry, a less capital intensive approach also required the transfer of a major portion of that steel investment to other industries, particularly in the private sector. The probable results of such a strategy were unknown at that time. Finally, arguments in favor of a different strategy assume that the noneconomic objectives of the Plan, such as national integration and political development, were not important or could also be achieved with alternative economic programs.

Given the prominence of foreign assistance and the difficulty of either political or economic adjustment to substitute growth strategies, it is not surprising that the rapid reduction in foreign aid after the Third Plan had a major depressing effect on the economy. Net foreign resource inflow into India declined from 1.3 billion dollars in 1965–66 to 225 million in

---

[11] The government of India decided to import about four million tons of foodgrains each year during the Fifth Plan period and made contracts for the purchase of three million tons of wheat from the United States by May 1974 (*Economic Times* [Bombay] 14:61[May 13, 1974] and 14:76 [May 29, 1974]).

1969–70—a decrease reflecting reduced gross aid, sharp increases in debt repayment, and a substantial increase in reserves, perhaps prompted by the uncertainties accompanying the decline in aid. This is an average decline of 260 million dollars a year and is equal to 31 percent of the average annual increments to gross investment from 1960–61 to 1965–66. This choice of years perhaps exaggerates the rate of reduction, since in 1966–67, an unusually large proportion of net foreign resource inflow was accounted for by the imports of PL 480 wheat for relief of the effects of the major drought of the two preceding years. If the predrought year of 1964–65 is selected as the beginning of the aid decline, the average annual decrease in foreign resource transfer was 179 million dollars a year, equal to 21 percent of the average annual increments to gross investment in the period 1960–61 to 1965–66.

So great a decline in foreign assistance has three crippling effects on short-run growth. First, it directly reduces the funds and the resources available for investment—equivalent, in this case, to a major portion of the expected increments to savings. Second, given the previous strategy and the role of foreign assistance in that strategy, it imposes a proportionately larger share of adjustment on producers of capital goods in the public sector, whose characteristics of scale and capital intensity are particularly ill-suited to rapid adaptation. The third effect follows from the decline in investment: the reduction has a potential for at least a partial multiplier-accelerator consequence of reducing demand, income, and therefore further investment. The last result becomes much more likely, since the drop in foreign assistance was associated with the significant decline in national income accompanying the great drought of 1965–66 and 1966–67. Indeed, even without a multiplier-accelerator effect, a reasonable set of assumptions shows net investment falling sharply after the record dry period and then ascending very gradually until the end of the decline in aid six years later, at which point investment begins to grow again at the old pace. That would place the beginning of resumed rapid growth in 1972—just as another drought, and then the drastic increase in oil and grain prices, occurred, presumably postponing the recovery an additional year or two.[12]

---

[12] The stated result occurs from the following assumption: from 1964–65, net investment aid from abroad declined 0.2 billion dollars per year and ceases declining at zero, in 1970–71; net investment from domestic savings falls sharply, on the assumption of a marginal propensity to consume of 0.2 from 1964–65 to 1965–66, holds unchanged for one

The Commodity Composition of Foreign Assistance

Foreign aid to India was largely directed to industrial rather than agricultural development and to increased imports of capital goods rather than wage goods and raw materials. The composition of foreign aid was, therefore, consistent with the underlying Indian plans for growth and indeed may actually have reinforced them. Foreign aid came from many different sources, most of which were insignificant compared to both the foreign exchange used for the maintenance of imports and to total investment; thus Indian officials were able to manipulate the allocation of aid to fit the plans. It is likely that, in general, the aid donors not only sympathized with the growth strategy, but in many cases may have actively promoted it.

Foreign assistance was of particular importance in filling an exchange gap created by rapidly increasing imports of machinery. Annual imports of machinery and transport equipment rose by 625 million dollars between 1955–56 and the peak aid year of 1965–66 (Appendix, Table 11)—an increase equal to nearly two-thirds of the total rise in net foreign resource flows between the two years. Foreign aid provided these goods directly, as in the case of specifically financed steel mills provided by the Soviet Union, Britain, and Germany; in the form of unearmarked foreign exchange which could be allocated to them; or as financed imports of raw materials and wage goods previously supported from other sources of foreign exchange. Each contributed to the capital intensive strategy.

Although aid donors have in recent years paid at least lip service to agricultural development, agriculture received a considerably smaller proportion of overall aid funds than was allocated in the Indian development plans.

According to the *Report on Currency and Finance*, from 1951–52 to 1970–71, only 2 percent of foreign loans and credits were earmarked for agricultural development, compared to 61 percent for industrial develop-

year, and increases at an annual rate of 5.0 percent thereafter. In 1964–65, national income is at a level of 40 billion dollars and declines sharply to a level of 36 billion dollars in 1965–66—consistent with the drought—holds constant for one year, and rises thereafter. From these calculations, total investments decline sharply in 1965–66, moderately in 1966–67, hold relatively stable for five years, and then increase sharply in 1971–72. These movements both down and up would be expected to be magnified by an accelerator-multiplier effect. Similar effects would be extended by the effects of the large oil and grain price increases of the early 1970s.

ment. Consistent with this, the World Bank loans to developing countries for agricultural development have been less than 4 percent of the total lending of 25 billion dollars during more than a quarter century of its operations.[13] In contrast, the Indian government, much criticized by foreign observers for underemphasizing agriculture, allocated 17 percent of investment in this period to agriculture and irrigation (Appendix, Table 2).

Aid donors neglected agriculture ostensibly because they preferred projects with a large foreign exchange component, of which the Indian plans provided an ample selection in the industrial sector and little in agriculture. Actually, the emphasis probably grew from a basic sympathy for the Plan approach. Neglect of agriculture could more correctly have been based on the lack of technology for providing high returns to incremental investment and an early stress on the building of institutional structures, an activity which initially can absorb relatively little investment. In fact, the requisite institution building did receive substantial attention from the United States government and private sources and was an effort that would eventually pay off handsomely.

Agriculture has recently been receiving a greater proportion of foreign aid, as much because of the new problem of loan repayments as because of the increasing recognition of its importance. The very characteristic of low foreign exchange requirements which justified the previous foreign aid neglect now emerges to support agriculture. A government which receives foreign exchange for agricultural purposes may use it for loan repayment or for maintenance imports, while it allocates domestic resources to the agricultural projects. There is, of course, the danger that under the influence of foreign aid, investment would be more capital intensive than it would otherwise have been—a danger of less consequence in the old industrial-oriented growth strategy, whose structure of industrial investment offered little scope for choice of technology.

If foreign assistance had played an active role in the selection of a more labor intensive strategy of development, it would have emphasized the financing of foodgrain imports to back the increased consumption expenditure accompanying increased employment, as well as of raw materials and intermediate products. In practice, although food aid was sub-

[13] Robert S. McNamara, address to the Board of Governors, Nairobi, Kenya, for the World Bank Group, International Bank for Reconstruction and Development (Washington, D.C.: World Bank, September 24, 1973), p. 14.

stantial, it was largely a passive reaction to the leakages from the capital intensive program rather than a positive force for accelerated growth in employment.

Foodgrain imports remained roughly the same from 1950–51 to 1963–64. Thus, even though food aid averaged 27 percent of total assistance from 1955–56 to 1963–64 (Table IX-2), it seems to have largely substituted for commercial imports that would, in any case, have been politically necessary, even within the strategy of slow growth in agricultural production and in employment. Food aid thereby released foreign exchange for the purchase of capital goods and was therefore consistent with the capital intensive, not the employment-oriented, plan of development.

When in practice, if not by design, employment growth accelerated in

Table IX-2. The relative importance of food aid, India, 1955–56 to 1972–73

Year	P.L. 480–665 assistance (million U.S.$)	P.L. 480–665 assistance as a percent of		
		Food imports *	Net foreign resource transfer	All imports
1955–56	10	9	8	1
1956–57	106	116	18	6
1957–58	241	136	29	11
1958–59	195	93	28	11
1969–60	295	54	30	10
1960–61	392	87	39	17
1961–62	185	60	21	8
1962–63	257	68	27	11
1963–64	387	86	43	15
1964–65	454	67	41	16
1965–66	501	67	40	17
1966–67	477	51	39	17
1967–68	456	59	42	17
1968–69	209	49	28	8
1969–70	226	53	100	11
1970–71	118	33	89	5
1971–72	154	59	47	6
1972–73	6	3	†	–

* Based on incomplete figures, due to the operation of a special system of clearing foodgrain imports on government account.
† No net foreign resource transfer.
Sources: Column 1: Government of India, Ministry of Finance, *Economic Survey,* various issues. Column 2: Calculated on the basis of data in Appendix, Table 13, and in Government of India, Central Statistical Organisation, *Monthly Abstract of Statistics,* various issues. Column 3: Table IX-1. Column 4: Based on data in Appendix, Table 11, and in Reserve Bank of India, *Report on Currency and Finance,* various issues.

the Third Plan period, food aid did rise rapidly to provide a substantial share of the added demand for wage goods. Indeed, the rate of increase of foodgrain production was slower than previously and subsequently, while that of foodgrain supplies was, because of food aid, faster than at any other time between 1950 and 1972. Accordingly, the stepped-up rate of growth in employment during this period depended significantly on larger food aid shipments. Even the relative importance of food aid as a proportion of total aid rose during this period, despite the increase in total foreign resource transfers (Table IX-2). Food aid maintained its share of total aid during the drought years of 1965–66 and 1966–67, averaging 41 percent of net foreign resource transfers for the three years 1965–66 to 1967–68. Once again, the food aid was not part of a strategy for increasing employment; it was a means of meeting greatly reduced production growth rates and, in a sense, unplanned growth in demand, through temporary imports. It was a diversion from the capital intensive strategy, not a change in that strategy.

The political importance of food aid may well have been immense. In short-crop years, the government of India has consistently had great difficulty in obtaining domestically the foodgrains needed to maintain adequate supplies for the fair-price shops serving the urban labor classes. Imports have typically met much of this need. Of the total public distribution in the poor crop years of 1957–58, 1965–66, and 1966–67, 71 percent was from imports and 29 percent from domestic procurement. Food aid was probably the key to preserving the existing political balance without massive diversion of foreign exchange from capital goods to food imports.

Technical Assistance

Technical assistance, or trained manpower transfer, represents one of the most important means of accelerating growth—whether it be "catching up" with respect to installation of a modern steel mill or petrochemical plant, or using modern science to provide high-yield crop varieties adapted to local environments. A difficult form of aid to provide, it underscores the basic conflicts between objectives of givers and receivers.

Trained manpower is a critical complement to both capital goods and labor; its scarcity depresses returns to the other resources and therefore slows growth. Although trained manpower can be imported from high-income countries, lack of an efficient institutional structure may constrain the productivity of that manpower. The manpower to build institutions is hard to find and harder to transfer; the institutions must be consistent with local conditions—a goal difficult to achieve even when those conditions are well known and understood.

Conflicts of interest between the countries involved have brought technical assistance under considerable attack, perhaps to the extent of excessively reducing its utilization. The receiving country wants to determine the pattern of newly built institutions in light of broad political and economic relations and to maintain control of patronage with respect to jobs and the purchase of supplies. The donor countries wish also to control job patronage; to specify plant requirements to the advantage of home country suppliers in furnishing original equipment, repairs, and parts; and to create ties with the home country which increase both economic and political power. Technical assistance may also provide a longer-term political and cultural dependence than is desired by the recipient. Insofar as the staffs of the international agencies are dominated directly or indirectly by attitudes of nationals from high-income countries, those agencies, too, will tend to be responsible for similar conflicts of interest that in the long run reduce the extent and effectiveness of technical aid. The critical role of technical assistance, not only in accelerating development, but in attaining the broader and potentially conflicting objectives of donor and recipient countries, gives it attention out of all proportion to its small share of total foreign assistance budgets.[14]

In the first big push toward industrialization, the disadvantageous aspects of technical aid were insignificant to India and the gains considerable. The desired rate of expansion of steel production was probably well beyond the technical capacity of the existing private sector plants, and certainly beyond the management capabilities of the technically inexperienced civil service in the public sector. Finances were available from foreign exchange reserves and foreign aid; domestic labor was obtainable; but technical aid was needed to mobilize these resources into a productive system. The development of the steel industry epitomizes these processes:

[14] Up to March 31, 1965, technical assistance comprised only 5.3 percent of aid from the U.S., 0.5 percent of aid from the United Kingdom, 0.6 percent of aid from West Germany, and 0.5 percent of aid from Canada (P. J. Eldridge, *The Politics of Foreign Aid in India* [London: Weidenfeld and Nicholson, 1969], ch. ii). If one assumes 0.5 percent of technical assistance from other sources, technical assistance up to March 31, 1965, forms 3.3 percent of the total aid utilized.

Russian, German, and British builders each used different approaches to technical assistance, but each provided a large complement of manpower.[15] Although technical aid was inefficient in absolute terms, it is doubtful that a more efficient alternative was initially apparent. The potential costs of such aid became much clearer as Indian competence increased. The issue is dramatized by the Bokaro steel plant. Padma Desai documents the conflicts between the Indian need to develop and utilize indigenous design and production capacity and the interests of potential foreign financiers of the plant, often paralleled by the influence of controlling politicians and bureaucrats.[16] By 1962, when foreign assistance for Bokaro was being negotiated, India clearly had developed a substantial indigenous capacity to design steel mills, particularly in Dastur and Company, a private Indian firm. But no major aid provider, whether the United States or the USSR, would fail to insist that the basic design be made by its own nationals. This insistence was justified, not by the technical assistance needs of India, but by the political and economic requirements of the donor country. It was clear that national interests of the donors would determine the choice of suppliers for much of the machinery and equipment.[17] In this case, the domestic portions supplied from India would be larger if the aid were Russian rather than American, but this was primarily because the Indian suppliers had been established by the Russians through previous aid programs.

Technical assistance in agriculture has apparently involved less conflict with Indian objectives. The introduction of technical change in agriculture depended most heavily on trained personnel. The lack of substantial import content in most of the complements to trained manpower offered little incentive for donors to influence markets in India. Of particular relevance, in view of the starring role of the United States in technical assistance, is the fact that agricultural technicians, even in the United States,

[15] For example, the contract for Bokaro provided for technical services of 450 to 500 Soviet specialists at the peak of construction activity, in addition to the services of suppliers, representatives, and other service personnel, amounting in total to Rs. 123 million expenditure for the first stage (Padma Desai, *The Bokaro Steel Plant: A Study of Soviet Economic Assistance* [New York: American Elsevier, 1972], p. 59). This is a careful, copiously documented treatment of critical aspects of technical assistance.

[16] Ibid.

[17] For example, the cost reduction study on the Bokaro Steel Plant project prepared by M. N. Dastur and Company, Private, Ltd., worked out a reduction of foreign exchange cost amounting to Rs. 1075 million, yet the net reduction agreed upon as a result of an Indian delegation's visit to Moscow amounted to only Rs. 95 million (ibid., p. 64).

are located primarily in the public or quasi-public sector. The use of such technicians is thus more in harmony with the evolving Indian system than is the case with industrial experts.

Two particularly outstanding successes exemplify the potentials for effective technical aid in agriculture. Most important, a large foreign input helped significantly to develop the high-yield varieties which formed the basis for the "green revolution" and, even more important, stimulated the reform of agricultural research institutions at a time when Indian attention was directed largely elsewhere. Although India has a long history of distinguished work in the agricultural sciences, dating back to the Imperial Agricultural Research Institute formed in the 1920s, which pyramided into an extensive set of research stations, there was little cooperation, coordination, or even sense of direction within the system. In a very striking effort spanning more than a decade, the Rockefeller Foundation provided technicians and helped evolve an effective set of operating procedures which facilitated the development of the various coordinated research schemes now recognized as necessary to modern agriculture. Those undertakings, supplemented by massive foreign training of scientists by the Rockefeller Foundation, the Ford Foundation, the United States government, and other agencies, provided the basis for a rapidly growing and vigorous research establishment.[18] The care with which this structure is being built is probably one of the best examples of technical assistance executed sensitively and intelligently.[19] Similar endeavors in other countries greatly enhanced the value of this work, creating the opportunity for an integrated international system of agricultural research.

The major American effort to introduce in India a system of agricultural universities initially patterned rather precisely after American land grant universities provided an apparently more heavy-handed approach to technical aid. Although such a direct transplant of foreign institutions to a low-income country was fraught with danger, the system was attuned to the institutional needs for agricultural development, and was eventually properly adapted to Indian conditions by Indian administrators. No doubt,

[18] See, for example, Carroll P. Streeter, *A Partnership to Improve Food Production in India,* a special report from the Rockefeller Foundation (New York: Rockefeller Foundation, December 1969), p. 87.

[19] The career of Dr. Ralph Cummings, as Indian Program Director for the Rockefeller Foundation and more recently as director of the International Research Center in Hyderabad, India, affords ample illustration of effective technical assistance procedures.

rigid minds wasted a part of this input by attempting an excessively meticulous transfer of the system. In total, however, the project is supplying a large proportion of the high-level manpower crucial to growth of the institutions of agricultural development.[20]

Foreign agencies made sizable efforts to enlarge programs to which the Indian government was already committed. Most noticeable was the large foreign contribution (particularly through the United States Agency for International Development [USAID] and its predecessor agencies, as well as the Ford Foundation) to the Community Development Program. Various extensions of those endeavors included the Intensive Agricultural District Programme and the high-yield-varieties projects.

Much of the past technical aid has in practice supported a rural-led approach to economic development. In an employment-oriented strategy, the most important technical assistance is that which will spur the growth of agriculture. Fortunately, whether or not consistent with the past program of development, such technical assistance has already been successful in building the basic institutions. Now they need to be expanded to cover larger geographic areas and intensified. Large rewards might well accrue to a number of foreign technicians, perhaps larger than in the past, working within the currently growing institutional structure.

Existing sensitivities make mandatory a highly imaginative approach to develop a basis for expanding technical assistance. The continued rapid extension and internationalization of the International Research Institutes offer good prospects, not only for the coordination of national research efforts but also for increasing the total number of people working on crucial scientific problems. Similarly, greater care in defining areas of more traditional technical assistance in terms of mutual acceptability could be profitable as well. There is a continuing danger that the necessary and productive effort to develop indigenous capability will detract from the effort to develop complementary foreign technical assistance. That is one of the most pressing problems facing the international effort to accelerate growth, not only in India, but generally in the low-income nations.

[20] For an intensive and corroborating analysis of one of the more successful agricultural universities, see Richard L. Shortlidge, Jr., "The Labor Market for Agricultural Graduates in India: A Benefit-Cost Case Study of G. B. Pant University of Agriculture and Technology," Cornell Agricultural Economics Occasional Paper No. 69 (April 1974).

Grappling with Indebtedness

The end of old-style foreign assistance to India has not ended the problems created by that assistance. Contrary to the popular impression, what has been called "aid" has been largely loans. India had, by March 1970, an outstanding debt to foreign countries of approximately 8 billion dollars.[21] In 1971–72, repayment of principal and interest on that debt totaled 639 million dollars, equal to nearly one-third of the total export earnings in that year.[22] Adjusting to a rapid decline in net aid subsequent to the 1965–66 high point was a major cause of India's economic stagnation up to 1971–72. Failure to eliminate or reschedule debt repayment could prolong that period, with potentially disastrous implications for the political system and human welfare.

Ironically, it is doubtful that the aid-giving countries wish to run up balance of payments deficits with India, by constantly importing more from India than they are exporting, so that India can acquire the foreign exchange to meet repayment requirements. The lenders do not want repayment (in the only sense in which it can have economic meaning) and India presumably does not wish to repay—at least for the present. The situation is surprisingly similar to the circumstances about which Keynes warned, after World War I, in *The Economic Consequences of the Peace*.[23] Keynes noted, with respect to the World War I peace treaty, that debt repayment and reparation payments would require a net balance of exports over imports for the losers which would not be tolerated by the winning countries. At the same time, therefore, that there was to be great tension because the losers were not repaying, the continued imposition of policies and trade restrictions would make repayment impossible. Similarly, in the foreign assistance context, insistence on repayment, increased control of the Indian economy through negotiated project loans, and trade and growth policies that make repayment difficult or impossible offer potential for tensions.

In 1970, five nations plus the World Bank group held over 90 percent of India's external public debt. Over one-third, or 2.7 billion dollars

[21] The data in this section are from unpublished sources. They are, however, consistent with published data for earlier periods. See, for example, Reserve Bank of India, *Bulletin*, March 1971, p. 355.

[22] Government of India, *Economic Survey, 1973–74*, Tables 7.6 and 6.1.

[23] John Maynard Keynes, *The Economic Consequences of the Peace* (New York: Harcourt, Brace and Howe, 1920).

(excluding PL 480 food aid), was owed to the United States, the principal donor. The second largest outstanding debt was to the World Bank group, a total of 1.5 billion dollars. Third in rank was the USSR—0.9 billion dollars repayable in rubles, but nearly half to be earned through specific trade agreements with the USSR. The other major debtors were the United Kingdom and Germany, 0.7 billion dollars each, and Japan, 0.4 billion.

Substantially dissimilar terms for loans somewhat alter the ranking of nations with respect to immediate repayment requirements. The United States still ranks first, with close to 100 million dollars in repayments obligated in 1972. But while the United States holds nearly 34 percent of the external debt repayable in foreign currency, it requires only about one-fifth of current reimbursement. The World Bank group, with about one-third of its debt in stiff-term, essentially commercial IBRD (International Bank for Reconstruction and Development) loans, and only two-thirds in soft-term IDA (International Development Association) loans, imposes basically the same obligations for the near future as the United States. Consequently, with about 53 percent of the debt, the United States and the World Bank group have about 40 percent of the repayment requirements. Japan, which ranks sixth in size of the debt outstanding—about 15 percent as much as the United States—has repayment liabilities in the near term of about three-quarters as much as the United States. These calculations do not include the reimbursements to East European countries which, in total, are about as large as those to the United States but for which specific trade provision is made, nor does it count the rupee restitutions to the United States in accordance with PL 480, most of which were renegotiated in 1973.[24]

The difference in repayment burden relative to debt emphasizes the unequal aid content in loans from various countries. The amount of true aid in a loan is a function of how much less than the market level of interest is charged and the time period for repayment. The Japanese assistance has contained relatively little true aid. If we assume as the commercial rate, for the period of the 1960s, the interest rate paid by the World Bank in its commercial borrowings on the international money markets to be, say, about 7 percent, and the terms of the Japanese loans to be 5.84 percent interest and repayment in fifteen years, then the present value of the

[24] For details on the disposition of PL 480 funds, see the *Economic Times*, 13:278 (December 14, 1973).

subsidy on a 100 million dollar loan is only about 8 million dollars. In sharp contrast, according to the same calculation but using IDA terms of 0.75 percent interest, a ten-year grace period, and fifty years for repayment, the present value of the subsidy on 100 million dollars is 74 million, in a sense three-quarters as good as a grant. United States loans have also had favorable terms and include a present subsidy value, per 100 million dollars, of 53 million—or 46 million if one estimates, as was perhaps appropriate in the 1960s, that requiring that the money loaned be spent in the United States raised costs by 20 percent. In the past, United Kingdom and German loans averaged close to 5 percent interest and therefore had a low subsidy element like Japan's.

The repayment problem for India traces from the low and slow returns to investment and the lack of advancement of export-oriented industries— all due primarily to the strategy of growth, the stage of development, and the attempt to accelerate expansion through foreign assistance.

Simplistically, if loan proceeds are invested profitably and repayment can be spread over the life of the investment, the depreciation allowance will repay the principal, and the net returns on the investment will pay the interest. If the rate of profitability is greater than the interest rate, there is a surplus for further investment, and foreign loans are then a cause of accelerated growth. Thus, foreign assistance of 13 billion dollars at a 15 percent rate of return, on the surface not an unreasonable expectation for a country with India's initial start in manufacturing and trade, would have generated annual increments to national income of 2 billion dollars, even without the benefit of compounding. That is nearly equal to the total average annual increments to national income for 1967–68 to 1970–71. Such a level of efficiency in spawning growth of national income would surely have also bred capacity for greater export expansion; yet in practice, India's repayment problem has been compounded because so little investment was made in export-competitive industries necessary for payment in foreign exchange. If India's exports had grown between 1955–57 and 1971–72 at a rate of 10 percent per year instead of the actual 3.3 percent, interest and repayment of 639 million dollars would have comprised a little over 11 percent of exports instead of 31 percent. The higher growth rate would have added 571 million in export earnings in 1972–73 alone, an increment nearly equal to the repayment requirements in that year. In contrast, the 3.3 percent rate of increase in exports achieved between 1955–56 and 1971–72 would have added only 69 million dollars in 1972–73, equal to only about one-tenth of the current debt-servicing requirements.

Given the conditions of India's economic development, rates of return on investment, and the annual growth of national income, exports sufficient to pay commercial interest rates and the near-term reimbursement of principal should not have been expected. Thus, loans were not then an appropriate mechanism of foreign assistance. At the present stage of development, however, and with a change in strategy, they might become a timely means of assistance, except that the overhead of the earlier loans is a heavy burden for the economy to carry. It should be noted, however, that the rapid international price inflation of the mid-1970s did serve to sharply decrease the size of the debts relative to the present value of production and exports and in effect to convert more of the debt to grants.

The capital intensive growth strategy was bound to produce low rates of return on investment in the short run. And, starting in the 1950s, even an employment intensive approach would probably have done no better because of the slow, laborious process of building the necessary institutional structure, particularly in agriculture. Large capital investment in the rural infrastructure of irrigation, power, and communication was not likely to provide high rewards until the research, education, and supply organization became productive. As a result, although export industries might have prospered and loan repayment would have been less difficult than at present, reimbursements would still have placed a heavy burden on further growth.

The presumed objective of foreign development assistance is to accelerate growth beyond the rate that would otherwise be attained, and to do so in the environment of a politically acceptable strategy of advancement. This buying of time, in achieving a given income level sooner, is bound to depress returns to investment as a faster pace of growth spurs resource imbalances, particularly with respect to the capacity of institutions to manage effectively. The example just cited of a temporarily low rate of return on investment in irrigation made prior to the availability of research from experimental institutions is apt. In addition, less efficient allocation of resources is likely to follow accelerated investment rates for the same reason. A potentially compounding problem, in the case of loans and the consequent pressure to generate near-term funds for repayment, is the added urgency for immediately productive investment in preference to the slow processes of building institutions and training manpower that may give higher long-run returns.

Therefore, foreign assistance grants, rather than loans, seem much more appropriate in the context of the Indian Second and Third Plan periods. At that stage, instead of borrowing on the terms available, India might have been better advised to proceed more slowly, build its infrastructure a little more fully, and then to move into larger-scale, even commercial, loans in order to support an accelerated rate of growth later. Similarly, of course, ten to twenty years of rapid development, even without new net aid, would make the present debts manageable —providing, of course, that a case can be made for a moratorium on interest and repayment.

At present, debt servicing is handled, in part, by new loans and, in part, by rescheduling the payments—although the latter comprised only 15 percent of debt servicing from 1967–68 to 1971–72. New loans are, to a larger extent, tied to specific projects and may, in a sense, be costly because of the sizable (and scarce) administrative input in their negotiation; because of inappropriate project specifications by uninformed or, perhaps, self-seeking foreign lenders, and because of reduced flexibility incident to the terms of the loan.[25] The more such aid is tied to a specific country and to certain commodities, the higher the cost to India. Such costs should provide India with a strong incentive not to take small amounts of net aid. It may be better not to receive aid and to bargain for the rescheduling of debt.

All these lessons, of necessarily low returns in early stages of growth, consequent problems of repayment, and resultant international tensions, can still be learned and applied to the many countries in earlier stages of development than India. The lessons as to how to deal with the problem will have relevance to more and more countries as they enter the period of large repayment obligations.

Foreign Assistance in the New Strategy of Growth

As the transition is made to more rapid expansion in employment, the urgency of accelerating agricultural production growth increases, as does

[25] For a discussion of this point, see John W. Mellor, review of J. P. Gittinger, "Economic Analysis of Agricultural Projects," *Journal of Economic Literature*, 12:1 (March 1974), 136–138.

the vulnerability of the economy to sharp, weather-related changes in that production. Foreign assistance could provide the guarantees of food supplies which would aid a shift to higher rates of increase in employment, even as the early stages of faster agricultural growth are reached.

Even though the new strategy will reduce capital intensity, accelerated growth will nevertheless place pressures on the supply of capital. In particular, a rapid increase in demand for transportation and power—with respect both to trunk lines and to primary capacity, as well as to distribution and feeder lines in rural areas—will require large investment. Accordingly, foreign assistance for specific capital goods can, if carefully chosen, facilitate the employment-oriented strategy. But India will move toward the employment intensive approach via the resolution of a complex set of forces. The greater the total capital available to the nation and the less costly that capital, the greater the tendency of those forces to be directed toward the capital intensive approach. Thus, a portion of any foreign assistance will, in effect, allow increased investment in capital intensive industries that help meet various nongrowth objectives. If the foreign donors wish to avoid tipping the balance further in that direction, they must at least avoid earmarking funds for developing capacity to produce capital intensive products which could be imported. That will essentially limit specific capital intensive assistance to electric power and communications. It should hardly need stating that India may still then make such capital intensive investments, but entirely on its own—without the expectation that such funds would be unavailable for other purposes.

Given the high level of current servicing requirements, the primary need in providing foreign assistance is to remove the negative ''aid'' of repayments on past loans. Since these loans were, in effect, for projects with low rates of return and long periods of construction, and since it is to the current economic interests neither of India nor the donor countries to have net repayment of loans and interest at this time, the logical first move is to cancel the existing debt. If that is not acceptable to either side, then a major rescheduling should postpone all debt repayment and interest for a substantial period of time, say ten to twenty years. For example, rescheduling for twenty years, an interest moratorium during that period, complete repayment in another ten years, and a market rate of interest of 7 percent during the repayment period provide a present value, discounting at 7 percent, of only 26 million dollars per 100 million of debt. That would, in effect, write down the 8 billion dollars of outstanding debt to

2.1 billion in present value. Assuming a discount rate of 15 percent and all terms as above would write it down to 489 million. As payments came due, each donor would convert them in accordance with the above terms. The greatest percentage concessions from present loans would come from Japan, the United Kingdom, and Germany. The IBRD loans may pose a special problem because of concern with the effect on the Bank's bond markets. One alternative would be to convert IBRD loans to new IDA loans as repayment is required, perhaps with the understanding that there would be no further IDA loans to India. The latter would have a salutary effect in bringing commercial considerations to decisions about new World Bank borrowings, concerns that seem appropriate for India at this stage in an employment-oriented growth strategy, even though they may not have been suitable earlier. For that reason, converting old IBRD debts to IDA loans and making new IBRD borrowings are preferable to making new IDA loans to allow repayment of old IBRD borrowings.

If the old debt problem could be put out of the way, potential donors might then choose from among several devices for providing a new flow of resources to India. The choice will be the product of compromise between the interests of India and each donor country; the various agreements will differ in consort with the diversity in resources and economic and political interests among the assisting nations. Allowing for differences in approach among contributors, bilateral negotiation is fitting; and the old Aid India Consortium, which played a useful role in developing mutual pressures to raise aid to India, would lose its positive purpose.

National bilateral assistance programs from the Western countries could stop focusing on charity and buying allies and get back to economic self-interest through a higher competitive position in long-run commercial transactions. The credibility of such an interest depends on the expectation that India will achieve self-sustaining economic growth and become an increasingly large commercial market, eventually commensurate with its present approximately 600 million people and its future billion or more. The over 10 percent annual rate of gain in Indian trade implicit in the employment-oriented strategy of development offers potentials that were not conceivable under the old capital intensive approach. Within this context, special export subsidies, commercial credits, specific commodity agreements, and technical assistance programs will have value.

A general export subsidy granted by a high-income nation, arranged on a bilateral basis and made expressly to develop long-run export potential, could be a mutually attractive arrangement. For the donor, as long as there are not too many restrictions, it provides entry into, and possible future advantages in, a potentially large market. Since a low-income country has more elastic demand for most commodities than a high-income country, the result of the subsidy is the differentiation among markets preferred by any producer; therefore, the recommendation has merit even if all high-income countries act in concert. While the export subsidy would be tied to the nation granting it, to be most beneficial to the parties involved it should not be bound additionally to either projects or goods. Then India would be able to bargain for terms on individual commodities on a competitive basis among the granting nations and among firms and commodities within those nations. Equally important, the commodities, because of increased exports resulting from the scheme, would be those in which the subsidizing nation had a natural comparative advantage, thereby encouraging exactly those exports which have a potential commercial future.

In 1972–73, India's total imports from the high-income nations—defined as the OECD (Organisation for Economic Co-operation and Development) nations—were worth 1.5 billion dollars. A 20 percent general export subsidy would provide a grant of approximately 300 million dollars, completely tied to the various grantors and presumably encouraging growth in the grantors' exports. The subsidy could, of course, be made more effective for the interests of the grantor by raising the percentage substantially and tying it to increments to exports above those of a base period. This would have the considerable disadvantage to India of providing smaller grants initially, although they would grow over time, while the greatest problem might be adjusting to the first years of a new strategy. The addition of more complex stipulations to the grant terms could, of course, reverse that tendency.

A second element of a new aid program would involve expanded commercial credits, such as those of the United States Export-Import Bank, which would finance capital goods exports. Such commercial credits are relatively short term and would lead to even worse repayment problems than now exist if the old strategy of growth was still in effect. However, starting from India's present stage of economic development with a change in approach, investment returns should be so much higher and quicker that, if the current high level of debt and repayment could be eliminated, progress from here on could be largely on a commercial basis. Such credits may usefully and safely compound over time at a pace related to the Indian growth rate for national income and exports. The large loans from Iran and, to some extent, other oil exporters, though tied to a specific raw material, are quite consistent with this proposal—if the Indian growth strategy is indeed changing to facilitate repayment.

A third element of bilateral assistance would recognize specific problems of so-called commodity surpluses, particularly with respect to agricultural production. Those problems arise because once agricultural production in high-income countries, such as the United States, expands to a particular level or a particular rate of growth is achieved, the cost of a substantial proportion of that production is much lower than the price which government policy will endorse. Especially for agricultural commodities, there are large cyclical variations in the extent to which there appear to be surpluses. Therefore, an agreement dealing with these surpluses must be written in an appropriate set of years. The period 1969 to 1972 would have been a good time for writing such an agreement; the years immediately following would not. Indeed, in 1974, it was widely thought that the world would never again face the old types of surpluses. But even by mid-1975, agricultural prices in the United States had dropped to a level already suggesting the efficacy of support operation. Another good crop year would reinforce that suggestion. A concentrated effort to increase employment and hence the demand for food in India could engender a strong mutuality between American and Indian interests.

Bilateral agreements for technical assistance can also be mutually beneficial—the donor obtaining political prestige and economic influence, the receiver achieving faster growth while maintaining final control of the choice and institutionalization of technical assistance. Agriculture offers particular opportunity for such aid; so does education. Small-scale industries could be assisted in a manner similar to agriculture, although few, if any, institutions exist in high-income nations for specifically fostering such industries.

None of the preceding approaches is suitable for an international agency such as the World Bank, whose staff is of a size justified only by specific sector- and project-related loans requiring intensive appraisal and development by its own staff. The outlines for appropriate activities for the World Bank are, however, clear. First, it should, as already explained, eschew loans for capital intensive industry, excepting power and transport, the output of which cannot be imported. An employment-oriented strategy of growth would, of course, require massive investment in power and transport. Second, the World Bank should offer a major technical service in the development of projects which might or might not have a dominant foreign exchange component. Insofar as there was not a foreign exchange element, loans would, in effect, provide foreign exchange for general import purposes, thereby assisting the necessary import of capital intensive intermediate products. The technical assistance aspect of project loans would increase the emphasis on scientific ability to develop undertakings suited to specific environments. Such a policy would, of course, entail the reversal of tendencies toward employing the "generalist" and favor, instead, use of the technically competent specialist—a need which India itself shares.

Accordingly, one might envisage up to 300 million dollars in export subsidies; another 200 million per year, growing at a compound rate, for the Export-Import Bank type of commercial credits; between 50 million and 100 million dollars per year in reduced prices, as a result of commodity agreements; and 400 million to 600 million dollars for World Bank loans—for a total of 1,000 million to 1,200 million dollars in annual net resource transfers. This amount would increase over time. That is roughly as large as the maximum amount of past net aid. In addition, the oil exporters might, in this context, continue to finance a substantial portion of the cost of oil imports.

The current programs of the Eastern bloc countries have much in common with this set of procedures. Payments on past loans are made only on the basis of trade agreements providing India a surplus of rubles. Trade is on the basis of bilateral agreements which allow pricing according to the specific supply and demand relationships and other factors relevant to that trade.[26] Although these arrangements may not be as efficient as unfettered multilateral trading, they may be more efficient than the operation of presently controlled markets.

In the several years following 1967, large and effective foreign assistance could have facilitated a change in the structure of Indian growth which would have sustained much of the old pattern while the new was developing. Those were years when agricultural production was increas-

[26] For discussion of how trade with the Eastern bloc is carried on see Hasan Masood, *India's Trade Relations with Rupee Payments Countries* (Aligarh: International Books Traders, 1972).

ing rapidly yet public resources could not finance further major expansion of the capital intensive sector. The time was ripe for a change in the structure of incremental investment. Instead, the decrease in foreign assistance ensured the stagnation and even the decline of the heavy industries sector, while short-run resource bottlenecks restrained the growth of the potentially increasing consumer goods sectors. Those problems of adjustment continued until the drought of 1972–73 to 1973–74. After close to ten years of stagnation, transition to a new strategy of development had probably become both politically and economically more difficult. Nevertheless, the opportunity does remain for a change in approach, and foreign assistance can still play a useful role in facilitating that shift.

X "A Life Fit for the Dignity of Man"

Broad participation of the low-income laboring classes in a strategy of economic growth will not, by itself, relieve the intense poverty which is so well known in India and which is also so pervasive in the bulk of low-income countries. The strategy should be supplemented to meet their needs. And the question may arise as to whether or not the demands of the poor can be met by special low-cost programs without a basic and complex change in the overall orientation toward development.

Poor health, short life expectancy, little formal education, and numerous children per family are the classic features of poverty. Each is both a cause and an effect of poverty; amelioration of each condition is a potential target for specific programs to reduce poverty. For nations with average incomes as low as India's, which includes a high proportion of the world's poor, the choice and effectiveness of such programs depend very much on the level and distribution of income and the strategy of growth. These factors, as well as the nature of increased welfare programs, depend, in turn, on the political system and the apportionment of power. Detailed proposals for health, education, and family planning are unlikely to be meaningful unless they are combined with a major redistribution of income or a major shift in the approach to development.

Improved Health

Health epitomizes the complex interaction of production, employment, consumption, and human well-being. Increased production of food provides the most basic requisite for improved health. More employment can put money to buy more food into the hands of the poor. A better diet creates a more favorable environment for health education and direct programs of health improvement. A pattern of growth which offers widespread job opportunities requires a large, productive, healthy labor force.

As was generally the case in low-income nations, during the past two decades, each of these interacting elements was bound to fare badly in India, given the capital intensive approach to development and the realities of income distribution. Since food production barely kept up with the increase in population, only substantial imports or rationing of supplies to upper-income groups could upgrade the diets of the poor; the one was inconsistent with the chosen strategy of economic development; the other contradicted the realities of the political power structure. Employment, too, grew little faster than population; thus the paucity of food was balanced with a paucity of low-income purchasing power, and the equilibrium was further reinforced at a poor level of health. The presence of a labor surplus lent little importance to the argument that improved health would provide a larger, more productive labor force. Concurrently, the rural power structure provided an inhospitable environment for specific programs of nutrition improvement to reach the poor.

Dwarkados observes, "There is more sickness in the lower paid workers of the unskilled groups than among the better paid semi-skilled and skilled group—poverty, malnutrition, under-nutrition and bad housing with next to no sanitary conveniences all combine to create this condition." [1] Wyon and Gordon, in a set of villages in the relatively prosperous Punjab, found the death rate nearly twice as high among the low-caste agricultural laborers as among the higher-caste owner-cultivators—twenty-three per thousand compared to fourteen per thousand. [2] Similarly, 20 percent of the owner-cultivator families reared all their live-born children, contrasted with only 4 percent of the labor-class families; and 36 percent of the owner-cultivator families had lost three or more children, compared with 67 percent of the laborer families. [3]

The pervasiveness of health problems among the poor is emphasized by data from the Punjab, a region which by world standards has relatively high and broadly distributed income. The detail and accuracy of data from the Punjab facilitate making the important points clearly and, it happens, dramatically. All too often data focus on the average income or diet of a nation, leaving little impression of the extremely difficult condition for a substantial minority or even majority with below average income,

[1] Kanji Dwarkadas, *Forty-five Years with Labour* (London: Asia Publishing House, 1962), p. 256.

[2] John B. Wyon and John E. Gordon, *The Khanna Study: Population Problems in the Rural Punjab* (Cambridge, Mass.: Harvard University Press, 1971), pp. 195–96 and Table 33.

[3] Ibid., p. 197.

diet, and health. This chapter concentrates on exposing the problems of that group.

In his study, also in the Punjab, of infants aged six months to twenty-four months, Levinson found frequent cases of significant malnutrition in all income and caste groups, reflecting a lack of knowledge as well as a lack of resources. But malnutrition was much more widespread among the laboring classes than the landowning classes. Of the latter, nearly 4 percent suffered third-degree malnutrition (essentially calling for hospitalization) while over 12 percent of the laboring class children suffered third-degree malnutrition. For the sum of second- and third-degree malnutrition, the proportions were 39 percent and 57 percent, respectively. In the same age class, Levinson found the incidence of diarrheal infection 30 percent higher in the laboring than the cultivating class.[4] These sharp contrasts occur among the very young, for whom the relative importance of parental care and knowledge would appear to far outweigh the small financial requirements of good diet.

Extreme poverty presents three major obstacles to improved health. First, levels of income insufficient to provide basic caloric requirements tend to aggravate other nutritional and health problems. Second, the mothers of small infants work long hours, reducing the potential for adequate child care—a serious problem in a poor society lacking convenience foods and labor-saving household devices. Third, dependency for employment on the village elite reduces political power and therefore the ability of the poor to influence health programs so as to meet the special needs of their income, employment, and social position.

Dandekar and Rath find one-third of all rural people and about half of all urban people in India with incomes too low to obtain enough food for adequate nourishment and activity.[5] An earlier survey, conducted by Sukhatme, and using the Nutrition Advisory Committee recommended requirement of 2,400 calories per day per person, estimated 25 percent of the Indian population as deficient in calories.[6] Malnutrition prejudices all

[4] F. James Levinson, *Morinda: An Economic Analysis of Malnutrition among Young Children in Rural India* (Cambridge, Mass.: Cornell-MIT International Nutrition Policy Series, 1974), ch. iv, particularly Tables 7 and 15.
[5] V. M. Dandekar and Nilakantha Rath, "Poverty in India," *Economic and Political Weekly*, 6:1 (January 2, 1971), 29–30.
[6] P. V. Sukhatme, "The Food and Nutrition Situation in India," *Indian Journal of Agricultural Economics*, 17:2 (April–June 1962), 1–28, especially pp. 20–21; and 17:3 (July–September 1962), 1–34. See also Uma J. Lele, "The Green Revolution: Income Distribution and Nutrition," *Proceedings—Western Hemisphere Nutrition Congress III*, Philip L.

other health programs as it interacts with and reinforces the direct effect of disease and is closely associated with protein deficiency.

Redistribution of the existing foodgrain supply is unlikely to solve the problem of hunger. The average per capita availability of the past two decades has provided little leeway over the minimum requirement. Perhaps more important, a simple one-to-one transfer of income from the rich to the poor cannot be effective in improving calorie intake of the poor because of sharply different patterns of expenditure. Accordingly, transfer of one rupee of income away from the upper-income class (the top 10 percent) will reduce the foodgrain expenditure by only about Rs. 0.04; while a rupee of increased income for the lowest (20 percent) income class will raise expenditure on foodgrains by Rs. 0.59 (Table VII-1). With an equal transfer of income, the rich will release only 7 percent of the foodgrains the poor desire and attempt to purchase. These problems of balance in supply of real goods are exemplified at a sharply higher level of real income by the food problems in Chile when substantial increase in incomes of lower-income people forced food prices sharply higher. For a higher-income country the range of food commodities receiving this pressure may be greater than in a country like India, but the overall effect is surprisingly similar.

Of course, a drastic leveling or near leveling of incomes would roughly equalize consumption. The same effect could be achieved by statutory rationing. In both cases, however, not only the urban middle classes but also the rural cultivator classes would have to reduce consumption markedly—an unlikely prospect as long as those two groups retain substantial political power. Only importation or—more reasonably—increased domestic production can provide more meals for the Indian poor. Once additional foodgrain supplies become available and larger purchasing power is placed in the hands of the poor, normal expenditure patterns and the private market distribution system can effectively apportion the greater supply.[7] Indeed, it is doubtful if direct-distribution programs can match

---

White, ed. (Mount Kisco, N.Y.: Futura, 1972); and Alan Berg, *The Nutrition Factor* (Washington, D.C.: The Brookings Institution, 1973).

[7] See Chapter III, above, for comment on the efficiency of the private market system in times of adequate supplies. For a more substantial treatment, see Uma J. Lele, *Food Grain Marketing in India: Private Performance and Public Policy* (Ithaca, N.Y.: Cornell University Press, 1971), and Uma J. Lele, "Marketing Integration: A Study of Sorghum Prices in Western India," Part I, *Journal of Farm Economics*, 49:1 (February 1967), 147–59.

the efficiency of increased income in moving calories to the hungry.[8] Additional food production, increased income to the poor, and the use of the private distribution system not only set the stage for health education plans and delivery programs for target groups, but leave public institutions and other resources available to fulfill those special functions.

Ill health and high mortality strike the children of the poor, frequently because they lack the proper care. The solution requires increased labor productivity, not greater employment alone.

On the basis of intensive observation in villages of the prosperous Punjab, Taylor comments that inadequate maternal care of children, especially of female offspring by multiparous women, "was not so much a deliberate neglect infanticide, as a result of numerous competing claims on the overworked mothers' time and attention." [9] Observing the life of women in Senapur village, in poor Uttar Pradesh, Luschinsky notes the heavier outdoor occupations of lower-caste women—in the fields or in caste-prescribed work. In their families, she found that "girls of five or six years and up often tend their youngest siblings." [10] Minkler notes that in both urban and rural India the need to supplement existing incomes clearly forces the majority of women from low-income households to seek remunerative employment outside the home and leave young children unattended or in the care of older siblings or an aged mother-in-law.[11]

In rural landless laboring families, the mothers work when employment is available, typically averaging 131 days of labor per year.[12] As incomes

[8] Note the large leakages of expenditure implied in the analysis of nutrition programs in Gunvant M. Desai and V. R. Gaikwad, *Applied Nutrition Programme: An Evaluation Study* (Ahmedabad: Indian Institute of Management, Centre for Management in Agriculture, 1971). In contrast, note the high proportion of added income the poor spend on food in Table VII-1, above.

[9] Carl E. Taylor, C. Desweemer, I. S. Uberoi, A. Kielmann, and M. List, eds., *Malnutrition and Infection in Weaning-Age Punjabi Children* (Baltimore, Md.: Johns Hopkins University, School of Hygiene and Public Health, 1972), p. 17.

[10] Mildred Stroop Luschinsky, "The Life of Women in a Village of North India: A Study of Role and Status" (Ph.D. dissertation, Department of Anthropology, Cornell University, 1962), p. 519.

[11] Meredith Minkler, "Fertility and Female Labour Force Participation in India: A Survey of Workers in Old Delhi Area," *Journal of Family Welfare,* 17:1 (September 1970), 31–43.

[12] *Agricultural Labour in India: Report on the Second Agricultural Labour Enquiry, 1956–57* (Delhi: Government of India, Ministry of Labour and Employment [Labour Bureau], 1961), pp. 88–89.

in the laboring classes rise, the amount of female work declines, reflecting societal values and the pull of other activities. The result is more time available for child care. For example, from survey data in Badaun and Nainital districts, which undoubtedly understate the relative work pressure on women in low-income families, Richard Shortlidge estimates that 12 percent of the rural women in landless homes worked in nonhousehold jobs, compared to 6 percent for those households with up to five acres of land.[13]

The effectiveness of many public programs for health improvement postulates available time on the part of the participants. Children must be free to attend activities where feeding is provided; women must be free to grow kitchen gardens to add to vitamin supplies; men need access to ponds and time to fish to add to protein; women need time to prepare more labor-requiring but nutrition-conserving foods. Since such programs have more feasibility for families of leisure than for families of poverty, they probably serve to widen rather than to narrow human welfare disparities. These problems of excessive burden on the time of low-income women are widespread in low-income countries and are little understood, in part because of the widespread but incorrect view of idleness among the poor, and hence merit careful study if effective, ameliorative programs are to be mounted.

Policy statements in India indicate awareness of these realities. The report of the subcommittee examining primary health centers in 1960–61 stated:

Success of a health programme entirely depends on whether it is integrated into a social process of general economic development or applied to a status of economic stagnation. The maximum effect of a health programme also depends on whether and to what degree coordinated efforts at the same time are set to work in the fields of education, food, housing and particularly general economic development.[14]

Similarly, Asok Mitra, then secretary to the Planning Commission, stated that the first priority "in the field of nutrition will thus continue to be the program of the Green Revolution, multiple cropping, and the intensive

[13] From unpublished data collected by Richard L. Shortlidge, Jr. For a description and analysis of these data, see "A Socioeconomic Model of School Attendance," Cornell Agricultural Economics Occasional Paper No. 86 (January 1976). For a discussion of women in the nonagricultural labor force, see Dwarkadas, pp. 91–143.

[14] *Summary Proceedings of the Tenth Meeting of the Central Council of Health* (Nasik: Government of India, Ministry of Health, 1964), p. 130.

cultivation of high yielding varieties of cereals." He also recommended priority for programs to increase the purchasing power of the lowest (40 percent) income group, and urged further emphasis on drinking water, sanitation, and completion of "the unfinished public health revolution." [15] Only after the achievement of these goals would he support special programs for expectant mothers and infants, even though he recognized their absolute importance. But while the conceptualization of programs and priorities has been clear and sound, the specific programs have had limited impact because the key conditions of increased agricultural production and larger purchasing power of the poor have not been met.

Despite the unfavorable environment in the past, the recommendations and experience of health programs provide useful lessons for future application and state clearly the set of problems encountered in nearly all the low-income nations as they attempt to improve health for the mass of their people. The Bhore Committee Report, published in 1946, comprehensively reviewed various aspects of public health in India and formed the basis for post-independence policy. The Bhore Committee rated unsafe drinking water as the principal cause of ill health.[16] Although the First Five-Year Plan put heavy stress on safe water supplies, the funds actually available in each successive plan were meager. Long-range plans stated the objectives and general means for improving water supplies; overall economic strategy provided no basis for financing such activities, and the political development of rural government did not furnish effective political pressures for making such expenditure.

The Bhore Committee and each of the Five-Year Plans have stated the need for expanded health centers, particularly in rural areas. The core of the medical effort was to be a Primary Health Center with an integrated staff including medical officers, compounders, and midwives. By December of 1961, about 3,000 centers were operating, but over two-thirds were without their regular complement of doctors, "lady health visitors," nurse-midwives, and public health nurses.[17] By March 1969, 68 percent

[15] Asok Mitra, "The Nutrition Movement in India," in *Nutrition, National Development, and Planning,* ed. Alan Berg, Nevin S. Schrimshaw, and David L. Call (Cambridge, Mass.: M.I.T. Press, 1973), pp. 358, 360–361.

[16] See *The Health Survey and Development Committee Report* (Bhore Committee Report) (New Delhi: Government of India, 1946).

[17] *Summary Proceedings of the Tenth Meeting of the Central Council of Health,* pp. 132, 172.

of the community development blocks (village groups) were covered by a center, but presumably many were still without doctors. Each center served an average of over 78,000 people—in sharp contrast to the Bhore Committee recommendation of one fully staffed center per 10,000 to 20,000 people.[18] A shortage of trained personnel and the failure of the government to spend money on safe water and sanitation sharply limited the possibilities for treating a large number of poorly nourished people.

The trained personnel problem illustrates the general political and institutional difficulties of meeting the needs of the poor. India commenced independence with an average of one doctor per 6,300 people and a rural average of less than one per 25,000 people.[19] As of 1956, only 11 percent of the registered doctors worked in rural areas, and 82 percent of those licensed had completed the "licentiate" four-year medical course given to matriculates.[20] It would seem that the logical way to break the manpower bottleneck would be through a crash training program for paramedical personnel. Carl Taylor and his co-workers argue (on the basis of work at the Rural Health Research Center in Narangwal, Punjab) that "with adequate supervision, safe medical care can be practiced by auxiliaries who treat 80–90 percent of illnesses of children and refer the rest." However, they point out that "the whole notion of using paramedical personnel to diagnose and treat illness at first met with major resistance from the Indian medical profession." [21] The problem of resistance to such an approach is, of course, widespread. Unfortunately, as in much of the world, the trend in India seems to have been away from massive training of paramedical personnel. The licentiate course was abolished by the central government at the insistence of the Medical Council in 1956, in order to provide "one standard" for medical education. This has inevitably reinforced a typical urban-oriented, Western-pattern style of medical training, combined with a sprinkling of rural clinic experience.[22]

In the First Five-Year Plan, officials foresaw the expanding need for auxiliary health personnel. The government admitted, at the same time,

---

[18] Ibid., p. 133; *Fourth Five-Year Plan, 1969–74* (New Delhi: Government of India, Planning Commission, n.d.), p. 390.

[19] Jean Joyce, *Health in New India: The Story of Free India's War against Disease, 1947–1961* (New York: Ford Foundation, 1961), p. 3.

[20] *Doctors in India* (Delhi: Government of India, Planning Commission, Manpower Studies No. 14, August 1959).

[21] Taylor et al., pp. 14–15.

[22] See *Doctors in India*.

that it would not be able to cope with the entire problem and suggested seeking the help of voluntary agencies to provide training.[23] "The Second Five-Year Plan for the first time put training of health personnel high on its list of priorities. Yet the targets set and the funds allotted were still far too small. . . . No effort was made, except for training village midwives, to train personnel with limited skills to serve as health assistants."[24]

During the Third Five-Year Plan period, efforts were made to revive the licentiate course. The draft outline of the plan suggested that training of licentiates would make more medical help available to villages. A *Times of India* editorial of November 4, 1960, asserted:

> It is high time the relevant authorities in the States and at the Center revived the licentiate course in medicine and surgery and took steps to end the cruel maldistribution of available medical personnel in the country. The situation is plainly shameful. In Uttar Pradesh there are 218 dispensaries without doctors. According to the Health Minister of Orissa there are 54 hospitals which are being run without doctors . . . and in Madhya Pradesh there are another 200 such dispensaries. . . . One wonders what kind of planning has gone into the health schemes that have been launched in the past 10 years.[25]

Despite such expressions of support, the suggestion of the draft Fourth Plan for reviving the licentiate course failed to appear among the final proposals. Specific mention was made of expanding the existing pattern of medical instruction, with particular reference to strengthening postgraduate education in order to keep up with the need for medical teachers. Paramedical personnel mentioned in the Plan are nurses and family-planning-program workers. Participation of medical and public health personnel in rural health care was envisaged as increasing via better residential accommodations and higher salaries, rather than rapid enlargement of the total supply.[26]

A final point regarding the relationship between a rural-led approach to growth and the adequacy of trained personnel in small towns and villages should be noted. It is often stated that educated people do not like to live in rural areas. Certainly, the low priority given to rural development has resulted in a continuing lack of sufficient transport, communication, elec-

---

[23] *First Five-Year Plan* (New Delhi: Government of India, Planning Commission, 1952), p. 495.

[24] Joyce, p. 46.

[25] *Times of India* (daily), November 4, 1960.

[26] *Fourth Five-Year Plan*, pp. 388–90.

trification, and income to support consumer services. Altering the strategy of growth could substantially diminish the disadvantages of rural living.

As rising incomes enable the poor to spend more time caring for their families, the environment for health education programs becomes favorable. The considerable variation in the state of health care, even within the upper-income groups of rural India, demonstrates the need for such programs. Although Levinson's study shows much more infant malnutrition in the families of the lower-income laborers, it is still significant among the cultivator classes; 35 percent of their children suffer second-degree malnutrition.[27] People in the cultivator classes can amply afford an adequate diet for the whole family and sufficient time for the care of children. Education in nutrition is necessary for better health in these income classes, just as it will be for currently low-income families once their general economic status is improved.

Pregnant women, nursing mothers, and infants are the groups most vulnerable to malnutrition. Special programs to reach them would make effective use of limited resources. Such programs must struggle with the continuing problem of calorie deficiency and the scarcity of mothers' time for effective participation in health education and other programs. Moreover, operating procedures are frequently insensitive to the needs of the poor. In their study of a child-feeding program, G. M. Desai and V. R. Gaikwad point out the flaws resulting from the distribution of food largely through specially organized village children's groups called *balwadi*s.

There was no restriction in admission to balwadis. Despite this about 75 percent of the children in the age group of three to six years were not attending balwadis. The children attending balwadis came mainly from relatively better off families in the villages. Very few children from the families of small cultivators, or agricultural and other laborers attended balwadis. Interviews with many households revealed that nonparticipation in the balwadis by children of the low income groups was not due to any class or caste restriction for admission but to the need for older children at home to look after the younger ones when the womenfolk went to work. Thus it is clear that balwadi was not the most appropriate institution through which a supplementary or welfare feeding scheme should have been implemented. Most of the children attending balwadis came from a background where there was no acute need for supplementary feeding while the children in maximum need of some assistance did not get any benefit of the scheme.[28]

[27] Levinson, Table 7.   [28] Desai and Gaikwad, p. 129.

The same study documents similar problems for other programs, from vegetable raising to water supply. Some efforts, of course, do reach the poor. Vaccination for smallpox is almost universal. But such procedures should be extended—for example, to include tetanus—which is the fourth most important cause of death in India.[29]

A basic dilemma in improving welfare in the context of maldistribution of wealth, income, and power is making the programs appropriate to the *specific* needs of the poor. That goal could theoretically be achieved by decentralizing the administration of programs. The local political bodies through which the decentralization proceeds are almost everywhere dominated by the prosperous cultivator classes. For increasing agricultural production, there is much to be said for placing power in the hands of these groups. But the wealthier classes will, at worst, subvert programs for the poor in order to gain the benefits for themselves and to ensure against the organization and strengthening of the lower classes. At best, they simply will not understand the particular needs of the indigent and the means of fulfilling them. Under present political conditions, decentralized administration seems unlikely to enhance the effectiveness of welfare programs in reaching the poor. More centralized control will require intensive, systematic study of the problems as a substitute for intuitive knowledge that would be made accessible by including the poor in decision making.

Increased Participation in Education

No effective poverty program can ignore education. Education increases access to jobs, production resources, and power. By improving labor productivity and the efficiency with which resources are utilized, it contributes to higher national income. It is important for improving the quality of life and is a logical means of enhancing health. As a rule, the poor participate least in education and get the fewest benefits from their schooling.

The poor—particularly the rural poor—fail to attend school largely because job opportunities are unfavorable. It will not pay the poor to attend school until an employment-oriented strategy of growth increases the demand for educated people. Only then will it become economic to increase the availability of instruction and achieve the broader social pur-

[29] See Wyon and Gordon, pp. 173–76, particularly Table 17.

poses of education in company with the individual goals of improved job opportunities and income.

At the beginning of the period of independence India had one of the world's lowest literacy and primary school attendance rates; the nation has since spent sums on education which, relative to national income, are high according to international standards. But a continuing elitist tradition and the slow growth in demand for educated manpower have placed a particularly large share of the money at the upper income levels, thus tending to reinforce class differences in educational attainment.

At the inception of the First Five-Year Plan in 1951, India's illiteracy rate was reported by UNESCO as 83 percent; it was 72 percent in 1961. Pakistan was comparably high at 81 percent in 1951, and in sharp contrast to Taiwan at 50 percent in 1950; the Philippines at 40 percent in 1948; and Thailand at 48 percent in 1947. Most Latin American countries reported illiteracy rates much lower than India's: Brazil, 51 percent in 1950; Chile, 20 percent in 1952; and Venezuela, 48 percent in 1950. The Indian proportion was more comparable to that reported for a number of African countries: Nigeria, 89 percent in 1953; Uganda, 75 percent in 1959; and Algeria, 92 percent in 1954.[30]

The evidence about illiteracy belies the official data on school enrollment. The number of boys aged six to ten years enrolled in primary school increased from 60 percent to 99 percent during the period 1950–51 to 1965–66. The corresponding increase for girls in the same age group was from 25 percent to 56 percent.[31] These attendance data are inflated by the repetition of grades, particularly among the poor, by the inclusion of children in primary school who are outside the age range of six to ten years, as well as by a general tendency to overestimate the actual number of children in school.

A more precise view of school attendance is available from a village survey, conducted by Shortlidge in the villages of Badaun and Nainital districts.[32] Of a weighted sample of 4,258 children in the age group six to twenty-one years, 32 percent were in school, 11 percent had attended school at some time in the past, and 57 percent had no previous school-

[30] *Statistical Yearbook, 1965* (Paris: UNESCO, 1966), Table 4.

[31] Mark Blaug, Richard Layard, and Maureen Woodhall, *The Causes of Graduate Unemployment in India* (London: Allen Lane, 1969), Table 2.2, p. 44.

[32] For data and further discussion of school participation in India, see Shortlidge, "A Socioeconomic Model of School Attendance."

ing. The proportion of girls in school remained at approximately half the overall participation rate of boys in each age group, except in the group aged seventeen to twenty-one, in which the proportion of girls who had *never* attended school (76 percent) was significantly higher than the proportion of boys (44 percent).

From 1950 to 1965 the share of India's GNP allocated to education had risen from 0.8 percent to 2.6 percent.[33] By 1965, India's proportion of GNP spent on education was nearly twice that of Pakistan; about the same as that of the Philippines and Thailand, with much higher per capita incomes; and less than half that of the United States and the United Kingdom. But India puts an abnormally high percentage of its educational budget into the universities—24 percent in 1966, compared to 13 percent in Taiwan in 1965, 12 percent in Thailand in 1968, 11 percent in Japan in 1965, and 12 percent in the USSR in 1965. The Indian percentage spent on advanced education is comparable to that of high-income countries such as the United Kingdom, West Germany, and the United States, as well as the elitist countries of Latin America—for example, Venezuela and Chile.

According to the Education Commission Report, from 1950–51 to 1965–66 the proportion of current education expenditure allocated for primary instruction declined from 49 to 44 percent; for secondary education, it held constant at 28 percent; and for higher education, it rose from 23 percent to 29 percent. The size of the allocation for higher education reflects the greater costs of such schooling, as well as the elitist tradition. The Education Commission Report suggests that it costs over ten times as much per person, per year, to teach a student at the higher-education level as at the primary level.[34] Since upper-income people fill the majority of positions in higher education, such an expenditure pattern tends to widen income and welfare disparities.

The aristocratic tradition in education has deep roots in Indian history. Both the Hindu Brahmanic and the Moslem Maktab traditions gave elitist reverence to education. The British influence reinforced these tendencies. For example, although the local indigenous educational system was lim-

---

[33] These and the following data on education expenditure by country are from UNESCO, *Statistical Yearbook, 1970*, Tables 2.19 and 2.20; and ibid., 1972, Table 5.2.

[34] See *Report of the Education Commission, 1964–66: Education and National Development* (New Delhi: Government of India, Ministry of Education and Youth Services, 1966); and Supplementary Volume II (1970).

ited and reached only a select few, the British government's emphasis on the establishment of quality institutions, even at the primary level, actually reduced the number of children completing elementary schools in 1901–02 from the number in previous decades of the nineteenth century.[35]

Changing British attitudes toward education—and growing Indian control—did eventually bring substantial, but slow, progress.

Quinquennial statistics for compulsory education are available and they make painful reading, showing how slow progress has been. In 1921–22 when education was transferred to Indian control, compulsory education had been introduced in eight towns only and not even in one village, although India is predominantly a rural country. By 1936–37, compulsory education had been introduced in 167 urban areas (6.18 percent) out of 2,703 and in 13,062 (2.00 percent) rural regions out of 655,892.[36]

Thus, despite continued growth of the educational system, at independence India was a nation comprised largely of illiterates, and it possessed no better than a rudimentary primary school system.

Although the post-independence surge in education expenditure greatly increased the school population, the slow growth in employment has created the distinct danger that a low-level equilibrium has been reached, or will soon be reached, between the supply and the demand of educated people. If so, pressures for further expansion of the educational system would likely be resisted by the already favored elite. At this point, the social objective of broadened participation in schooling challenges the political objective of the existing elite to preserve its position through access to education. Meanwhile, the present growth strategy provides ominously slow increases in employment. These relationships explain the sluggish participation of the poor in education—a condition most critical at the primary school level. For primary school is not only the entry point to higher education; it also furnishes the basic skills of literacy and the ability to calculate. Girls and the poor are the least likely to enter primary school and the most likely to drop out; consequently, existing social patterns are reinforced.

Nationally, the primary school dropout rates have been relatively stable

[35] K. G. Saiyidain, J. P. Naik, and S. Abid Husain, *Compulsory Education in India* (Delhi: Universal Book and Stationery Co., 1966), p. 23.
[36] Ibid., p. 37.

over the years, with about half of the males and one-quarter of the females who start first grade continuing to grade five.[37] But school participation rates vary sharply according to the standard of living. In Badaun district, Shortlidge finds that in 1971, among children aged six to twenty-one years from families owning no land, 54 percent of the males and 90 percent of the females had never attended school. In contrast, only 25 percent of the male children and 72 percent of the female children from families owning ten acres had not attended school.[38] These data are qualitatively supported with regard to other north Indian villages by Oscar Lewis and the Wisers.[39] The latter, though noting improvement from the decade of the 1930s to the 1950s, nevertheless reveal that poor children still tend not to go to school. Education is too costly; its rewards are too limited as far as poor families are concerned.

The relative cost of education is much higher for the needy than for the upper-income classes because of the importance of foregone income. In Shortlidge's Badaun and Nainital district survey, the opportunity cost of sending a child to primary school was shown to be approximately Rs. 140, compared to over Rs. 400 for high school. As a result, a high proportion of the poor may start school and then drop out after a few grades. Among the laboring class a high proportion of the children perform important household chores, such as child care or cattle herding.[40] Even erratic employment produces unsatisfactory attendance records, one of the most important causes of dropout. Unfortunately, key school examinations are often scheduled at harvest time, as in Badaun—a matter of no consequence to nonworking children from prosperous families but crucial for children of the poor, whose income from labor is essential in the peak periods when work is available. In addition, needy children attending school must spend extra money for clothing and supplies that the rich would buy in any case. The very low income of the poor creates a problem of obtaining cash to finance education that, in effect, discounts potential rewards to a much greater extent than for the well-to-do.[41]

A number of studies show rates of return to investment in primary edu-

[37] Blaug et al., Figure 2.1.
[38] Shortlidge, "A Socioeconomic Model of School Attendance."
[39] See Oscar Lewis, *Village Life in Northern India: Studies in a Delhi Village* (Urbana: University of Illinois Press, 1958); and William H. Wiser and Charlotte Viall Wiser, *Behind Mud Walls, 1930–1960* (Berkeley: University of California Press, 1963).
[40] Shortlidge, "A Socioeconomic Model of School Attendance."
[41] Blaug et al., pp. 130–35.

cation considerably higher than to other levels of schooling.[42] From these studies, as well as the knowledge that large numbers of children still do not attend primary grades, it would seem that additional elementary schools would offer the highest return to educational investment. However, the studies are based largely on experience in urban areas, where a much larger percentage of children attend primary institutions, which are substantially superior to those in rural districts.

In the outlying areas, in order to obtain economic rewards, further schooling must follow primary education. For additional education, a large proportion of rural people would have to move their children to an urban area. In 1971, according to Shortlidge's survey in Badaun district, the total of direct and indirect costs to send a child to primary school was Rs. 168 per year, or approximately three-quarters of the average landless laborer's annual per capita income; for attending middle school, the total cost rose to Rs. 343—more than the average laborer's annual income.[43]

Each of the circumstances discouraging school attendance is even more serious for girls from poor families than for boys. The alternative cost of the girls' labor is high, because they would normally be caring for younger siblings while their mothers work. Furthermore, for girls the practical rewards of a primary education are nil; choice jobs require secondary education, and both cost and social custom enjoin girls from leaving the villages for secondary schooling. Interviews in Badaun suggest that the chance that more education will provide a more desirable marriage for a poor girl is slim. For a girl from a wealthier family, the possibility of a better marriage as a result of further education is greater.

Higher-income children are more likely to be attending urban schools. Among the landless class, only 13 percent of the children in primary school attended local urban schools, compared with 24 percent of children of landowners with more than ten acres. The superior quality of urban schools benefits not only urban people, but also wealthier rural people. In Badaun and Nainital districts, student-teacher ratios for rural

---

[42] See Richard L. Shortlidge, Jr., "The Profitability of Educational Investments in India" (M.S. thesis, Cornell University, Department of Agricultural Economics, June 1970); V. N. Kothari, "Returns to Education in India," in Baljit Singh, ed., *Education as Investment* (Meerut: Meenakshi Prakashan, 1967), pp. 127–40; Arnold C. Harberger, "Investment in Men versus Investment in Machines: The Case of India," in C. Arnold Anderson and Mary Jean Bowman, eds., *Education and Economic Development* (Chicago: Aldine, 1965), pp. 11–50; and Blaug et al., op. cit.

[43] Shortlidge, "A Socioeconomic Model of School Attendance."

schools averaged 38.8, 56 percent higher than the average of 24.9 for urban schools. Furthermore, the estimated value of the school building and other assets per student averaged Rs. 366.8 for the eight urban schools, nearly six times more than the average of Rs. 63.6 for the eleven rural schools.[44]

The pronounced contrasts in enrollment between economic classes at the university level are similarly associated with greater costs and lower rewards for the poor. However, the cost and rewards of the well-to-do are reinforced at the higher-educational level by the effects of the earlier, inferior educational experience of those from lower-income classes. For example, at G. B. Pant University of Agriculture and Technology, one of the better agricultural universities, which provides very high returns to education investment, the monthly parental income of the July 1971 graduating class averaged Rs. 823. In 1971, only 4 percent of the urban households and 0.9 percent of the rural households in India earned more than Rs. 500 per month. Similarly, the median size of holding was thirty acres, compared to the all-India average of five acres.[45] The striking feature of this high average family income of students is that the university is seriously trying to increase enrollment from lower-income groups. It reserves 18 percent of its undergraduate positions for members of scheduled (low) castes and tribes with annual incomes of less than Rs. 5000; it awards entrance points to applicants from rural schools and those whose families have less than twelve acres of land; and it provides liberal scholarships. But the low participation of the poor is rooted in more basic social and economic phenomena. At the very least, the problem traces back to primary education and the lack of incentive for the rural poor to undergo schooling.

It is clear that full participation of the poor in education cannot be achieved simply by adding primary school facilities within a rural environment of economic stagnation and extreme poverty. Fundamental economic and, possibly, social changes are needed. Since modern development has made education an increasingly important avenue to power, access to education may become something of a battleground between the haves and the have-nots. Even in villages, land becomes a more tenuous

[44] Unpublished data collected by Richard L. Shortlidge, Jr.
[45] Richard L. Shortlidge, Jr., "The Labor Market for Agricultural Graduates in India: A Benefit-Cost Case Study of G. B. Pant University of Agriculture and Technology," Cornell Agricultural Economics Occasional Paper No. 69 (April 1974), pp. 11, 22.

source of power under the threat of land legislation and the growth of nonfarm jobs, while education provides access not only to government programs and subsidies, but also to a wide range of jobs which themselves provide economic and social power. A strategy of growth which emphasizes rural development and increasing rural incomes would raise the demand for a literate labor force, improve the rewards of education through better job opportunities, decrease the cost of schooling as higher incomes reduce the necessity of using child labor, and enlarge the availability of funds to finance education.

Vigorous rural development will accelerate the demand for educated people. The data from Badaun and Nainital districts show a substantial incidence of education among employees of small manufacturing and service firms. In a study of 79 concerns in Rudrapur city and 93 in Badaun city, the average years of schooling completed by employees was 6.5 years and 6.2 years, respectively. Moreover, education was found to be one of the important determinants of monthly earnings. However, it became significant only at the middle school and higher levels, suggesting that the villagers' negative attitude toward the benefits of education which terminates at the primary level has foundation in reality.[46]

It would be possible to use the school system to serve other social objectives such as health education and family planning. Such programs will never reach the impoverished if they lack economic incentive to attend school. Efforts to improve attendance by increasing the relevance of instruction must recognize that most children who are not in school are from families whose only vocational opportunities are the performance of physical labor on land owned by others. Education cannot be meaningful to them without the prospect of better jobs. For children of the landowning classes, primary school attendance normally leads to higher levels of education and then to better jobs. The test of relevance is thus based on the entrance requirements at the successive levels of schooling. That may be the pertinent test for the poor as well.

Furthermore, once the needy are attracted to school, it becomes important to make changes to keep them there. These would include a shift in the timing of the school year to conform to demands for labor; textbook and instructional methods of greater practical significance; greater refer-

[46] Richard L. Shortlidge, Jr., "Is Human Capital an Important Determinant of Earnings in Small Manufacturing and Retail Firms in India," Cornell Agricultural Economics Occasional Paper No. 85 (January 1976).

ence to the experience and needs of lower-income rural students; increased adult education; larger expenditure per pupil on higher salaries for teachers; and more and better trained teachers.

The basic alternative to a rural, employment-oriented growth strategy for providing incentive to expand rural education—as for improvement in health—is a radical redistribution of assets and income, and a change in the objective of education toward direct social purposes. Without a modification either in the strategy of growth or in the socioeconomic structure of society, the poor will not participate in education above the present low level.

Family Planning and Family Size

Family planning and lower birthrates are usually justified on the basis of national interests. Decreased rates of population growth relax pressure on limited natural resources and capital supplies and facilitate a rise in the savings rate. Fewer people dividing the national income accelerate expansion in the per capita level of living. These national gains have their individual analogues: fewer children per family allow the wage earner's income to provide better diet, clothing, and housing per child; improved health and more investment in education per child promote a later increase in family income. In addition, smaller families make possible more personal attention to children and better health for the mother. For those families owning productive assets such as land, there is a further reason for small family size: to avoid dividing the tangible resources and consequently reducing the proportion of income earned from property relative to that earned from labor.

But national and individual interests may also diverge. Unlike specific families, national authorities do not fear that the birthrate may drop so low that, with existing death rates, the nation will have no children to carry on name and tradition and to provide future income security. Individual families do have that fear. The average of 2.5 surviving males per family that Wyon and Gordon report for the Indian Punjab does not seem excessive, given the randomness of death and the average mortality rate of 40 percent of the children before the mother passes childbearing age.[47]

In addition, for that 20 to 40 percent of the Indian population comprising the landless laboring class, the cost of bringing up children until they

[47] Wyon and Gordon, ch. vii, particularly Table 10, p. 140.

are of working age is relatively lower than for higher-income classes; and alternative means of saving and investing essentially do not exist. Entrance into the labor market at an early age substantially reduces the expense of raising a child, and that cost occurs when the parents are young and most able to earn a living from physical labor. High death rates and low potential rewards from education discourage spending more money per child on a few children, rather than less per child on several. For the individual family, unlike the class as a whole, additional laborers promise greater income to the household. For the laboring-class family, there is clear incentive to produce large numbers of children.

Maybe the poor would prefer to have a small number of well-fed, healthy, and better educated children. But if the strategy of growth offers only a slow increase in employment and little opportunity for the needy to participate in that growth, this option is not open. As in the case of health and education, receptivity to family planning is a function of the strategy of development. The program that includes the poor may provide an eventual bonus of accelerated growth in per capita income through reduced rates of population expansion.

Analysis of traditional Indian family size and structure reveals three features of importance to modern family-planning programs. First, limitation of family size *is* traditionally practiced in India. Second, the extent of control of family size is closely related to death rates, income, and material assets. Third, modern techniques of birth control may merely substitute for old methods, with little further reduction in birthrates.

Wyon and Gordon present striking contrasts between age-specific birthrates of women in the Punjab town of Khanna and the American Hutterites, a small religious sect with maximum birthrates. Prior to age twenty-two the difference in birthrates between the two groups is small, but even at that age, the middle- and upper-income cultivating classes of Khanna evidence significantly lower birthrates than do the Hutterite women. Most striking is the decline in birthrates among Khanna women beyond age twenty-two, while the birthrate for the Hutterites continues to a level nearly 50 percent higher than that of the Khanna women by age thirty. Wyon and Gordon marshal considerable evidence with respect to practices of cohabitation following the birth of children and among the older age groups which suggest conscious efforts to reduce family size on the part of Khanna families.[48]

[48] Ibid., pp. 165–67 and ch. v.

Wyon and Gordon also document the fact that age-specific birthrates of wives in the upper-income cultivator castes are consistently lower than those of the low-income laboring castes, reinforcing the conclusion that there is deliberate birth control. Similarly, the combination of stillbirths and abortions was consistently higher for the cultivator castes than the laboring castes, despite a level of health, nutrition, and home environment more favorable to live childbirths. In a survey of women over forty-four, married once and with husbands still alive, they found for the cultivator class an average number of seven live-born children per family; for the lower-caste laborers, an average of eight children per family.[49] Data on family size and composition in Senapur village in eastern Uttar Pradesh are consistent with this finding.[50]

High child mortality encourages a larger number of births. Strikingly, despite substantial differences in the number of births in the two socioeconomic classes in the Wyon-Gordon study, the average number of live male children per family was almost exactly the same: 2.5 for the cultivator class and 2.4 for the laborer class. Given the strong social drive to beget male survivors to operate farms and to support parents in their old age, it seems likely that high death rates among children would prevent major decreases in birthrates below present levels.

Improved income, nutrition, health, and education will encourage acceptance of better methods of birth control. Similarly, if better education and employment prospects for girls reduced the drive to beget sons, overall birth rates might be lowered. There is a Punjab saying that "no son begets many daughters." Frequently, a couple that has produced two sons makes successful efforts to reduce the number of subsequent children.

In the Wyon and Gordon survey, inquiry was made concerning reasons for and against contraceptive practice. The most important reasons people gave for adopting birth control measures were inability to afford more children and regard for the health of the mother. A concern was also expressed regarding the division of family land. Those who refused to accept contraceptive practices, of whom 30 percent had no living sons, said they wanted more sons or more children.[51]

[49] Ibid., Table 10, p. 141.
[50] Sheldon R. Simon, "The Village of Senapur," Part IV of John W. Mellor et al., *Developing Rural India* (Ithaca, N.Y.: Cornell University Press, 1968), pp. 297–339.
[51] Wyon and Gordon, pp. 146–47.

The awkward traditional methods of birth control in Khanna, though effective, call for improvement. Long separation of husband and wife through visits of the wife to her home village, and lack of contact for lengthy periods after childbirth, reduce birthrates. The average spacing between children is twenty-two months. There are extremely low rates of coitus after the mid-thirties, as compared to populations in the United States. High death rates for girls cause a low ratio of females to males—an average 15 percent of the males never marry.[52] In other areas of India, social influences, such as a ban on the remarriage of widows, may be significant.[53]

Gradual change is occurring in traditional practices which affect birthrates. For example, during the period 1956 to 1969, Wyon and Gordon report the average age of first cohabitation after marriage increased from 17.5 years to 20 years.[54] It is still quite common for marriages to occur at a rather early age, after which the respective man and wife return to their families for a considerable period of time; later, a second ceremony occurs, at which time cohabitation may begin.

New methods of birth control may simply substitute for old procedures—increasing human welfare, but not causing a reduction in birthrates. Wyon and Gordon find evidence of this; 20 percent of their sample accepted modern methods of birth control, with no observable decline in birthrates.[55]

But since old techniques may be the product of complex, slow-acting social processes, economic factors which increase the number of families wishing to reduce birthrates may have a much more rapid effect when they occur in conjunction with new methods of birth control. In that case, there may be a high degree of complementarity between general programs which broaden participation in economic growth and specific programs of family planning. Further improvement of birth control technology could play an important role. In a manner analogous to efforts to expand agricultural production, it is quite possible that the importance and the potentials for scientific advances in birth control have been understated and underemphasized by the world community when providing funds and technical manpower.[56]

---

[52] Ibid., p. 155 and Table 33.   [53] See Simon, in Mellor et al., pp. 297–339.

[54] Wyon and Gordon, p. 298.   [55] Ibid., pp. 137–151, 245–47.

[56] Bhaskar D. Misra draws specific attention to "a lack of suitable contraceptive technology for Indian conditions" ("Family Planning: Differential Performance of States," *Economic and Political Weekly*, 6:39 [September 29, 1973], 1769–79). A. R. Kamat notes: "In spite of the great scientific advance of the last twenty years, most of the available contracep-

Taiwan and Korea illustrate the interaction of the pattern of growth with vigorous programs of family planning. Korea's birthrate dropped by one-fifth from 1955–60 to 1965–70, and Taiwan's by one-third from 1959 to 1969.[57] These records offer hope to India and other low-income countries as the drop occurred much more swiftly than in countries developing in earlier periods, and commenced at relatively low levels of per capita income. However, in 1969, Korea's per capita income was over twice that of India, and Taiwan's was nearly four times as high. In both Taiwan and Korea, the percentages of literate females, of females attending school, and of doctors per capita were all much greater than in India. In general, Korea and Taiwan had experienced rapid growth in per capita income, and, more important, the population had participated broadly in that growth through a fast expansion in employment and a quickly growing system of primary education. It is noteworthy that birthrates dropped sharply in Korea and Taiwan even while they were dominated by a large rural population.

In India, each successive Five-Year Plan increased the allocation of expenditures for family planning until, by 1972, it took 3.7 percent of the national budget, which is high by world standards.[58] Recent policy pronouncements indicate a clear understanding of the importance of family planning, an explicit intent that financing will not limit efforts, recognition that the endeavor will be restricted only by available scientific knowledge and by manpower resources, and a desire to proceed pragmatically, learning from domestic experience with minimum intrusion from the outside.[59]

But the situation with respect to family planning is reminiscent of plans for agriculture, small-scale industries, and rural public works. The specifics of the problem are understood, a substantial administrative structure has been built, yet the results are meager. As in the other programs, there

---

tives (except sterilisation, abortion and IUD insertion) require much understanding and patience on the part of the user and a level of living much more above that of the common people in our [India's] rural or urban areas" ("Family Planning Programmes: A Reassessment," *Economic and Political Weekly*, 6:13 [March 27, 1971], 726).

[57] See United Nations, Department of Economics and Social Affairs, *Population and Vital Statistics Report*, 18:1 (January 1966); and United Nations, Statistical Office, Department of Economic and Social Affairs, *Demographic Yearbook*, 1969 and 1970.

[58] *Reports on Population/Family Planning* (Population Council, New York), 6:2 (December 1974), Table 12. This compares with 0.2 percent of the national budget for Taiwan (1970); 0.1 percent for South Korea (1974); and 1.0 percent for Indonesia (1973).

[59] See *Fourth Five-Year Plan: A Draft Outline* (New Delhi: Government of India, Planning Commission, 1966), pp. 346–49.

is considerable evidence of administrative failing. Misra states: "The administrative defects and bureaucratic problems that involve a lack of commitment on the part of family planning staff, result in lack of co-ordination, supervision, and follow-up activities." [60] As in many of the programs, during the time the underlying strategy of growth fails to include participation of the mass of people, family planning efforts can have, at best, very limited success. It is then difficult to know whether the failures in execution are due solely to the lack of a favorable environment or present an additional problem that needs attention as other conditions start improving.

With increased breadth of participation in growth, a whole set of beneficial forces comes into play. Higher income will extend the motivation to limit family size to a larger proportion of the population. Wider access to education will spread the knowledge of means to reduce both death and birth rates, and the incentive to invest in more education for fewer children will increase. Specific family-planning programs can then effectively reinforce the underlying tendencies. At that point, the past efforts to build the requisite institutions, knowledge, and manpower can provide substantial rewards.

Toward a "Fair and Just Society"

John Locke, quoting the theologian Richard Hooker, states that the justification for "men uniting themselves . . . in politic societies" is the provision of "a life fit for the dignity of man." [61] The extent and the rapidity with which people of various economic strata attain such a life is a complex function of society's sense of justice and fairness; the state of knowledge of the needs and the means of growth; the distribution of resources; the effect of the division of political power on both future policies for the apportionment of income and the choice of programs for growth; and the initial level of income and its disposition.

In India, extreme poverty grips a vast proportion of the population, and the average per capita income barely exceeds the minimum subsistence level. The vicious circle of poverty leads from low labor productivity, insufficient income, and lack of food to poor health, little education, and high birthrates, and back to extreme poverty. That circle cannot be bro-

---

[60] Misra, p. 1769.
[61] John Locke (quoting Richard Hooker), *The Second Treatise of Government*, Sec. 15.

ken solely by minor levies on the rich to provide low-cost programs targeted toward specific aspects of health, education, and family planning. Such programs cannot be useful to the poor unless a much larger income places a much greater supply of goods in their hands. In this context, the cost of compassion must fall both heavily and widely.

Knowledge is available about the means of restructuring the processes of development to provide greater and earlier participation of the poor. Accelerated growth in food production by the reallocation of physical and institutional resources, and the reshaping of industrial development toward greater labor intensity by changes in consumption, trade, and investment patterns, would provide the incomes and the goods required by the needy. These processes would diminish poverty much more rapidly than has the past strategy of development, though, of course, not as quickly as would radical redistribution of existing flows of income.

Shift to a growth strategy with participation by the poor involves risks of failure as well as uncertainty concerning the precise dynamics of change in the power structure. It additionally requires the substantial price of revising many of the rules and precepts of development. There may be resistance to a change to a new approach toward growth. Perhaps more important, when decisions are made by the prosperous, the implications to the poor may inadvertently escape attention, as, for example, in the capital- and urban-oriented strategies of growth. It is all too common to fail to recognize that, in choosing tactics, it is upper-income bureaucrats rather than the rich capitalists who may find a conflict of interest with the poor. It is perhaps even more common to advocate radical redistribution that is unlikely to occur, owing to concerted action against it by large vested interests, and to ignore changes in strategy which are less dramatic and less widely known, but which might bring less complete opposition.

The reason people are reticent in making these choices is well set forth by John Rawls when he states that a "fair and just" society is conditioned on a "social contract"—the implicit and explicit rules by which a community operates—written in "a veil of ignorance" of the writer's future position in society. Thus, "no one knows his situation in society nor his natural assets, and no one is in a position to tailor principles to his advantage." [62] Such a society would not necessarily be one of equal

[62] John Rawls, *A Theory of Justice* (Cambridge, Mass.: Harvard University Press, 1971), pp. 136–42. See ch. iii, esp. pp. 136–42.

wealth, but it would provide much greater equality of opportunity than is available in most contemporary communities, and it would surely result in a much more thoughtful appraisal of the effect of various policies and strategies on the poor.

XI | Planning and the Strategy for Growth

A rural-led, employment-oriented strategy of economic growth is now feasible for India and many other countries as well. This strategy has major political and social ramifications, requires substantial changes in planning and implementation of policy, and presents significant risks.

The Choice of Strategy

Choice of growth strategy for any country is substantially the product of politics—domestic and foreign. Alternative policies indirectly influence the structure of national political power by their impact on the relative rate of income growth for various socioeconomic classes and, therefore, the relative and absolute distribution of income among those classes. More important, the choice of strategy directly affects the ability to exercise political power by determining the nature of the planning process, the mechanisms for allocating resources, and, accordingly, the authority over those allocations.[1] The extent of political centralization is defined by the strategic concentration of national resources and the structure of industrial output. Fulfilling the related international objectives of self-sufficiency and relative military and economic power also may depend on the rate of growth and therefore on the total wealth that may be devoted to these objectives over time. Similarly, the nature of foreign alliances influences the size and composition of available resources, which in turn influence the optimal choice of strategy—and conversely.

Successful implementation of the employment-oriented strategy clearly

---

[1] See Warren F. Ilchman and Norman T. Uphoff, *The Political Economy of Change* (Berkeley: University of California Press, 1969), pp. 242–43.

accelerates the earnings growth rate of the low-income laboring classes—reason enough for opposition to the strategy from conservative landowning interests.

Even though the employment-oriented strategy raises the absolute level of income of the poor, it is much less clear that it increases their relative incomes. The extent to which income disparities widen is a complex function of the rate of change in agricultural productivity, the amount and nature of change in consumption patterns, the elasticity of the labor and capital supply in the nonagricultural sector, and the level of nonagricultural output. It does seem likely that accelerated growth of agricultural production and of small- and medium-scale industry will sharply increase incomes of peasant landowning classes and of the small capitalist-cum-entrepreneur class, quite possibly at the expense of the owners and managers of large-scale public and private industrial enterprises. Thus, the support of the peasant landowning classes for the employment-oriented strategy may be equivocal, because of a balance between income gain and possible reduction of absolute power over the laboring class, while the laboring and small-to-medium-size business classes would be unequivocable gainers.

Enthusiasm for the opposing capital intensive strategy comes substantially from the politicians and bureaucrats who derive power and profit from the attendant planning procedures and controls. The big industrial concerns may also lend their support to the strategy that structures the economy toward industries with major economies of scale.[2] The urban intellectuals, too, may identify their interests with centralized power and direct allocation of resources, for which they can provide rationale, operating procedures, and economic models—all less necessary and less feasible under the more diffused employment-oriented strategy with its greater reliance on market mechanisms. It is also quite possible that the urban upper class feel intellectually and emotionally more comfortable with the large industrialist and the higher-level bureaucrat than with the

---

[2] For example, Jagdish N. Bhagwati and Padma Desai note that "the success of the licensing regulation system in checking the concentration of industrial ownership and in promoting a competitive system was no greater [than in achieving balanced growth] . . . and, paradoxically, the system is almost certain to have worked in the contrary direction in many respects" (*India: Planning for Industrialization* [London: Oxford University Press, 1970], p. 269). See also R. K. Hazari, *Industrial Planning and Licensing Policy* (New Delhi: Government of India, Planning Commission, 1967), for evidence on the effects of licensing control.

peasant landowner and the small businessman. Although their social values and even political party affiliation may be different, there is a natural congruence of interest between the politician, the bureaucrat, the big industrialist, and the urban intellectual. A likely alliance to provide effective political control then would be between these groups and the landed peasantry.[3] The latter, of course, may gain immense income from a change to a rural development strategy, but in the alternative strategy, the more powerful among them can be offered continued control of land, special access to scarce production inputs and technology, continued dominance over the laboring classes, and a share of the spoils of office through representation in the political process.[4]

It is the delicate and changing balance of these blocks that so conditions choice of strategy. It is the power of these groups, often so disproportionate to numbers or social deprivation, which raises legitimate question about the efficacy of the common democratic systems for meeting mass needs—a view equally relevant to political events of the mid-1970s in India, Ethiopia, Tanzania, the Philippines, and several other countries.

Apart from its power and patronage appeals, the central planning of the capital intensive approach promotes the objectives of national unity so significant in the early years of independence. Thus, K. Santhanam wrote, at the end of India's Second Five-Year Plan, that "planning has superseded the Federation and our country is functioning almost like a unitary system in many respects," [5] and Krishnaswami described the harmony of political centralization with the style of Indian planning:

This combination of circumstances—the bias in favor of the Centre, the extra-Constitutional influence exercised by the organization and functioning of the

[3] George Rosen comments that "political power within the national and state legislatures and within the party has shifted [from educated urban groups] to a coalition of members of landowning dominant castes and of the small town middle class combined with the upper class of larger cities, especially the new industrial and commercial groups" (*Democracy and Economic Change in India* [Berkeley: University of California Press, 1966], p. 72). This has been empirically supported by A. C. Mayer, "Rural Leaders and the Indian General Election," *Asian Survey,* 1:8 (October 1961), 23–29, who found a shift within the Congress Party from urban leadership to "an uneasy partnership of rural and urban leaders"; and by M. Weiner, "Political Leadership in West Bengal," *Economic Weekly,* 11:28–30 (July 1959), 925.

[4] See the similar analysis by Michael Lipton, "Strategy for Agriculture: Urban Bias and Rural Planning," in Paul Streeten and Michael Lipton, eds., *The Crisis of Indian Planning* (London: Oxford University Press, 1967), p. 142.

[5] K. Santhanam, *Union-State Relations in India* (London: Asia Publishing House, 1960), p. 56.

Congress Party, the setting up the Planning Commission and the enveloping process of planning—has tended to bring about a degree of centralization far beyond what was dreamt of even by the makers of the Constitution.[6]

From the start, Indian planning was also presented as a means of achieving widespread social reform and more equitable distribution of income. Thus, the First Plan stated:

The central objective of planning in India at the present stage is to initiate a process of development which will raise living standards and open out to the people new opportunities for a richer and more varied life. . . . economic planning has to be viewed as an integral part of a wider process aiming not merely at the development of resources in a narrow technical sense, but at the development of human faculties and the building up of an institutional framework adequate to the needs and aspirations of the people.[7]

and, the Second Plan:

. . . the pattern of development and the structure of socio-economic relations must be so planned that they result not only in appreciable increases in national income and employment, but also in greater equality in income and wealth. . . . The benefits of economic development must accrue more and more to the relatively less privileged classes of society, and there should be progressive reduction of the concentrations of income, wealth and economic power.[8]

Similarly, the Third Five-Year Plan sought "to establish greater equality of opportunity and bring about reduction in [social and economic] disparities." [9] By the 1970s it was abundantly clear that these equity objectives were not being achieved. Indeed, the very nature of the plans and the associated strategy were inimical to the fulfillment of these goals.[10]

Drive for national self-sufficiency and international political power may continue to justify the capital intensive approach. But self-suf-

---

[6] A. Krishnaswami, *The Indian Union and the States* (Oxford: Pergammon Press, 1964), p. 23.

[7] *First Five-Year Plan* (New Delhi: Government of India, Planning Commission, 1952), p. 7.

[8] *Second Five-Year Plan* (New Delhi: Government of India, Planning Commission, 1956), p. 22.

[9] *Third Five-Year Plan* (New Delhi: Government of India, Planning Commission, 1961), p. 48.

[10] S. K. Arora has commented that "while plan-making and plan-implementation become increasingly technicalized—and, albeit, more 'scientific' and 'rational'—the overall vision which had been the impetus for planning in the first place appears to have been discarded" ("Policy-Making and Social Indicators," *Economic and Political Weekly,* 6, Special Number [1971], 1559).

ficiency is a mirage—for India as well as for other developing nations. It involves, for example, important trade-offs among commodities at a given time and over time. Food self-sufficiency, a particularly attractive goal in the context of national integrity, may be achieved at the expense of increased dependence on other nations for fertilizer imports; steel or petrochemical self-sufficiency may have to sacrifice autonomy in food. And so on.

The basic trade-off between the capital intensive and the employment-oriented strategies in obtaining international power is one of time horizons. Clearly, the capital intensive approach has given to India a large heavy industry base with important power connotations. Nevertheless, the more rapid short-term growth rate of the employment-oriented program might provide the larger national income from which savings and investment could be generated at a pace sufficient for soon achieving even faster growth of the heavy industry section. Choosing an optimal time horizon for national survival is perhaps inevitably biased toward the short run and consequently the capital intensive policy.

The interaction between choice of growth strategy and choice of national alliances can be only partially and simplistically illustrated here. For example, the capital intensive, central planning strategy may be forwarded by close relations with the USSR because of similarity of bureaucratic structures and power. It is further reinforced by the facility of the Soviet Union in assisting large-scale public sector firms, and in trading on a bilateral exchange basis.

On the one hand, in the case of India, the now successful unification of the nation, the rising political power of the poor, and the failure of the past strategy to meet welfare objectives argue for a change in approach. On the other hand, the entrenched positions of the vested interests in the present policy and the nature of international power relations may argue against it. With this complex set of balances, the outcome may well depend substantially on unpredictable developments in agricultural research—and the weather. Technological breakthroughs combined with favorable rainfall could establish a powerful momentum toward the labor intensive policy. Thus, the outline of such a shift would involve new agricultural technology raising the demand for fertilizer and for water, inducing import of one and investment in the other. Increased agricultural production would then generate the income to stimulate investment in rural infrastructure and small- and medium-scale industry which, in turn, would exert pressure for the allocation of foreign exchange to support these efforts. While more savings and exports would be generated, co-opting domestic savings and foreign exchange at least in the short run, much of the capital intensive investment would be precluded. Failure to make such a change in strategy could stem from commitment of resources to the "core" sector of capital intensive industry sufficient to appropriate the bulk of domestic capital and foreign exchange. Inability to finance adequate fertilizer imports, investment in irrigation, rural infrastructure, and support of more labor intensive industry would constrain agricultural production, small- and medium-scale industry, exports, and other more employment-oriented policies. It should be clear, in this context, that foreign aid can play an important role in affecting the choice of strategy by its influence on the quantity of resources and the form in which they are made available.

Planning Models and the Capital Intensive Strategy

Multisectoral planning models designed to obtain long-term self-contained consistency in the strucuture of industrial production have been closely identified with Indian planning. In its ascendancy, which covered the period of the Second and Third Five-Year Plans, 1955 to 1965, the approach was a mutually reinforcing product of the political needs of the times, the strategy of growth, and the evolving planning technology.

The policy of the Second and Third Plans was based on direct allocation of the nation's resources through central authority. The approach was consistent with the political needs, rationalized by P. C. Mahalanobis' conceptual framework, itself explicitly based on direct allocation of physical resources and simplified by the planning assumptions of poor prospects for exports and agriculture—the two sectors least suited to such an orientation. Bureaucrats were to allocate resources through a system of licensing industrial and import capacity, theoretically based upon instructions from the formal, technical planning models. The two basic questions concerning the planning models were: (1) the degree (and duration) of accuracy with which the economic objectives and the technical and demand relationships could be estimated and (2) the extent of detail the systems could contain to provide the necessary degree of guidance for the given level of administrative competence.

The Mahalanobis multisector model showed how resources would be allocated within an economy comprised of four sectors (see Chapter I).

This was succeeded by increasingly sophisticated and complex versions which were to provide the instructions for running the economy. The approach initially used Leontief-type input-output systems to state a mutually consistent set of production levels for each industry for a given amount and composition of final demand. Sukhamoy Chakravarty, later a member of the Planning Commission, criticized these consistency models on the basis that elements of choice "may be filled in a very casual manner or in a manner in which their rationality is not quite evident." An alternative, more sophisticated approach was followed by Chakravarty, Louis Lefeber, R. S. Eckaus, and K. S. Parikh, who formulated a set of utility maximization models which combined programming techniques with input-output analysis.[11] Further elaboration of the models attempted to deal with a number of simplifying assumptions by adding sectors, introducing nonlinear relationships and technological change, and by dividing the economy into different regions. The systems were also elaborated to deal with increasingly difficult problems, such as deriving investment magnitudes endogenously to the model, and to treat the complex aspects of intertemporal allocations.

The developers of these models, in particular, recognized and stated the technical problems as well as the highly restrictive nature of the assumptions. Nevertheless, they had an impression that incorporation of more and more complex and sophisticated mathematical techniques would contribute to solution of the technical problems and provide a model useful and relevant for planning purposes. What they were striving for is perhaps best expressed by Frisch, one of the early and vigorous proponents of scientific economic planning.

What is of crucial importance today is to insist that a definite attempt be made to assure that the next plan shall come as close to the optimum solution as is possible to get with the available statistical and technical information. In order to do this, it is necessary to apply existing scientific techniques fully. But this must be done in such a way that the responsible political authorities maintain control over the whole thing at every stage of the work. . . . Scientific planning means coordinating everything in one simultaneous (and integrated) piece of analysis and doing it on some optimum basis. It involves solving the whole nexus as one simultaneous problem, where everything determines everything else.[12]

[11] S. Chakravarty, *Capital and Development Planning* (Cambridge, Mass.: M.I.T. Press, 1969), pp. 7–8. This work contains the theoretical exposition of the approach developed by Chakravarty et al. See also T. N. Srinivasan, "A Critique of the Optimizing Planning Model," *Economic Weekly,* Annual Number (February 1965).

[12] Ragnar Frisch, *Planning for India* (London: Asia Publishing House, 1960), pp. 1–2.

The view articulated by Frisch and implicitly accepted by the other model builders was, of course, a major factor in the political acceptability of their approach and helps explain why the attitude continued in such favor even as its practical problems of implementation became increasingly apparent. Imperfectly constructed in accordance with the level of development of the art, the models could not provide a basis for effectively operating the Indian economy, because they rested on assumptions both narrow and faulty.[13] Their applicability to smaller economies for which trade is more necessary and complex was even less appropriate—raising question as to why they have so dominated the development literature for so long.

The assumption that export possibilities were severely limited permitted a simplification of the planning models to include an assumed fixed rate of growth of exports. This naive assumption of course also made it unnecessary to make demand estimates for a market notoriously difficult to predict. And it provided the basis for developing norms for domestic production to meet the bulk of increased demand for each commodity. With scant allowance for imports to supply unanticipated demand for a commodity, the model had to detail estimates of future needs, at least for commodities which domestic production could provide only after long periods of time required for plant construction. Since the models, of course, would not provide much direction for the promotion of exports, the export sector was likely to perform badly—in practice, even worse than the assumptions on which the rest of the Plan was based.

The supposition that investment in agriculture yields slow and uncertain returns justified maintaining relatively fixed technology, and, consequently, fixed input-output relationships for that sector.[14] The key role of technological change renders agriculture least subject to prediction and least susceptible to the planning process described by Frisch. Therefore, the models give few guidelines for rural development, distract attention from planning and implementation in that sector, and, if the assumption about lack of "wage-goods constraint" proves incorrect, may result in

[13] For a comprehensive critique of planning models as used in the Plans, see S. P. Gupta, *Planning Models in India* (New York: Praeger, 1971), pp. 121–23.

[14] This assumption is implicit in most of the works cited above, but has been formally stated by James Mirrlees, "Targets and Investment in Industry," in Streeten and Lipton, eds., *The Crisis of Indian Planning*, pp. 63–82.

major inconsistencies between the supply and demand of agricultural commodities.

The limited role for agriculture was reinforced by the conjecture of the Chakravarty-Eckaus-Lefeber-Parikh models that it is possible to "ignore labour as a factor of production since production possibilities are not restricted by the amount of labour available." [15] In this context, Chakravarty dismisses the "wage-goods constraint" on the basis that "the government or the planner is in a position to redistribute consumption among the different sectors of the economy so that minimum consumption demands are satisfied everywhere." [16] Chakravarty of course fully recognizes the political aspects of this assumption. But nevertheless, as stated and applied, the assumption leads the models to focus on a single factor of production, namely capital, and avoid the vastly more complex problem of allocating resources between capital goods production and consumer goods production, with the latter enabling increased utilization of labor. The resulting program reduces the number of sectors to be analyzed and the detail of that analysis—but of course with adverse outcome for the rate of growth and the participation of the poor in development. The concentration on capital formation in the industrial sector, particularly in the capital goods sector, further reinforced the neglect of agriculture.

Since the models form the basis for planning and implementation of growth, they require increased central control of the economy, and, hence, ex post justification of the underlying assumptions outlined above. For example, the assumed stagnancy of the agricultural and export sectors will tend to become self-fulfilling, because of the lack of resources allocated to those sectors; furthermore, assuming away the "wage-goods constraint" in the model may necessitate rationing, procurement, and reduced farm prices, and, consequently, the institution of powerful disincentives to increased agricultural production. [17]

These problems stem basically from the assumptions underlying the models. From the standpoint of planning and implementing procedures,

[15] Chakravarty, *Capital and Development Planning,* pp. 1–2.

[16] Ibid., p. 11.

[17] Uma J. Lele, *Food Grain Marketing in India: Private Performance and Public Policy* (Ithaca, N.Y.: Cornell University Press, 1971); see also Uma J. Lele, "Agricultural Price Policy," *Economic and Political Weekly,* 4:35 (August 30, 1969), 1413–19.

the limitations of the models themselves as to the number of sectors which the mechanics of data collection and processing will allow contribute even more serious problems. There was not enough detail to guide the bureaucracy in its tasks of allocation of resources. And yet, because the technical elaboration and the size of the Indian planning models have been considered as unusually well developed, the failure of the planning process to live up to expectations was usually attributed not to the Plans themselves, but to faulty implementation. Barbara Ward was among those subscribing to the belief that "from the beginning Indian planning . . . [was] stronger on formulation than on implementation." [18]

But if, as Frisch believed, the purpose of the planning model was to provide detailed instructions with respect to the allocation of resources and the use of administrators as managers to carry them out, the fault lay not in the administration but in the Plans themselves. Indian administrators in the colonial era had a deserved reputation for ability to carry out orders, and the plans should simply have provided a new set of directors and instructors. But the Plans used questionable data and an inadequate number of economic sectors. These deficiencies, partly predetermined by the quality of the available analytical tools, could not have been avoided without a change in orientation.

Lewis describes the situation well as follows:

The principal danger of macroeconomics exercises lies in its propensity to dazzle. The more figures there are in a Plan, produced by an army of professionals who have laboured mightily to make them consistent, the more persuasive the Plan becomes. Attention shifts from policy to arithmetic. Consistency can be mistaken for truth. Revision is resisted. Yet the plan is not necessarily right merely because its figures are mutually consistent. . . . the value of the macroeconomic exercise depends on how much confidence one has in the figures. Even in countries which are rich in statistics, forecasts of the economy have usually turned out poorly. In poor countries, the econometrician has to invent many of the crucial figures. . . . Many important magnitudes in economics are found by subtractions involving two nearly equal quantities. . . . Relatively small errors are therefore easily magnified. [19]

Bhagwati and Desai elaborate further:

Given perfect foresight and total accuracy of information, combined with full specification of the utility function, time horizon, and other relevant variables,

[18] Barbara Ward, *Plan under Pressure: An Observer's View* (New York: Asia Publishing House, 1963), p. 31.

[19] W. A. Lewis, *Development Planning* (New York: Harper and Row, 1966), pp. 16–20.

one could in principle generate the optimum time path of all industrial investments in detail. However, we live in a world of imperfect information (on technological coefficients, substitution possibilities, etc.) and imperfect foresight (concerning technological progress, changes in world market conditions, foreign aid availability, vagaries in the natural elements determining agricultural harvest, etc). It is therefore impossible, in practice, to draw up a detailed investment plan which is truly optimal; and even the task of drawing up a reasonably consistent, realistic and detailed investment plan would seem to require more sophisticated tools of analysis, and sharper data gathering systems, than are available at the moment.[20]

Within the context of the capital intensive strategy, the Indian planning models might have furnished general guidelines to those sectors which should expand and to the respective administrators who would act as technicians to make the allocations. However, for such a system to work efficiently would have required a type of administrative structure that India did not have.

Useful diagnosis of the administrative problem must first distinguish between those errors that trace from ineptness in carrying out a clearly stated policy and those that trace from incomplete instruction. The allocation of resources without a detailed model makes administrative judgment substitute for the arithmetic of the model. In that case, the need is for technically astute people, highly experienced with the economic subsectors for which they make allocative decisions. The Indian administrative service was not designed or equipped to do this. The limitations of the efforts to upgrade technical competence—by new recruiting criteria and by greater longevity in particular job assignments—were costly to the planning and implementation process, and to the operation of public sector enterprises involved in related aspects of resource allocation.

During the limited period of the Second and Third Five-Year Plans, the total effects of the lack of adequate statistical detail on the level of efficiency in industry may not have been large because of the relative simplicity of the economy and because of the gross allocation of resources made at that time. The Plans provided for a major distribution of resources to the steel industry and to closely related heavy machinery industries. Misallocation of the remaining resources, modified as it was by market forces, was probably not so serious a source of inefficiency in the economy as the inefficient management of resources in the select, empha-

[20] J. Bhagwhati and P. Desai, pp.480–81.

sized industries. But as the economy became more complex, the inadequacies in allocation became more serious.

The rigidity interacted with the pessimistic assumptions about agriculture and trade to the detriment of the planning approach and its underlying strategy. By making long-term restrictions on resources the Plans left insufficient means for taking advantage of a sudden opportunity for agricultural growth or for increasing exports. While investment in agriculture may indeed provide low returns under traditional technology, a breakthrough in new varieties may suddenly create a surge in the possibilities for highly profitable investment in fertilizer and water. The Plan framework, particularly as stated by Frisch, could not accomoodate such fortuitous change. Export opportunities also tend to be unpredictable. Accordingly, bad luck, such as poor weather, failure of a major industrial plant, or a shift in terms of trade within the Plan context was necessarily accepted, with little occasion for substitution. This "heads you win, tails I lose" aspect is bound, in an uncertain world, to be costly to the overall rate of growth.

Planning in India, particularly after 1966–67, undoubtedly lost some of its luster as a result of severe economic crises—including the droughts of 1965 to 1967 and 1971 to 1973, and the decline in foreign assistance—which was exogenous to the strategy and to the Plans. Disillusionment might also have been engendered by slow economic growth, dependence upon foreign aid, and incompetent allocation of resources—all products of the strategy. Insofar as Nehru was responsible for creating the highly centralized planning system, his death probably contributed to the disintegration of planning in conjunction with the continued rise of state and district level power. Pressures to weaken the power of the Planning Commission grew. Hanson notes that the trend toward localization, stronger after Nehru's death in 1964, culminated in the 1967 election, which reflected the erosion of dominance by the Congress Party and a shift in the balance of power from Delhi to the state capitals.[21] Organized opposition to central control appeared in the report of the Administrative Reforms Commission (1966) with the recommendation to remove ministers from the Planning Commission and reduce it "to the status of a purely technocratic body."[22]

[21] A. H. Hanson, "Power Shifts and Regional Balances," in Streeten and Lipton, eds., *The Crisis of Indian Planning*, pp. 19–60.
[22] Ibid., p. 49.

The years from 1951 to 1965 formed a period of increasing analytical and political power for the traditional, formal systems of centralized planning. The period from 1966 to 1971 witnessed the disintegration of such planning, with a plan holiday, and then some periods of one-year plans and the virtual abandonment of sophisticated model-building techniques as the basis for operating the economy. The controversies about the Fifth Plan and its frequent revision represent a debate over whether India should return to traditional "scientific" economic planning or shift to a more pragmatic, less centralized approach.

Determining Public Policy for Employment-Oriented Growth

Four elements underlying the new strategy of growth require a departure from multisectoral planning models as a basis for resource allocation.

First, economic growth is seen as a function of two factors of production. The economic problem is not simply one of mobilizing resources to produce capital goods, but one of mobilizing resources to produce both wage goods and capital goods and to allocate those resources optimally between the two.

Second, the new prominence of technological innovation makes change in the technical coefficients of production a significant part of the growth process, ruling out the common simplifying assumptions with respect to fixed coefficients and the lack of emphasis on means of inducing technological advance.

Third, as growth in consumer income, prompted by an increase in agricultural production, stimulates a demand for expansion in other sectors of the economy, the importance of consumer goods industries makes shifts in the pattern of consumption difficult to predict.

Fourth, greater involvement in international trade mandates flexibility in production.

The first three characteristics make it difficult to define the objective function of growth and the technical coefficients of production for a planning model. The fourth renders the whole exercise of domestically balanced consistency models less necessary. It should be added that the assumptions necessary to the large planning models were of doubtful validity even for an immense country like India. The assumptions and policies of an employment-oriented strategy have a much broader validity not only for India but for the bulk of developing nations. The succeeding paragraphs specify these new planning assumptions and approaches in a broadly applicable form, occasionally illustrated by Indian examples.

The quite different assumptions of the new strategy for development have three important implications for planning processes, each a road block to management by a centralized bureaucracy.

First, the kind of economy implicit in the new strategy is from a planning point of view far more complex than that envisioned in even the most complex multisectoral models. The potential number of industries involved will undoubtedly be greater because of the increased attention to wage goods and consumer goods in general. In addition, since the scale of firms is smaller, the number of concerns will be considerably larger. And the emphasis on agriculture itself may introduce the task of dealing with a great many cultivators widely scattered across the country.

Second, implementation of the new development strategy must be more responsive and more flexible. Technological change in agriculture is a highly erratic process; it is hard to foresee which crops or which regions will experience the most substantial opportunities for technological advance at any given time. And the greater emphasis on growth in consumer incomes reduces the predictability of the structure of demand at the same time that it is gaining importance as a source of expansion. Certainly, the new stress on imports and exports adds an element of pragmatism to purchases of imports, and to meeting rapidly changing export needs.

Third, and even more devastating to past bureaucratic systems, is the loss of the old basic rules of thumb. Under the old capital-oriented strategy, for both imports and domestic production, capital goods were to be preferred to consumer goods because the former added to production and the latter did not. In the new strategy, that distinction does not hold. An alternative guideline—favoring labor intensive over capital intensive products for domestic production, and the opposite for imported goods—has potential for convenience but is probably also highly subject to misinterpretation and evasion.

Controversy flourishes among planners over how much resource allocation can be stated by economic models and how much must be left to the market. The resolution depends on how efficiently the markets operate, how complex the economy is, and how much of that complexity the models can reflect. Obviously, the choice of planning technique interacts with the choice of growth strategy. The rural, employment-oriented program puts more of the growth effort in the small-scale sector where competitive market forces are more likely to prevail and creates a multiplicity of economic relationships less adaptable to a model. Therefore, it argues for greater reliance on the market and less central allocation of resources.

Economists and planners have largely mistrusted market forces. Rosenstein-Rodan, for example, has commented, presumably with the Indian case very much in mind:

The automatic responses of the market economy do not ensure an optimum allocation in two out of four markets. They allocate efficiently stocks of consumers' goods and supplies of these goods flowing from stocks of equipment, but they do not function efficiently in the fields of investment and monetary equilibrium.[23]

Rosenstein-Rodan's argument for public allocation of capital is strengthened by the general distrust of private entrepreneurial activity so common in low-income nations, and the view that such activity is limited largely to "zero-sum" gains from an activity, which are balanced by losses so there is never a net gain from activities (particularly speculation and real estate dealing) which do not increase production and which might have welfare-reducing implications.

In corroboration, small-scale industrialists have received frequent criticism for overemphasizing the trading aspects of their business. Even more striking is the documentation of this view with respect to the buying and selling of grain and the history of repeated public takeover of the grain trade not only in India, but in modified form in a high proportion of low-income nations.[24]

Thus, the role of planning shifts substantially, in the new strategy, from "engineering" tasks—constructing quantitative models of the economy—to economic analysis to provide a broad policy framework within which the market can be made to assist in reaching societal objectives. Only a highly pragmatic planning structure can take advantage of the capricious technical, demand, and trade shifts which are part of the rural-led, employment-oriented strategy of growth. Such a planning structure is diffuse, varying according to the specific conditions of time and place. There must be mechanisms for setting the broad strategy at each level of decision making, for defining the technical aspects of executing the strategy, and for implementation.

---

[23] P. N. Rosenstein-Rodan, "The Flaw in the Mechanism of Market Forces," in Gerald Meier, ed., *Leading Issues in Economic Development,* (2d ed; New York: Oxford University Press, 1970), p. 680. See, however, the very contrary view of Meier in ibid., pp. 682–87.
[24] See Lele, *Food Grain Marketing in India,* pp. 225–37.

Determining the national strategy of growth is largely a political decision, logically made by a cabinet-level body on the basis of implicit or explicit objectives of development and the technical knowledge from the respective ministries. Such a planning commission would perhaps be not unlike those of India's early Five-Year Plans, of which 50 percent of the members were drawn from the national cabinet and over which the Prime Minister presided. Since governments seem unable to pursue effectively more than a few major policy thrusts at once, the goal of the Planning Commission would be to define only a small number of key programs within a basic strategy of growth, some of whose components would be chosen as most strategic for governmental effort at given times. Decision making of the Planning Commission, or perhaps more properly, the National Economic Policy Commission, would be a continuous process reflecting imperfect knowledge and the changing nature of objectives and technology. Just as it determined the strategic elements, so the Planning Commission would decide how much to temper the basic strategy because of other considerations—e.g., balanced regional development or national defense, particularly with respect to short-run self-sufficiency in certain elements of capital intensive industry.

Areas of Priority

Given the preceding strategic considerations and a rural-led employment-oriented strategy, the *first* priority is to accelerate growth in the agricultural sector. The basic priorities, within agriculture, are probably surprisingly similar across the low-income nations. First would be ensuring ample fertilizer supplies, presumably by predominant allocation of foreign exchange and possibly long-term purchase contracts, with estimates of needs based on recognition of a high inventory situation that encourages vigorous sales efforts and takes ready advantage of new technology. The strategic emphasis, in effect, should recognize uncertainty and therefore focus on ensuring ample supplies of key inputs that err on the side of excess rather than deficit—instead of trying to calculate a precise optimum. Second would be rapid and massive investment in water control, with stress on small-scale, well-controlled schemes, including investment in rural electrification as needed and particularly in high population density areas. Third would be a major expansion of research, monitoring of conclusions, and slashing of red tape to ensure expenditure wherever it has a reasonable chance of producing meaningful results. Fourth would be a large effort, inextricably bound to the success of the others, to broaden participation in rural growth by expanding supplies of trained manpower to staff programs for assisting the small farmer. Each of these subpriorities would be refined and administered by the Ministry of Agriculture, but since each subpriority competes for a major quantity of resources with other sectors, the allocative decisions must be set at the national level and worked out in view of interministerial conflicts.

The *second* priority would be to facilitate the expansion of small-scale industry, particularly through investment in the infrastructure of transport and power, which are so essential to its success. Investment in these categories interacts with the agricultural strategy, first, in producing commodities with a comparative advantage in export and thereby providing foreign exchange for the importation of capital intensive intermediate products and raw materials; second, by enlarging the base for the development of institutions to support both agriculture and small-scale industry; and third, in providing the increased employment so necessary to expanding markets for increased agricultural production.

The *third* priority would be the expansion of exports to pay for the growth of capital intensive imports. This priority follows from the enlargement of domestic markets and the increase of imports. It is likely that the joint demands of agriculture and small- and medium-scale industry for investment in transportation, power, and irrigation would place burdens on national resources which co-opt a high proportion of public funds and preclude much alternative investment. The key sectors would be pursued at substantial expense to other sectors on the presumption that those with less strategic value would be dealt with through imports. The critical role of small- and medium-scale industries would also, in the period of transition from existing strategy, give priority in import policy and materials allocation to the raw material needs of such firms, to the institutional requirements for funneling short-term credit to them, and to providing infrastructure through industrial estates. In the longer run, change to a more market-oriented strategy would make these public efforts less necessary.

Initially, this priority would require reducing the barriers to exports arising from controls on imports and production. In the longer run, emphasis would be on major investment in port facilities and development of institutions to foster exports by market analysis and promotion that would assist private producers, particularly in the small- and medium-scale sectors.

These priorities have two profound implications. First, they are almost certainly in short-run conflict with the allocation of resources consistent with the past old capital-oriented strategies of development. Second, they require major change in the procedures of planning and implementation.

Given the savings rates current in most low-income nations, following the capital intensive industry emphasis of the old strategy and still epitomized in India's Fifth Plan *Approach* almost certainly precludes full pursuit of the strategic objectives stated above. Large imports of capital goods for capital intensive industry would maintain a tight foreign exchange situation, which would almost certainly restrict imports of fertilizer for agriculture and raw materials for small-scale, labor intensive industry. Of particular importance, investment of a major portion of domestic savings in large-scale, heavy industry requiring the intensive use of electric power will reduce the quantity of capital available for investment in agriculture and small- and medium-scale industry (as well as electric power generation) while placing heavy demands on the now more limited supplies of electric power, as well as on transportation and other elements of infrastructure. Similarly, foreign aid, which supports capital intensive growth, is likely further to tighten the resource constraint on the employment-oriented strategy as it calls for increased domestic resources to be absorbed in the capital intensive sector, leaving less for other sectors. Conversely, foreign aid that finances import of capital intensive intermediate products relaxes that foreign exchange constraint and allows more domestic resources to be mobilized for growth of labor intensive sectors. Thus, choice of key factors in a strategy does require resolution of major conflicts in the use of resources at the highest policy level and may entail some compromise between elements of different strategies.

Developing the Details

The second stage of the planning process is logically conducted in the functional ministries and interacts with the choice of strategy by feeding information to the Planning Commission and then planning and executing the details implicit in the statements of priority. The functional ministries assume a powerful role in a pragmatic approach to planning because they are necessarily the reservoirs of intuitive knowledge that grows from implementing programs. The interaction between planner and implementor is crucial to effective policy.[25] It is precisely here that the British system of general purpose administrators creates difficulty for the pragmatic approach, because that system gives little place to the development of technical expertise.

The new growth strategy suggests that ministries be defined functionally so as to facilitate growth of scientific and technical knowledge. The strategy also suggests two nontraditional sectors of ministerial-level importance: small-scale industries and medium-size population centers. Small-scale industries play a major role in the program and have unique policy requirements. The growth of medium-size population centers is so important and involves such complex problems of physical and institutional infrastructure development that it, too, would merit a special concern.

Planning at the ministerial level would be concerned with the interacting functions of improving the efficiency with which activities are performed and the levels of inputs to those activities. For example, questions about research would be raised: What is its progress? Is it operating effectively? Could it be expanded efficiently? To what extent are fertilizer plans consistent with the research output expected as well as with the irrigation program? Such a procedure is not an additive exercise in quantities of inputs, but a multiplicative process of interaction between efficiency and input level across many complementary functions. From that analysis would come allocation of funds, administrative personnel, and institutional capacity to research, fertilizer distribution, marketing cooperatives, and so on.

Within each ministry, strategies and priorities would need to be set, presumably by a process similar to that at the national level. At the ministerial level, a professional interdepartmental committee would be appropriate, representing the various technical elements: for example, in the case of agriculture, the committee would embrace research, extension, higher education, irrigation, infrastructure, marketing, credit, small-farmer programs, and so forth. The interdepartmental committee would also require a secretariat or planning body to provide analysis of broad overview questions. A National Commission on Agriculture could perform such a role. In line with the pragmatic approach, it would be a con-

---

[25] In this connection, W. A. Lewis has observed: "It is necessary to change the bias of the bureaucratic machine. . . . Local and regional experience must be fed back into the planning process" (pp. 74–75).

tinuing body, supported by a permanent staff and by the various technical departments, providing a basis for continuous development and modification of programs.

Once the points of emphasis have been defined within the overall strategy, the specific tasks to be performed must be described, their execution divided between the public and private sectors, policies determined for dispatching tasks in the public sector and facilitating those to be performed in the private sector, and decisions made as to the governmental level—national and subregional—at which tasks would be implemented.

The decision on allocating the execution of functions between the private sector, presumably largely market-oriented, and the public sector is the major means of reducing the burden on the government's limited manpower, financial, and physical resources, so that it may effectively complete essential tasks the private sector is unlikely to perform adequately. Those tasks are particularly numerous in a recently modernized agriculture. Unfortunately, ideological considerations threaten to complicate this issue.

There remains considerable ignorance concerning the operations of the private sector and the extent to which it can be manipulated for social purposes.[26] Bureaucrats and politicians still want to increase their own powers. In most low-income countries the vast inequities in the distribution of assets and the refusal to opt for effective measures of redistribution have made the restraint or closure of private sector activities a tempting solution.

The division of planning and implementation efforts among different governmental levels raises problems of coordinating activities at the "action" level. For this purpose, the Indian district-level organization is well suited to a role of primary responsibility. Ideally, a political body at the district level would set the goals of local development within the constraints of national objectives and have a staff of technicians for implementing policy and a planning group to coordinate development activities across functional lines. The district-level body is necessary to modify plans to suit highly variable local conditions. It may be that local priorities will diverge from national ones. Such dilemmas can only be resolved through negotiation and subsidy.

In summary, the new strategy would utilize a three-tiered structure of

---

[26] For a full exposition of this subject in the context of the marketing sector, see Lele, *Food Grain Marketing in India.*

planning and implementation: a national planning commission that sets broad objectives and strategies; commissions comprised of the leaders within the technical ministries that develop the sectoral strategies; and district-level agencies to coordinate, develop, and implement those strategies at the local level. Feedback must occur at each of these levels.

The logic of national-level planning and a local-level diagnostic and coordinating body seems clear. A more difficult problem arises for a country the size of India—determination of the role of a body at the state level that would set an intermediate degree of detail in the strategy between the extremely general national plan and the extremely specific local requirements. A role for the states seems logically and politically essential, but its implementation lacks the simple logic of the other two levels, and faces difficult political questions of division of power and responsibility. Perhaps the states must perform the function of determining regional strategy, as the ministries determine the sectoral strategy.

A major objective of most planning procedures is to maintain consistency and conformity among various parts of the development process. In this connection, three problems arise: achieving consistency between the tasks allocated to the public sector and its resources for carrying them out, consistency between planned consumption, savings, and investment, and consistency between physical resource requirements and the availability of supplies. Planning processes in general and the Indian procedures specifically have emphasized the last of these.

Imbalance between public sector responsibilities and the availability of resources is particularly likely, yet receives little explicit attention in planning exercises. Government employees as planners, and politicians as decision makers, have a vested interest in the expansion of the public sector, but personnel resources are often tightly limited by past and present educational and employment policy; and public sector financial resources are restrained by the political and economic cost of higher taxes and the very inefficiency which arises from overexpansion of the public sector relative to its resources. Since the public sector must perform some functions crucial to rapid growth, it is important that the limited public resources be carefully allocated so as not to jeopardize the continuation of essential services.

The achievement of consistency between planned consumption, savings, and investment as a fiscal problem received inadequate attention in the Indian plans and resulted in imbalances that—for example, in 1962 to

1964—drove up relative foodgrain prices to politically uncomfortable levels. Such imbalances have been common in many other low-income countries which have consequently been plagued by high rates of inflation. In India, returns received from public sector investment, plus taxes, were lower than needed for conformity with the plan. And worse, the corresponding price changes occurred in sectors and in such conditions of resource availability that remedial production adjustments were all but impossible. The employment-oriented strategy will enable correctives of imbalance to work through prices and market forces.

In the new strategy, uneven supplies of raw materials for use in domestic production are much less limiting than in the old strategy because of the trade option. This is fortunate because the planners have not been particularly effective in achieving materials balances. The need for consistency models arises primarily from the long "incubation" period involved in building capacity for capital intensive production and the Plan's assumption that domestic demand for such products must be met from domestic production. In a more open economy, imports can meet needs with relatively little forward planning. There are, however, two advantages to having reasonably accurate estimates of future demand for major imported commodities: first, a desire, for national defense reasons, to ensure the fulfillment of at least a portion of needs from domestic plant capacity or by stockpiling; second, particularly for capital intensive intermediate products such as steel, fertilizer, and petrochemicals, the potential advantage in making long-term contracts for supplies. Although even for an immense country like India demand for such commodities will not, for a long time, comprise a major portion of world exports, that demand is large enough to offer some potential of lower prices. In addition, long-term contracts should reduce the degree of uncertainty to both buyer and seller and therefore lower the cost to the buyer. The combination of the planning models and political processes has provided poor measurement in the past. The new strategy places less emphasis on growth of capital intensive industry, so that there is less necessity to make overly optimistic estimates of production growth. Also, the new strategy would earn more foreign exchange. Thus, there may be less political and economic pressure to make overly optimistic estimates of import requirements.

Setting and reaching targets are crucial elements in the formal planning model approach, because of the obligation to achieve balance in the supply of materials. They may play a useful role in a less formal, more pragmatic approach as a goad to administrators and as objectives for evaluation, but targets should be more a by-product of the planning effort than the final result, and must be re-examined for consistency with changing goals. A pragmatic planning process does presume learning by doing, and thus, evaluation according to the standards of an explicit set of objectives. Given the employment-oriented strategy, these objectives are probably usefully stated in growth rates of output by sectors, including agriculture, industry, and the infrastructure of power and communications; by regions; and, to some extent, by socioeconomic classes. Therefore, the evaluation process would measure growth rates and continually question why faster rates had not been achieved. After some period of accelerated development, when the most basic employment and food consumption problems have been mitigated, the objectives will surely become more complex and hence the targets more numerous, involving many considerations of public services expenditure, rural versus urban development, and overall patterns of consumption.

The role of economists in the pragmatic strategy of growth is potentially large, but perhaps less apparent than in the formal model approach. Economists appeared to dominate in the old strategy, with politicians perhaps providing information as to objectives and technicians supplying data on the coefficients of production. The economists then built the models.

In the pragmatic approach to planning, the task of the economist is more diffuse and less formal. Each functional ministry would use a substantial number of economists on such microproblems as calculating optimal types of roads, irrigation systems, sources of supply of fertilizer, and size of town for small-scale industrial development. Because of the emphasis on the allocation of resources among processes of development, rather than on the choice of technology, the old strategy used relatively few economists in this manner. Economists may also have some comparative advantage in the broad analysis of choice of policies, although they will have to be more then economists to perform this task. Finally, the formal economic models can be adapted to an employment-oriented strategy and provide useful consistency checks based on assumptions about technical change and growth in income.

Thus, economists will make key contributions to the Planning Commission secretariat, the policy groups in the ministries, and the various technical divisions. They will increase in importance and number as technical aspects of growth become relatively less important and as a wider range of choices evolves as to the type of society and patterns of consumption desired.

Planning procedures interact with the choice of strategy. The employment-oriented strategy, having jettisoned the requirements for simple operating rules, specific long-term objectives, and technical coefficients, presses for a pragmatic approach with major emphasis on microanalysis within the functional ministries and coordination occurring at the cabinet level nationally and at the district level locally.

A Concluding Note

The two distinguishing advantages of a rural-led, employment-oriented strategy of growth are: (1) a large net addition to national income through technological change in agriculture and a consequent multiplier effect on growth; and (2) a change in the level and structure of demand as a manipulable variable which can increase total output and its distribution by shifting the relative demand for factors of production toward underemployed factors, particularly labor. This change in the demand structure originates from change in domestic demand and in international trade.

The strategy is directly applicable to India because it has a labor force still used at low levels of productivity. Moreover, India possesses a dominant agricultural sector apparently ready for substantial, continuing technological change in which land is distributed broadly enough to translate increased farm incomes into demand which can be met largely by increased domestic production. The policy would be facilitated by the breadth of India's existing industrial, institutional, and physical infrastructure. The last not only enables domestic production to respond to demand growth, but provides a wider option for the necessary export growth. The basic environment is favorable for success of the employment-oriented strategy. It is clear from these characteristics that the strategy is broadly applicable in the developing world. The constraints of embryotic industrial structures and limited infrastructure are probably less constraining to this domestic demand, consumer goods–oriented strategy than to the old capital-oriented strategy.

The employment-oriented strategy may appear intricate and subject to failure because of lack of coordination among the agricultural, industrial, trade, and planning components. That danger is much less real than apparent, for unlike the capital intensive strategy, the employment-oriented strategy is much more nearly self-adjusting through market mechanisms, leaving less for the public hand to manipulate. The more likely sources of failure are in the areas of technology and national will.

The recommended strategy is throughout highly dependent on new agricultural technologies. It is conceivable that such innovations will not, even under the best of conditions, appear at the required pace. It is more likely that failure on the agricultural front will occur because of lack of administrative desire to foster success in research and lack of political impetus to allocate sufficient resources to irrigation, power, and transport.

The total resource requirements of the new strategy are large, but the reduced pressure on public resources lessens the likelihood of a domestic resource constraint. A problem of foreign exchange shortage may arise as a legacy of the old strategy. Former "aid" donors may cause repayment requirements to fester; and the previous neglect of exports may create a lag in export performance leading to foreign exchange gaps sufficient to frighten national policy away from the loosening of controls so essential to the new strategy. Foreign aid could be the deus ex machina ensuring movement through such a crisis period; added capital would give greater assurance of supply of key capital intensive inputs, such as fertilizer and, possibly, steel and petroleum products.

To facilitate the new strategy, the international priorities must shift toward (1) relaxation of tensions so as to dissuade low-income countries from short-run pursuit of the capital intensive requisites of national defense and self-sufficiency; (2) provision of a relatively open trade situation with short-term credits for financing raw materials and capital intensive intermediate products; (3) increased technical aid, particularly for agriculture; and (4) renewed capital assistance for those minimum capital intensive investments still essential to the labor intensive strategy.

Most important, the strategy may fail unless sufficient attention is given to development of positive government agencies to provide export promotion, small-farmer credit, agricultural extension, and small-business credit and advisory services. The strategy cannot survive the continuation of strangulating and corrupt government regulation through restrictive licensing. The political atmosphere must be oriented away from past ineffective forms of redistribution toward encouragement of entrepreneurship by the peasant farmer and the small businessman.

Finally, in judging the success of the transition to the new strategy, it must be remembered that the required acceleration in foodgrain production is small compared to the annual, weather-induced fluctuations in foodgrain production. Not only may the strategy appear to fail when, in fact, it has not, but that very appearance of failure may weaken the will and the means to proceed with the new strategy. This may be the greatest danger of all to the success of the strategy, and this is where the compassion of rich nations with ample food supplies could make a contribution of incalculable value to the people of the developing nations.

The will for a change in strategy must come first from those nations. Only then can the rich countries contribute to the steady progress toward broadly participatory economic growth by acts of assistance consistent with a higher set of social values.

APPENDIX

Appendix Table 1. Agricultural work force, India, 1961 (in thousands)

Category	Number of workers			Percent of total workers	Number of households	Percent of total households	Total area operated (acres)	Percent of total area operated	Percent of gross value of output	Percent of gross output marketed	Percent of total marketed surplus
	Male	Female	Total								
No land	17,324	14,197	31,521	24	17,324*	27	0	0			
Less than 1 acre	5,018	2,359	7,377	6	5,338	8	4,281	1			
Subtotal	22,342	16,556	38,898	30	22,662	35	4,281	1	26	34	26
1–2.4 acres	12,943	6,678	19,621	15							
2.5–4.9 acres	14,666	7,205	21,871	17							
Subtotal	27,609	13,883	41,492	32	22,273	34	57,076	18	25	27	20
5–9.9 acres	15,400	7,376	22,776	17	10,115	15	64,819	20	11	23	8
10–14.9 acres	7,070	3,529	10,599	8	4,243	7	45,012	14	19	33	19
15–29.9 acres	7,360	3,852	11,212	9	4,110	6	71,978	22	9	41	11
30–49.9 acres	2,494	1,361	3,855	3	1,300	2	42,201	13	10	51	16
50 acres and over	1,291	668	1,959	1	651	1	39,602	12			
Unspecified	223	129	352	0	–	–	–	–	–	–	–
Subtotal	33,838	16,915	50,753	38	20,419	31	263,612	81	74	61	74
Total agricultural work force	83,789	47,354	131,143	100	65,354	100	324,969	100	100	35†	100

* The census does not give the number of households of agricultural laborers. We have therefore assumed that the number of these households is equal to the number of male agricultural workers (i.e., those workers who spend most of their time working on another person's land without exercising any supervision or direction in cultivation).

† Average.

Definitions: Those with no land are landless laborers, persons who work on another person's land without exercising any supervision or direction in cultivation for wages in money, kind, or share of produce but have no right or lease or contract on land on which they work. All others cover both owner and tenant cultivators. Cultivation includes ploughing, sowing, and harvesting but does not include fruit growing or keeping orchards or groves or working for plantations such as coffee, tea, rubber, chinchona, and other medical plantations.

Sources: Government of India, Census of India, 1961, Part III (ii), Table B-XI; Government of India, National Sample Survey, Sixteenth Round, July 1960–June 1961, No. 159, p. 64; and Dharm Narain, Distribution of the Marketed Surplus of Agricultural Produce by Size-Level of Holding in India, 1950–1951, Occasional Paper No. 2. Institute of Economic Growth (Delhi, 1961).

Appendix Table 2. Planned financial provisions, first four five-year plans, India, 1950–51 to 1970–71

Planned provisions	First Plan Rupee crores	First Plan Percent	Second Plan Rupee crores	Second Plan Percent	Third Plan Rupee crores	Third Plan Percent	Fourth Plan Rupee crores	Fourth Plan Percent
Agricultural programs	233	9.9	294	6.1	688	8.5	1,944	12.2
Agricultural production					226	2.8	720	4.5
Minor irrigation	197	8.3	170	3.5	177	2.2	520	3.2
Soil conservation					73	0.9	218	1.4
Animal husbandry	22	1.0	56	1.1	54	0.7	142	0.9
Dairying and milk supply					36	0.4	59	0.4
Forests	10	0.4	47	1.0	51	0.6	122	0.8
Fisheries	4	0.2	12	0.3	29	0.4	113	0.7
Warehousing, marketing, and storage	–	–	9	0.2	42	0.5	50	0.3
Community development and cooperation	124	5.2	274	5.7	403	5.0	466	2.9
Cooperation	8 *	0.3	47	1.0	80	1.0	206	1.3
Community development	90	3.8	200	4.1	294	3.6	260	1.6
Panchayats	26	1.1	27	0.6	29	0.4		
Irrigation and power	661	28.1	913	19.0	1,680	20.7	2,994	18.7
Irrigation	384	16.3	381	7.9	599	7.4	849	5.3
Flood control	17	0.7	105	2.2	61	0.8	115	0.7
Power	260	11.1	427	8.9	1,020	12.6	2,030	12.7
Industry and minerals	179	7.6	890	18.5	2,147	26.5	4,306	26.9
Industries and minerals	149	6.3	690	14.4	1,882	23.2	3,936	24.6
Village and small industries	30	1.3	200	4.1	264	3.3	370	2.3
Transport and communication	557	23.6	1,385	28.9	1,655	20.4	3,010	18.8
Social services	533	22.6	945	19.7	1,416	17.5	3,210	20.1
Miscellaneous	69	3.0	99	2.1	110	1.4	70	0.4
Grand total	2,356	100.0	4,800	100.0	8,099 †	100.0	16,000	100.0

* Includes Rs. one crore for "miscellaneous" agricultural programs.

† Excludes a provision of Rs. 200 crores for "inventories."

Note: One crore is equal to 10 million.

Sources: First and Second Plan periods: *Second Five-Year Plan* (New Delhi: Government of India, Planning Commission, 1956), p. 51; Third Plan period: *Third Five-Year Plan* (New Delhi: Government of India, Planning Commission, 1961), pp. 85–88; Fourth Plan provision: *Fourth Five-Year Plan: A Draft Outline* (New Delhi: Government of India, Planning Commission, 1966), pp. 41, 72–74, 185, 219, 227, 242, 257, 297.

Appendix Table 3. Availability of foodgrains, India, 1951 to 1974

Year	Net production of foodgrains *	Net imports of foodgrains	Withdrawal (−) or addition (+) to buffer stocks	Net availability of foodgrains †	Per capita availability
	million metric tons				grams per day
1951	48.2	4.8	+0.59	52.4	394.9
1952	48.7	3.9	+0.62	52.0	384.4
1953	54.1	2.0	−0.48	56.6	412.4
1954	63.3	0.8	+0.20	64.0	457.5
1955	61.9	0.7	−0.75	63.3	444.3
1956	60.7	1.4	−0.60	62.7	430.9
1957	63.5	3.7	+0.86	66.2	447.1
1958	58.3	3.2	−0.27	61.8	408.9
1959	69.0	3.9	+0.49	72.4	468.5
1960	67.3	5.1	+1.40	71.0	448.3
1961	72.0	3.5	−0.17	75.7	468.7
1962	72.6	3.6	−0.36	76.1	461.0
1963	70.3	4.6	−0.02	74.9	443.8
1964	70.6	6.3	−1.24	78.1	452.6
1965	78.2	7.5	+1.06	84.6	480.2
1966	63.3	10.4	+0.14	73.5	408.2
1967	65.0	8.7	−0.26	73.9	401.4
1968	83.2	5.7	+2.04	86.8	460.1
1969	82.3	3.9	+0.46	85.7	445.2
1970	87.1	3.6	+1.11	89.5	455.1
1971	94.9	2.0	+2.57	94.3	469.0
1972	92.0	0.5	−4.70	96.2	467.4
1973	84.9	3.6	−0.66	89.2	424.5
1974	90.7	4.8	−	−	448.5

* Net production is equal to 87.5 percent of gross production, 12.5 percent being provided for feed, seed requirements, and wastage.

† Net availability = net production + net imports + change in buffer stocks.

Source: Government of India, Ministry of Finance, *Economic Survey* (New Delhi), various issues.

Appendix Table 4. Production, area, yield, and irrigated area for wheat, rice, and other foodgrains, India, 1959–60 to 1973–74 (official estimates)

Year	Production thousand tons	Gross area thousand hectares	Yield per hectare kgs.	Gross irrigated area thousand hectares	Percent of area irrigated	Percent of total foodgrains production
			Wheat			
1959–60	10,324	13,380	772	4,262	31.8	13.5
1960–61	10,997	12,927	851	4,233	32.7	13.4
1961–62	12,072	13,570	890	4,326	31.9	14.6
1962–63	10,776	13,590	793	4,593	33.8	13.4
1963–64	9,853	13,499	730	4,724	35.0	12.2
1964–65	12,257	13,422	913	4,945	36.8	13.7
1965–66	10,394	12,572	827	5,404	43.0	14.4
1966–67	11,393	12,838	887	6,125	47.7	15.3
1967–68	16,540	14,998	1,103	6,457	43.0	17.4
1968–69	18,651	15,958	1,169	7,772	48.7	19.8
1969–70	20,093	16,626	1,209	8,611	51.8	20.2
1970–71	23,832	18,241	1,307	9,829	53.9	22.0
1971–72	26,410	19,139	1,380	10,268	53.6	25.1
1972–73	24,735	19,464	1,271	n.a.	n.a.	25.4
1973–74	22,073	19,057	1,158	n.a.	n.a.	21.3
			Rice			
1959–60	31,676	33,820	937	12,146	35.9	41.3
1960–61	34,574	34,128	1,013	12,523	36.7	42.2
1961–62	35,663	34,694	1,028	12,985	37.4	43.1
1962–63	33,217	35,695	931	13,361	37.4	41.4
1963–64	36,998	35,809	1,033	13,254	37.0	45.9
1964–65	39,308	36,462	1,078	13,556	37.2	44.0
1965–66	30,589	35,470	862	13,121	37.0	42.3
1966–67	30,438	35,251	863	13,375	37.9	41.0
1967–68	37,612	36,437	1,032	13,861	38.0	39.6
1968–69	39,761	36,967	1,076	13,729	37.1	42.3
1969–70	40,430	37,680	1,073	14,652	38.9	40.6
1970–71	42,225	37,592	1,123	14,971	39.7	38.9
1971–72	43,068	37,758	1,141	14,675	38.9	41.0
1972–73	39,245	36,688	1,070	n.a.	n.a.	40.4
1973–74	43,742	38,011	1,151	n.a.	n.a.	42.2
			Other foodgrains *			
1959–60	34,672	68,623	505	5,436	7.9	45.2
1960–61	36,447	68,526	532	5,309	7.7	44.4
1961–62	34,971	68,968	507	5,137	7.4	42.3
1962–63	36,158	68,559	527	5,436	7.9	45.1
1963–64	33,791	68,113	496	5,361	7.9	41.9
1964–65	37,791	68,228	554	5,442	8.0	42.3
1965–66	31,364	67,061	468	5,732	8.5	43.3
1966–67	32,400	67,213	482	6,342	9.4	43.6
1967–68	40,900	69,986	584	5,786	8.3	43.0
1968–69	35,601	67,505	527	6,551	9.7	37.9
1969–70	38,978	69,264	563	6,285	9.1	39.2

Year	Production thousand tons	Gross area thousand hectares	Yield per hectare kgs.	Gross irrigated area thousand hectares	Percent of area irrigated	Percent of total foodgrains production
			Other foodgrains *			
1970–71	42,365	68,483	619	6,845	10.0	39.1
1971–72	35,690	65,726	543	5,779	38.9	33.9
1972–73	33,047	63,126	523	n.a.	n.a.	34.1
1973–74	37,797	69,061	547	n.a.	n.a.	36.5

* For area, production, and irrigated area, other foodgrains was computed as total foodgrains minus wheat and rice. Yield for other foodgrains was computed by dividing production by area.

Sources: Columns 1, 2, 3, and 6: 1972–73 and 1973–74 were taken from Government of India, Directorate of Economics and Statistics, *Agricultural Situation in India,* 29:8 (November 1974); all other years based on Government of India, Directorate of Economics and Statistics, *Estimates of Area and Production of Principal Crops in India* (New Delhi), various issues. Columns 4 and 5: 1959–60 through 1967–68, Government of India, Directorate of Economics and Statistics, *Statistical Abstract of India* (New Delhi), various issues; 1968–69 and 1969–70, *Agriculture in Brief,* 12th ed. (New Delhi: Government of India, Directorate of Economics and Statistics, 1973); 1970–71, *Estimates of Area and Production of Principal Crops in India, 1972–73;* 1971–72, *Estimates of Area and Production of Principal Crops in India, 1973–74.*

Appendix Table 5. Area under different crops, India, 1969–70, 1978–79, and 1983–84 (in thousand hectares)

Crops	Official estimates 1969–70	Potentials 1978–79	Potentials 1983–84
Foodgrains			
Rice			
Irrigated HYV *	4,519	12,299	16,148
Irrigated local	9,596	3,075	–
Unirrigated HYV	–	5,189	9,022
Unirrigated local	23,565	20,754	18,317
Total rice	37,680	41,317	43,487
Wheat			
Irrigated HYV	6,100	12,563	17,099
Irrigated local	1,114	–	–
Unirrigated HYV	–	1,559	1,875
Unirrigated local	9,412	6,235	3,806
Total wheat	16,626	20,357	22,780
Other foodgrains			
Irrigated HYV	1,369	2,519	3,510
Irrigated local	4,690	5,002	5,084
Unirrigated HYV	746	9,550	16,037
Unirrigated local	62,459	54,505	48,791
Total other foodgrains	69,264	71,576	73,422
Total foodgrains			
Irrigated HYV	11,988	27,380	36,757
Irrigated local	15,400	8,077	5,084
Unirrigated HYV	746	16,298	26,934
Unirrigated local	95,436	81,494	70,914
Total foodgrains	123,570	133,249	139,689
Nonfoodgrains	29,208	31,577	33,151
Plantation crops	678	827	939
All crops	153,457	165,653	173,779

* HYV = High-yield variety

Source: Gunvant M. Desai, "Nitrogen Use and Foodgrain Production, India, 1973–74, 1978–79 and 1983–84," Department of Agricultural Economics, Occasional Paper No. 55, Cornell University USAID Employment and Income Distribution Project (March 1973).

Note: Estimates of cropped area were prepared from published data in *Estimates of Area and Production of Principal Crops in India, 1969–70,* Summary Tables (New Delhi, Government of India, Directorate of Economics and Statistics, 1970). At the time of computation estimates of irrigated area were available up to 1967–68 only. Therefore the 1969–70 figures were estimated by projecting the growth rate of irrigated area from 1960–61 to 1967–68 for each crop. In all cases, unirrigated area was defined as the difference between cropped area and irrigated area.

The growth rates for total and irrigated areas were assumed to be the same for the 1970's and 1980's as for the 1960's. See text Table III-1 for the growth rates used.

The assumptions concerning the areas under HYV's were as follows:

Cereal	Percent of cultivated area under HYV 1969–70 (official)	Percent of cultivated area under HYV 1978–79	Percent of cultivated area under HYV 1983–84
Rice			
Irrigated area	32	80	100
Unirrigated area	–	20	33

	Percent of cultivated area under HYV		
Cereal	1969–70 (official)	1978–79	1983–84
Wheat			
Irrigated area	85	100	100
Unirrigated area	–	20	33
Other foodgrains			
Sorghum			
Irrigated area	75	100	100
Unirrigated area	–	20	33
Millet			
Irrigated area	100	100	100
Unirrigated area	6	33	50
Maize			
Irrigated area	52	80	100
Unirrigated area	–	20	33

HYV's for additional foodgrains were assumed to be unavailable.

The assumptions concerning the spread of HYV's reflect judgments based on observation of the past record, including analysis of micro data, and discussions with biological scientists with regard to the potentials for scientific innovation.

For details on the calculations and data for nonfoodgrains and plantation crops, see Desai, cited in source.

Appendix Table 6. Nitrogen use on various crops, 1969–70, 1978–79, and 1983–84 (in thousand metric tons)

Crops	1969–70 (estimate)	Potentials 1978–79	Potentials 1983–84
Foodgrains			
Rice			
Irrigated HYV	135.6	737.9	1,291.8
Unirrigated local	239.9	107.6	–
Unirrigated HYV	–	155.7	360.9
Unirrigated local	70.7	207.5	348.0
Total rice	446.2	1,208.7	2,000.7
Wheat			
Irrigated HYV	366.0	1,005.0	1,538.9
Irrigated local	27.9	–	–
Unirrigated HYV	–	54.6	75.0
Unirrigated local	28.2	62.4	72.3
Total wheat	422.1	1,122.0	1,686.2
Other foodgrains			
Irrigated HYV	31.4	100.7	175.4
Irrigated local	44.6	79.1	111.8
Unirrigated HYV	11.2	233.7	539.3
Unirrigated local	62.5	313.7	541.1
Total other foodgrains	149.7	727.2	1,367.6
Total foodgrains			
Irrigated HYV	533.0	1,843.0	3,006.2
Irrigated local	312.4	186.7	111.8
Unirrigated HYV	11.2	444.0	975.2
Unirrigated local	161.4	583.6	961.4
Total foodgrains	1,018.0	3,057.9	5,054.6
Nonfoodgrain crops	337.0	732.5	1,057.5
Plantation crops	44.7	65.2	80.3
All crops	1,399.7	3,855.6	6,192.4

Source: Gunvant M. Desai, "Nitrogen Use and Foodgrain Production, India, 1973–74, 1978–79, and 1983–84," Department of Agricultural Economics, Occasional Paper No. 55, Cornell University USAID Employment and Income Distribution Project (March 1973).

Note: Nitrogen used on any crop *i* during any year *t* (N_{it}) can be expressed as a product of (1) area under crop *i* in the year *t* (A_{it}), (2) proportion of area under crop *i* fertilized in year *t* (P_{it}), and (3) average rate of nitrogen application on crop *i* in year *t* (R_{it}), i.e.,

$$N_{it} = A_{it} \cdot P_{it} \cdot R_{it}$$

For the series A_{it} used in the table above, see Appendix Table 5.

The series P_{it} used above assumes that in 1969–70, 100 percent of the irrigated area under wheat, rice, sorghum, millet, maize, and barley was fertilized, and that 10 percent of the irrigated area under other cereals and pulses was fertilized. These proportions were expected to remain constant through the 1980's, except for other cereals and pulses, which were assumed to rise to 33 percent by 1978–79 and 50 percent by 1983–84.

Concerning the proportion of unirrigated foodgrain area fertilized, the series P_{it} used above assumes the following (in percent):

Foodgrain	1969–70	1978–79	1983–84
Rice and wheat			
Unirrigated HYV	100	100	100
Unirrigated local	20	50	76

Foodgrain	1969–70	1978–79	1983–84
Sorghum, millet, and maize			
Unirrigated HYV	100	100	100
Unirrigated local	10	33	50
Barley and other cereals and pulses			
Unirrigated local	10	33	50

The series R_{it} used above with regard to foodgrains was based on the following assumptions:

Foodgrain	Average rate of nitrogen application (kilograms per hectare)		
	1969–70	1978–79	1983–84
Rice			
Irrigated HYV	30	60	80
Irrigated local	25	35	37
Unirrigated HYV	20	30	40
Unirrigated local	15	20	25
Wheat			
Irrigated HYV	60	80	90
Irrigated local	25	35	37
Unirrigated HYV	25	35	40
Unirrigated local	15	20	25
Sorghum, millet, and maize			
Irrigated HYV	25 (sorghum 20)	40	50
Irrigated local	15	22	25
Unirrigated HYV	15 (maize 17)	25	35 (maize 30)
Unirrigated local	10	20	25
Barley and other cereals and pulses			
Irrigated local	15	20 (barley 22)	25
Unirrigated local	10	15 (barley 20)	17 (barley 25)

For details on the assumptions for nonfoodgrains and plantation crops, see Desai, cited in source.

The assumptions used in calculating Appendix Table 6 were developed by drawing on the findings of micro studies and information on recommended rates of fertilizer application. For further discussion, see Desai cited above and his *Growth of Fertilizer Use in Indian Agriculture—Past Trends and Future Demand,* Cornell International Agricultural Development Bulletin 18, New York State College of Agricultural and Life Sciences (Ithaca, N.Y.).

Appendix Table 7. Production of different foodgrains under various categories of farming conditions, India, 1969–70, 1978–79, and 1983–84 (in thousand metric tons)

Foodgrain	1969–70	1978–79	1983–84
Rice			
Irrigated HYV fertilized	7,988	27,276	40,656
Irrigated local fertilized	14,136	4,837	–
Unirrigated HYV fertilized	–	6,620	12,437
Unirrigated local fertilized	4,166	9,587	13,419
Unirrigated local unfertilized	14,139	7,783	3,297
Total rice	40,430	56,103	69,809
Wheat			
Irrigated HYV fertilized	14,811	35,525	51,711
Irrigated local fertilized	1,127	–	–
Unirrigated HYV fertilized	–	1,764	2,234
Unirrigated local fertilized	1,143	2,017	1,987
Unirrigated local unfertilized	3,012	1,247	365
Total wheat	20,093	40,553	56,357
Other foodgrains			
Irrigated HYV fertilized	2,721	6,165	9,699
Irrigated local fertilized	4,586	5,864	6,875
Irrigated local unfertilized	839	469	–
Unirrigated HYV fertilized	597	11,609	21,048
Unirrigated local fertilized	4,977	15,289	21,355
Unirrigated local unfertilized	25,757	16,799	11,234
Total other foodgrains	39,477	56,195	70,211
Total foodgrains			
Irrigated HYV fertilized	25,521	68,966	102,126
Irrigated local fertilized	19,849	10,701	6,875
Irrigated local unfertilized	839	469	–
Unirrigated HYV fertilized	597	19,993	35,719
Unirrigated local fertilized	10,286	26,893	36,761
Unirrigated local unfertilized	42,908	25,829	14,896
Total foodgrains	100,000	152,851	196,377

Source: Gunvant M. Desai, "Nitrogen Use and Foodgrain Production, India, 1973–74, 1978–79, and 1983–84," Department of Agricultural Economics, Occasional Paper No. 55, Cornell University USAID Employment and Income Distribution Project (March 1973).

Note: Production of foodgrain *i* under category *j* in year *t* (Q_{ijt}) can be expressed as a product of (1) area under foodgrain *ij* in year *t* (A_{ijt}) and (2) average yield of foodgrain *ij* in year *t* (Y_{ijt}), i.e.,

$$Q_{ijt} = A_{ijt} \cdot Y_{ijt}$$

For the series A_{ijt} used in the above table, see Appendix Table 5.

For 1969–70, Y_{ij} was assumed to be a proportion of the average yield of crop *i* on irrigated fertilized area under HYV (Y_{ih}), the proportion being the ratio of the rate of nitrogen application on foodgrain *ij* (R_{ij}) to the rate of application on foodgrain *ih* (R_{ih}), i.e.,

$$Y_{ij} = \frac{R_{ij}}{R_{ih}} \cdot Y_{ih}$$

Yield of foodgrain *i* in the irrigated fertilized HYV category (Y_{ih}) for 1969–70 was estimated by using data for actual production (Appendix Table 5), the series on areas under different categories (Appendix Table 5), the series on rates of nitrogen application on these areas (Appendix Table 6), and assumed yields of local varieties on unfertilized areas. For wheat and rice these assumptions were 4.0 quintals and 7.5 quintals per hectare.

For 1978–79 and 1983–84 yields of different foodgrains ($Y_{ijt'}$) were calculated by adding increments in yield to the 1969–70 figures (Y_{ijt}). These increments were calculated by multiplying the increment in rate of nitrogen application (Appendix Table 6) by certain "yardsticks," K, i.e.,

$$Y_{ijt'} = Y_{ijt} + (K_{ij} \cdot R_{ij})$$

where K_{ij} equals the increment in yield of foodgrain ij resulting from one additional unit of nitrogen.

The "yardsticks" (K_{ij}) used in calculating wheat and rice yields for 1978–79 and 1983–84 ($Y_{ijt'}$) were as follows (in kgs. per hectare):

Category	Wheat	Rice
Irrigated HYV	20	15
Irrigated local	12	10
Unirrigated HYV	12	10
Unirrigated local	8	8

These "yardsticks," although attached to increments in the use of nitrogen fertilizer, carry the effect of phosphorus and potassium application, as well as any improvement in varietal response and agronomic practices. (From 1969–70 to 1973–74, an average of 0.32 kgs. of phosphorus and 0.17 kgs. of potassium were consumed for every kilogram of nitrogen fertilizer used.) The different yardsticks attached to various crops and varieties reflect the preceding factors as well as differences in natural conditions.

For a detailed explanation of these calculations, see Desai, cited above.

Appendix Table 8. Components of growth in foodgrain production, India, 1969–70 to 1978–79 and 1978–79 to 1983–84 (in thousand metric tons)

| Foodgrain | Growth due to increment in area | Growth due to increment in yield | | Growth due to simultaneous increase in both area and yield | Total increment |
| | | On various categories of farming condition | Because of shift in area among different categories | | |
		(percent of total increment in parenthesis)			
1969–70 to 1978–79					
Rice	3,902	3,931	6,803	1,037	15,673
	(24.9)	(25.1)	(43.4)	(6.6)	(100.0)
Wheat	4,507	2,948	10,080	2,925	20,460
	(22.0)	(14.4)	(49.3)	(14.3)	(100.0)
Other foodgrains	1,635	3,550	10,341	1,193	16,719
	(9.8)	(21.2)	(61.9)	(7.1)	(100.0)
All foodgrains	10,044	10,429	27,224	5,155	52,852
	(19.0)	(19.7)	(51.5)	(9.8)	(100.0)
1978–79 to 1983–84					
Rice	2,947	4,686	5,536	537	13,706
	(21.5)	(34.2)	(40.4)	(3.9)	(100.0)
Wheat	4,827	2,728	7,082	1,167	15,804
	(30.5)	(17.3)	(44.8)	(7.4)	(100.0)
Other foodgrains	2,102	1,652	9,667	595	14,016
	(15.0)	(11.8)	(69.0)	(4.2)	(100.0)
All foodgrains	9,876	9,066	22,285	2,299	43,526
	(22.7)	(20.8)	(51.2)	(5.3)	(100.0)

Sources: Appendix Tables 5, 6, and 7; and Gunvant M. Desai, "Nitrogen Use and Foodgrain Production, India, 1973–74, 1978–79, and 1983–84," Department of Agricultural Economics, Occasional Paper No. 55, Cornell University USAID Employment and Income Distribution Project (March 1973).

Note: Column 1 (ΔQ_i^A) was calculated as the change in area under foodgrain i (ΔA_i) multiplied by the average yield in the base year (Y_i).

Column 2 (ΔQ_i^{Yc}) was calculated as the change in yield of foodgrain i in the various categories of farming (ΔY_{ij}) times the area of foodgrain i in the respective categories in the base year (A_{ij}).

Column 3 (ΔQ_i^{Ys}) was calculated as the change in yield of foodgrain i (ΔY_i) times the area under foodgrain i in the base year (A_i), minus the change in yield due to increment in yield on various categories of farming (ΔQ_i^{Yc}).

Column 4 (ΔQ_i^{AY}) was calculated as the change in area of foodgrain i (ΔA_i) multiplied by the change in yield of foodgrain i (ΔY_i).

Column 5 (ΔQ_i) was calculated as the sum of columns 1 through 4, i.e.,

$$\Delta Q_i = \Delta Q_i^A + \Delta Q_i^{Yc} + \Delta Q_i^{Ys} + \Delta Q_i^{AY}$$
$$= (\Delta A_i \cdot Y_i) + (\Delta Q_{ij}^Y \cdot A_{ij}) + [(\Delta Y_i \cdot A_i) - (\Delta Q_{ij}^Y \cdot A_{ij})] + (\Delta A_i \cdot \Delta Y_i)$$

Appendix Table 9. Estimated annual contribution of various inputs to total foodgrain production and estimated total marketings, India, 1949–50 to 1983–84
(in million metric tons)

Year	Unirrigated land	Labor on unirrigated land	Irrigated land	Labor on irrigated land	Intensification of labor	Inorganic fertilizer	Total production	Total marketings
1949–50	18.9	28.6	4.7	8.6	0.0	0.0	60.8	31.0
1950–51	18.3	27.6	4.9	9.0	0.4	0.2	60.4	30.8
1951–52	18.2	27.6	4.8	8.9	1.2	0.2	61.0	30.9
1952–53	19.2	29.1	5.1	9.3	1.1	0.4	64.2	32.6
1953–54	20.6	31.1	5.3	9.8	1.0	0.6	68.6	34.9
1954–55	20.3	30.7	5.4	9.9	1.8	0.7	68.7	34.9
1955–56	20.8	31.5	5.5	10.1	2.1	0.8	70.8	35.9
1956–57	21.0	31.7	5.4	10.0	2.9	0.9	72.0	36.4
1957–58	20.5	30.9	5.6	10.4	5.1	1.1	73.6	36.8
1958–59	21.6	32.6	5.7	10.5	5.1	1.4	76.9	38.6
1959–60	21.8	32.9	5.8	10.7	6.2	1.9	79.2	39.6
1960–61	21.7	32.7	5.9	10.8	7.6	1.8	80.5	40.0
1961–62	22.0	33.2	6.0	11.0	8.1	2.3	82.6	41.1
1962–63	21.9	33.0	6.2	11.5	8.8	3.0	84.4	42.1
1963–64	21.8	32.9	6.2	11.4	9.7	3.7	85.7	42.8
1964–65	21.8	32.9	6.4	11.7	9.8	4.3	87.0	43.6
1965–66	21.0	31.8	6.5	11.9	11.8	5.0	88.0	44.0
1966–67	20.7	31.3	6.9	12.7	12.0	8.2	91.8	46.8
1967–68	22.1	33.3	6.9	12.8	11.6	8.1	94.9	48.5
1968–69	21.4	32.3	7.5	13.7	13.3	11.9	100.1	52.1
1969–70	21.8	32.9	7.8	14.5	13.2	14.5	104.7	55.2
1970–71	21.5	32.4	8.5	15.4	13.0	15.9	106.7	56.7
1971–72	21.0	31.5	8.7	15.8	14.7	19.1	110.8	59.5
1972–73	20.0	30.1	8.9	16.2	16.9	19.7	111.8	59.7
1973–74	21.3	32.4	9.1	16.6	15.5	20.3	115.0	61.8
1974–75	21.8	32.9	9.0	16.3	16.3	23.4	119.7	65.0
1975–76	22.0	33.2	9.1	16.6	16.9	27.6	125.4	69.2
1976–77	22.3	33.5	9.3	16.8	17.5	32.5	131.9	74.0

Appendix Table 9 (continued)

Year	Unirrigated land	Labor on unirrigated land	Irrigated land	Labor on irrigated land	Intensification of labor	Inorganic fertilizer	Total production	Total marketings
1977–78	22.5	33.8	9.3	17.1	18.2	38.4	139.3	79.5
1978–79	22.7	34.2	9.5	17.3	18.9	45.2	147.8	85.9
1979–80	22.7	34.2	9.8	17.9	19.4	50.0	154.1	90.4
1980–81	22.7	34.2	10.1	18.5	20.1	55.3	161.0	95.5
1981–82	22.7	34.2	10.4	19.2	20.8	61.1	168.5	101.1
1982–83	22.7	34.2	10.8	19.8	21.5	67.6	176.7	107.2
1983–84	22.7	34.2	11.1	20.5	22.2	74.8	185.5	113.8

Source: John W. Mellor, Uma J. Lele, Debra Biamonte, and Arthur Goldsmith, "Estimates of Foodgrain Production and Marketings from Input Estimates 1949–50 to 1973–74 and Projections to 1983–84, India," Department of Agricultural Economics, Occasional Paper No. 83, Cornell University USAID Employment and Income Distribution Project (September 1975).

Note: In this table foodgrain production is defined as an additive function of the four inputs of irrigated land, unirrigated land, labor, and inorganic fertilizer. All other inputs, such as other types of fertilizer, improved seed varieties, and improved animal power, are implicitly assumed to move proportionately with these four major inputs. A response coefficient has been attached to each input such that the sum of the products of the four inputs and their respective response coefficients provide an estimate of total output for that year. The response coefficients were estimated on the basis of data for 1949–50.

The response coefficients for land were determined by using official Indian estimates for foodgrain production, total area under foodgrains, and irrigated area under foodgrains in 1949–50. They also assume a yield increment of 30 percent on irrigated acreage. The response coefficients thus derived were 0.5815 metric tons/hectare for unirrigated land and 0.7559 metric tons/hectare for irrigated land.

The response coefficient for labor was calculated by first determining labor flow, which in 1949–50 was estimated to be 14,073.2 million man-days or 153.5 days per laborer. Assuming 40 percent additional labor required per irrigated hectare, labor coefficients of 0.101 days/unirrigated hectare and 0.141 days/irrigated hectare were derived. To determine the response coefficient to labor output it was assumed that a linear relationship existed between labor and output and that the response coefficient was the same as the marginal productivity of labor and the wage rate. Thus, assuming a wage rate of Rs. 1.5 per day, the total value product of agricultural labor in 1949–50 was Rs. 16,117.3 million, which when divided by the average price per ton of foodgrain, yields a total physical product of 37.1898 million metric tons. The response coefficient for labor was thus determined to be 0.00346 metric tons/man day of labor input.

For inorganic fertilizer a response coefficient of 10 metric tons of grain per metric ton of fertilizer nutrient was used.

Using the above response coefficients, foodgrain production was estimated for 1949–50 to 1973–74 on the basis of land, labor, and fertilizer input. Official Indian sources were used to determine the actual irrigated and unirrigated areas through 1970–71. Irrigated area for 1971–72 to 1973–74 was estimated by assuming that irrigated acreage grew by 2.4 percent per year, i.e., the average annual growth rate of irrigated area for all crops from 1960–61 to 1967–68 (see Table III-1). The agricultural working population in each year was estimated on the basis of available census data. The proportion of farm labor devoted to foodgrain production was assumed to be the same as the ratio of foodgrain acreage to total agricultural acreage.

(For 1972–73 and 1973–74 the ratio was assumed to be 0.745.) Fertilizer use on foodgrain production was assumed to be 61 percent of total fertilizer consumption from 1949–50 to 1961–62, rising to 73 percent by 1969–70, and remaining at that proportion through 1973–74.

The estimates of potential production for 1974–75 through 1983–84 were made by using the same response coefficients and estimates of the various inputs in the respective years. Irrigated and unirrigated areas were projected on the basis of the previously determined 1973–74 figures and the 1978–79 and 1983–84 figures cited in Appendix Table 5. Using the respective compound growth rates, acreage for the intervening years was derived. Estimates of agricultural labor population were projected by assuming that the 1961-to-1971 growth rate of 1.8 percent remained constant through 1983–84, and that 74.5 percent of that labor was allocated to foodgrain production. Inorganic fertilizer use was estimated on the basis of nitrogen fertilizer consumption for 1978–79 and 1983–84 cited in Appendix Table 6. Total inorganic fertilizer consumption (i.e., including phosphorus and potassium) for these two years was computed by dividing the nitrogenous fertilizer consumption by 0.676. (The divisor 0.676 was obtained by taking the average ratio of nitrogenous fertilizer to total fertilizer consumption from 1967–68 to 1972–73, based on official estimates). Using 1973–74 as a base year, fertilizer input through 1983–84 was determined on the basis of the respective growth rates.

The estimates of foodgrain marketings were derived by separating the inputs into three categories—total labor (on irrigated and unirrigated acreage, and intensification of labor); total land (irrigated and unirrigated); and fertilizer. It was assumed that output attributable to each input was paid to that input and that a particular expenditure pattern characterized each of the input categories.

For labor the assumptions were that 30 percent of the returns to labor would be marketed, 70 percent being consumed in the home. This pattern approximately reflects the average propensity to spend on foodgrains of the poorest 20 percent of the population. For land it was assumed that 84 percent of the returns to land were marketed and only 16 percent consumed in the home. This assumption reflects the higher income of landowners and is based on the estimated marginal propensity to consume of the 6th, 7th, and 8th income deciles. For fertilizer it was assumed that 30 percent of the total returns to fertilizer was marketed to pay for the fertilizer; 10 percent of fertilizer returns was considered to be allocated to labor and 60 percent allocated to land. The fertilizer returns allocated to labor and land were assumed to be expended in the normal pattern, i.e., 30 percent of the returns allocated to labor and 84 percent of the returns allocated to land were assumed to be marketed.

A detailed list of the sources and a further description of the calculations is given in Mellor et al., cited in the source for this table.

Appendix Table 10. Changes in fixed capital, productive capital, employment, value added, and output in registered industries, India, 1951–1965 (in Rs. 100,000, employment in 100 persons)

Industry group	1951					1957				
	Fixed capital	Productive capital	Employment	Value added	Gross output	Fixed capital	Productive capital	Employment	Value added	Gross output
Group 20 Food mfg. industries except beverage ind.	13,242	25,451	4,900	9,818	62,647	14,442	25,779	5,471	15,742	81,338
Group 21 Beverage industries	342	529	78	297	628	229	380	56	247	518
Group 22 Tobacco mfg.	829	2,774	1,434	1,462	8,180	789	2,911	2,062	2,316	10,073
Group 23 Mfg. of textiles	18,751	43,607	13,549	25,505	84,623	21,753	40,531	13,707	23,662	85,202
Group 24 Mfg. of footwear, other wearing apparel, & made-up textile goods	400	799	264	675	1,807	188	593	199	406	1,780
Group 25 & 26 Mfr. of wood & cork; mfr. of furniture & fixtures	447	685	261	481	1,207	711	1,425	450	957	3,294
Group 27 & 28 Mfr. of paper & paper products; printing, publishing, & allied industries	3,846	11,237	1,079	2,617	5,413	4,687	7,059	1,398	3,545	8,885
Group 29 Mfr. of leather & fur products except footwear & other wearing apparel	169	852	230	412	3,288	272	411	219	408	2,679
Group 30 Mfr. of rubber products	328	969	166	506	1,838	420	1,192	307	1,834	5,038

Group 31 Mfr. of chemicals & chemical products	3,589	7,135	1,044	3,591	10,463	6,156	10,458	1,290	5,635	17,076
Group 32 Mfr. of products of petroleum & coal	69	199	16	458	786	814	806	34	969	3,380
Group 33 Mfr. of nonmetallic mineral products except products of petroleum & coal	2,213	3,631	1,094	2,187	4,390	4,734	6,261	1,240	2,918	7,164
Group 34 Basic metal industries	2,931	4,824	682	2,898	5,394	2,044	3,178	505	2,441	5,879
Group 35 Mfr. of metal products except machinery & transport equipment	2,673	5,217	1,109	2,399	6,979	6,611	11,254	1,771	7,743	21,215
Group 36 Mfr. of machinery except electrical machinery	415	248	150	256	589	667	1,244	249	803	1,795
Group 37 Mfr. of electrical machinery, apparatus, appliances, & supplies	2,801	4,990	1,123	2,191	4,424	4,034	9,001	2,196	5,145	14,294
Group 38 Mfr. of transport equipment	1,924	4,519	856	1,682	4,612	3,942	7,489	1,385	3,913	12,100
Group 39 Miscellaneous mfg. industries	4,192	8,641	2,341	3,140	10,063	4,305	7,828	2,367	4,416	15,533
Group 51 Electricity, gas & steam	11,577	12,103	300	1,516	2,516	9,299	9,903	348	1,984	5,360
Total	70,739	138,410	30,676	62,091	219,848	86,087	147,703	35,254	85,083	302,602

Appendix Table 10 (continued)
(Rs. 100,000, employment in 100 persons)

Industry group	1961					1965				
	Fixed capital	Productive capital	Employment	Value added	Gross output	Fixed capital	Productive capital	Employment	Value added	Gross output
Group 20 Food mfg. industries except beverage ind.	18,469	37,580	5,373	14,715	107,121	25,572	47,705	5,941	18,570	150,186
Group 21 Beverage industries	607	1,080	105	524	1,341	1,107	1,959	118	1,161	2,909
Group 22 Tobacco mfg.	778	3,749	1,696	2,719	13,027	954	4,597	1,314	3,500	19,186
Group 23 Mfr. of textiles	28,034	48,000	13,367	32,989	115,306	44,691	68,199	13,829	42,457	162,854
Group 24 Mfr. of footwear, other wearing apparel, & made-up textile goods	120	351	135	294	1,241	226	858	214	571	2,420
Group 25 & 26 Mfr. of wood & cork; mfr. of furniture & fixtures	1,666	2,884	696	1,853	5,420	2,161	4,567	797	2,055	7,481
Group 27 & 28 Mfr. of paper & paper products; printing, publishing, & allied industries	8,134	11,974	1,721	5,475	15,642	15,112	21,641	2,081	8,213	24,612
Group 29 Mfr. of leather & fur products except footwear & other wearing apparel	221	1,006	198	514	4,321	361	1,700	200	598	5,110
Group 30 Mfr. of rubber products	1,456	3,241	402	2,873	8,267	3,253	6,027	522	3,774	13,824
Group 31 Mfr. of chemicals & chemical products	18,809	29,122	1,548	9,899	33,987	31,961	51,061	2,026	16,843	64,715
Group 32 Mfr. of products of petroleum & coal	4,255	8,089	83	1,932	6,174	15,467	20,846	171	1,864	10,702

Group 33 Mfr. of nonmetallic mineral products except products of petroleum & coal	8,231	12,710	1,880	4,662	14,710	13,686	19,915	2,260	7,454	24,557
Group 34 Basic metal products	24,478	35,474	2,187	9,314	36,187	95,045	126,985	3,557	20,628	77,756
Group 35 Mfr. of metal products except machinery & transport equipment	3,114	6,873	1,036	3,195	12,079	6,304	12,552	1,432	5,371	19,535
Group 36 Mfr. of machinery except electrical machinery	6,135	10,877	1,664	5,107	14,599	18,821	29,442	2,633	12,427	35,095
Group 37 Mfr. of electrical machinery, apparatus, appliances, & supplies	3,712	8,386	920	4,055	12,624	12,432	24,236	1,583	8,704	30,651
Group 38 Mfr. of transport equipment	13,599	21,342	3,221	9,439	33,323	22,617	37,065	4,443	17,732	57,091
Group 39 Miscellaneous mfg. industries	1,537	3,021	566	1,585	4,878	3,421	5,821	879	2,888	8,851
Group 51 Electricity, gas & steam	25,420	27,756	524	4,475	12,047	169,984	192,285	2,804	13,979	36,014
Total	168,775	273,515	37,322	115,619	452,293	483,175	677,461	46,804	188,789	753,549

Source: Uttam Dabholkar and Arthur Goldsmith, "Changes in the Composition of Capital, Employment, Value Added and Production, by Industry Group, India, 1951–1965," Department of Agricultural Economics, Occasional Paper No. 84, Cornell University USAID Employment and Income Distribution Project (October 1975).

Note: This table was developed from data presented in the Indian Government's Annual Survey of Industries (A.S.I.), and refers to the total registered industrial sector, i.e., the sample and the census sectors. The sample sector includes all firms employing more than 10 and less than 50 workers with the aid of power, and those employing more than 20 and less than 100 workers without the aid of power. The census sector covers all firms with more than 50 workers with the aid of power and those with more than 100 workers without the aid of power.

The definitions and terms are those used in the A.S.I. and are briefly as follows: Fixed capital: the book value of land and buildings and of plant, machinery and tools. Productive capital: the total book value of fixed capital and working capital. Employment: the number of persons employed, including production workers and supervisory or managerial personnel, but excluding owners and proprietors. Value added: the book value of net operating surplus plus the book value of depreciation during the period of reference. Gross output: the book value of the output plus the book value of depreciation during the period of reference.

Appendix Table 11. Indian imports by commodity, in million U.S. dollars, 1951–52, 1955–56, 1960–61 to 1973–74

Commodity group	1951–52	1955–56	1960–61	1961–62	1962–63	1963–64	1964–
TOTAL IMPORTS	1,838	1,365	2,356	2,290	2,377	2,569	2,83
I. Food	547	111	450	309	377	450	67
a. Cereal and cereal preparations	483	37	381	246	303	377	59
b. Food other than cereal and cereal preparations	64	72	69	63	74	73	8
II. Beverages and tobacco	7	5	2	4	4	2	
III. Crude materials, inedible, except fuels	367	191	326	273	267	262	26
a. Raw cotton other than linters	292	120	172	132	120	103	12
b. Crude materials other than raw cotton	75	71	155	141	148	159	14
IV. Mineral fuels, lubricants	151	117	146	201	185	220	14
V. Animal and vegetable oils and fats	15	15	10	18	12	10	1
VI. Chemicals	139	139	180	189	211	201	19
a. Fertilizers manufactured	7	4	20	26	56	72	6
b. Chemicals other than fertilizers	132	135	160	163	155	129	13
VII. Manufactured goods	224	321	492	465	429	421	45
VIII. Machinery and transport equipment	333	409	699	772	814	918	1,00
a. Machinery other than electric	140	187	427	498	526	591	65
b. Electrical machinery	64	79	120	138	136	178	19
c. Transport equipment	129	143	152	136	151	149	15
IX. Miscellaneous manufactured goods	29	38	37	46	64	70	4
X. Residual imports	26	18	15	14	15	14	2

Sources: 1951–52 to 1971–72 from Ram P. Yadev, "An Econometric Model for the Foreign Trade Sector of India, 1960/61–1971/72," Ph.D. dissertation, Cornell University, Ithaca, N.Y., January 197 Appendix Table 3.5; based on data from Reserve Bank of India, *Report on Currency and Finance* (Bombay), various issues; Government of India, Department of Commercial Intelligence a Statistics, *Monthly Statistics of the Foreign Trade of India* (Delhi), various issues; and Government India, Department of Commercial Intelligence and Statistics, *Accounts Relating to the Foreign (Se Air, and Land) Trade and Navigation of India,* March 1954 and March 1956; 1972–73 and 1973– calculated on the basis of figures in Reserve Bank of India, *Bulletin,* 28:9 (September 1974).

1965-66	1966-67	1967-68	1968-69	1969-70	1970-71	1971-72	1972-73	1973-74
2,959	2,771	2,677	2,545	2,109	2,179	2,416	2,311	3,555
744	941	772	537	428	362	263	198	667
677	868	691	449	348	284	175	73	430
67	73	81	89	80	78	88	125	237
1	1	2	1	1	–	–	–	–
259	266	255	253	236	267	284	235	102
97	75	111	120	111	132	151	112	63
162	190	143	133	125	135	133	123	39
144	84	100	178	184	181	259	253	683
29	20	46	26	39	51	62	31	79
221	262	363	378	260	256	290	320	429
82	120	185	186	103	82	108	120	198
139	142	178	192	157	175	182	201	231
454	330	339	334	307	460	586	556	647
1,034	768	671	685	528	526	606	659	767
701	544	449	488	374	344	357	369	508
185	141	114	109	86	94	136	166	151
148	83	108	88	68	88	113	124	108
39	31	37	33	34	43	43	45	49
35	69	91	119	93	31	23	14	132

Appendix Table 12. Indian exports by commodity, in million U.S. dollars, 1951–52, 1955–56, and 1960–61 to 1973–74

Commodity group	1951–52	1955–56	1960–61	1961–62	1962–63	1963–64	1964–65
TOTAL EXPORTS	1,503	1,242	1,349	1,387	1,440	1,666	1,715
I. Food	298	340	416	449	491	525	549
a. Tea and mate	197	229	260	257	270	259	262
b. Fruits and vegetables	29	33	54	53	56	63	75
c. Food other than tea and mate, and fruits and vegetables	72	78	102	139	165	203	212
II. Beverages and tobacco	36	25	33	32	40	47	54
III. Crude materials	233	244	236	249	233	277	289
a. Metalliferous ores and metal scrap	38	42	82	77	67	107	122
b. Crude materials other than metalliferous ores	195	201	153	172	166	170	167
IV. Mineral fuels, lubricants	23	12	16	12	14	21	26
V. Animal and vegetable oils and fats	44	72	21	14	29	43	16
VI. Chemicals	30	20	15	16	16	14	22
VII. Manufactured goods	807	489	553	567	560	671	686
a. Leather and manufactures of leather	54	48	53	53	47	55	57
b. Cotton textiles	128	140	121	102	97	114	135
c. Jute manufactures	570	248	277	295	319	323	377
d. Manufactured goods other than leather, cotton and jute	56	52	103	117	96	179	117
VIII. Machinery and transport equipment	4	9	15	10	14	15	19
IX. Miscellaneous manufactured goods	14	16	25	22	24	38	42
X. Residual exports	14	14	21	17	20	15	12

Sources: 1951–52 to 1971–72 from Ram P. Yadev, "An Econometric Model for the Foreign Trade Sector of India, 1960/61–1971/72," Ph.D. dissertation, Cornell University, Ithaca, N.Y., January 1975, Appendix Table 3.8; based on data from Reserve Bank of India, *Report on Currency and Finance* (Bombay), various issues; Government of India, Department of Commercial Intelligence and Statistics, *Monthly Statistics of the Foreign Trade of India* (Delhi), various issues; and Government of India, Department of Commercial Intelligence and Statistics, *Accounts Relating to the Foreign (Sea, Air, and Land) Trade and Navigation of India,* March 1954 and March 1956; 1972–73 and 1973–74 computed on the basis of figures in Government of India, Central Statistical Organisation, *Monthly Abstract of Statistics,* 27:10 (October 1974).

1965–66	1966–67	1967–68	1968–69	1969–70	1970–71	1971–72	1972–73	1973–74
1,692	1,542	1,598	1,810	1,884	2,047	2,091	2,431	3,021
506	470	483	486	461	550	550	656	812
241	211	235	209	166	197	208	260	301
70	73	69	97	94	87	94	100	110
195	186	180	180	201	266	248	296	402
46	30	47	45	45	43	60	79	86
284	278	259	283	309	335	321	327	434
125	129	132	151	158	189	161	156	190
159	149	127	132	151	146	159	171	245
20	17	12	16	13	17	11	40	19
9	4	6	16	7	9	10	33	38
23	20	21	32	41	49	43	50	69
721	654	681	801	840	821	882	1,008	1,203
60	83	71	97	109	96	121	216	209
133	98	106	117	115	130	133	126	236
370	320	301	279	269	246	345	205	187
158	150	203	308	347	349	283	460	571
24	21	29	60	75	111	97	105	140
46	37	49	62	85	102	110	140	211
14	11	11	10	11	9	9	–	8

Appendix Table 13. Indian imports by selected countries and regions, 1951–52, 1955–56, and 1960–61 to 1973–74

Year	All countries		U.S.A.		Canada		United Kingdom		Federal Republic of Germany		Other Western European countries	
	% of total	Million U.S. $	% of total	Million U.S. $	% of total	Million U.S. $	% of total	Million U.S. $	% of total	Million U.S. $	% of total	Million U.S. $
1951–52	100	1,838	33.6	617	2.2	41	18.6	341	3.3	60	8.7	160
1955–56	100	1,365	13.8	188	1.1	14	26.6	363	9.3	127	13.7	187
1960–61	100	2,356	29.2	688	1.8	42	19.4	456	10.9	257	9.3	218
1961–62	100	2,290	23.4	537	1.7	39	18.4	421	11.3	258	9.6	219
1962–63	100	2,377	30.7	729	1.5	35	16.4	390	8.7	207	7.6	180
1963–64	100	2,569	36.8	945	2.0	50	14.0	360	7.4	190	6.6	171
1964–65	100	2,834	37.8	1,072	2.0	56	12.1	344	8.1	230	7.0	198
1965–66	100	2,959	38.0	1,124	2.1	64	10.7	315	9.7	288	7.2	214
1966–67	100	2,771	37.7	1,044	4.4	123	8.0	221	7.8	217	8.7	241
1967–68	100	2,677	38.7	1,036	4.9	131	8.1	217	7.2	192	7.9	211
1968–69	100	2,545	30.0	763	5.2	132	6.7	170	6.3	160	8.3	210
1969–70	100	2,109	29.5	623	4.7	100	6.5	137	5.3	113	7.4	155
1970–71	100	2,165	27.5	595	7.2	156	7.7	168	6.4	143	7.0	147
1971–72	100	2,416	23.0	555	6.2	150	12.0	289	6.9	165	8.6	207
1972–73	100	2,311	12.6	291	5.8	133	12.7	294	9.2	214	11.0	254
1973–74	100	3,555	16.9	602	4.0	141	8.4	298	6.7	239	10.1	359

Year	USSR % of total	USSR Million U.S. $	Eastern European countries % of total	Eastern European countries Million U.S. $	Japan % of total	Japan Million U.S. $	Other Asian countries* % of total	Other Asian countries* Million U.S. $	Africa % of total	Africa Million U.S. $	Other countries† % of total	Other countries† Million U.S. $
1951–52	0.2	3	0.4	8	2.9	53	16.6	305	9.5	175	4.1	75
1955–56	1.0	13	0.7	10	5.1	70	12.0	164	10.9	149	5.9	81
1960–61	1.4	33	2.8	60	5.4	128	10.6	249	6.3	149	3.3	77
1961–62	3.7	84	4.4	100	5.5	125	12.3	280	5.9	135	4.0	93
1962–63	5.2	123	4.6	108	5.7	136	11.9	283	5.0	118	2.8	67
1963–64	5.6	144	5.0	128	5.4	138	10.0	259	4.2	107	3.0	77
1964–65	5.8	166	4.9	139	5.8	164	9.2	260	4.9	138	2.4	67
1965–66	5.9	175	5.2	155	5.6	167	10.0	294	4.0	117	1.6	47
1966–67	5.5	152	5.6	155	5.2	143	11.2	309	4.1	115	1.9	52
1967–68	5.5	148	5.5	148	5.4	145	9.0	241	4.7	126	3.1	83
1968–69	10.0	256	6.2	157	6.0	154	11.2	285	7.8	198	2.4	61
1969–70	10.8	229	7.9	150	4.3	90	12.2	257	8.9	189	3.2	68
1970–71	6.5	140	7.5	162	5.1	111	11.2	241	10.5	226	3.6	77
1971–72	4.5	109	6.6	160	8.9	215	11.0	266	7.9	192	4.4	106
1972–73	6.1	142	6.3	145	9.6	221	11.9	275	8.8	204	6.0	140
1973–74	8.6	306	4.9	174	8.8	312	14.2	504	5.7	204	11.8	419

* Including the Philippines, Australia and New Zealand.
† Including the Middle East.
Note: Errors in summation are due to rounding.

Sources: 1951–52 to 1971–72 from Reserve Bank of India, Report on Currency and Finance (Bombay), various issues; 1972–73 and 1973–74 from Reserve Bank of India, Bulletin, 28:9 (September 1974); and Government of India, Central Statistical Organisation, Monthly Abstract of Statistics, 27:10 (October 1974).

Appendix Table 14. Indian exports by selected countries and regions, 1951–52, 1955–56, and 1960–61 to 1973–74

Year	All countries		U.S.A.		Canada		United Kingdom		Federal Republic of Germany		Other Western European countries	
	% of total	Million U.S. $	% of total	Million U.S. $	% of total	Million U.S. $	% of total	Million U.S. $	% of total	Million U.S. $	% of total	Million U.S. $
1951–52	100	1,503	18.5	278	2.3	34	26.5	399	1.3	20	6.3	94
1955–56	100	1,242	14.7	183	2.4	30	28.1	349	2.5	31	8.0	100
1960–61	100	1,349	16.0	215	2.8	37	26.9	362	3.1	42	5.9	80
1961–62	100	1,387	17.5	243	2.7	37	24.4	338	3.1	43	5.8	80
1962–63	100	1,440	16.7	240	3.2	47	23.8	343	2.4	34	5.3	84
1963–64	100	1,667	16.4	273	2.7	45	20.6	344	2.5	42	6.8	113
1964–65	100	1,715	18.0	309	2.1	37	20.5	352	2.2	37	6.1	104
1965–66	100	1,693	18.3	310	2.5	43	18.1	306	2.3	38	5.8	99
1966–67	100	1,542	19.0	293	2.7	41	17.5	270	2.3	35	6.6	102
1967–68	100	1,598	17.3	277	2.5	40	19.1	305	1.9	30	6.8	108
1968–69	100	1,811	17.3	313	2.2	40	14.8	269	2.0	35	7.4	134
1969–70	100	1,884	16.9	317	1.9	35	11.7	220	1.9	40	6.3	119
1970–71	100	2,047	13.5	277	1.8	37	11.1	227	2.1	43	5.6	114
1971–72	100	2,092	16.8	351	2.5	53	10.8	225	2.4	50	6.9	144
1972–73	100	2,431	14.0	341	1.4	35	8.8	214	3.2	77	10.1	246
1973–74	100	3,021	13.8	418	1.2	38	10.4	315	3.3	100	11.5	348

Year	USSR		Eastern European countries		Japan		Other Asian countries *		Africa		Other countries †	
	% of total	Million U.S. $	% of total	Million U.S. $	% of total	Million U.S. $	% of total	Million U.S. $	% of total	Million U.S. $	% of total	Million U.S. $
1951–52	1.0	15	0.2	4	2.1	31	22.9	344	7.1	106	11.9	179
1955–56	0.6	7	0.4	4	5.1	64	19.5	243	8.6	106	10.2	126
1960–61	4.5	61	3.2	44	5.5	74	16.7	226	7.6	103	7.9	107
1961–62	4.9	68	4.8	66	6.1	85	14.5	202	8.5	118	7.7	106
1962–63	5.6	80	7.9	114	4.9	70	13.8	199	7.3	105	8.6	124
1963–64	6.6	110	7.2	119	7.4	124	15.9	265	5.8	97	8.1	135
1964–65	9.6	164	8.1	139	7.5	128	14.2	244	5.7	97	6.2	106
1965–66	11.5	195	7.9	134	7.1	100	12.6	214	7.7	130	6.1	104
1966–67	10.7	165	8.9	137	9.3	143	11.6	179	6.2	96	5.3	82
1967–68	10.2	162	8.7	139	11.3	181	11.3	180	5.9	94	5.2	83
1968–69	10.9	198	8.7	158	11.7	211	13.5	245	5.4	97	6.2	112
1969–70	12.5	235	9.3	175	12.7	239	14.1	265	6.2	118	6.5	122
1970–71	13.7	280	9.9	203	13.3	271	13.5	276	9.1	186	6.6	134
1971–72	13.3	278	8.6	180	11.6	243	12.9	270	8.4	176	5.9	123
1972–73	15.5	377	8.4	204	11.1	269	17.7	431	5.1	125	4.6	112
1973–74	11.1	346	7.8	237	15.0	432	15.2	458	4.1	123	6.8	203

* Includes Philippines, Australia, and New Zealand.
† Includes the Middle East.
Note: Errors in summation are due to rounding.
Sources: 1951–52 to 1971–72 from Reserve Bank of India, Report on Currency and Finance (Bombay) various issues; 1972–73 and 1973–74 from Reserve Bank of India, Bulletin, 28:9 (September 1974); and Government of India, Central Statistical Organisation, Monthly Abstract of Statistics, 27:10 (October 1974).

Appendix Table 15. Simulation of the proportion of incremental employment in various sectors according to various assumptions
(in percent)

	Alternative foodgrain growth rates				
	Assumption Set 1				
Year	Foodgrain agriculture	Nonfoodgrain agriculture	Agricultural sector	Nonagricultural sector	Total
5	30.5	17.2	47.7	52.3	100
10	28.7	17.8	46.6	53.5	100
15	27.2	18.6	45.7	54.3	100
20	25.8	19.3	45.1	54.9	100
25	24.6	20.3	44.9	55.1	100
30	23.5	21.3	44.8	55.2	100
35	22.6	22.4	44.9	55.1	100
39	21.9	23.4	45.2	54.8	100

	Assumption Set 2				
Year	Foodgrain agriculture	Nonfoodgrain agriculture	Agricultural sector	Nonagricultural sector	Total
5	32.4	18.9	51.3	48.7	100
10	30.2	19.8	50.0	50.0	100
15	28.4	20.8	49.2	50.8	100
20	26.7	22.1	48.9	51.2	100
25	25.3	23.7	48.9	51.1	100
27	24.7	24.2	49.0	51.0	100

	Assumption Set 3				
Year	Foodgrain agriculture	Nonfoodgrain agriculture	Agricultural sector	Nonagricultural sector	Total
5	21.0	22.9	44.0	56.0	100
10	19.9	25.9	45.8	54.3	100
12	19.5	27.1	46.6	53.4	100

Alternative technologies

Assumption Set 4

Year	Foodgrain agriculture	Nonfoodgrain agriculture	Agricultural sector	Nonagricultural sector	Total
5	4.3	23.1	27.4	72.6	100
10	7.2	28.8	36.0	64.0	100

Assumption Set 5

Year	Foodgrain agriculture	Nonfoodgrain agriculture	Agricultural sector	Nonagricultural sector	Total
5	35.4	22.9	58.3	41.7	100
10	32.5	24.5	57.0	43.0	100
14	30.6	26.0	56.6	43.4	100

Alternative population growth rates

Assumption Set 6

Year	Foodgrain agriculture	Nonfoodgrain agriculture	Agricultural sector	Nonagricultural sector	Total
5	20.8	26.2	47.0	53.0	100
9	19.6	29.9	49.5	50.5	100

Assumption Set 7

Year	Foodgrain agriculture	Nonfoodgrain agriculture	Agricultural sector	Nonagricultural sector	Total
5	21.1	19.9	41.0	59.0	100
10	20.2	21.4	41.6	58.4	100
15	19.6	22.6	42.1	57.9	100
19	18.9	24.3	43.2	56.8	100

Note: This table shows, under sets of various assumptions, the proportion of employment in various sectors at 5-year intervals and at the final year in which full employment is reached. For the assumptions concerning the yield growth rate in the modern and traditional foodgrain sectors, the rate of population growth, and the rate of transfer of land from the traditional to the modern sector, see Table VII-5.

Sources: Adapted from John W. Mellor and Mohinder S. Mudahar, "Simulating a Development Economy with Modernizing Agricultural Sector: Implications for Employment and Economic Growth," Department of Agricultural Economics, Occasional Paper No. 76, Cornell University USAID Employment and Income Distribution Project (August 1974).

General Index

Agricultural production, effect on industrial expansion, 107-8, 140

Agricultural Research Institute, 230

Agriculture, technological change in, 29, 47; capital needs of, 163; cost-decreasing effect of, 16; demand for labor, 94-96, 97-99; growth linkages of, 163; initial benefits of, 79-82, 108; rural poverty and, 78-79; transfer of resources to other sectors, 177-81

Agriculture, traditional: diminishing returns to, 161; high risks of, 26-27

Agro-Economic Research Centres, 83

Aid India Consortium, 238

All-India Coordinated Rice Research Scheme, 58

Annual Survey of Industries, 111, 114, 119

Approach to the Fifth Plan, see *Fifth Plan, Approach to the*

*Balwadi*s, 252

Bhore Committee Report, 249

Birth rates: class differences in, 263; effect of economic development on, 95, 265

Brazil, 95, 254

Bureaucracy, Indian: economic planning, 279; export expansion, 208; management of industry, performance of, 147-48; reform needed, 150; technical knowledge of, 149; vested interest of, 270

Capital constraint on industry, relief of, 143

Capital goods industries, production of, 151

Capital intensive development strategy: exports, effect on, 207; imports, effect on, 195; reason chosen (India), 222; repay-

ment problems and, 235; rural welfare, effect on, 244; vested interests and, 273-74; *see also* Second Five-Year Plan, Indian

Capital intensive industry, 111-14; *see also* Electrical power industry; Large-scale industry; *and* Steel industry, India

Children, participation in rural labor force, 91, 247-48

Chile, 143, 246, 254, 255

Civil service, *see* Bureaucracy, Indian

Commodity surplus problem, 240

Community Development Program, Indian, 30-32, 38, 222, 231

Consumer goods industries, India: exports of, 206-7; labor intensity of, 17, 175-76; production of, 132, 137

Consumption pattern, India, 164-68, 246; policies to influence, 171-72

Cooperatives, agricultural, 35-38, 87-88

Crash Scheme for Rural Employment, 102

Credit, agricultural, 35-37, 87-88

Dairy industry, 88, 109, 173-74

Dandekar-Rath poverty line, 76, 245; *see also* Income distribution, India, *and* Land distribution, India

Demand, structure of, 108-9, 163-68; employment growth, consistency with, 118-19, 176; income distribution, effect of, on, 168-70; manipulation of, by public policy, 162

Development Assistance Committee, 218

Development strategy: political factors determining choice of, 20-21, 270-73; prospects for change in India, 19; *see also* Capital intensive development strategy *and*

Index of Persons

Library of Congress Cataloging in Publication Data
(For library cataloging purposes only)

Mellor, John Williams, 1928–
  The new economics of growth.

    "A Twentieth Century Fund study."
    Includes index.
    1. India—Economic policy—1966–   2. Under-
developed areas—Economic policy.   I. Title.
HC435.M39   338.954   75-38430
ISBN 0-8014-0999-3